Unintended Consequences

Unintended Consequences

A Twentieth Century Odyssey

Edward Harper

Rutledge Books, Inc.

Bethel, CT

Rutledge Books, Inc.
8 F.J. Clarke Circle, Bethel, CT 06801

Manufactured in the United States of America

Cataloging in Publication Data
Harper, Edward, 1926-
Unintended consequences : a twentieth century odyssey / Edward Harper.
p. cm.
ISBN 1-887750-42-8
1. Harper, Edward, 1926- . 2. Diplomats—United States—Biography. 3. Diplomatic and consular service, American. 4. United States—Foreign relations—1945-1989. I. Title.
327.20971—dc21 LC 96-71054
CIP

Books by Edward Harper

As Edward Harper

The Assassin
Janine

As Edward McGhee

The Chinese Ultimatum
The Last Caesar
The Orpheus Circle
The Heracles Commando

Il faut combatre juesqu'au dernier moment la nature et la fortune et ne jamais desesperer de rien, jusqu'a ce qu'on soit bien mort.

Voltaire to d'Argentail August 31, 1977

For

Mary Lee

Don't Speak to me of love
Nor yet of passion
But of a gray winter's day
When, for a moment,
You held the dark at bay

Introduction

A memoir is an exercise in picking lint from the navel of history.

Anonymous

This book is intended both as a personal Odyssey through the perils of the middle years of the twentieth century and a commentary on the comedies and tragedies I witnessed on the margins of power. It is not a formal history of the era but rather a series of impressions frozen in time. It is deliberately anecdotal. Conventional historians belittle such an approach as unscientific. But history is, by its very nature, subjective.

It is a memoir of the concrete versus the abstract, experience versus theory. It is also an attempt to reveal the gulf between the intellectual pretensions of our time and the crude reality of the individual caught in the web of an increasingly cruel, dehumanized and alienated world. In the end it is the story of a survivor, existing in the interstices of power.

It is a picaresque journey in which the protagonist, like Don Quixote, is often unseated from his Rosinante by the lance of the Law of Unintended Consequences. The leitmotifs running through it, like the proverbial red thread, are hubris, egomania and self-delusion. Armed with the lessons of history and the tools of Cartesian logic, political leaders of our time have nonetheless careened from one disaster to another. Intellectuals have embraced supposed utopias of indescribable cruelty in the belief that evil means can lead to benevolent ends, little realizing that means are the ends for those millions sacrificed on the altar of some dubious idealized state or polity.

The tragic irony of good intentions leading to repeated disasters is not a new phenomenon, but in the twentieth century it has reached new heights of absurdity. The primitive propaganda machine of Joseph Goebbels came to be the paradigm of our time. Words, the opiate of the intellectual, unattached to actions, became the reality.

Diplomacy was once the playground of cynics, a stage where the actors sought to win national advantage short of war. In our time it has become less an attempt to take the geopolitical high ground and decayed into a collusive facade constructed by international bureaucracies interested only in the petty perquisites of the trade. Winning for this cadre is, as in a marriage, often losing, as the end of the Cold War has so poignantly revealed.

Beginning in the sixties, vast numbers of young people came spewing out of universities imbued with half-digested revolutionary philosophies often possessing little information and no useful skills but nonetheless demanding highly paid employment. Generational dissonance enters here with a vengeance. The defining event for my generation was the Second World War. For this sixties cohort it was Vietnam.

For me, at the time, this obscure skirmish was little more than a blip on life's screen, particularly since I spent thirteen of the fifteen years between 1960 and 1975 outside the United States. At a distance, the immense emotional upheavals accompanying this sideshow in the U.S. - Soviet contest for world dominance were difficult for me to grasp. It was even more incomprehensible for our European allies, for centuries inured to the use of force in the furtherance of their national interests.

True, more than 50,000 men died in the far away jungles, but 600,000 were killed in three days at Verdun. And thirty million perished in the Second World War. Our leaders, in the grip of history, knew that had the French confronted Hitler in the Rhineland, he might well have been overthrown by his contemptuous generals and the war avoided. They sought to block Soviet expansion short of war. But one of the problems with using history as a guide to action is that you are always in danger of learning the wrong lesson.

In this case, a better lesson might have been learned from the Athenian expedition to conquer Syracuse. Like Vietnam, this minor war came to obsess the Greek leadership, eventually leading to its downfall. Similarly the effects of our engagement in Vietnam has poisoned our political culture and sapped our will, leaving us a hamstrung giant.

It is one of the oldest axioms of international politics that all actions are interconnected. Nothing exists in isolation. By far the most important result of Vietnam was that the supposed lessons of this relatively peripheral geopolitical rumble came to dominate our political culture, inhibiting the use of American power and handcuffing any action which could have resulted in the loss of even one American life. Ironically, we now even cringe from the use of the mercenary army we created, although these are men and women who have voluntarily contracted to fight and die.

During the three hundred years between 1650 and 1950, Great Britain fought ceaselessly in minor conflicts from The War of Jenkin's Ear to Afghanistan to the kingdom of the Ashanti in Ghana and a myriad of others. It fought first to preserve and expand its empire but also to maintain a minimum of political civility in the world to protect its trading interests. It went with the turf as the only genuinely global power.

We inherited that responsibility by default. The only alternative would have been to turn over the role to the Soviet Union which waited in the wings with a seductive ideology and immense military might for just that opportunity. Until Vietnam, we performed reasonably well. However, our failure of will in Southeast Asia could have resulted in disaster. That it didn't is more a factor of luck, Niccolo Machiavelli's famous *fortuna*, than calculation. Our enemy, the Soviet Union, in an irony of history, turned out to have been a clumsy, staggering political cripple, unable to contain the empire it had and incapable of grasping the opportunity we presented.

The geopolitical imperatives for making a stand in Vietnam were impeccable. Control of the raw materials and sea lanes of Southeast Asia were essential to maintaining our strategic position in the region. China and Russia had not yet come apart. Or, more accurately, we did not know they had. In 1965, Indonesia, with a population in excess of one hundred million and immense natural wealth, was almost taken over in a bloody coup d'état by pro-communist rebels. Malaysia and the Philippines were torn by communist-supported rebellions which came very close to bringing down their governments. Had we not intervened in Vietnam, supplying backbone to the area's threatened regimes, the whole region might have fallen under Soviet influence, effectively isolating Japan, our essential Pacific ally.

In retrospect, it seems clear that these fears were exaggerated and we were drawn into a war which probably was unnecessary. But in 1965 the cracks in the Soviet monolith were not apparent. Its alliance with China seemed firm. Three years earlier Khrushev had risked war in attempting to emplace medium range missiles in Cuba which could have destroyed our major cities in a matter of minutes. Continued attempts to draw third world governments, such as India and the newly emerging states in Asia and Africa, into the Soviet orbit were having considerable success.

The liberal and enlightened men around Presidents Kennedy and Johnson were not war hawks. Soviet tyranny was a formidable enemy. It had to be confronted, its power blunted, its expansion contained. They made their decisions based on the facts at their disposal and with the perhaps flawed lessons of very recent events as a guide. History is unlikely to fault their actions.

Their error was in ignoring the new environment which had arisen in the seemingly endless spiral of prosperity which began in the early nineteen-fifties and produced a narcissistic society rich beyond the hope of previous generations. This, in combination with an explosion of visual media, made war—any war—an unpalatable option. Body bags, ghastly wounds and the look of terror on the faces of young infantrymen in combat brought the battlefield into every living room in America with the evening news.

It was a hard war to explain. Vietnam was far away, seemingly unimportant, incomprehensible to any but those with the most informed and sophisticated understanding of our national interest. In addition, it offended the American sense of fair play. What were we, a mastodon of a nation, doing beating up on these poor peasants in black pajamas? The romantic infatuation of the sixties generation with the slogans of the revolutionary left led to an increasing crescendo of criticism.

The military were unable to follow Admiral Ernest King's advice on how to handle the press in World War II. "Don't tell them anything. After it's over tell them we won."

Some of this rhetoric was genuine idealism. More was cynical self-interest. The idea that sixteen million Americans had marched off with gritted teeth and idealism to defeat fascism in the Second World War is one of the more enduring myths of our time. Had the thousand men on the carriers I served on in that war been told why we were fighting and offered the opportunity to stay and fight or go home, more than ninety percent would have trampled anyone between them and the gangway to freedom. The desertion rate was far higher in that war than in the Vietnam conflict.

The unwillingness of the sons of the middle and upper classes to officer our armies in Vietnam, historically one of the first signs of slackening national will and societal degeneracy, was a shock. Their eagerness to hide out on university campuses, while the sons of the lower and lower middle class took their places to die in tropical jungles, left a bitter taste in many mouths. The hollowness of the ideals advanced in defense of this refusal were exposed when the campus riots protesting the war ceased on the day the draft ended.

Looking back on the experience of the United States in Vietnam and the Soviet Union in Afghanistan, it becomes more and more clear that mass societies in the visual media age are unable to pursue political ends through grinding wars of attrition. The coffins on television will always outweigh geopolitical logic.

The upheavals of 1968 in Europe, and the proliferation of anarchic terrorist groups in all the industrialized nations, sent a trenchant message to their governments. The situation was similar to that in Europe between World War I and World War II, when extremists of all stripes proliferated among restless young intellectuals left without hope by a seemingly endless economic crisis.

In the sixties and seventies, leaders of western democracies, eastern tyrannies and third world states of various political configurations all recognized the danger of revolutionary uprisings if their restless and often violent youth were not placated. Their solutions were the same: bribe them.

The result was a proliferation of highly paid bureaucracies, both public and private, to staff international organizations with vaguely defined goals and large amounts of money. Foundations, most of whose funds went for managerial expenses, financed endless arcane scholarly studies. Multinational corporations, bloated by a seemingly bottomless demand following the years of wartime deprivation, followed suit, adding layer after layer to their hierarchies.

In the beginning, an increasingly productive industrial base provided funds to finance the essentially useless work of this new mandarin class of semi-intellectuals. But as the twentieth century approaches its end, this process had led to an arteriosclerotic paralysis and the proliferation of talmudic exercises involving more and more economists and political theorists in debates about invented problems with no relation to the real world.

The reaction of an increasingly sophisticated populace, harassed by the arrogance of office and the expense of maintaining its bureaucratic oppressors, was finally to revolt. The result is the rapid implosion of these bureaucracies throughout the industrial world.

Meanwhile, academe, with its cherished Marxism discredited, has become obsessed with vicious feuds between the politically correct, seeking to impose the ideologically rigid theorems of post structuralism, and a traditional establishment still insisting on a smorgasbord of ideas, leaving to the student the decision of which he will accept and reject. Multiculturialism has become a vehicle for the dilution of academic excellence and the encouragement of ethnic enclaves outside the main currents of American society.

Each new generation of historians seeks to rewrite history to fit the currently fashionable ideology. But the present revisionist school has carried this exercise to the outer limits of the tolerable, cynically distorting facts to absolve the Soviet Union of responsibility for the Cold War and casting Western leaders in the role of villains. The historian Robert Conquest fought virtually alone against this intellectual phalanx, reviled and ridiculed by his critics, only in the end to have been proven right.

At the same time, and almost unnoticed, a general unease seems to have spread through the restless citizenry in Asian nations enjoying a prosperity undreamed of in any other epoch. No longer forced into daily combat to supply the minimum needs of food and shelter, these populations, too, seem to be demanding that some outside force guarantee them personal fulfillment, something beyond the reach of any government.

The age is further marked by an addiction to "solutions": economic, political and personal. The eighteenth century Rousseauist belief in formal, generalized axioms leading to perpetual prosperity and happiness had been revived in a restless search for fulfillment. Radical individualism—the shedding of the inhibitions enforced by ancient tradition and belief—and an all-pervasive narcissism, combined with a fashionable addiction among intellectuals to angst and alienation, has splintered even further the eroding base of agreed values.

The inability of the majority northern European culture of the United States to absorb and integrate increasing numbers of immigrants from nations whose values are often radically at odds with the dominant group, has led to further ethnic and linguistic separatism. This sense of difference was compounded by the internal emigration of large numbers of blacks from southern rural backwaters to the great metropolitan conglomerates where they became a disoriented, hostile and indigestible element in an increasingly discrete society.

The unifying aim of the "melting pot" and the consequent pressures to conform to the majority culture in its broadest form, died in the late decades of the twentieth century, replaced by pride of ethnic origin and the deification of racial, cultural and linguistic differences.

The centrifugal forces driving this crumbling of any consensus, in another example of the Law of Unintended Consequences, may, with exquisite irony, destroy the very attraction American society has held for those energetic immigrants who have contributed so much to the rich diversity of the nation.

But the real danger, and the leitmotif of this book, if it has one, is the proliferation of bureaucracies, both private and public, which have gathered to them immense power as society has become more complicated. Unproductive, protected from dismissal by various forms of tenure, arrogant in their cocoons of petty power, they have gradually sapped the creativity and dynamism of a culture whose genius has always been its ability to meet new challenges.

This may well be a natural phenomenon. Societies, like people, age. Veins become clogged, energy and creativity diminish and decline results. This systemic arteriosclerosis combined with the proliferation of meaningless verbiage—the Bullshit Factor—causes societal ischemia.

It is against this background that my personal history unfolds. It attempts to tell the tale, in Leopold von Ranke's inimitable phrase, *wie es eigtentlich gewesen*—the way it was.

One

When in doubt, run in circles scream and shout.

Julius Caesar

William Butts Macomber, United States ambassador to Turkey, gripped the telephone like a life preserver, beads of sweat popping out on his forehead. "Mr. Prime Minister, don't do anything rash. I have a call in to our ambassador in Greece which should come through at any moment. He will be in contact with Papadopoulos as soon as possible."

Macomber grabbed for the other phone, covering the mouthpiece of the first against his side, spittle gathering at the edges of his mouth. "Henry, how are you? What? It's three o'clock in the morning? Well sorry to wake you, but Ecevit says there's a Greek destroyer heading for the Turkish fleet off the north coast of Cyprus. He says either it turns away or he's going to sink it. Can you get hold of the prime minister and find out what's going on?"

Macomber held the phone away from his ear. Henry Tasca was a no-nonsense career officer near the end of his career. He had repeatedly recommended that the United States step in and mediate the crisis over the island of Cyprus between its two Mediterranean allies. Nobody in Washington was listening. The Watergate crisis was entering its final agony, and everybody, including Secretary of State Henry Kissinger, was trying to save their skin.

Tasca's guttural voice boomed over the speaker phone. "Christ, Butts, calm down. I doubt if the Greeks have a rowboat off Cyprus. They're pissing in their pants. But hang on. I'll see if I can get somebody. Try to stall Ecevit."

"Mr. Prime Minister? It will only be a minute. Our ambassador in Greece is contacting Papadopoulos. Please ask your people to hold off. What? Yes, I realize you can't trust the Greeks, sir." He listened as the Turkish Prime Minister rattled off a list of grievances against the United States, winding up repeating his demand for support for the Turkish invasion of Cyprus.

"Butts?" Tasca's voice came over the second phone. "Listen, I just talked to the prime minister. He says the Greek navy doesn't have a destroyer within a hundred miles of the Cyprus coast. If the Turks have something in their sights, they can sink it as far as he's concerned."

We were in the immense mansion the United States supplies its ambassador to Ankara. It sits on a ridge overlooking the pollution-ridden city in the bowl below. Macomber had transferred the embassy's operations to his home when the Cyprus crisis degenerated, and the possibility of riots against us became acute. I was the embassy press spokesman. For seventy-two hours I had fended off hundreds of press queries and arranged briefings for the flood of reporters and television commentators converging on the city as Turkey and Greece, two crucial U.S. allies, moved toward war over the divided island.

I had slept an hour or so occasionally in one of the overstuffed chairs in Macomber's living room, but he forbade me to leave to bathe and change my shirt, although I lived about five hundred yards down the road.

At the residence, chaos reigned as a dozen or so embassy staffers milled about trying to find work space. A few hours earlier, Macomber had convened his staff and begun a raging tirade, incoherent and with no seeming point, until it finally became clear that he was ripping the administrative officer to shreds for not having cleaned up an oil slick in the driveway between the mansion parking lot and the street.

The administrative officer, jowls quivering with terror, had somehow found and brought in a backhoe which was noisily tearing up the driveway as dawn broke outside. Once again the direct line to the prime minister's office rang.

"Mr. Prime Minister? You want to see me at once? You've sunk the destroyer? Oh, my God." Macomber put down the phone. "He sank it. Get my car. I've got to go down there."

At the front door Macomber stopped abruptly at the sight of the backhoe which had ripped a wide and impassable hole in the driveway between the immense residence parking lot and the street. All the embassy's cars, including the ambassador's bullet-proof limousine, were immobilized behind a pile of stained asphalt.

The admin officer quailed as Macomber advanced on him, prepared—or so it seemed—to beat him to a pulp. He was pulled away by the deputy chief of mission who led him to the small red Fiat of a secretary who had parked on the street, the only vehicle available.

Watching Macomber fold himself into the tiny car, I thought back to another scene more than twenty years earlier which had led me to this surrealistic comedy.

There were five of them facing me around a semi-circular table. Men in their fifties and sixties. Two in pinstriped suits with vests, the others in tweed jackets. A sixth, much younger, sat behind them. The room was in an annex of the State Department, a nondescript cube with a picture of then President Harry Truman looking over their shoulders. All of them had stood when I came into the room and held out their hands across the table.

The Board of Foreign Service Examiners met once a year to select between ten and thirty beginning career diplomats. The candidates had already taken and passed a four-day written examination until recently held only in Washington. The first three days, each lasting six hours, covered history, economics, general information, vocabulary and an essay based on a set of facts about a hypothetical problem in a mythical country. The fourth day was devoted to a language test.

In 1951, two thousand seven hundred people took the written exam and a hundred and three passed. The final selection was made in an oral exam given only in Washington. It was an obscure procedure, not widely advertised, and most of the candidates were graduates of Ivy League colleagues with a few from elite private regional universities. They were usually all male, white and members of the middle and upper classes, dressed in Brooks Brothers suits, button down shirts, wingtips and discreetly patterned silk ties. Several years before, women had begun to be accepted.

The candidates were all dedicated students of international relations who had prepared themselves for the exam for five or six years. Most had graduate degrees and had attended Georgetown University's cram course on the exam.

I was a ringer. My family were southern kulaks, land rich uneducated rural proletarians. Fierce Scots-Irish anarchists, violent and embittered by the aftermath of the Civil War which had left them impoverished and vengeful. I arrived in the examination room wearing a hand-sewn blue serge suit, my father's gift to me when I graduated from the University of Georgia two years earlier, the first of my clan to achieve this distinction. I had gained fifteen pounds in the interim, and the suit refused to button. The cuffs of my heavily starched shirt were held together by platinum cuff links, another graduation gift of my father's, which bore the initials of their previous owner who had left them unclaimed at Sam's Pawn Shop on Atlanta's Decatur Street.

An unlikely Odyssey had brought me to this room. I had escaped from the university, after completing a four-year course in two, with the complicity of a faculty desperate to be rid of the horde of grim-faced veterans who had ripped to shreds their somnolent existence and seemed intent on draining them of all knowledge. For six months after graduation I had manned the radio desk of the United Press in Atlanta from midnight to eight a.m. The radio desk took the morning newspapers and rewrote them in sentences no longer than ten words for the radio wire. My fingers rarely lifted from the ancient Underwood.

I had just been offered the job of bureau chief in the one-man office of UP in Jackson, Mississippi, at no increase in pay, when a college friend called to say he was heading for France. Would I like to come along? The GI Bill would enable us to live like princes in a Europe plunged in poverty. I did not hesitate.

Eighteen months later I had stood humbly before the personnel officer of the American Embassy in Paris, GI Bill subsidy exhausted, hungry, broke, having cashed my ticket home two months before, applying for a menial job in the bowels of the great building just off the Place de la Concorde, ready to do anything to stay in France.

"I wouldn't give you a job cleaning urinals," the lady said, surveying my scraggly red beard and worn, none-too-clean clothes. "Get the hell out of here." As I left I noticed a discreet announcement for the upcoming Foreign Service Examination. I filled out the form, having only a vague idea what the foreign service was, and dropped it in the box, promptly forgetting it.

Six months later an embossed envelope landed on my desk at the Sanford Florida Herald. Report to the central post office building in Atlanta for the exam, the letter read. My agreement with the paper's editor, Roland Dean, allowed me only one week's vacation a year, but Roland was a reasonable man. He had to be. His father had traded the Miami Herald for the Sanford paper in 1912, not believing that the insect-ridden swamp of south Florida had a future.

Roland, a graduate of Yale, was in the habit of playing solitary polo in the spacious field at his mansion on the outskirts of town. I was the telegraph editor of his five-day-a-week, twelve-page paper, meaning I edited all wire copy and wrote all headlines. But I also covered all sports, wrote a daily sports column, "Straight from the Horse's Mouth," handled publicity for the dog racing track and covered the five weekly lunch meetings of the Kiwanis, Rotary, Lions, Chamber of Commerce and Jaycees. The publicity perk paid me two hundred dollars and the lunches were free which was just as well, since my salary was still forty dollars a week. I was able to further supplement it with the three dollars I got for being official scorer at seventy Class D league baseball games. In my free time I helped our aging reporter, Willard, cover the city hall and the police beat.

Roland was an elegant gentleman, and he looked at me with what in retrospect can only have been pity when I told him I needed to go to Atlanta for the exam. I was clearly not diplomatic material. "Sure. Take a week off. I'll do the paper." He advanced me bus faire, and I arrived in Atlanta, bunking with an old college friend to avoid one of the periodic marital crises during which my parents savaged each other with white hot fury.

In the exam room I recognized two former Boys High School classmates, one who had received the coveted full scholarship to Emory, the local equivalent of Harvard; the other a graduate of Princeton, then, and for a century or so before, the Ivy League school of preference for the southern rich.

At eight a.m. the exams were passed out. Thick books, the first third of which were given over to identification questions, the rest multiple choice. Thumbing through the pages, I was appalled at their difficulty but even more at the kicker: if you guessed and missed an identification question, it counted off a point. Missing a multiple choice counted off a quarter.

The questions rambled across the landscape from "which direction do the winds in an anti-cyclone blow in the southern hemisphere" to "who wrote the Decline of the West" and "who was Effie Briest?" The only Effie I had ever known ran the officially sanctioned brothel in Athens, Georgia. It was also clearly a physical impossibility to answer more than two-thirds of the questions even if you knew the answers. I was on the verge of closing the book and leaving, when I noticed the look of supercilious contempt on the Emory scholar's face as he finally recognized me.

I had learned little during my short stay at the University of Georgia, but in self-defense I had made an in-depth study of the science of passing exams without any information. The one before me, a diabolically clever one, offered only two possible avenues of attack. First, I went through it as rapidly as possible, answering every question I was reasonably sure of. Then I returned to the beginning and worked my way through the rest, eliminating those about which I knew nothing, and attempting to reduce the choices from four to two on the others, shifting the odds in my favor. Then I guessed.

Fifteen minutes before the time was up, I turned in my exam book. Around the room sweat-moistened faces bent over the books as serious candidates grappled with the subtle textures on the questions. Was Pericles: a) a dictator b) chief oligarch c) secular priest d) a democratically elected leader e) none of the above.

I passed the general interest section on the basis of a vacuum cleaner mind which had engorged masses of useless information, barely got by the history cum political science by having read *Time Magazine* from cover to cover since I was twelve, failed miserably on the economics and clobbered the essay which was based on a set of facts about an imaginary country in the throes of a civil war. A revolutionary group of dubious legitimacy was attempting to overthrow a more or less democratically elected government.

The essay was supposed to analyze the situation and culminate in a recommendation for U.S. action.

Again I watched the agonized faces of the intelligent, highly-educated, dedicated young men around me as they attempted to disentangle the subtleties hidden among the raw facts, seeking a general concept to guide them. And I remembered the definition of a diplomat's task given in a lecture by Andre Siegfried at the Ecole Libre des Sciences Politiques in Paris. Seek out the sources of power, define their motivations and forecast their actions.

I then wrote what was basically a United Press radio news story, laying out the premises for a series of Cartesian syllogisms, then using them as impeccably logical building blocks for the conclusion. I ended it in two sentences pointing out that, since no evident U.S. interests were involved in the conflict, our best course was to take no action whatsoever, while maintaining contacts with both sides in the conflict. We could then, I wrote, painlessly resume relations with the eventual winner.

The paper was permeated by the kind of chilly realpolitik which so offends the politically correct in our time. But in 1951 we were a nation of arrogant warriors, intent on bending the world to our will. I scored a ninety on this section which barely tipped me over the seventy which was the overall passing grade.

The oral exam started badly and went rapidly downhill. The chairman of the examiners, a former ambassador to Afghanistan named Dreyfus, began by saying that as far as he was aware I was the first graduate of the University of Georgia to appear before the board. Perhaps I would like to tell them why I wanted to join the Foreign Service? I gave the usual boilerplate about being dedicated to serving my country in these perilous times. I answered in the carefully enunciated accent I'd cultivated since one of my professors at the University of Grenoble had informed me, with that unconscious insolence of the French, that before she could teach me French I would first have to learn English.

Dreyfus mentioned that for graduates of some universities they had favorite questions which some past victim had missed. Princetonians, for example, were always asked in which direction the river Tiber flowed on its way to the sea. Did I know the answer? I did not. And for the next half hour I knew very few answers. The battle of Cannae might as well have been between Nathan Bedford Forest and Sherman as far as I was concerned, since the only Cannae I'd ever heard of was in Tennessee.

I had taken four years of Latin? Did I know the author of the quotation: "Yield not to misfortunes, but press forward the more boldly in their face." I didn't, but I guessed Virgil. It turned out to be Cicero. And on into the maze of economics in which I was quickly lost.

They gave me forty-five minutes, but I knew it was hopeless after the first fifteen. A certain bored, patronizing tone entered their voices. And I fell into what a professor at the University of Georgia, a native of Maine, once described to me as the Southern Defense. The accent deepens, becoming virtually impenetrable, the grammar verges on the bizarre, convoluted garrulousness defies logic and a vacuous grin spreads across the features. Years later I laughed when I read that Eisenhower used the same technique with the press, sowing obfuscation and confusion and convincing them of his stupidity.

At about this point, a slender bespectacled examiner, with what seemed to me to be a slight English accent, leaned forward in his chair. "Mr. Harper, at midnight on the night of October 1, 1950 you were involved in a serious automobile accident outside," he glanced down at his notes, "Spartanburg, South Carolina. Could you perhaps describe the circumstances of this accident?"

"Yes, suh. Ah wuz driving' down to Atlanta where I had a date next mornin' with an ole girl friend. I was running kinda hot, you know, since I only had thirty-six hours fore I had to git back tuh wuk."

"How, er, hot were you running, Mr. Harper?"

"'Bout eighty. Had me a 1948 Hudson Coupe." I pronounced it in good southern fashion, coo-pee. "Real nice. Not as good as the old 'forty Ford I had in college, but real nice. That Ford was a bootlegger car. Had to stuff a chunk of concrete in the trunk, keep the troopers off my back."

My interlocutor was an earnest fellow, typical of many political officers I was to know over my career, and he had their insatiable curiosity for the trivial. "And why did putting concrete in the trunk keep the troopers off your back?"

"Well, uh, you know, all bootlegger cars got their springs built up so's the poh-lice won't know they got a load like they would if the rear end was dragging the ground. So, you ain't got no whiskey in the back, they ride up real high on them special springs."

"I see," the poor man said. "Please continue, Mr. Harper."

"Anyways," and at about this point I had begun to sound like a fugitive from Tobacco Road, "I was chuggin' along when I see this sumbitch pullin' out of a tavern on the rite hand side. I mean there wasn't no place to hide. Head on there woulda been blood all the way to Greenville, so I try to cut behind this fella into the yard of the tavern."

I stopped at this point, remembering waking up with the Hudson's still smoking engine rammed into the seat beside me, the steering post planted in my chest, its wheel bent double where my hands had gripped it.

"Yes?"

"Well, suh, I didn't quite make it. I hit this here cuvert sideways and it pushed the engine up right beside me on the seat."

"You hit a what?"

"A cuvert. You know. One of them pipes water runs through."

"A culvert?"

"Yes, suh. Like I said."

There was a silence as the five examiners looked at me from across the room, clearly trying to figure out how I had gotten there.

"One final question, Mr. Harper," Dreyfus said. "Could you tell us who you have been reading recently?"

I didn't have anything left to lose, so I looked them all in the eye in turn as I spoke, although looking people in the eye in the South is insolent and regarded as an invitation to fight.

"Spengler, Thucydides, Machiavelli, Hegel, Sartre, Camus, Celine, Radiguet, Stendahl, Koestler, Orwell, Simenon, Flaubert, Dostoevksi, Miller, Grosser, Mounier and James T. Farrel, Theodore Dreiser and Ernest Hemingway."

"And the books you admired most?"

"Voyage au Bout de la Nuit, Le Rouge et Le Noir, Le Diable au Corps, Tropic of Cancer and the *Studs Lonigan Trilogy."*

The examiners exchanged a glance in the succeeding silence, and I was about to get up and leave when the slender young man sitting behind the board tapped Dreyfus on the shoulder and whispered something in his ear. He was wearing a double-breasted gray chalkstripe and the round little metal-framed glasses I associated with French intellectuals. Dreyfus looked at me, shrugged and nodded.

The question was in French, the crystalline French of the educated elite, rolling over me, as it always did, like oil over a hot blister. Had I ever read the French newspaper *Le Monde?* I had. Every day for two years.

Would I describe the third force strategy of this paper? In French, please. I would and did, pointing out that the editor, Hubert Beuve-Meury, in recommending that France lead a third force coalition of European nations in developing a neutral buffer zone between the Soviet Union and the United States, was proposing romantic nonsense. France had neither the population, economic resources or armed forces necessary to defend such a position, and, in any case, neither Germany nor any other European country was prepared to give up the protective shield of the United States for such an adventure.

I went on to say that France had no alternative but to accept its changed position in the world as a third-rate power whose ability to influence events was minimal. It, and Germany and Britain as well, must bend to the fact that there were only two world powers, Russia and the United States, as De Toqueville had forecast a century earlier, and adjust to the reality that they could have an impact on events only by influencing one of these two superpowers.

Needless to say, a slanging match of some force developed during which the young French diplomat, for such he was, acting as an observer to our selection process, and I covered the horizon of French postwar political and cultural thought from DeGaulle to Sartre, Mauriac, Thorez and Aron, occasionally digging into history to cite the French masters of realpolitik, Thiers, Michelet, de Toqueville and de Maistre. All the while exchanging quotes from Richelieu and Talleyrand.

I had spent a year and a half at the Ecole Libre des Sciences Politiques in Paris absorbing the mannered logic so dear to the French soul, constructing unbreakable syllogisms utterly divorced from reality but infinitely pleasing in their clarity and elegance. Sitting in the examination room I forgot where I was in the thirst for bare knuckle intellectual combat, so alien to the compromising American soul, provoking my opponent with facts and figures indicating France's political and economic impotence and the necessity to submit to American dominance.

He bobbed and weaved, concocting a maze of convoluted defenses designed to obfuscate the facts, showing the same skill Napoleon exhibited in his brilliant but losing defensive campaign of 1813 at Bautzen and Leipzig. It was an exhibition of the virtuosity France was to sustain over the next half century, using will power and intellectual brilliance to project the illusion of a power it no longer possessed and repeatedly winning against all odds and logic.

Dreyfus finally intervened, indicating that the next candidate was waiting. I left the examiners and almost did not wait for their verdict. There was no way I was going to be accepted. But I finally sat down. Two hours later Dreyfus emerged with my impeccable successor, shaking hands with him and inviting him to lunch at the Metropolitan Club. He then turned to me.

"Mr. Harper, the board is happy to inform you that you have been accepted as a member of the career foreign service. Congratulations," he said, extending a huge paw. "I hope you'll be free to join me with several other members of the board at lunch?"

"You're kidding," I said.

Dreyfus smiled. "We're democratizing, Mr. Harper." If he hadn't been so old I think I might have hit him. However, looking back on the whole thing, I can only be deeply impressed with the broad-minded tolerance of these upper class men, under orders to broaden the base of their little club, in accepting me, particularly when forty years later I read the FBI background reports in my personnel file to which they had access.

In it, the lifelong combat between my mother and father was vividly documented as it spilled over into the public domain. In 1933, in the parking lot of Atlanta's Piedmont Hotel, then the city's finest, my mother, a gentle lady barely five feet tall, took five shots at the red-headed paramour of my father. In the FBI file the incident is described in dry police terms. No complaint was made and the case was closed.

Reality was a little different. The incident was described for me by Sam Redwine, a friend of my father's when deep in his cups.

"Ed," Sam, a slender, elegant southerner of the old school, said. "Your daddy had just come down from meeting his lady friend and was settling in for an afternoon of poker when we heard these shots. I was standing by the window, and I see this red-headed lady running like hell into that little hut the boys who park the cars keep warm in." In a metaphor no longer allowable, Sam described the scene.

"Eva, your mother was right behind her lettin' fly with this little snub-nosed thirty-two revolver. When the redhead scuttled into that hut, the boys came flying through the windows like a flock of crows. Your daddy, Alec, he got on his horse and gets down there just as your mother's figured out how to reload the pistol, and takes it away from her."

"How come she wasn't arrested?"

"Well, you know how it is. Half the town is related either to your daddy or your mother, and the judge didn't see much point in making a big deal out of it, since she didn't hit anybody. He just told her not to do it again."

It didn't end there. In another incident twenty years later my mother was restrained from beating in the same lady's door with an ax in search of my father. And then there was the murky history of the death of my father's real estate and construction business. With a fourth grade education, he had built every filling station in Atlanta before 1930 and was, on paper at least, by then a millionaire.

Over the next three years compulsive gambling, wenching, marital discord and the deepening depression led to the failure of his business and, worse, accusations of fraud which were probably true. In any event, he didn't wait for trial and left town with us in tow for a seven-year odyssey until the statue of limitations had run its course.

In retrospect he was clearly an eccentric genius, combining intelligence, energy, duplicity, an amoral humor and a lust for life, all colored by the corrosive cynicism of a born hustler. Returning to Atlanta shortly after the beginning of the Second World War, he became a business outlaw, gambling in an ever rising property market with other people's money for a small percentage of the profit.

He used an uncanny ability to judge real estate values to wheel and deal on the margins of a growing, dynamic city. He never paid an income tax, using a gothic collection of street people, whom he called, with total realism, his "bums", to sign all legal papers. At the end of the year he scrupulously filed pauper's oaths in their names, relieving them of the necessity of facing the Internal Revenue Service. Their loyalty to him was total.

He was endlessly convoked to interviews by the IRS which he refused to attend. With no evidence against him, the frustrated civil servants were unable to obtain subpoenas. During this period, always paying cash, he and my mother traveled extensively to the Kentucky Derby and Florida race tracks and lived with a certain lavishness—while avoiding any taxes.

Paradoxically, he wasn't particularly interested in money other than as a sort of score card. I once, on a rare visit home, told him in exasperation that money would not buy everything.

He laughed and replied: "You're right, boy. It won't. But what it won't buy ain't worth having."

He was a mine of one-liners. Of a straight-laced friend he said: "You couldn't drive a needle up his ass with a sledgehammer."

Or, when I told him my foreign service salary: "Hell, boy, I can make more money than that looking for pocket books."

Describing another friend he said: "He's as clumsy as a one-legged man in a kicking contest."

And, maybe his best advice: "It's the spouting whale that gets harpooned."

He subscribed throughout his life to the bank robber's iron rule: Get in, get the money, get out.

I asked him once if he had a goal in life. He grinned and said: "Sure, boy. Live to ninety-seven and get hung for rape."

Over the years this corrosive cynicism I fought so hard to escape has colored my view of the world, tempering the utopian idealism of youth and making more bearable the bitter disappointments of age.

As a child I was more or less oblivious to the vengeful chaos which had descended on my parents' marriage. Until I was about five, I probably believed Will Davenport, one of my father's workmen, was my father, since I saw more of him than anybody else. He taught me to skate, ride a bicycle, field a ground ball and play a mean game of marbles. Will was a gentle giant, a painter and a carpenter, who for some unfathomable reason had been assigned as my baby sitter.

Year's later, after my encounter with the South Carolina culvert and while I was having my face and teeth repaired in Atlanta, I worked with Will rehabilitating a half dozen black slum apartment houses my father had acquired in one of his various deals. Will had disappeared from my life, leaving a great void, about the time I started kindergarten. Much later I learned that, in one of the Saturday night saturnalias which characterized the black ghettos of the time, he had used his straight razor to deadly effect, slicing the throat of an opponent.

Despite a massive effort, my father was unable to get him acquitted, and Will was sent up for murder. Fourteen years later he was released, a worn and broken old man, face seamed with age and razor scars, a hopeless alcoholic. He shared his fruit jar of white lightening with me as we climbed the ladders and sloshed a vile green paint, bought from an army surplus store, on the rickety shacks. By late afternoon we were both blind drunk.

We took our time, often sitting in the shade sipping whiskey from a mason jar. Will was a superb raconteur and a mine of southern jokes. "You hear the one about the Yankee who come south and bought hisself a farm out to the Lick Skillet?"

"No, tell me about it Will."

"Well this here Yankee took to settin' on his porch. Didn't do no work. Evah day he seen Mistuh Sam, his neighbor, come by with his hog goin' down to the mudhole to let the hog roll around. Yankee finally stopped Mistuh Sam."

"'Tell me, sir,' sez the Yankee, 'you have plenty of water in your well. Why don't you make a mudhole for the pig on your farm?'"

"Mistuh Sam, he scratch his head and look at the Yankee."

"'Now why would I do that?'"

"'Well,' sez the Yankee, 'think of the time you'd save.'"

"Mistuh Sam, he look puzzled. 'What's time to a hog,' he sez."

It was a great summer until one of the religious ladies of the neighborhood ratted on us to my father. But by then the houses were painted and sold to a slum landlord, and I took the fifteen hundred dollars my father paid me as my share of the profit, bought a car and headed south to the Sanford Herald.

Between the time Will went to jail and our summer idyll, the United States had entered a decade of unrelieved economic agony. One of the phenomena of the time was a great migration of peoples in search of work or simply seeking survival. My hegira began at the age of seven when I was sent to live with my aunt in a rural slum on the outskirts of Atlanta in a place called Lakewood. My mother's older sister, a school teacher, had married an uneducated carpenter who had built a small wooden cottage on land owned by his brother, Jubal Morris, named after the one-legged Confederate general, Jubal Early, under whom his grandfather had served.

The Morris clan was immense, as least ten children ranging from two or three to twenty swarmed in a rambling old house next door to my aunt's. They lived in a state of slovenly chaos, resented by the half dozen other families in the little neighborhood, running wild in the surrounding wilderness. I had been pulled out of the second grade at Smiley Grammar School, located in an upper class area where the teachers were gentle and caring, the classes small, the children obedient.

The Lakewood school was an unpainted clapboard shack, full of wild young Scots-Irish anarchists. The teachers ruled by the rod, and I was beaten mercilessly on my first day. Let go, I ran, with tears streaming down my face, home to my aunt. My memories of what happened next are vague, but I was returned to school every day for several weeks and, refusing to "give in", was beaten regularly, escaping time and again to the sanctuary of my aunt's house.

The school finally gave up on me, and my aunt returned with me to Smiley Grammar School. I was to be allowed to study there, although it was illegal, taking an hour's streetcar ride each morning and walking the ten blocks to the school, returning the same way in the evening. This curious arrangement lasted for more than a year until I was reunited with my mother and father in Birmingham, Alabama.

On one memorable day, the terror still seared in my memory, I lost my return streetcar ticket and stood at the stop, staring up at the motorman, tears streaming down my seven-year-old face. He descended, picked me up and let me ride home sitting on his lap, hands on the brass levers worn and polished by time and use.

Oddly, my memories of Lakewood are fond ones. My cousins took me under their wing, teaching me to smoke a weed called rabbit tobacco, to roam the forests surrounding us using a three-dollar single shot Sears Roebuck .22 rifle to massacre squirrels and rabbits used to make succotash stew and to trap, clean and roast the quail and pheasant which we lured into the deserted farmlands by seeding them with corn and illegally trapped. And we would crawl on our bellies into the neighboring farmer's field and slice open ripe watermelons, eating only the sweet hearts.

The school I transferred into, when I joined my mother and father in Birmingham, was a paradigm of the next few years. On the first day, I was confronted in a deserted corner of the schoolyard by the class bully and beaten mercilessly. My father, listening to my tearful tale, shrugged and told me to fight back. I did, for several days, winding up bloodied and punished by the teachers as my tormentor accused me of being the aggressor. But my father was right. Fighting back, even losing, eventually obtained for me a certain respect, and I was soon left in peace. It was a dance often to be repeated and probably seeded the thread of violence which ran through my later life.

My father then had a piece of luck. One of his old gambling acquaintances had opened an illegal operation in Jacksonville, Florida. It as modest. Two rooms and five poker tables above a grocery store. My father was hired as a dealer, playing for the house. Although he'd lost a small fortune betting on horses, he was a shrewd and implacable poker player, with an instinctive knowledge of the odds, immense patience and a photographic memory for the cards dealt in the classic draw, five-card stud and blackjack games which were then in favor.

I brought him his lunch each day and stood behind his chair as he dealt the hands, and the nickels, dimes and quarters were thrown on the table by anxious work hardened hands.

The five housemen often played each other during the slow daytime hours. One, a slim dark-haired part Cherokee was never allowed to deal. He could pick up a new deck, spill the cards on the table and allow the others to cut and shuffle, then deal five hands of straight flushes, long graceful fingers moving with lightning speed.

I asked my father once how he did it.

"Watch him the next time. That ring on his left hand has a miniature mirror in it. Del has Indian eyes. He can see the hairs on a gnat's ass. He turns the ring over and holds the mirror under the deck, slides the top cards over it until he finds one he wants and holds it back dealing the card underneath. It's called dealing seconds. They ever catch him doing it, they'll take him out in the alley and break those pretty fingers."

Once, on a bet, Del took a new deck and dealt six draw poker hands face down and then read off the cards, back up, never missing.

Occasionally, the dealers would let me into the game, giving me chips instead of money. Teaching me to watch the cards and catalog those dealt in the stud games. Reciting the odds on winning hands. Telling me to fold low cards quickly and bag the ante, never go for an inside or three-card straight or flush. Never hold a kicker. Patience. Wait for the cards. Watch their eyes in draw. And the hands. Some men begin to twitch when they get a good hand. Others yawn. A few suddenly get poker faces. Everybody has his tics.

"Watch them long enough and you can read them like through clear glass," Del said.

"A poker face don't mean sitting there like a goddamn mummy in a museum," he used to say. "All you gotta do it confuse the bastards. You got a full house one time, you jump around like a roach on a hot skillet. Next time you sit like a stone. Poker ain't about winnin' anyway," he said. "It's for fun. The money's just the gravy on the grits."

One of my most vivid memories of the time was the bootlegger. He made his deliveries wearing a huge overcoat, his inventory of flat, curved bottles stashed in neat rows of pockets inside his overcoat. He carried a little sawed off .22 rifle.

"Shoot the eye out a chicken at ten yards," Del said.

Years later, in a replacement depot in Norfolk, Virginia, in 1944, waiting for a carrier to which I was assigned to dock, I was invited to join a game of grizzled chief petty officers who needed a sixth. I had been winning in the nickel, dime and quarter games and had a stash they planned to lift.

It was serious poker. Table stakes. No small talk. Each player started with a hundred dollars, big money then. A third class petty officer made sixty a month. I played for three weeks and wound up fifty dollars ahead. Probably the least money for the hardest work I ever made. In two years at sea I won another three thousand dollars in nickel, dime and quarter games.

Recently, at the Institute for Advanced Study in Princeton, New Jersey, where my wife had a two-year grant, I played nickel, dime and quarter poker for the first time in thirty years against six of America's finest academic minds. It was the most emotional, illogical game I can remember, totally lacking in discipline, elementary knowledge of odds and, mostly, patience. I won forty dollars in one evening and dropped out of the game. Watching their antics offended my sense of the fitness of things. They played for fun, not understanding that poker is a holy ritual.

My father gathered together enough money in Jacksonville over a two-year period to move to New Orleans, where he and my mother opened a restaurant which rapidly went broke. They then moved to Nashville where he ran a wholesale grocery business for another year. I spent most of these years living with my grandmother and a maiden aunt in Atlanta, all of us supported by my aunt's pitiful wages as a hat maker. My mother soon joined us, and my father hit the road. We didn't see him for two years when a phone call came from a place called Alton, Illinois. It was 1939. The economy was beginning to move. He had a job selling cars. My mother and I joined him.

The three years in Atlanta had been in many ways an idyll. I'd discovered books and read my way through the Carnegie Library junior section, immersing myself in the adventure books of Henty and the historical tales of sir Walter Scott and Fenimore Cooper. I still vividly remember one of Henty's tales, *Tros of Samothrace*, about a swaggering Greek pirate, which aroused an interest in Greece which has never waned.

Finally obtaining permission to use the adult section, I read indiscriminately, an entire shelf of Dumas, living in the skin of D'Artagnan, Athos and the other musketeers. I read Tom Sawyer, Huckleberry Finn and Dickens, masses of Dickens, finally graduating to *For Whom the Bell Tolls, Tender is the Night,* Dreiser's *An American Tragedy* and Dorothy Sayers' mystery novels. I also discovered Mencken and his six volumes of prejudices, Dos Passos and Willa Cather.

The Library, a Greek classic imitation with a copy of the Winged Victory on the monumental staircase leading to the second floor, was a refuge and escape from the grim day-to-day reality of the time. City council vandals tore it down in a frenzy of urbanization in the nineteen eighties.

At one point I read somewhere about a book which had been banned as pornography. The librarians, always pathetically eager to help any youth who showed some interest in books, often frowned on my choices but were amazingly tolerant. I had discovered that some of the younger women were, in fact, nothing but gophers, not really aware of the library rules. One day I passed over to one of them the name of this book which I knew to be on the restricted list and pointed back into the reserved stacks.

"It's in there." I said. "Probably just got brought back. Look in the shelf on the right." The young woman did as she was told, and I suddenly had in my hands a pornographic book. It took me several days to get used to the author's odd style, but I ploughed through it until I was rewarded by Molly's epiphany. By then I was so absorbed in Bloom's life that this ode to lust was, and continues to be, oddly unmoving.

All this time I was running with a tough bunch. Harold, whose mother was a waitress and, as I look back, probably a part-time prostitute, lived in a red brick apartment house abutting the ancient wooden row house my grandmother and aunt rented. He was a tall, slender boy who already smoked when he could steal his mother's cigarettes. He was often outside, shivering in the cold while his mother entertained a friend.

He and Linwood, a gentle, freckled, red-haired boy who, when aroused, fought with a vicious ferocity we all admired, were my only friends. We rode our bicycles through the city's streets, stealing scuppernongs from the garden of one of the big deserted old mansions across Ponce de Leon, the boulevard which divided the slums from the upper class, swimming in Piedmont Park in the summer and playing pickup games of baseball and football.

A friend of my father's, Tom Osler, a prosperous real estate man who was probably a secret admirer of my pretty mother, took me under his wing and introduced me to the YMCA, paying my dues. Looking back I think he must have realized I was running wild, having been almost expelled for fighting, the three women unable to control me.

At the "Y" I learned to lift weights, play handball. And box. It was here that I picked up a lifelong habit of working out in gyms, the mindless effort becoming a crutch, a sort of daily session with a shrink, draining off aggression and frustration in the aging iron and sweat-and-blood-stained punching bags. An old professional, a wizened lightweight whose face was seamed and scarred, ears cauliflowered from slipping punches, taught us the moves which have long since become quaint in the modern sport. Slip right and counter with a straight left. Hook off a jab. Circle right against a right hander, away from his power, left against a southpaw. Slip left against a straight left and counter with a right cross over the extended arm, the punch with which Schmelling defeated Joe Louis in their first fight.

The old boxer took me aside once, after losing a bout with a boy I should have beaten. "You're going to have to take some punches to win, son. You're quick and you're smart, but you don't like to get hit. Getting hit is part of life. You're a hustler, kid. Hustlers always lose."

The Second World War had started by now, and I was terrified it would be over before I could get in. I went to summer school in 1942 and advanced my graduation to January 1943. On February 20, my birthday, I volunteered for the navy. My classmates, all in high school ROTC, graduated in January a year later, just in time to finish basic training and Officer Candidate School before the European invasion. Many died and more were wounded on the beaches of Normandy, while I rode out the war on jeep carriers in relative safety.

It was my second encounter of many with The Law of Unintended Consequences.

Two

First Soldier: *I wonder what future historians will say about the Second World War.*

Second Soldier: *They'll probably say, "The first half of the twentieth century was marked by unrest and wars."*

Private by Lester Atwell

The radar shack of the U.S.S. Bogue, CVE-13, was packed as the pilots' voices came over the loudspeaker. It was early winter off the coast of Newfoundland. Four Avenger bombers were lost under an overcast hugging the sea, almost a fog. The skipper had broken radio silence and was on the bridge, trying to talk them home. They were on the last leg of anti-submarine sweep when the clouds, last remnants of a tropical disturbance which had turned into a vicious winter storm, rolled in across the rising swells, whitecaps clipped off by a gale approaching fifty knots. The ship bucked and heeled as the helmsman tried to hold it head-on to the sea. Our five corvette escorts gathered close like hounds protecting their master.

"I can hear your engines, Larrimore," the skipper said from the bridge, trying to talk them down. "Bear left. You'll have to get right down on the deck to see us. Visibility is five hundred yards."

The four stumpy torpedo bombers had lost sight of each other minutes earlier when they plunged into the clouds trying to find the ship.

"Your engines are growing fainter," the skipper said. "Bear hard left and circle back."

"My gas gauge is on empty, sir."

Another voice broke in. "Nelson here, sir. Engine just stopped. I'm ditching."

Seconds later Larrimore came on. "That's it, sir. Ditching."

"Johnson here, sir. Ditching."

Campbell here, sir. Ditching."

Eight men were dead. Four pilots and four bombardiers. They flew off what the navy called a CVE, tankers converted into small aircraft carriers. Marine postage stamps with four-hundred-foot wooden decks barely long enough to contain the obsolete Navy F-4Fs and TBFs on cruises designed to deny German submarines a shot at the massive convoys carrying U.S. invasion forces and materiel to Europe.

The pilots were nineteen and twenty-year olds, those who survived the training. Fearless and funny on the surface. Frightened near children underneath. I was seventeen years old when I joined the ship in Norfolk, Virginia that winter. An Aerographer's Mate third class, an enlisted meteorologist.

Aside from the chief warrant officer, a thirty-year navy veteran, I was the ship's only trained weatherman. I drew up the maps from encoded weather observations, entering temperatures and pressure readings and tracing the fronts and air masses in on the maps. It all looked very professional except information was usually twenty-four hours old and came mostly from U.S. coastal areas and a half dozen weather ships scattered over thousands of miles of ocean.

The chief, who had learned his meteorology by the seat of his pants, forecast more by instinct and experience than the erratic science at our disposal. We sailed in winter seas a half degree above the freezing point. Contact with an air mass loaded with moisture only a few degrees warmer resulted in fog so dense the bow of the ship was invisible from the bridge. Winds as high as 75 knots often whipped up giant waves, flipping the top heavy ship about like a ponderous chip. On one cruise a monster wave caught the bow as it plunged and rolled up the front of the flight deck like a rug.

The skipper, one of the first Navy pilots to qualify to land on a carrier, had retired before the war and been brought back to command the ship. He knew more weather than anybody else on board and had an instinctive feel for storms. Earlier that day he had stood over my map staring down at the neat whorls designating the frontal system of a degenerating tropical disturbance.

"How fast is it going?"

I pulled out the previous map, six hours older and let him compare the almost stationary storm. "How come it's not moving?"

"Bermuda high, sir," I said, circling the high pressure area named after the island of Bermuda, which sometimes funneled weather north along the Atlantic coast. It had moved across the storm's path, slowing it almost to a halt.

"What if the high shifts offshore?"

"The movement of the front will accelerate, sir."

He glanced at me and nodded. "You bet your ass it will. What's your last observation report?"

I pulled the last coded sheets toward me and folded them under the numbers in the code book, subtracting one from the other and writing down the weather code in the clear. It was a system designed to keep weather data from the German subs we hunted, but they had long since broken it. I selected five stations along the Jersey and New England coast and entered them rapidly next to the previous readings. I was quick and good and I knew it.

"What do you think?"

"There's a tertiary front developing behind the main storm, sir." I didn't get any further.

"Cut the crap, son. Can we fly or not?" He didn't wait for a reply. "Get the Chief up here. I want to see him on the bridge." An hour later the planes took off. Two hours later, the new weather reports began to trickle in. The storm had taken off and was moving northward at ten to fifteen knots. Worse, its core had begun to diffuse, spreading out over a larger and larger area. The Bermuda High had shifted further out over the Atlantic, leaving the coastal funnel open.

I went down to the Chief's quarters and woke him up. He listened impatiently and told me to go back and work up the chart.

The planes had reached the end of their outward leg when I finished, and the Chief, yawning, came in to crouch over the scrawls.

"It looks bad, Chief. He'd better get the planes back real quick."

The Chief, a slim swarthy man with slicked back black hair touched with gray and a pencil mustache, paled. "Why the fuck didn't you wake me sooner, you little shit," he said, grabbing the map and heading for the bridge. I followed him up onto the cramped semi-circle, looking out over a sea already beginning to heave as the swells rose ever higher in response to the winds of the onrushing storm.

Breaking radio silence, the skipper ordered the planes to end their sweeps and head straight for home. The ship turned its back on the storm and raced ahead of the stratus overcast, heading for the rendezvous point, bucking quartering seas all the way. Winds on the deck reached thirty knots which meant at the five thousand foot ceiling they were fifty to seventy-five. Our flank speed was sixteen. We would never outrun the storm.

The cruise was almost over when the planes went down, and the skipper was ordered to cut it short, heading for our home port, Norfolk, Virginia, and the naval inquiry board which would be convoked. I was dazed with guilt, and two days before we hit port, the Air Officer, a retired navy enlisted pilot recalled to duty and given a temporary commission as commander, called me into his office.

"Harper, you realize you face a court martial in the death of eight men? You were negligent in not waking the Chief in time to abort the mission. Had you alerted him to the storm's speed, they would still be alive. You realize that, don't you?" he said, leaning across the table, his thin, hawklike face pitted with acne scars only inches from mine. He was a man we all admired. A fair, good-natured man, ever tolerant of the undisciplined civilian citizen sailors surrounding him.

"Yes, sir."

He nodded. "Well, I've talked to the skipper and the Chief about you. We've decided you didn't really mean any harm. Just the negligence of youth. So we're going to wipe the slate clean. You'll be transferred to the Norfolk replacement depot for reassignment. I want you off the ship the minute we tie up. And Harper."

"Yes, sir."

"I think the best thing would be if you never mentioned this incident to anybody. You understand? Anybody."

"Yes, sir."

I carried with me a paralyzing sense of guilt even though I had awakened the Chief as soon as the storm reports came in. For years I woke in the middle of the night, the captain's dialog with the pilots racing through my mind. It eased, and then only partially, when a couple of decades later I told the story to a navy pilot whom I had come to know. When I finished, he shook his head.

"You realize what happened? The two old chiefs knew if you testified before an investigation panel, nobody would try to hang this on you. It was the chief warrant officer's responsibility to monitor that storm. He should have been on deck, not in the sack. The Air Officer should have been informed by him of the danger. And finally the captain knew damn well he was taking a risk." He shook his head. "Somebody's ass would have been grass if you had testified. Maybe all three. Without your testimony, they got together and cooked up a plausible story. Green pilots were dying all the time. We were in a war. They closed the case. The navy has a lot of problems, but nailing seventeen-year-olds for their superiors' incompetence is not one."

I'd volunteered for the navy the day I turned seventeen, partially to escape from the increasingly virulent atmosphere of hatred and vengeance between my parents but mostly because I was afraid the war would be over before I was drafted. My mother had rejoined my father in late 1939 in Alton, Illinois, where he had found a job selling used cars. I followed at the end of the school year. During the next three years their bitter marital squabbling turned to outright war.

Alton was a mill town. A grim, late nineteenth century place of small clapboard houses and cramped, vermin-ridden four-unit apartment houses of dirty red brick. One of our neighbors was a lady wrestler who periodically beat up her husband, an unemployed boilermaker. Another was a prostitute. The town's population was made up of second generation immigrants whose parents had been recruited by press gangs ranging through the outlying fiefs of the Austro-Hungarian Empire. These recruiters, aided by the local police, rounded up the criminals, mentally deranged and trouble makers and shipped them across the sea. Poles, Hungarians, Rumanians, Slovenes Croats, Czechs, Slovaks and south Europeans now joined with the impoverished descendants of the original German and Anglo Saxon settlers who had left the land to work in the factories.

It was a union town. Strikes, lockouts and layoffs had hardened the men and worn out the women over the long years of the depression. There was a desolate, beaten look to the place. We were part of a new element in the area. As the Second World War began, southern Scots-Irish migrants from the worn out fields of the Appalachian highlands, escaping an even deeper poverty, had invaded the border areas of the industrial states, working as scabs in the struck factories, earning the hatred of the ethnic enclaves, jeered and sneered at for their strange accents and funny foods. Later, during the war, southern blacks arrived to occupy the lowest rung in the ladder, and race riots erupted across this industrial heartland.

Redneck hillbilly was the epithet applied to us. I entered the ninth grade, the first year of high school, that fall expecting the worst, and it wasn't long in coming. A squat youth whose thick mop of black hair began about an inch above his eyebrows walked up at the first recess and, without preamble, swung a roundhouse right which I barely managed to duck.

At the time I was convinced he was made of concrete, since my straight lefts bounced off his face doing more damage to my knuckles than to him. Fortunately, he was slow and clumsy, and I survived long enough for one of the monitors to intervene. More important, I'd managed to stand off one of the tougher kids on the playground, and it quickly became known that I was fighting in the local Golden Gloves bouts arranged by the YMCA. For several months I was left alone.

Then, at a weekly assembly one of the football players, sitting in the row behind me, refused to take his foot off my folding seat, and I was left standing, humiliated, to the amusement of the multitude. I then made a serious mistake. Taking out a miniature knife I used to sharpen pencils, I poked the boy's ankle with the tip.

He came up out of his seat with a roar of rage, arms like logs, swinging rhythmically. There was no place to hide, and any minor skill I had was useless. I fought back, trying to stay inside his wild swings, punching furiously until I was draped, bleeding and battered over the back of the seat and a teacher managed to fight his way through the packed students to rescue me. I still bear the scars of his fists on my lips.

The next thing I remember is sitting with my tormentor in the principal's office on a low couch looking up at this bespectacled man who stared down at us from what seemed a great height, although he was rather short. Years later in the Foreign Service I worked for a nasty semi-dwarf, named Tom Tuch, who always placed visitors to his office on a low couch, the legs of which had been sliced off enabling him to look down on them. I suspect that our principal had had similar surgery performed on this couch.

He had tented his hands and was staring down at my miniature knife which lay on the table between us. "Harper," he said, "you have committed a crime. You have used a knife in a fight with a fellow student. I'd like to know what you have to say."

I glanced over at my opponent who was smirking at me in obvious delight. I had at least cut him above one eye and left it black. There wasn't anything to say. I'd learned early to keep my mouth shut in crises and let other people do the talking.

"Your father is on his way over here, Harper. I hope you realize that I don't have much choice but to expel you for this infraction."

At that moment, my father, a medium-sized but muscular man with an immense animal presence, surged into the room. He stood staring at the scene, taking it in, recognizing my little knife.

"Mr. Harper," the principal said, "I regret to tell you that your son drew this knife in a fight with a fellow student." He stopped expectantly.

My father turned to me, face congested, southern accent exaggerated. "Boy, how many times, I told you? You pull a knife, you use it." At which point he turned and stalked out of the office. I stared after him, probably with an open mouth. He had never advised me on anything, certainly not on knife fighting.

The principal stood transfixed. He motioned to my opponent to leave and sat down to face me from his eminence. "Well, Harper, I just don't know what to say. I've looked at your record with us, and you've already had one schoolyard fight. However, your teachers tell me you are an honor roll student." He glanced down at a paper on the table in front of him. "You have a straight A average over six months," a fact I'd managed to conceal from my peers. I always sat in the back and never volunteered.

"What are we going to do with you?"

I sat silent. The idea of being expelled filled me with panic. I'd already figured out that an education was the only way out of the family morass which engulfed me. There seemed to be a glimmer of hope in his question.

"What is your church, Harper?"

"My church?"

"Where do you worship?"

I hadn't been in a church since I was seven, but we were nominally Methodists.

"Methodist?" he said, nodding. "Do you know anything about the Episcopal Church?"

I shook my head. All I knew was that my mother said they were fake papists, but it didn't seem to be the time to bring that up.

"Well, Harper, I'm going to make a suggestion. If you are willing to come to our church here and participate in the programs we have for troubled boys like you, I think I can see my way clear to allowing you to continue your schooling. On strict probation, of course. If you will bring me your parents' written consent to this tomorrow, I'll introduce you to our priest."

It took a while. In fact it took two days, but I finally persuaded my mother I was going to be expelled if she didn't agree. I think the thought of having me underfoot was decisive. It would have interfered with her vendetta against my father. She signed me over to what she called the "papists" and never brought up the subject again.

It was, of course, all a hustle. The Episcopal church in Alton catered to the town's minimal upper class. Factory managers, lawyers, doctors, professors at nearby colleges. St. Paul's was a small stone structure, built in the late nineteenth century in a vaguely gothic style, now dirty gray from the pollution of the surrounding factories. The priest was a young man with a pretty wife and baby who had recently graduated with a doctorate in theology from a Wisconsin seminary. He was small-boned, bespectacled and gentle. He was, as well, very high church.

He insisted on having a service each morning, and he needed an acolyte for this ceremony. Since the acolyte was not allowed to eat before taking communion, virtually none of the young *jeunesse dore* of the town were willing to get up and arrive at the church at six a.m., hungry and sleepy. The solution was to dragoon young delinquents from the local high school into joining the congregation, under pain of expulsion, and enlist them as acolytes.

There were six of us, plus a tall young man who walked down the center aisle of the church on Sundays swinging a baroque object emitting incense. I met my confreres in the vestry on the first Sunday. Sons of mill workers who were congenital troublemakers at the school, either for fighting, stealing or disrupting classes, smoking in the hallways, skipping school or any of the other myriad pastimes of rebels without a cause. It was an innocent time. No guns or knives. Nobody would think of questioning a teacher's authority or threatening him or her.

I was a member of the inmates' elite, convicted of fighting a very large football player to the bitter end and using a knife. Once the lighting of the candles was completed, and the young priest had begun his sermon, the dice appeared. A half hour later several of us left the game to assist at the offering of communion and, finally, to extinguish the candles.

The early morning weekday sessions were shorter editions of the Sunday ceremony. A couple of candles, the blessing of the wine and wafers, the ritual sip from the common cup. The priest and I were almost always the only people in the church. And this presented a minor problem. The young servant of God was an incipient alcoholic and tended to pour a liberal libation into the ornate chalice. On occasion he would absentmindedly present it to me for several healthy gulps. At fourteen, on an empty stomach, the result was a pleasant buzz which lasted for much of the morning.

Following the service the priest's wife would give us breakfast. He was a shy, intelligent and tortured young man who made an immense effort to come down from his existential confrontation with his doubts about the existence of God and meet us on our own terms. I followed my usual hustler's technique of saying whatever I thought he wanted to hear, and it worked reasonably well for about six months.

Then one morning, having swilled about half a cup of sacramental wine, I made the mistake of mentioning Robert Ingersoll's answer to Anselm's proof of the existence of a divine being. I guess if you had given the young priest a goose with a cattle prod he might have jumped higher, but he definitely lifted out of his chair.

Ingersoll, now long forgotten, was a turn-of-the-century atheist who was lashed together in deadly combat with the fundamentalist preachers of his time. He was the favorite writer of my atheist uncle, Marvin McGhee, with whom I had spent many a summer on the remnants of the family farm near a village called Lick Skillet outside Atlanta.

Lick Skillet had been the site of a civil war battle as Sherman approached Atlanta in 1864, and our farm contained a line of crumbling earthworks behind which the outnumbered confederates had fought until outflanked and forced to retreat. Pursuing Yankees burned the farm before my five-year-old grandmother's eyes. The farm's fields were seeded with Minie balls, rusted rifles, bayonets and the detritus of war which I collected and piled in the unused barn. Shelby Foote describes this southern defeat, on pages 489-90 of the third volume of his masterly study, of what my father always called The War of Northern Aggression.

In my youth this conflict was still a vivid memory in the South. In the thirties and early forties the remnants of the two thousand acre farm were worked by my Uncle Marvin, in fact my mother's double first cousin in southern parlance, since they were the children of two sisters who had married brothers. Marvin was an autodidact and a noted eccentric, intellectual, storyteller and humorist in the area. He had returned from the First World War, where he had served honorably in France, with his surplus army issue Springfield and a diagnosis of terminal tuberculosis.

I spent my summers on the farm following him as he plowed behind a nameless Jack mule which must have been more than twenty years old. This animal and Marvin treated each other with wary deference. But toward me, the beast showed a contemptuous and lethal hatred. Despite his gray muzzle and arthritic bones, his hind legs lashed out with deadly force whenever I came near him. I can still see the strained yellow teeth snapping at me as I attempted to harness him.

My mother's family—Scots driven off their land after the rebellion of 1745, into an exile which first took them to Northern Ireland, then to Maryland and finally to a land grant in central Georgia at the beginning of the nineteenth century—were hard-bitten, religious fanatics. The patriarch, Fletcher Thompson, known as Bashee, freed his eight slaves as a matter of principle in the mid eighteen-fifties, although they represented virtually all his capital, and was the only Republican in a sea of Democrats at the time the war began in 1861.

My father's family history is murky. His grandfather was a penniless, illiterate, barefooted Irishman who landed in Terminus, the end of the rail line which later became Atlanta, sometime in the eighteen forties. By the turn of the century his son owned a prosperous farm near Jonesboro, south of Atlanta, and a string of livery stables between Atlanta and Chattanooga.

His mother, a school teacher, was descended from French Huguenots who wound up in Charleston after the revocation of the Edict of Nantes in 1686. Their name was, according to old records, D'Oyle, but the apostrophe disappeared at least two centuries ago.

The South in my youth was a poverty-stricken backwater which saw itself as oppressed and beaten down by the victorious Union, obsessed by vengeance, self-pity and a romantic vision of the gallant loser immortalized in the saccharine pages of the novel *Gone with the Wind*.

My first encounter with the hated Yankee came when I was seven or eight, during my morning walk from the streetcar stop to school. A large black car halted and its elegant lady driver leaned out to ask, "Young man, can you tell me the way to Ponce de Leon boulevard?" She spoke in an accent which sounded like crystal glasses touching. And she pronounced the great explorer's name Pon-see day Lay-owne, rather than our Ponce dee Lee-on, but I figured it out and pointed out the way. It was my first inkling that the North and South were not only divided by a brutal war but also by a common language.

Uncle Marvin was a true original. Pictures of him at the time show a tall, handsome young man with the straight black hair, high cheekbones and brown eyes of his Cherokee grandmother. He had brought with him, when he came home to die a pretty young nurse who had cared for him at an army hospital. My mother took the young bride, as she assumed her to be, under her wing and the two women set out to make Marvin's last months comfortable.

Marvin, however, had other ideas. He resuscitated the old copper still tucked away in the barn and began to make corn whiskey with the intention, as he told my father, of drinking himself to death. Marvin may have been one of the few people who genuinely puzzled my father, who prided himself on being able to isolate any man's weaknesses and work them to his advantage.

The nurse, who was not Marvin's wife but—as my mother put it later—his "whore", left after a year on the isolated farm with the dying, continually drunk young man immersed in Ingersoll, Voltaire, Hobbes, Kant, Hegel, Tacitus and Schopenhauer. He had virtually no needs, growing his own food, and he spent most of his disability pension on books. His heavily annotated copies of Thucydides and Machiavelli were my first introduction to geopolitical realism.

"He'd make up a batch of whiskey and fill up a dozen or so old oak nail kegs he'd caulked up," my father said. "Then he'd give me one, a couple to the sheriff and another couple to the county judge. He was a war hero, dying of tuberculosis. Nobody even thought about bothering him. Add to that he made the purest corn whiskey in north Georgia."

In the mid-twenties Marvin got into an altercation at the little cross-roads grocery in Lick Skillet. His opponent announced that he was going home to get his gun and kill him. Marvin went back to the farm, took out the old army Springfield and sat on the front porch in his rocking chair. When the man came onto his property carrying a double-barreled shotgun, Marvin lifted the rifle and, when he kept coming, shot him dead.

In the south of the time, it was an open and shut case not only of self-defense but stupidity. You didn't go up against a man armed with a rifle with a shotgun. The judge dismissed the case.

In 1932, again as my father told the tale, Marvin was convoked to the Veterans Administration hospital after some bureaucrat noticed that a man who should have died fourteen years earlier was still collecting his pension. X-rays showed some scarring of the lungs but no active tuberculosis. The doctors pronounced him cured and discontinued his pension. Marvin went home, closed down his still, gave away what whiskey he had in stock and never took another drink.

"The damn fool," my father would occasionally lament, "put cement around dozens of his extra nail kegs of whiskey and buried them. Only trouble was he always too drunk to remember where he put it." When the farm was later sold to become a subdivision, my father continued to fantasize about the thirty-year-old whiskey kegs which must be rising to the surface during excavations.

By the mid-nineteen thirties, when I began to spend summers on the farm, Marvin was making enough on cotton and corn crops to survive, selling timber when he needed a new Ford or was forced to pay back taxes. At the time he kept an immense boar hog as a pet. The animal followed him around the farm like a dog.

"Pigs are the smartest animals there are," he told me once. "They think just like people." The pig answered to the name Judas, and at its sound, bellowed out by Uncle Marvin, he would come trotting across the fields to snuffle at my uncle's feet, to accept an ear of corn and have his ears scratched.

Marvin's atheism was well known, and the local Methodist and Baptist preachers would often join him at sundown for debates on the existence of God, Marvin quoting from obscure Greek pagans, delightedly citing biblical passages of patent absurdity and lancing their arguments from the twelve volumes of Bob Ingersoll in his library.

I was there one summer evening when a carload of divinity students from Emory University, then the site of one of the most prestigious Methodist theological seminaries in the South, drove up in an antique Maxwell. Six young men and their professor, whom Marvin greeted as an old friend, piled out and joined him on the porch.

"Marvin, I've come to get my young preachers blooded."

"Always welcome, Cyrus. Always welcome. Can't offer you the corn squeezin's of yesteryear, but I have some blackberry wine this young man's mother made me. Guaranteed non-alcoholic." He was a terrible liar. The stuff was laced with some of his leftover corn whiskey. He would occasionally give me a sip to "get me used to whiskey", and I have no doubt that the blackberry wine was the first alcohol that had passed the young men's lips.

The Emory preachers and Marvin sat on the porch until midnight, discussing everything from Paul's epiphany on the road to Damascus to Jansenism, the French Cathars and the evils of the Papists, which was about the only thing they agreed on.

He punctured their attempts at proof of a personal God by

forcing a return to first causes. "It's all blind faith, son," he would say. "You got no proof. Read Fraser's *Golden Bough*. Religion ain't nothing but an attempt by scared people to explain what they don't understand. Started out with lightning but now it's death. Everybody's afraid of dying. Most folks will believe anything to keep from facing death. The priests throughout history were either deluded fools or cynics using God to oppress the people." Somehow his cornball southern diction disappeared as he talked, quoting from his books. "All your so-called proofs start with the same first premise: believe."

As I sat across the breakfast table in the Alton, Illinois parsonage, blurting out Marvin's remembered reasoning to the young priest, I watched the increasing horror on the face of his wife who came to stand behind him, hands resting gently on his hunched shoulders as he listened to the old atheist speaking through my lips.

"Out of the mouths of babes," he murmured, reaching up to hold his wife's hand.

A few months later I suited up for a church basketball game with a team from a neighboring parish. Our coach, a fat, red-faced math teacher at the high school, crammed our six-man team, mostly acolytes, into his ancient but impeccable Model A Ford and drove us to and from the games. I was always the last one he let off.

On this evening, when we were alone in the car, he placed a hand on my bare thigh at the bottom of my shorts and, hyperventilating, said: "You know, you have legs like a girl."

At fourteen I wasn't sure exactly what a queer was, but as the Supreme Court justice said about pornography, I knew one when I saw one. When he stopped at a corner, I opened the door and slid out, never returning to the church. As far as I was concerned Marvin had it right. There was no God, religion was a hustle and dust to dust is all there is.

I've never since given God more than a passing thought.

Three

She's so Silky
She's so Sweet
She makes things stand
That ain't got feet

Doggerel written on a urinal wall
of the USS Card, CVE-11, January 1945

"How come women can jerk you about the way they do?" the young sailor asked of nobody in particular, one evening as we gathered around a 40 MM. gun mount on the USS Card, CVE-11, sailing into the sunset toward the Pacific war zone, obsessed by lust. It was a lucky ship. We arrived too late to take part in the Battle of Leyte Gulf, in which Admiral Halsey cold-bloodedly sent sixteen of his jeep carriers against a vastly more powerful Japanese fleet to protect the troops landing on the beaches at Leyte. One carrier and three destroyers were sunk and the others took a fearful beating.

"'Cause they got all the pussy," a lanky southern torpedo-man, face pitted by deep acne scars, said, cupping his hands around his cigarette to keep it out of sight of the officer on the bridge. He was, relatively, an old man, a career sailor in his mid-thirties. Quiet, tough, broken-nosed.

"You know the chief petty officer's dream of the ideal wife, boy?"

"No."

"A nymphomaniac who's deaf and dumb and owns a liquor store."

I had been transferred from the Bogue to the U.S.S. Card,

CVE-11, after six weeks in a replacement depot in Norfolk. The Card was a famous ship. In 1942 its task force had brought to the surface a wounded German submarine. The crew, instead of surrendering, had come out fighting, very nearly overpowering the startled crew of the corvette which had come alongside to rescue them.

The average age of the thousand sailors on board was nineteen. Most of us lived with permanent erections, despite persistent rumors of saltpeter in the food. I had gotten laid for the first time when I was seventeen, during a refueling stop of the USS Bogue in Liverpool. The skipper had relented and given us port and starboard liberty instead of allowing the usual one-third of the crew ashore.

A sister ship, the Block Island, had just taken a torpedo off Casablanca and gone down like a lead balloon. We were suddenly confronted with our mortality. Or scared shitless, as a torpedoman from the Bronx named Tatarski put it.

Before leaving the ship, the chaplain had passed out a little booklet entitled *Proper Behavior for American Servicemen in the British Isles.* I glanced at the introduction before tossing it away. "The British," it said, "are a reserved, conservative and well-mannered people not given to public displays of emotion. They speak in quiet voices, and, although polite, do not encourage conversation with strangers. They are, as a people, moderate in all things, not given to excess."

Liverpool was a broken down nineteenth century mill and port city, wracked by fifteen years of economic depression and war. It was a uniform color of dirty gray, and its people had taken on the same hue. There were almost no automobiles, and the streetcars looked as if they had been in service since the turn of the century. It was mid-winter and cold. Biting damp cold that cut through our peacoats and chilled the marrow.

One of the Old Salts, a youth of twenty, had been to Liverpool before. "Come on. All they got to drink is gin, but nobody asks for IDs. And the place is full of horny women. No men. They're all in North Africa or Burma or somewhere, fighting the war." He led us past the deserted Red Cross canteen, offering coffee and doughnuts, and into the center of the town.

"This is Mount Pleasant Street," he said. We walked up a slight incline past dusty tailor shops, stores offering handmade shoes and a grim looking Woolworth's to a pub, The Hound and Horn. "Sailors ain't welcome in the gents bar," the Old Salt said, passing up an elegant salon decorated with hunting prints, and leading us into a dark wood-paneled room ringed with scarred booths and half a dozen ancient tables surrounded by creaky Thonet chairs. We bellied up to the ornate wooden bar with a brass foot railing and ordered gin with beer chasers. A decade later, when I was peddling flour for Pillsbury Mills on the West Coast of Africa and often flew up to Liverpool on business, I tried to find the place without success.

"Welcome to Liverpool, Yanks," the bartender said. Down the bar two British soldiers picked up their glasses and moved away. "When do the girls get here?" the Old Salt asked, his Bronx accent cutting through the lower murmur of the surrounding conversation like a rusty saw.

"Won't be long, boys. Won't be long," the bartender said. "Factory closes at five."

"Goddamn Yanks," one of the soldiers said. "All they think about is fucking."

There were four of us and two of them, and the Old Salt swaggered over to stare in the soldier's face. "You got a problem, limey?"

"Yeah. Yanks," the Brit said, climbing down off his stool. As he did, the bartender, whose arms were the size of small tree trunks, brought out an odd shaped wooden club from under the bar. Years later I saw one like it for sale at the Shannon Airport. A shillelagh. Named for an Irish town in Wicklow County.

"And what's wrong with Yanks?" the Old Salt asked, eyeing the club.

An elderly man playing cards at one of the tables looked up and cackled. "You're oversexed, overpaid and over here."

The Old Salt laughed. "And you're undersexed, underpaid

and under Eisenhower." He turned to the bartender. "Give these two Limey heroes a drink on me, Jack."

The soldier was getting set to belt the Old Salt, when the bar door opened and half a dozen young women blew in from the cold. They were in their late teens and early twenties, pasty-faced, overweight, dressed in shapeless woolen skirts and heavy handknit sweaters, feet encased in high-topped work shoes, thick woolen socks rolled down over them.

They moved giggling to a booth along one wall. We circled for a few minutes, finally moving in. They drank gin neat and spoke a virtually unintelligible patois. I found myself next to a red-cheeked young woman missing several teeth on the right side of her mouth. Her breasts, the size of small melons, were swelling out of her blouse. She had clearly never encountered a deodorant and seemed to have had only a passing acquaintance with a bathtub. And she drank like a fish, running her hand down the inside of my thigh as they evening wore on.

"When do you have to be back to the ship, mate?" she asked at one point.

"Midnight."

"Turn into a bloomin' pumpkin if you don't, will you?" she asked as her friends broke up into gales of laughter. At eleven, when the bartender called "Time, gentlemen," she pushed me out of the booth, pulled on her sweater and dragged me out into the now Arctic night air. Only the juniper flavored anti-freeze kept me alive.

"You live near here?"

"Around the corner, love, but we can't go there. Me old dad wouldn't approve now would he?" She dragged me into a darkened alley, drawing me toward her, running a work chapped hand into my crotch, undoing the rectangle of thirteen buttons of the navy issue pants, pulling up her skirt and running my hand between fat thighs.

Even if I'd been sober I wouldn't have known what to do. "What's the matter laddie?" she asked. "Not the first time is it?" her body suddenly shaking with laughter. "Just my luck, dearie, a bloody virgin. Here now, push me panties away," she said, directing my hand to push aside the coarse loose-fitting drawers. "Give him to Mazie, that's a good boy. We'll put him in a nice warm place out of the cold."

It didn't last long, but she appeared not to mind, big body pumping against mine, letting out a pleased little whimper of pleasure at the end. "Come on, sailor. Button up. Wouldn't want the little bugger to freeze." As we emerged from the alley, other couples disengaged and moved through the blackout to the port.

"Here, Mazie," one of the women called out in the dark. "That skinny little thing of yours. I bet you couldn't pick him up."

"You're on for a gin, dearie," she said, and reached down, slipping an arm behind my knees and under my shoulders, lifting me off the ground and staggering up to the gate with me in her arms like a large baby.

I was mildly retarded as far as girls were concerned, although I'd fallen madly in love with Geneva Holton when I was twelve, ignoring my mother's orders to stay away from what she called "that little slut."

She lived in one of the identical row tenements two doors down the street with her parents and three older brothers. They were, in my mother's eyes, poor white trash. Detritus littered their minuscule front yard and a broken-down old brown sofa sat on the front porch. Inside the house was filthy, and nobody seemed to mind.

Geneva had coal black hair, green eyes, high cheekbones and a honey-beige skin. At twelve she was wise far beyond her years. We played house, hiding down in the fields and "necking" as it was then called. My mother said I was besotted with her. Then, without warning, she moved away. Once, a year later, when we were both thirteen, she came back to the neighborhood. Different. Older. She took me by the hand and led me down into the vacant lots across from the row houses into our secret niche and kissed me, running her hands over my body and inside my shirt.

I had no idea what do, how to start, although I had a vast amount of information, much of it erroneous, about the details of what we universally called screwing. Finally, Geneva laughed, kissed me gently on the mouth and led me home.

The next time I saw her it was 1942, and all the young men were in the army. The age for lifeguards was lowered to sixteen and, although a mediocre swimmer, I rowed around Piedmont Park lake pulling gasping swimmers out of the water. Four people drowned that summer. I watched helplessly as the head lifeguard tried to bring them back to life.

One day, I saw Geneva. She was a child no more. Her girl's body had swelled into a woman's. She wore a tight one-piece bathing suit, leaving little to my overheated imagination. Three or four older boys circled her like country dogs around a bitch in heat. Another, older, lifeguard watched with amusement.

"She puts out for anybody who asks. One of the guys says she even screws her brothers." As he spoke, Geneva disappeared with a boy under one of the floats. I felt a sudden attack of nausea welling up in my throat and turned away.

Earlier, at fourteen. I had once again fallen madly in love. This time with a pretty young English teacher who stood out in the drab Alton High School scene like an exotic flower. Her husband was a resident at the local hospital, a handsome, elegant young man who drove a dark blue Buick convertible.

Over the years I had developed a defensive strategy in school. The classes were effortless for me, except for mathematics in which I had less than no interest. I enjoyed reading Shakespeare, memorizing the great soliloquies. Wordsworth left me cold, but Byron and Shelley sent me into a kind of orbit. But nothing was more fatal than to be regarded as a grind, and I normally took my seat in the back row with the jocks and half-wits, hiding out from the probing questions of the teachers.

But in Mrs. North's class I sat in the front row, savoring a hopeless lust as she perched on her desk on one shapely hip, skirt stretched across the bulge of the catch on her garter strap, reading a Herrick love sonnet and pointing out the arcane rhyming patterns. An occasional whiff of her perfume reached us in the front row. I assume she knew, and was amused by, the effect she had on the boys in that class, all of whom were rearranging their pants to accommodate the erections as we rose to leave.

Moving from one town to another in adolescence is a particular form of torture. Shallow friendships are formed and broken as you go from one school to another, but the fierce bonding typical of the time never occurs.

When we finally returned to Atlanta in 1942 I entered the elite Boys High School. In those days of merit-based schooling, this was the top of the statewide pyramid. Here were formed the budding doctors, lawyers, professors and intellectuals of the region.

The school's enrollment had grown to two thousand since the First World War when its few students were housed in the solid old brick building which was its centerpiece. As Atlanta's population exploded in the late nineteen twenties, the city administration had acquired a large number of old prefabricated wooden army barracks. These had been erected surrounding the main building with the intention of replacing them with brick structures. The depression intervened, and by 1942 the barracks were decaying sieves, literally falling apart.

The situation was further complicated by the fact that the Technical High School, designed to teach manual skills to the intellectually lazy or, as we said then, stupid, occupied the same site, divided only by the jointly used athletic fields. Four thousand adolescent males pullulated in this space. The town's schools were completed by the genteel Girls High School and the co-ed Commercial High, devoted to training secretaries, accountants and clerks. Inconceivable today, in an era of false egalitarianism, the system seemed normal and sensible at the time.

Oddly, Boy's High was by far the most successful school athletically, its football team, coached by one of my first cousins, "Shorty" Doyle, going undefeated year after year. The hero in my time was a handsome, tow-headed, not very bright, youth named Clint Castleberry who later starred as a freshman half back at Georgia Tech. He was killed a year later trying to fly his navy trainer under a bridge.

It was a male environment par excellence, despite the high academic standards. In the midst of the school was a shallow depression called "the pit", where altercations were settled, often bloodily, with fists and without interference by the teachers. I was, of course, immediately challenged, but in a rather odd way.

My cousin, Coach Doyle, called "Shorty" because of his six feet five inches, taught American history, using a fairly simple method. A laconic Lincolnesque figure with black Irish coloring, he read from a book by a famed southern historian, finger moving across the page. The book gave about ten pages to the American history before the War of Northern Aggression and another ten to the period following it. The middle three or four hundred pages were a hymn to southern culture, chivalry and military prowess, overwhelmed by the cowardly demographic and economic superiority of the North with its mongrel armies of Irish and German emigrants. If you missed his final session you would have left the course firm in the belief that the South had won going away.

Needless to say the class was packed with his football players, assured of a passing grade. At the end of the first week, I made the mistake of answering a question from our esteemed professor at more than necessary length. One of the football players, who must have outweighed me by forty pounds, turned and called me a sissy shithead. I told him to fuck off, at which point he rose and invited me outside.

We never made it to "the pit". As we left the classroom I was formulating a strategy known in boxing as "stick and run", essentially fending him off with a straight left while hoping to move fast enough to survive. It was, alas, not to be. We were no sooner out the door than he had me by the shirt front, twisting it and choking me, lifting me off the ground until barely my toes were touching, jamming me against the wall. I remember the dialog, and the humiliation, to this day.

"You want your fuckin' head knocked off, kid?"

"No," I said, weak with terror, staring at his crew cut bullet head set into shoulders with no apparent neck.

He led me back into class, and within seconds I was the

object of total and complete contempt, exceeded only by me own shame. The laughter of my peers still rings in my years more than a half a century later. At the end of class I bolted from the door, took off my glasses, posed them on my books and, as my tormentor came through the door, challenged him to fight me there and then. It was, in many ways, a pathetic performance. The skinny, desperate grind challenging the class bully.

He started toward me as the crowd surrounded us, blocking the view of any stray teachers but also shutting off any possibility of maneuver. I had prepared myself to take an impressive beating when one of the other football players, a large fat tackle with a sense of humor, stepped in and stopped it.

The odd result of this was that I achieved by desperation more than an honorable descent into the "pit" would have. I had challenged one of the toughest kids in the school and was generally left alone for the remainder of the year.

This was almost certainly the beginning of an insight which was to serve me well over the years. I'll call it Harper's Second Law. It goes like this: in confrontational situations, the man willing to go the last inch will win ninety percent of the time. Once a reputation for reckless abandon is established, the more civilized or prudent opponents will be more and more reluctant to take on the perceived madman even if they possess more hierarchical or even physical power.

A caveat to this tactic, enunciated by my father was: "Boy, don't take on a man with nothing to lose." In later bureaucratic battles, with subtle and highly intelligent opponents accustomed to playing by rules of impressive intellectual virulence, the whiff of violence was a disconcerting addition to the equation. Highly courageous men recoiled from physical confrontation, not from fear, but because such behavior was outside the accepted canon of civilized behavior. Hierarchical superiors quailed from the prospect of going head-to-head with a subordinate seemingly oblivious to the sanctions they might exercise. Ferociously ambitious, they all had something to lose. Getting into a fist fight with a subordinate would soil their impeccably mediocre, but safe, records.

Western democracies have, in the political chaos of the twentieth century, suffered from similar inhibitions when confronted with regimes and revolutionary cabals exercising utterly ruthless tactics. Hitler, Stalin, the Red Brigades, the Weathermen, ETA, Sinn Fein and the various murderously effective national liberation movements have worked this strategy with great success while their opponents placated them and tried to maintain a semblance of the rule of law. Peace movements, pacifist and religious visionaries, all naive believers in reason and fair play, fell into their traps.

Obviously, such a strategy is, on a personal level, more useful in avoiding humiliation and retaining some sense of self-esteem than in rising slowly and cautiously through the bureaucratic morass to become, let us say, an ambassador. The unimaginative bureaucratic hacks will gang up on the maverick and he will die the death of a thousand cuts. In my case, Cyrano de Bergerac's great dying boast: *"Mais, j'emporte, malgre vous, mon panache"*, absurd though it might be, was generally more important than the satisfactions of supposed power.

I subscribed from a very early age to what might be described as the *Weltanschauung* of the unbelieving nihilist. The death of God negated the ethical system on which society was based, leaving one theoretically free to cheat, steal and gouge with gay abandon. Work, defined as any distasteful activity forced on you for survival, was to be avoided at all costs and, when unavoidable, to be subtly sabotaged.

I began, more or less unconsciously, building a personal ethic unchained by dogma. A totally artificial construct based on unswerving loyalty to certain individuals, designated friends, and a cold blooded willingness to betray or sacrifice all others, a rigorous avoidance of cant, a willingness to pay certain societal dues in return for concrete rewards, and to pay none if there were no rewards, and an anachronistic canon of personal honor. At the same time I began to subject the sacred verities of both the political left and right to a kind of mugwump cynicism.

Southerners of my generation were permeated by the myth of the Confederacy's brave and brilliant chevaliers defeated by the grinding mediocrity of a ponderous, unimaginative but implacable northern machine backed by industrial might and superior numbers. Losing with courage, wit and grace was more important than winning without honor. In the larger American world, where winning was, and is, the only thing, this quaint attitude has its disadvantages. Discarding the useless baggage of my youth took some time and effort as subsequent events will show.

The jeep carriers ranging the North Atlantic had, with the help of American technology, driven German submarines from coastal areas and made deadly any attempt to attack the heavily protected convoys streaming toward the European battlefields. Sonar devices tracked the submarines mercilessly from wide-ranging blimps and reconnaissance planes allowing the carriers' Avenger bombers to home in for the kill.

Even the German invention of the snorkel tube, a device enabling the U-Boats to breathe and recharge their batteries without surfacing, soon lost its effectiveness as soon as sonar was perfected. Occasionally one of the small carriers would be withdrawn and sent to cruise off Quonset Point, Rhode Island, to train young pilots in carrier landings. They normally flew the squat, reliable Hellcat fighters and Avengers, but sometimes squadrons of Corsairs, a graceful gull-winged aircraft used on the large carriers, would be sent out.

The ship always operated in a combat mode when recovering planes, and my general quarters station was as gunner on a twin 40 mm. anti-aircraft gun mount just forward of the bridge. Behind me was the first line of arresting gear, a fence made of cables to stop the planes before they skidded off the bow of the ship if their tail hooks didn't catch.

There were three lines of arresting gear on the Card type carriers. The first was by far the most important, since it had to be instantly dropped flat on the deck if the plane landing caught the final cable, otherwise the stretching cable would allow the plane to jerk forward into the arresting gear, destroying the propeller and probably the plane's engine. The sailor manning this piece of arresting gear had one of the most responsible jobs on the ship. Men's lives hung on his decision whether to drop the first line of cables, since the qualifying pilots often came in so fast that not even three sets of arresting gear were enough to hold the planes on board.

The Corsairs were particularly "hot", landing at much higher speeds than the Hellcats. In our last qualifying stint one came in high, its wings dipping wildly. The hook caught on the final arresting cable—and pulled loose from the pressure sending the plane hurtling into the arresting gear.

The sailor manning the gear had hesitated an instant too long in ducking below the level of the deck and, when the plane's propellers cut through the cables, he was still standing erect. One of the cables, stretched to full tension by the weight and momentum of the plane, snapped and wrapped itself around his body like a steel snake, crushing his chest, shutting off a beginning scream. He was dead before he hit the deck.

He belonged to the catapult crew, an elite group who held the pilots lives in their hands. Highly skilled, they attached the plane to the catapult, listened as the engines revved up to flight speed and hit the catapult release button as the pilot gave a thumbs up when the engine revolutions hit a certain speed. A mistake in sending the plane off dumped it into the drink, condemning the pilot to almost certain death in the icy North Atlantic water.

As we trudged through the snow toward what might be our last liberty, short of some desolate and womanless Pacific atoll, an ambulance bulled its way though the snow to an automobile parked in an alcove just off the road. Medics removed a male and female sailor, locked in lust, her legs wrapped around his body.

"Kept the engine runnin' while they was screwin'", a shore patrolman said as we gawked.

"Great way to go," the Old Salt said, laughing, pulling us away from the scene.

After Quonset Point, we returned to patrolling the North Atlantic. By late 1944 the German submarine menace was virtually eradicated, as the U.S. and British navies saturated the sea lanes and long range aircraft forced the dispersal of hunter-killer flotillas which had wreaked havoc on the convoys in 1942 and 1943. German losses had eliminated most of their experienced sub commanders, and their replacements were no match for the new technology.

In mid-summer the Card's planes had sunk U-233 and taken thirty prisoners, including the boat's fatally wounded commander. The escorts moved alongside the carrier later in the day to transfer the prisoners as the Card's entire crew, including the skipper, lined up with forbidden cameras at the ready, prepared to immortalize this great victory.

The Germans, with the uncut hair affected by their submarines on long cruises, looked like modern hippies. They stared up at us and began shouting "Kamm, Kamm!"

Phil Zimberg, the senior enlisted aerographer at the time, who spoke Yiddish, turned to me, face pale. "We'll never beat the arrogant bastards," he said. "They're asking for combs."

The next few months we patrolled the Caribbean and the Azores. At one point we pulled into the Brooklyn Navy Yard for minor repairs. I headed alone for Manhattan with a map and a USO-donated theater ticket to a play, "Harvey", staring Frank Fay. I had picked the play out of one of the *New Yorker* magazines, slender add-free versions printed for the troops, which I had begun to read with increasing fascination.

Mouth agape I walked for hours through the pulsating city, winding up after a tour of the Metropolitan Museum in a little Italian restaurant in the theater district. When the waiter, looking at my campaign ribbons, found out I was on an aircraft carrier he placed a half-bottle of Chianti on the table, the first wine I'd ever drunk. When I asked for the bill, the manager came over and told me in a thick accent that it was on the house, shaking my hand and wishing me luck.

Slightly blitzed, I sat through the play in a daze. By the end, the invisible six-foot rabbit had come alive as had a lifelong love affair with the theater.

With the submarine war winding down, the Atlantic Fleet

began shifting ships to the Pacific. When our turn came, a wave of desertions depleted the crew as news of the battle of Leyte Gulf battle spread. An average of ten percent of the crew deserted every time we hit a new port. They were following the shrewd observations of General Antoine Henri Jomini, the brilliant nineteenth century French rival to Von Clausewitz as a military theorist. In his *Traite des Grands Operations Militaires* Jomini observed that, confronted with the dangers of battle, any rational man would desert. Which is why about a third of all modern armies consist of military police patrolling the rear echelon.

On the way to the Pacific I suffered my one and only war wound. I acquired this badge of honor in the port of Colon, Panama, where, as was the custom, petty officers from the ship streaming through the canal teamed with members of the permanent Shore Patrol to police the place. These were typically older men who had in civilian life been policemen or sheriff's deputies. We were armed with .45 automatics, the ammunition clip uninserted, and a large billy club.

As a petty officer I had routinely done Short Patrol duty in half the ports on the Atlantic seaboard. Boston, New York, Philadelphia, and Norfolk as well as Liverpool and the most godforsaken hole I saw in the whole war, St. John's, Newfoundland. But the scariest was Casablanca. When no professionals were available, petty officers from the ships patrolled in pairs. It was a deeply flawed system, since none of us wanted to harass our shipmates. It was too easy to disappear over the side on some dark night. Fairly often, sailors would conceal their billy clubs and .45s under their jumpers and take off the white leggins and arm bands in order to fade away among the mass of other sailors.

In Casablanca, a renowned liberty port offering virtually any vice ever conceived by man or beast, two boson's mates off one of our corvettes had stashed their gear, with the exception of the .45s, with a friendly French shopkeeper and tried to drink the souk dry. At some point a difference of opinion developed between them and one belted the other. The hidden .45s suddenly appeared and from a distance it sounded as if the Afrika Korps was attacking in force, as the blasts of the automatics reverberated through the souk's narrow alleys.

Fortunately, they each had only one clip and when their ammunition was exhausted, nobody had been hit. From then on that clip was attached to our webbing, to be inserted only under threat of mortal attack.

The center of Colon seemed inhabited solely by sailors, whores and pimps, the latter barking out lewd advertisements for sex shows involving donkeys and even more obscene delights. One young woman, eight or nine months pregnant, offered "fuckee, suckee" and another stumped about on one leg. One wonders how much of the arcane sexual knowledge acquired by innocent mid-western puritans resulted in requests for similar caresses from their wives. The sexual revolution of the sixties and seventies may, once again, have been a result of the Law of Unintended Consequences.

Typically the ground floor of the buildings in Colon was a bar, the upper floors a bordello. After enjoying the favors of the whores, departing sailors where presented with a disposable tube of prophylactic which they were supposed to insert in their penises. Despite such precautions ten percent of the Card's crew were infected with gonorrhea when we left.

For most of the ships Colon would be their last port of call short of the war zone. It would be months before they saw a woman. Getting laid one last time was everybody's prime concern. The navy, ever pragmatic, tacitly cooperated in providing the means. The professional Short Patrol's main job was to prevent murder and mayhem among the drunken young men prowling the streets in search of surcease. Petty officers from the ships were reinforcements.

I was assigned to a tall former Alabama state trooper named Luke Taliaferro, pronounced Tolliver. Luke had played tackle for Auburn and, in his early forties, had developed a massive paunch. He was a genial, slovenly figure, ridiculous sailor cap perched on the back of a huge balding head like a yarmulke.

Our modus operandi was simple. We walked into each bar,

circled its tables and left. Projecting quiet menace, a police theorist might say. Or letting the men know the storm troopers were at their elbows. The reaction to our entrance was instant. Talk stopped, heads turned and the atmosphere thickened with hatred. In navy ports, only the well publicized hell of the naval prison at Portsmouth, stood between the Shore Patrol and a lynching. As it was, its members were occasionally lured into side streets and alleys and beaten unmercifully.

The early evening was uneventful until we walked into a bar cum brothel called El Toro Negro. Luke always arranged for me to enter first. As I started our paseo around the bar, a large raw-boned sailor with a prominent Adam's apple and bloodshot eyes, turned toward me, face congested with rage.

"I hate fucking Shore Patrols," he said, fumbling in the front pocket of his skintight, tailor made dress blues, coming up with a pair of worn iron knuckles. I was transfixed. He swung a roundhouse right which I could easily have ducked had I not been frozen with terror, but which caught me on the upper lip, laying it open like a butterflied shrimp. As his fist came around, Luke Taliaferro's long arm reached across my right shoulder and cracked his billy club across the sailor's skull, dropping him to his knees.

"Get the knucks, kid," Luke said, his whistle screaming rapid blasts for help into the night, as he played tune with his club on the heads of the surging mass of attacking sailors, while he pulled me with him toward the door behind us. Within seconds a phalanx of reinforcements surged into the bar, beating the guilty and the innocent indiscriminately, dragging off the blood smeared sailors to large, wire screened trucks. I watched Luke and two other professionals dispassionately beat the sailor who had attacked us, careful not to mark him, landing thudding blows on his back, arms and legs.

The corpsman who sewed up my lip grinned and told me I should apply for a Purple Heart. The ancient rust-pitted iron knuckles are on my desk as I write, a compact paperweight.

The Card had been scheduled to sail directly to Honolulu, to pick up our planes and air crews, but three days out of Panama the ship's engines began to cough and sputter, reducing our speed to about four knots. A week later we limped into San Diego for repairs. The rumor spread that somebody had thrown sand in the pistons. Whatever the cause, the ship was going into the yard for repairs for twelve days. The crew was transferred to shore barracks and those of us with leave were allowed to take it.

A shipmate, Albert, a stumpy youth so blond as to be almost albino, suggested I come home with him to a place outside Los Angeles called Santa Monica, a small scruffy seaside town. Rooms were cheap and there were girls galore. I had by this time accumulated a fair stash of poker winnings, and we got on the bus to Los Angeles. He led me to a shabby ten-room beachfront hotel, badly in need of paint, which was run by a cousin.

My shipmate and his cousin were part of an extended family which had migrated during the dust bowl from farms near Muskogee, Oklahoma. They had headed west in the depths of the depression to work as stoop labor in the vegetable fields. When the war started they moved into the defense industries, and by the time I met them the clan was reasonably prosperous.

"Boy," his cousin, who was 4F because of a hernia he refused to have repaired, said, "rooms are two dollars a night. You can bring girls in, but that's another dollar. Sheets changed once a week. I count the towels before you leave."

Al's family lived in a mixed lower middle class neighborhood of displaced Okies and illegal Mexicans. Nobody checked papers, since the defense industries and farms were desperate for labor. I bought cheap pants and a couple of plastic shirts and shucked my uniform, a court marshal offense in wartime, and Al took me along in the evening to an immense, barnlike dance hall just off the beach.

He introduced me around and disappeared into the mass of dancers. I found myself standing next to a young Mexican girl with hair as black as the night, makeup an inch thick and a black silk dress cut down to the navel. I asked her to dance. The rest of the evening disappeared as we downed rum and coke, gyrated to a curious mixture of hillbilly and Mexican music, she grinding her pelvis against me in a sort of impersonal sexual message. I blacked out at some point in the evening, and the next thing I remember is being awakened to her caress at sunrise.

She had turned on the ancient radio in the room and we made love as the sounds of a Mexican band sliced into my hang-over like a dull knife.

"I gotta go to work. You let me have five dollars for a taxi?"

She watched as I felt through my pants for the remnants of the twenty I'd had the evening before. All of it was gone. I lifted the linoleum from one corner of the room where I'd hidden my stash and handed her five dollars. She dressed, a cigarette hanging from her mouth. The night before she'd looked about fourteen. In the glare of the hard sun, it was closer to twenty-five.

"You want to see me tonight?"

"Sure."

She moved in that night with a small cloth suitcase, and I spent the next week walking on the cold beach waiting for her to get off from work. We'd go to a Mexican restaurant and wind up in the dance hall. I saw Al occasionally, usually with a prim young blonde.

"You doing real good, buddy. Hermione's a nice girl. She likes sailors." He hesitated. "Better use a rubber, though."

I did use a rubber. I stuffed my stash in it, closed it tightly with a rubber band and dropped it in the toilet tank. Advice an old chief, another of the ancients brought back from retirement, had given me to avoid being rolled. One day, after a week, Hermione packed her bag, took her taxi money and said she had to go home. Her family was giving her grief for being the *guero's* whore. And I'd better stay away from the dance hall. Her brother might put a knife in me. Until then all he'd done was hit me up every night for a loan which he never repaid.

At the door as she was about to leave, she turned and asked me with a grin. "Sailor, where you hide your money?"

I didn't have much left to hide by this time and, with nothing else to do, I wandered into the USO. Earnest young women were giving out invitations from families who had offered meals to servicemen, tickets to local movie houses and the addresses of churches which had welcome centers.

At one table, labeled University of Southern California, a young woman offered tickets to a basketball game. "You can come to the Tri Delt house afterwards for punch and cookies," she said. I went and watched the local heroes get clobbered by Stanford. The crowd was made up predominantly of young women, dressed in skirts and socks. After Hermione, they looked scrubbed and innocent, almost from another planet.

I was in uniform again, and as I left I was drawn into a group heading for the sorority house. The place was crowded with young women, soldiers and sailors dancing to a record player. Four or five older women sat along the walls trying to look inconspicuous. A darkened room off the entrance carried a sign: "Anything Goes As Long as Your Feet are Flat on the Floor" I started to laugh as one of the girls slipped her arm through mine and led me onto the dance floor.

"Where are you stationed?" she asked.

I told her.

"An aircraft carrier? Oh my God. You're a real sailor. Most of these guys are clerks out at the base." She dragged me over to a couch and asked me where I'd been, what I'd done, where I was going. She reached up at one point to touch the livid scar on my upper lip.

"Where'd you get that?"

"We crashed into the arresting gear," I lied. "I went through the glass." I had, in fact, ridden in the belly of a TBF a half a dozen times, getting in the four hours monthly flight time I needed to qualify for the fifty percent flight pay allowance aerographer's mates were given, using weather observation as an excuse. The money wasn't worth it, and when I started winning at poker I quit making the flights, forfeiting the pay if I couldn't cadge enough air time while we were in port.

"You could have been killed!"

I shrugged. I was a pale faced, slender young man who had

just spent a week screwing myself blind and in a post-alcoholic stupor. My hormones were still more or less appeased. The result was an appearance of sensitive vulnerability.

"Where are you headed?"

"We're replacing the carrier sunk off Leyte," I lied. The news of the battle had just been released to the public.

"Oh, my God." She looked at me, a slightly overweight girl exuding the tanned good health that sun and the right food gave the California upper middle class. She took me by the hand, led me into the darkened room under the sign and sat down next to me on the sofa, reaching up to bring my head down to hers. For the next half hour we groped and grappled. After pushing my hand away several times she let me undo her brassiere and fondle her breasts.

I finally ran my hand up under her skirt, gradually working my way upward. She was wet through her panties. "Please don't," she said, body arching to my touch. "I'd do it if we could, but there's no way."

"Sure there is," I said, remembering the cold alley in Liverpool. I led her into the furthest corner of the room against a wall, lifting her skirt as she protested, pulling down her panties, slipping them off. Around us the giggling sounds of necking couples came out of the darkness. I had gotten through about ten of the thirteen buttons on my pants when the lights suddenly flickered on and off. One of the chaperones stood at the door.

"It's midnight. The bus leaves for town in five minutes."

Four

Je ne blame, ni approve; je raconte.

Charles Maurice de Talleyrand-Perigord

"Now hear this. Drop your cocks and grab your socks," the drunken boson's mate, a lifer about to make chief, blared over the speaker system at 5 a.m. the day we were to leave San Diego for the Pacific war zone. The skipper, his normal sense of humor atrophied by a massive hangover, broke him to seaman and relegated him to the punishment detail, the red hat gang. Two months later his rank was quietly restored.

It was a somber crew that listened to the next command. "Now hear this. Single up all lines. Single up all lines." We were about to cast off from San Diego for the Pacific war zone. Most of the crew were lined up in the gun mounts and along the flight deck for one last look at home. Across the dock a large passenger ship was loading a nondescript mass of men weighted down with knapsacks, cheap cardboard suitcases and a bizarre collection of artifacts ranging from table lamps to bicycles.

We were leaving from a civilian docking area shut off from the town by a high wire fence. Hundreds of the men were clamped against it. Outside, a dense throng of women tried to fight their way to the fence to join others locked in embraces through the wire. A high pitched moaning wail rose from the crowd.

"What the fuck is going on?" a seaman named Skags asked, simian forehead knotted in his usual scowl. Skags was the most noticeable of the dozens or so psychopaths on the ship. He was a slab of muscle honestly earned as a lumberjack in the forests of

Washington State before the war. Nominally a boilermaker, he spent most of his time in the ship's red hat gang for insubordination.

He and a deck crew had just appeared to haul up the gangway. The one our commanding officer had climbed with alcoholic unsteadiness the night before to confront the newly-minted red-haired ensign who was officer of the deck and me, the senior petty officer on duty. Between us we were twenty years younger than the worn old officer brought back from retirement.

He had stood before us weaving from side to side. "Prepare to launch," he muttered, lurching onto the hangar deck where our twenty hellcats and Avengers were parked, wings folded upwards to conserve space, and tied down with cables. The skipper headed for one of the fighters with the two of us in his wake. He hoisted himself onto the wing and into the cockpit with remembered agility and began barking out orders.

"Where the hell is the catapult crew? The goddamn guns aren't armed. This barge is a fucking Chinese fire drill."

"Where are you going?" the desperate young ensign demanded as I started to run. I ignored him and slid down the ladder into the chief petty officer's quarters without touching the metal steps. Four of the paunchy noncoms were playing hearts in the small chief's galley.

"Oh, shit," a huge Irish machinist said, throwing in his cards and following me up to the hangar deck. He climbed onto the wing and began to talk in a low voice to the skipper who had slumped forward. He hauled him out of the cockpit, picked him up in a fireman's lift and carried him up to the captain's quarters.

The last watch before departure was always the worst as the Shore Patrol delivered a stream of drunk and battered sailors and the occasional tipsy officer into our hands. By dawn, the young ensign was in a state of catatonic shock. This was hardly the navy for which a crash course in navigation at Georgia Tech had prepared him.

"What the fuck is going on?" Skaggs repeated as he peered out from under heavy black eyebrows at the scene on the opposite dock.

"They're Italian prisoners of war," the ensign said. "They've been working on farms all over California since Italy surrendered."

Skags stared at him, uncomprehending. I doubt if he realized Italy had surrendered. Or had been in the war. "Who's them women?"

The ensign shrugged, trying not to be intimidated by the Neanderthal confronting him. "Girl friends," he said turning away.

"Girl friends," Skags screamed. "Goddamn dagoes screwing our women while we're fighting a war!" By this time the explanation of the bizarre scene had filtered through the ship, and, if the order to cast off had not been given, most of the crew would have swarmed across the dock to lynch the hapless Italian prisoners.

The ship was permeated by a restless fear. Details of the battle of Leyte Gulf were filtering through the fleet. The story we heard was that Admiral Halsey had deliberately exposed the defenseless jeep carriers as a decoy for Admiral Kurita's powerful force as it surged through the San Bernadino Strait. Our sister ship, The Gambier Bay, and the destroyers Johnston, Roberts and St. Lo went down immediately. Others were badly hit.

The facts were, of course, that Halsey had misjudged Japanese intentions. His aggressive move to the north had opened an opportunity for them to deliver a real blow to the American fleet and the invasion force about to land in the Philippines. The slender line of carriers and destroyers had delayed the attack. And the Japanese, also confused and misinformed, hesitated and were lost.

Marshal Frederic Saxe-Coburg's description of the fog of war has seldom been more apt: "War is a scene replete with shadows in whose obscurity one cannot move with assurance. Routine and prejudices, a natural consequence of ignorance, are its foundations."

Unknown to us, the Japanese fleet had suffered a mortal blow and was never again a major player in the conflict. The real danger lay in the suicide pilots, the Kamikaze, of which we were blissfully ignorant. In an irony of war, our friends and comrades who died at Leyte were to save us from the final bloody battles with the Kamikaze around Okinawa.

Before we arrived in Honolulu some strategist in the naval high command, after analyzing the Battle of Leyte Gulf, decided that the slow and vulnerable jeep carriers were not useful in surface warfare. The ship was stripped of its plane and seven hundred of the thousand-man crew, leaving only a nucleus of each division in the event of a return to combat. The three other aerographers mates and the weather officer were transferred, and I was assigned to quartermaster duties, standing for hours at the helm of the old rust-bucket staring out at the glassy Pacific Ocean.

There were times when we prayed for a typhoon to break the monotony. We moved at a snail's pace back and forth across the ocean, ferrying thousands of troops, fuel and materiel for the final campaigns of the war, loosely guarded by terrier-like corvettes on the watch for still lethal Japanese submarines.

At one point, the radar shack inherited a chess board with rudimentary rules from an officer being transferred. The game rapidly became an obsession, and my poker winnings were badly dented by losses on the chess board. Then, during a layover in Honolulu I bought a book on how to play the game by a man named Lerner. On the next cruise I began to win very quickly with fool's mate moves and Lerner's simple tactics for beginners.

Since nobody on the ship knew anything about chess, these wins seemed like some sort of magic. The smart players quickly figured out what I was doing, but by then I had moved on to the next stage, learning to vary the openings, control the board and attack from all angles.

I carelessly stored the book among the manuals in the weather shack where I continued to sleep, a privilege of the senior petty officer, thus avoiding the malodorous crew's quarters below decks. And keeping from being trapped in the bowels of the vessel like a rat below decks if a torpedo hit a ship which was basically nothing more than a floating torch ready to be lit. One of the literate radarmen, fumbling for something to read among my books, came across the chess book, and within minutes I was cornered by enraged players. Since most of them were yeomen and other shipboard intellectuals, I managed to avoid being thrown overboard, but only after promising to stand drinks for the entire radar shack.

They confiscated the book, but chess soon died, since, the few talented players came to dominate the rest of us.

In addition to my quartermaster duties, I was the ship's librarian, a choice slot, since virtually nobody on board except a few of the officers seemed to be able to read. The library was located in the deepest reaches of the ship and enclosed in a wire mesh cage. The books were a melange of donated volumes ranging from an almost complete selection of Zane Gray to the library of a deceased professor of English at the University of Pennsylvania. Among his contributions were *The Dance of Life* by Havelock Ellis, a portion of which became so sought after that I conducted periodic readings in it.

The scene which so enthralled and enraged my shipmates was a description by Ellis of a visit to the actress Ellen Terry in her rooms. At some point, during an animated conversation through an open door to her bedroom, Havelock looks up to find her standing nude in the doorway. Ellis, the most famous sexual psychologist of his time, wrote that he promptly "averted his gaze" to avoid embarrassing the actress, who had clearly become so engrossed in their conversation as to forget her state of undress. Howls of frustrated disbelief arose from listeners as I read this passage.

Under threat of death and destruction, I was told to search through the donated books, seek out the pornographic passages and either make them available or read them aloud. The collector who donated Havelock Ellis had also given the ship *Psychopathia Sexualis* by Dr. Richard von Kraft-Ebbing and a smuggled edition of Henry Miller's *Tropic of Cancer*. Strangely, many of my horny shipmates found Miller's vivid descriptions of his fantasies offensive, possibly because they mirrored their own too closely.

Kraft-Ebbing was also not very inviting as pornography in its raw state, but the book was a mine of ideas. Out of boredom I began using his research to concoct tales of gothic sex which had the animals rattling the library cage. To my everlasting regret, I gave away these first literary efforts as I used them.

The professor's library was an eclectic collection. An ancient edition of Shakespeare's works, in three volumes, absorbed me for months. And for a time I immersed myself in H.L. Mencken's six volumes of prejudices, Hemingway's *The Sun Also Rises, For Whom the Bell Tolls* and a superb short story collection. Here also were *The Great Gatsby* and *Tender is the Night*. Less impressive was William Faulkner, obviously one of the professor's favorites, since he had a whole shelf of the man's works.

I read them all and, at the time and ever after, Faulkner struck me as little more than a shrewd southern fabulist who had taken in the Yankee critics with the rich quasi-Shakespearean verbal culture which still permeated the south of my youth. The marvelous rhetoric of the King James Bible, the only thing a lot of these people ever read, was pervasive among my Uncle Marvin and his friends, telling tall tales on the porch of the country store. Still I have to admit that *Pylon* and *The Hamlet* were pretty good books.

On return trips from the periphery of war, the skipper introduced smokers, two-round boxing matches, among volunteers from the crew. We were all in lousy condition, since there was no organized exercise on board and life was generally sedentary. I volunteered and found myself in a series of four-minute wars with a squat young Irishman who had begun his navy career as a cadet pilot. He wound up serving six months in Portsmouth prison for adultery after being caught in the bed of an officer's wife.

According to Pat, the lady had screamed rape when her husband appeared, and he'd bolted through the window. The court marshal hadn't believed the rape, but in the interests of decorum and discipline had sentenced him to six months for adultery. He had been a celebrity in prison, since getting caught screwing an officer's wife was right up there with murder in the criminal hierarchy.

A case of beer was the reward for the winners of the boxing matches, and the first couple with Pat were seriously bloody. At a hundred and forty pounds, he was short and powerful, and I was a skinny wraith. It was my stick and run versus an endless attack by Pat. After we split the first two fights, and wound up sharing the beer on the beach of some godforsaken atoll where the ship was picking up or dropping off soldiers, we decided it was stupid to keep trying to kill each other.

From then on we put on a great show, reasonably careful to come out intact unless one of us got carried away and started pounding for real. Pat was, among his many talents, a stunningly successful cocksman. We usually picked up our load of soldiers for the war zone in San Diego, a port swarming with sex-starved sailors prowling for females. Or, as Pat put it, with his usual delicacy, "any aperture in a storm."

He always wound up with an attractive woman, usually considerably older than he was, married with a husband in the army or navy. He had an infectious Irish wit and exuded a kind of coarse vitality and a sensuality which women seemed to sense at a primitive, atavistic level. I once asked him for the secret of his success.

He shrugged. "First I pick the married ones who are missing their regular screwing. Then after getting them giggling I just ask them if they want to fuck. One out of ten usually says yes." Once, walking down a San Francisco street, a lovely young woman passed him. He called out. "Hey, you dropped something." She ignored him. "Okay, bleed to death," a remark which should have gotten him arrested. She turned, outraged, and for some reason, laughed.

The average age of the three hundred men left on the ship was probably under twenty. It was, as an older radar officer once remarked, a tanker full of testosterone waiting to explode. We cruised on the edges of the combat zone delivering planes and supplies to rear echelon areas such as Guam and Samar in the Philippines, rarely leaving the ship except for a beer party on a beach on some godforsaken atoll where the natives were separated by high fences to keep the sailors away from their women. Fights proliferated as boredom and inactivity led to endless poker sessions.

The meteorology office, unused, had become the site of one of the more serious games. The ex-lumberjack, Skaggs, bulled his way into it each payday and within hours had lost all his money. Sol Tatarski, one of the better players, was unable to control his contempt for his stupidity and often moved to the edge of suicide by provoking him. One night all of us were a little high on the alcohol, drained and strained through bread to remove the poisons, in the useless torpedoes which still lined the hangar deck. Skaggs, losing as usual, stood up after one of Tatarski's sallies, grabbed him by a skinny arm, twisted it behind his back and broke it. Nobody laughed at Skaggs again.

When the war ended the crew was reduced even more, and we began to transport thousands of troops home. Discipline crumbled. The soldiers were confined to the enclosed hanger deck except for supervised excursions onto the flight deck. They were served two meals a day at each end of the deck which was wall-to-wall with cots and gear. They called the ship the U.S.S. Kornflakes. Army military police were supposed to enforce strict separation of the crew and the soldiers. Nonetheless, a lively market in Japanese officers' swords, side arms and other military knickknacks developed.

A massive, disciplined military machine dissolved before our eyes as sixteen million men were rushed home to be discharged. At one point, we loaded the flight deck with dozens of new fighter planes in Guam. As we left the port we were suddenly ordered to dump them over the side. They were useless artifacts, not worth the cost of storing. On another cruise we carried a cargo of Japanese Zeros on deck, gifts to military museums around the country, a couple going into the private collection of an admiral.

By the time of my discharge in March of 1946 I had been accepted for the fall semester by Stanford University. I planned to use the three thousand dollars I had sent home to my mother in the course of the war to cover the difference between what the GI Bill would pay and the cost of tuition.

It was not to be.

Five

It is better never to trust anyone.

Henrik Ibsen

"I'd like to have the three thousand dollars I sent home," I said over breakfast on my second day home. My mother refused to look at me, glancing down at her hands knotted together in her lap. In the two-and-a-half years I'd been in the navy her hair had grown gray, and she had aged ten years.

"I don't have it, Edward. Your father had some bad luck, and I lent it to him. It's gone."

"You mean he lost it on the horses."

An hour later he drove up in a black 1940 Ford coupe and tossed me the keys as he came through the door. "All yours, boy. Homecoming present."

I started to say something when over his shoulder I saw the look of panic on my mother's face. I shut up and drove to my sister's house. "He's broke," she said. "They may lose the house. It's not that he doesn't make money. The banks pay him fifty dollars just to drive by a piece of property and give them an assessment. And I know for a fact he made fifteen hundred dollars on one deal last week. He gave mother five hundred and the rest is gone."

"Still playing the horses?"

"Yes. And I think he's seeing some woman. Mother thinks he is. All they do is fight. You're a damn fool to have sent her your money. You know he can get anything out of her he wants."

My sister, twelve years older, had been a senior at Washington Seminary, Atlanta's most prestigious girls school, when my father went broke. She had planned to "come out" in the fall after graduation and wound up a clerk in Lane Drug Store instead. Two years later she married a cotton classer and bore him three children, in the beginning living on the edge of poverty. Increasingly embittered and ferocious, she had begun to sell real estate, using my father's contacts, and when I returned from the navy had just managed to buy a small four-unit apartment house. She would quit thirty years later, a millionaire.

With no money for the extra tuition, any hope I had of going to Stanford was down the drain. I took the two hundred dollars I had left, bought a cheap sports jacket and pants and a pair of Thom McAnn wingtips and drove the sixty miles of winding pot-holed country road to Athens, site of the state university. It took me through a countryside devastated by erosion and the rural detritus left by the collapse of the South's corn and cotton culture. The overgrown fields were dotted with the deserted shacks of the sharecroppers, black and white, who had headed north to the industrial cities of the midwest. The sleepy small towns were slowly dying.

In those days Athens was a somnolent village, the university sprawled across its spacious lawns in a charming chaos of architectural styles dating back to its founding at the end of the eighteenth century. Victorian era mansions circled the center, many now housing fraternities and sororities. I pulled up at a bus stop and four girls piled in, giggling, sitting on each others laps.

"Uh, could you tell me where the administration building is?"

"Oh, damn," one said, as they piled out again. "We thought you were going to women's campus. The ad building is over there." She waved vaguely. "Just ask anybody."

I picked up my dormitory assignment and wandered down to a chaotic scene in the gymnasium where four thousand students were registering. The university's student body doubled that summer as veterans descended on it in hordes. The whole state university system was on the verge of collapse as tens of thousands, armed with the support of GI bill payments, demanded an education.

I had taken a series of examinations designed to allow those who could pass to skip freshman year. At twenty I felt an overwhelming urgency to get education behind me and attack the real world. With fifty of the two hundred hours necessary to graduate up front, I could, and did, graduate in two years by going to the summer sessions and taking the maximum twenty hours a quarter, winding up with ten hours more than the required two hundred.

There was an air of desperation among many of the older students, married, some with three children, living in trailers on the outskirts of town, battling for the few part time jobs available, their wives working. The GI Bill was one of a series of sops thrown to the sixteen million veterans who had to be reabsorbed into an economy winding down from the wartime expansion.

But its authors never anticipated what would happen. A whole generation of lower and lower middle class men were suddenly offered a onetime chance to obtain an education and climb into the bourgeoisie. They took it in hordes. And the university reeled under the shock of their energy, intellectual hunger and determination to fight their way into a better life. Toughened by military discipline, eager to obtain the edge that education would provide, they had nothing but contempt for the gentle humanism of many of the professors.

I came to Athens ahead of the game. I had read voraciously for a decade. Among the donated books in the USS Card library were two that decided me to be a newspaperman: *The Last Time I Saw Paris* by Elliot Paul and *A Personal History* by Vincent Sheehan, both foreign correspondents in Europe between the wars. These romanticized memoirs were reinforced as I devoured Hemingway, Fitzgerald, Dos Passos, Farrell, O'Hara, Ford Maddox Ford, Miller, Huxley, Waugh, Graves and the rest of the Lost Generation.

I found myself for the first time in a place where intelligence was not looked upon as effeminate. Through some fluke of scheduling I landed in the fall semester in a senior course on Spenser taught by a man named Davidson. He was a member of a famous literary family connected with the agrarian movement at Vanderbilt. A brilliant teacher, miraculously bringing life to the long dead poet's sonnets, he was sometimes unhinged by the literal seriousness of the aging veterans impatient with his languid style.

A requirement of the course was the creation of a Spenserian sonnet following one of the poet's complicated rhyme structures. I doodled away in class on this from the first week and discovered a fatal talent for doggerel verse. As the end of the quarter approached, my veteran classmates were in a state of panic, agonizing over the sonnets which would not come. I dashed off one for a friend and was suddenly in demand. I wound up writing more than a dozen at two dollars a shot.

"You have an "A" in my course, Mr. Harper," Davidson said on the final day of class when I showed up for my grade. "But you have not turned in your sonnet, and I will be obliged to drop you to "B-plus" if you do not let me have it today." I didn't bother. Grades were as meaningless to me then as performance ratings were many years later in the foreign service. Davidson was smiling his usual sardonic smile when he demanded my sonnet, and I sometimes wonder if he hadn't recognized my universally crude facility in the others.

Bob West, also a member of the Vanderbilt school, was another superb teacher and a master of brutal intellectual flagellation in his creative writing class. His critiques left you much like the fists of old time bare knuckle boxers who soaked their hands in brine to toughen the skin. His contempt for whiners, aesthetes and non-producers erased in me forevermore the concept of writer's block. He would have been a great believer in Woody Allen's great line, "eighty percent of success is showing up."

A large chunk of the next two academic years were absorbed by required courses in the journalism school. Most of the students were headed for small town newspapers. Many were second and third generation sons and daughters of editors and publishers of such papers. The curriculum was practical. Headline writing, copy editing, page make-up and above all, news writing of the who, what, when, where and how school of reporting. Objectivity, now a quaint concept from the dark ages of innocence, was an obsession.

The university newspaper was our practice field. Most of the professors were worn out former newsmen. The closest thing to the arcane theories which now predominate at schools of communications was a course in law of the press which we labeled "how to write lies and still stay out of jail."

Our maximum leader, Dean Drewry, was a pompous, vested figure of comedy among the students. He spoke in orotund paragraphs and was known as "D.E.", because of his obsessive use of the phrase "distilled essence" to characterize good news stories. I was stunned to read, years later, that his mousy wife had put three bullets into him and his graduate student paramour when she caught them *en flagrante*. Both survived, and he continued as dean for many years.

Advertising was taught by an escapee from the jungles of New York, an aging cynic, mustached, decadently handsome, burnt out and semi-alcoholic, who looked upon the invasion of the barbarians with sardonic amusement. The last thing he wanted or needed was a horde of ambitious, energetic believers ruining his declining years. His course demanded as a final product an advertising campaign from concept to research to completed copy with illustrations.

Coincidentally, in the sudden upsurge of the economy after the war ended, my father had begun, once again, to wheel and deal with considerable success. In one of the complex barters at which he excelled, he acquired a cemetery. Since neither he nor my brother, who worked for him, had any interest in running the place, I commuted to Atlanta on weekends to supervise the sales staff, a half dozen aging men who shuffled from house to house selling lots for two hundred dollars apiece, a quarter of which they were allowed to keep. I also audited the books, supervised the grave diggers and made sure the grass was more or less cut.

Mountain View Cemetery turned out to be a potential gold mine. It catered to a lower middle class clientele, upkeep was minimal and there was enough empty land to bring in several million dollars over time. My father offered me a fifty percent share in the place if I would take it over and run it. I was sorely tempted, estimating that in ten years I could make enough money to retire, and I used my course project to develop an advertising campaign for the place.

For the first time in living memory, the professor came alive. He invited me to come before the class and describe my campaign. "Mr. Harper," he said, when I finished, "has just given a superb exhibition of what advertising is all about. He has brought a dead subject to life. In his copy you can envision the myriad of happy corpses resting in eternal comfort in padded lead-lined coffins surrounded by their peers under a manicured greensward lovingly tended by servile darkies." This was, of course, long before the era of political correctness, and there were no "darkies" at the university. "Assured of perpetual care, they have no need to worry in their hermetic comfort." He lit a cigarette and slumped back in his chair, feet on his desk.

"In fact cemeteries are an excellent subject from which to approach the theoretical underpinnings behind advertising. Let's face it. What you've got here is a piece of dead meat, usually diseased, which has to be disposed of fairly quickly. Logically dead bodies should be ground up, sanitized and converted into fertilizer which is what the Chinese have done for millennia."

At this point a good half of his audience, the born again Christians and straight arrows, began to shift restlessly in their chairs. Nobody was foolish enough to confront him, however. His wit was like a razor blade dipped in acid.

"But to succeed in advertising," he continued, sucking in lungfuls of smoke, "the first thing you have to do is discard logic and rationality. The putrefying corpses pumped full of formaldehyde are symbols. By smearing them with makeup to simulate life, we negate death. By burying them in expensive coffins we are implicitly assuming they aren't really dead, that, comes the millennium, they will rise up and rejoin us in the fleshpots of eternal life."

At about this point I realized he must have been hitting the bottle before class. In the back row a hand suddenly shot up.

"Yes, Mr. Rivers."

"Sir, my father is an undertaker. You think we could tap into the same sort of stuff in our business?" From then on it was downhill.

I got an A-plus in the course, and an offer of an introduction to his old New York advertising agency. A couple of weeks later, when I went home to do the cemetery books, I discovered that my father had, as usual, reneged on his offer and sold it for a song. He was nothing if not a believer in the old Persian's adage—take the cash and let the credit go.

From this distance in time, the two university years have blurred, crew cut young faces in the yearbooks bearing the imprint of an era passing rapidly into history. It was an innocent time, before photographs resembling gynecological textbooks passed for pornography, beer was the drink of choice, drugs were unheard of and getting laid usually meant coughing up two dollars at the unofficially sanctioned brothel, Effie's place, to couple with fat farm girls.

I had joined the intellectuals fraternity, Delta Tau Delta, mainly because the Greeks controlled social life on the campus, and I was assured that sorority girls were easy lays. They weren't, and the Delts were not my kind of intellectuals. They were primarily grade grubbers whose obsession was coming in with a higher average than the Jewish fraternity which customarily won the scholarship prize.

The Jews were an odd phenomenon at the University of Georgia in these years. Most were refugees from the quota systems then in effect at the elite northern universities. Others came because Athens was an inexpensive place to live, and the GI Bill easily covered tuition, board and books. They were, with rare exceptions, energetic students. But mostly they were intellectually tough, intense and impatient, devoid of the phony southern courtesy which masked disagreement in a society where conflict often led to violence and where looking somebody in the eye could get you killed.

Into this shifty-eyed environment they suddenly descended, two or three hundred Yankee Jews with strange accents and a ferocious competitiveness. Most were imbued with the left-wing ideologies of the Eastern European environment from which they came. Many had attended a New York high school known as Odessa on the Hudson because of the large percentage of descendants of Russian Jews studying there. Trotskyists battled Stalinists and social democrats were regarded as running dogs of capitalism. They argued with a brutal directness, pumped full of information and a self-confidence which fascinated me.

In the beginning I was blown away. I was already saturated with the radical southern populism of my Uncle Marvin. Class conflicts were implicit in its rage at the capitalist bankers impoverishing farmers with high interest rates and a government whose protectionist economic policies favored northern industry over southern agriculture. I found theoretical confirmation of southern paranoia in Marx's Communist Manifesto and the tightly reasoned dialectic of his acolytes. The South was clearly an oppressed colony of the Yankee imperialists.

In 1946 Georgia's liberal governor, Ellis Arnall, had brought a suit to overturn a rail freight price structure which charged fifty percent more on manufactured goods shipped from the South than for those coming in from the North. The Supreme Court overturned the regulations and equalized freight rates. Virtually overnight the New England textile industry began to migrate southwards.

The equalization of freight rates combined with cheap nonunion labor over the next fifty years led to the closure of many obsolete northern mills and to the relative rejuvenation of the South. This awakening New South held curious seductions for many of the Jewish students. Anti-seminism, a brutish reality in the festering ethnic enclaves in northern cities, was a religious artifact in the South. And the somnolence of the natives opened seductive economic vistas to anybody with energy, brains and ambition.

Len Bagen, one of my roommates of the period, said: "Hell, Harper. The south is paradise for a Jew. As long as you're white, you're king down here." Behind the joke was a serious reality. Which is not to deny that there was anti-seminism. It was simply more confused and diffuse than in the seething northern ghettos.

Another friend, Howard Berk, later a screenwriter in Hollywood, was fascinated by my father, a true precursor of Tennessee Williams' Big Daddy. At a dinner with my family in Atlanta, where Berk was often a guest, my father looked at him across the table one Sunday and said: "You're a Jew aren't you, boy?"

Berk, blond, blue-eyed, six-feet-one and two hundred and twenty pounds, was a gentle, unaggressive giant. He smiled ingratiatingly as I prepared to get up and tell my father to cut the crap. "Yes, sir."

"Some of my best friends *are* Jews," my father said, approvingly.

Later, as I apologized to Berk, he put his arm around me and said: "But, Ed. It's true. Some of his best friends are Jews." And, in fact, they were.

Once, in high school, I had asked him why people disliked Jews. He said, without missing a beat, "Hell, boy, it's because they're smarter than most folks."

"How come you do so much business with them then?"

"They're smarter than most folks, but they're not smarter than me," he said, with that hustler's grin I knew so well. "Boy, never forget. You get somebody thinking you're stupid, you can take his money and leave him smiling. And the smarter they are, the easier it is."

Money, for him, was keeping score. With a redhead and a crippled horse thrown in here and there.

That first fall, I turned out for the boxing team, coached by an old pro named Pete Tarpley. Pete had gone seven rounds with Tony Zale a few years before, and his face looked as if it had been repeatedly battered by a shovel. The cartilage in his nose was gone, scar tissue was thick around his eyebrows and lips, and he twitched when a bell rang.

He had some fairly primitive ideas about boxing and held my stick-and-run style in contempt. To cure me, and others, of this cowardice he set up a variation of the old boxing custom of "coming to scratch". We were forced to stand toe to toe and hammer each other to learn to "take a punch". I slipped, blocked and rode punches during these exercises, much to his irritation.

At the time I weighed one-thirty-seven, barely able to make the lightweight limit. As punishment for my dilettantish ways, he would put me in the ring with the hundred-and-sixty-pound middleweight, a tough young redneck built like a fireplug who had fought since he was fourteen in rural smokers. Up to this weight level, with sixteen ounce gloves, its hard to hurt anybody. But middleweights can punch. As Joe Lewis said of a clever light-heavyweight, Billy Conn, "he can run but he can't hide." Lewis was right.

In the end, Tarpley cured me of stick and run, mostly because every time I threw a straight left, Hank, my sparring partner, would cross a right over it and knock me halfway across the ring. Unable to stick, I couldn't keep him off me, so I settled down in one session to fight it out, winding up suitably bloodied.

In a fight, early in the season, I tore a muscle in my left shoulder and was out for the rest of the year. In the spring, one of the boxers began to set up smokers in the rural counties of north Georgia, matching former members of the boxing team with local thugs. We got ten dollars for two two-minute rounds. Our opponents were mostly out of condition and came out swinging wildly. You circled the ring, letting them become arm weary, then moved in to punch in flurries. It worked reasonably well, even though we were usually outweighed by twenty pounds.

I finally gave it up after barely escaping with my life one memorable evening against a middleweight made of cement who knew a little boxing. He smashed my nose and almost broke my jaw. With the exception of a couple of experiences some years later, it was the end of my boxing career. I had finally entered an environment where masculinity wasn't measured by your ability to take and give a punch.

In the Spenser class I had become enamored of a graduate student named Marian Hine. She was a product of the American middle class family at its best. Educated, hard working, liberal, open minded and honest. Naturally, she rebelled, in a self-consciously ostentatious way. In the nineteen-sixties she would probably have joined the Students for a Democratic Society and slept with any man who asked. Through her I met a group of campus intellectuals who gathered in the cellar bookstore run by a student named Hugh Geeseling. He had the attraction of what the French call *nostalgie de la boue.*

Hugh, tall, skinny, with bad teeth and lank uncombed black hair, was usually unshaven and unwashed, invariably clad in dirty jeans and tennis shoes. He was in his mid-thirties and attended just enough classes to collect his GI Bill money. Twenty years later he would have been a hippie. He was also a total phony, cultivating his act to *epater les bourgeois* who gathered in his cellar to talk of Marx, Joyce, Faulkner, Hemingway, Dos Passos, Eliot and Pound. Don Marquis' *Archy and Mehitabel* and William Steig's *The Lonely Ones* were cult objects. I strung along in the vain hope of getting Hine, as she insisted on being called, into bed.

Beginning that first fall, my father's business picked up dramatically. He and my brother began to build houses, and the real estate market entered a boom which was to last for fifty years. My mother began to slip me a hundred dollars a month which, with the sixty-five from the GI Bill, made me one of the rich among the poverty stricken veterans.

Hine benefited from this largesse. She carried with her at all times a supply of candles which she lit in campus restaurants and beer joints. I was totally enamored and pressed my unsuccessful campaign to seduce her. This was the deep south in 1946. Good girls didn't sleep with you, or anyway, with me. I was deeply saddened twenty years later when she died of an embolism while working as a stewardess on an airline.

I sometimes think the Victorians may have gotten it right when they maintained that sex saps intellectual drive. In any event, raging unappeased hormones aside, it was a fascinating time. I read, as I had for years, uninterruptedly. Only now there was some guidance and structure, even in this provincial university whose dazed faculty was staggered by our thirst for knowledge.

I devoured Marx, Hobbes, Locke, Montesquieu, Adam Smith, Riccardo, Burke and Mill. In a superb class on classical logic, taught by a former Methodist minister in his seventies, I was introduced to Plato, Aristotle, Descartes and the eleven rules of the syllogism, invaluable tools when I was later confronted by the Cartesian logic of French intellectuals. I often played golf with the old boy, who shot in the high seventies, spotting me a stroke a hole and winning, offering up Uncle Marvin's iconoclastic cynicism to his positivist ethic. He smiled and hit his drives like arrows down the middle of the fairway.

Art appreciation was a course required for graduation, but all sections of it were filled in my senior year, and I was allowed to take a course in sketching as a substitute. It was designed to prepare high school teachers of art. Ten hours a week of drawing, mostly from life. Hine, curious, came by to watch one day and was recruited for a modest fee as a model. Dressed in a bathing suit, of course. Nude models were *verboten*.

The art school, directed by a conventional but tolerant painter named Lamarr Dodd, was staffed by bored young avant garde artists. We received virtually no guidance other than a curt introductory lecture. The instructor wandered among us, occasionally putting a few lines on our sketches, wordlessly.

The course was a revelation. As the weeks went by I began to see the bones in the model, to draw, however crudely, movement rather than a figure. I had no talent, but the intensive effort required to come up with anything called forth a furious concentration. I poured over the books of drawings of Picasso, Matisse, Manet, Derain, Dufy and Braque, attempting to duplicate the simplicity of the first two who seemed capable of creating life forms out of simple black lines.

Many years later, living and writing novels in a place called Los Boliches on the Costa del Sol, when it was still a collection of primitive villages, I met a painter named Maurice Grosser, author of a superb book called *The Painter's Eye*. Maurice was then in his sixties, a graduate of Harvard, scion of a rich Montgomery, Alabama family. He was a homosexual, a member of the nineteen twenties Lost Generation in Paris, and as he put it, "the best imitator of Corot alive."

We often sat in the fly-specked cafe on the main plaza of Fuengirola, then a village of stone houses put together with mud, after working all morning, sipping Manzanilla, eating olives and dissecting life. Maurice, more or less disowned by his family, had spent several years in his youth motorcycling through the south with an easel and paint box strapped to the back. He painted oil portraits of black sharecroppers and their children for a dollar apiece and fake Corots of the countryside. He also developed a taste for dark-skinned lovers.

"Most non-figurative modern art is wallpaper, design," he said. "It's like free verse, playing tennis without a net. None of them can draw. The whole thing is a hustle. Photography destroyed conventional painting for the masses. Now we're awash in self-indulgent crap put out by people who couldn't draw a hand if their lives depended on it."

If you've ever tried to draw a hand, you'll know what he meant. I have never since been able to look at an abstract painting without wondering if the artist could draw one.

Toward the end of my final year at Georgia, Hine introduced me to one of her friends, a beautiful young woman with a chip on her shoulder the size of Gibraltar. "Where are you from?" I asked, making conversation.

"Lakewood." She spat it out like a defiant oath. Lakewood was the rural slum where I had lived with my aunt.

"No kidding. I lived there when I was a kid," I said, mentioning where my aunt's house was located. She stared at me in astonishment and later told me that I was the first person she'd ever met who admitted to having lived in Lakewood.

"This bunch of snobs act like it's Tobacco Road," she said.

"Yeah, well, you can always come up with Nunnally Johnson's answer when people asked him about Tobacco Road." Johnson was a Georgian who wrote film scripts in Hollywood in the thirties and forties.

"What did he say?"

"Where I come from Tobacco Road was the country club set."

She was an original feminist, making Hine seem a pale imitation of the genre. Over a coffee she told me she intended to sleep with every member of the senior class at the law school and was well on the way to her goal.

One weekend I drove her home from Athens and we went out on the town after she fixed up a friend of mine with a blind date. Somehow we wound up at a lake in the middle of an upper class Atlanta neighborhood. The two of us swam, nude, out toward the middle of the lake and were about to get it on when a police car began flashing its lights and shining them on the lake. She swam quickly to shore and hid in the dense undergrowth as I came out, bare-assed to confront the police.

"Get your clothes on, boy, and get your ass out of here." I grabbed both my clothes and hers and we drove away, circling the lake without lights after the cop car disappeared. She came out of the underbrush and leapt in the car, giggling. From then until Monday morning it was a memorable weekend, and I showed up for my first class, Abnormal Psychology 404, in a state of catatonic exhaustion.

AbPsy—or Kooks, Klowns and Kinks as it was called—was taught by a Watsonian psychologist who held a radically mechanistic view of the human mind. In an early lecture he had pointed out that the human drives, in order of intensity, were: hunger, self-preservation, nurturing the young and sex. A young veterinary student commented in a stage whisper, "I ain't hungry, am well preserved and got no tits, but I shore could use a piece of ass."

The professor was completing, just before retirement, a lifelong research study on personality disorders which revolved around a series of questionnaires followed by a test of how much your finger trembled as measured by a machine he had built. It was, essentially, a square frame with strings attached which were joined at the middle around a small circle. The subject placed a forefinger in the circle which was then tightened to a measured tension. The amount of movement, tremor, in your finger was then measured and compared with your psychological profile.

On this morning I filled in the thirty or so questions on the questionnaire in a trance and held up my hand to the graduate assistant. After a couple of minutes, she looked at me, exasperated. "Are you dead, or something? The damn thing doesn't register."

"Busted," I said.

She called in the professor who tested the machine and once again inserted my finger. No movement.

"An anomaly, Miss Johnson. Discard these results, otherwise they will distort the conclusions."

I have, forevermore, distrusted the pseudo-scientific so-called disciplines of psychology and sociology.

In 1946 there was an election for governor of Georgia which was won by Eugene Talmadge, a charismatic racist demagogue of the old school, and a legend in Georgia politics. Unknown to the electorate, Talmadge was suffering from cancer. He had submerged his opposition in the democratic primary, which was tantamount to election in those days, and won easily in the general election. Rumors of his illness had surfaced between the primary and the election, and his son, Herman, later for many years a respected U.S. senator, entered his name on the general election ballot. He received the next highest number of votes after his father, among them a unanimous vote from the cemetery in the Talmadge fiefdom of Sugar Creek.

Eugene Talmadge died between his election in November and the scheduled inauguration in January. The state law clearly stated that the lieutenant governor, a nonentity named Thompson, and a distant relative of mine, would succeed in such circumstances. However, the apparatus of the state government, including the State Patrol and lower courts, were loyal Talmadge supporters. On inauguration day, Herman Talmadge was inaugurated and took over the governor's office and mansion with the support of the State Patrol which barred Thompson from the Capitol building.

A court case was immediately begun, but, given the power structure of the state, Talmadge seemed sure to win. At this time a plan was concocted by a small group of the more radical students on campus to mount a surprise attack on the State Capitol, physically remove Herman Talmadge and declare Thompson the legal governor. At Hine's instigation I was recruited into this enterprise, probably in the vain hope of adding some muscle to the intellectuals involved.

At the last minute most of the original instigators chickened out, leaving half a dozen of us in two cars to mount the attack. Despite everything, the nutty scheme might have worked at least temporarily, since we had discovered in a reconnaissance of the State Capitol that the governor's office was unguarded. But we were betrayed.

As we started up the Capitol steps, a dozen or so beefy State Troopers surrounded us and gave us a fairly gentle beating before escorting us back to the two cars, one of them my ancient black Ford, and warning us not to try again.

Thoroughly chastened we slunk away. No report of the attempt appeared in any newspaper, and there is no record of it that I have been able to find in the State archives. Three months later the Georgia supreme court declared Thompson to be the legal governor and Talmadge vacated the governor's office and mansion. He later spent eighteen years in the United States senate.

Thus ended the only attempted coup d'état in American history.

Six

An ambassador is an honest man sent to lie abroad for the commonwealth.

Sir Henry Wotton

"Oh, I say Ed, what the hell are you doing here?" Niko Henderson, British ambassador to the Quai d'Orsay, asked, leaning his hawklike visage down toward mine, hair uncombed, tie askew, Huntsman suit artfully rumpled.

"Helping with the press arrangements," I said. We were standing in one of the immense reception rooms of the Palace of Versailles waiting for U.S. President Jimmy Carter, and the president of France, Giscard D'Estaing, to emerge from double doors on the left to greet the two thousand guests scattered throughout the building.

"I absolutely must have a word with Carter," Mike said, predatory eyes searching the room. "My government will be chagrined if he doesn't exchange a few words with me."

"They're going to race through, Niko. They're already late for a formal dinner at the Elysee."

Niko's eyes lit on a short figure in a red fez and black floor-length soutane standing among the dignitaries in the front row. "Carter will stop there," he said, moving through the packed crowd with that practiced ease and courteous insolence typical of the British upper classes. When the door opened and Giscard strode through trailed by Carter and his wife, I thought Niko had, for once, miscalculated.

Roslyn had, however, spotted the massed television cameras

and, eyes flicking over the crowd, landed on the little orthodox priest. She reached forward, gripped Carter by the bottom of his suit coat and pulled. He turned his head and, without missing a beat, followed her nod toward the priest, swerved out of Giscard's wake and held out his hand to the little man.

In a second Henderson was on him, introducing himself as the representative of the queen in a voice loud enough to carry across the room to the bank of cameras and sound men. Giscard wheeled, annoyance turning to rage as he saw the Brit clamp an inescapable arm on Carter and turn him toward the BBC cameras. It took several minutes for the exasperated French president to free the bewildered Georgian and lead him through dozens of rooms decorated with priceless paintings on loan from the Louvre. Small chamber music groups of three to four military musicians playing French compositions alternated with sumptuous spreads of caviar, pate de foi gras and champagne.

I had known Niko well when he was ambassador to Poland and I was the American embassy press attaché, playing tennis on his grass court and attending the five-course lunches he gave for the Polish press, drinking the superb Manzanilla from his vineyard near Seville and, incidentally, providing him with precious access to the Polish media.

Giscard's orchestration of the Carter visit, which included a trip to the Normandy battlefields on the thirty-fifth anniversary of the D-Day landing, was done with the kind of pomp and circumstance that only the French can call up. It was designed to flatter and impress the little peasant from Georgia and nail into his skull the power and grandeur that was France. This would, to the elegant Cartesian mind of Giscard, turn him into silly putty when presented with unreasonable French proposals to subsidize its agricultural exports with Common Market funds to the detriment of U.S. farmers and, contrary to international agreements, enable France to underwrite the development of the Airbus, Boeing's potential competition, with French government research money.

One of Carter's deputy press secretaries, Paul Costello,

whom I had met when he traveled to Madrid with Vice President Mondale, had asked that I be sent to Paris on temporary duty to help with press arrangements.

I had already run press centers in Bucharest, Belgrade and Warsaw for Nixon visits as well as a half-dozen others for secretaries of state and vice presidents, and I wasn't really interested in diving once again into the ego-driven chaos and confusion generated by arrogant White House aides. But Paris was too great a lure. It was there, more than thirty years earlier, that the world had opened for me like a brilliant flower.

The United Press, then a light-footed competitor to the Associated Press, had hired me at forty dollars a week the day I graduated from the University of Georgia at the end of the winter quarter in 1948. It was one of the four best jobs available, the others being on the two Atlanta papers, the Journal and Constitution, and the Associated Press. I was assigned to the midnight to eight a.m. shift writing for the radio news wire.

UP, unable to afford an adequate reporting staff for local news, serviced its radio wire by rewriting the early editions of the local newspapers and handouts from local public relations outfits. It had recently issued a new radio style book, based on research which showed that listeners were unable to absorb sentences of more than ten words, none of more than two or three syllables. Short, pithy Anglo-Saxon based terms were preferred to Latin cognates. Passive voice was taboo.

Midnight to eight a.m. was a Stakanovite shift. My fingers rarely left the keys except to grab a sip of coffee, the taste and consistency of fusel oil, and gulp down an occasional doughnut baked from straw and sawdust. It was invaluable training. You learned to think with your fingers, always honing, cutting adjectives and adverbs to make the ten-word maximum, discarding nuance and verbiage.

After six months of this the bureau manager, a former foreign correspondent named Brooks Smith, called me in and offered me the one man bureau in Jackson, Mississippi, at no increase in salary. It was a promotion, a chance to write my own ticket.

Turning it down was unthinkable. But I had by this time become fed up with the South, permeated as it was with bitter memories of a long lost wars, innate racism and the ingrown provincialism of a region left behind as the American Dream began to be realized in the rest of the country.

Mississippi, dominated politically by a planter class still living in 1850, was last in every census category from individual income to literacy. At the time Brooks made me the offer, I received a letter from classmate Howard Berk telling me he was headed for a semester at the University of Grenoble in France. Why didn't I come with him? I agonized not. With almost two years left on the GI Bill, I could easily cover expenses in a France on the verge of starvation and where the dollar was God.

I sold my car for enough to pay the $200.00 passage money on the Nieuw Amsterdam and never looked back. It was certainly the most momentous decision of my life. I left that fall a twenty-two-year-old American primitive, head filled with a mass of undigested facts, a minor talent for clear crisp writing and the baggage of a Southern upbringing which had bred in me a quaint sense of personal honor, combined with the hustler's duplicity common among the politically downtrodden.

In a sense I was a three-time loser. A southerner, living with the memory of defeat in battle, I was descended on my mother's side from Scots brutally driven from their homeland by the English in the eighteenth century, their lands confiscated for hunting estates. On my father's, one ancestor was an illiterate Irishman who fled his nation to avoid starvation. Others were Huguenots who landed in Charleston after the revocation of the Edict of Nantes on October 18, 1685 and the subsequent massacre of Protestants throughout France.

In 1948, Americans headed for France tended to be from the northeastern upper classes, people with some connection to Europe and a reason for studying there. Most already had graduate degrees or were working toward them. All spoke fairly fluent French. I was an anomaly: a vagabond without a real goal. My southern accent was, as always, a source of considerable hilarity.

Several of the young women on board became disturbed at my apparent helplessness. How was I going to get to Grenoble without speaking French? Did I know which station to go to in Paris? How much money did I have?

It was another of many encounters over the years with the patronizing assumption inherent in all Yankees that southerners are fundamentally stupid, illiterate, culturally primitive and bigoted. At this point I was, in fact, an incipient anarchist, compulsive reader, obsessed with gulping down new intellectual sensations, and a self-conscious preacher of interracial marriage as a solution to the race problem.

Before leaving Atlanta I had called on an aging French lady, the war bride of a World War I veteran, who had taught French in the public school system for twenty-five years. She had given me detailed instructions on how to get to the Gare de Lyon—including an ancient but still valid map of the Metro system—written out half a dozen instructions in French for me to show to taxi drivers and ticket sellers, and loaned me a phonetic phrase book dating from 1910.

"Where can I find a WC?" was the first entry. To this day I cannot help laughing when I see the expression, since it was the first thing I asked when we landed at Le Havre amidst the type of chaos which I have come to associate with my beloved French. Vectoring in on a new building amid the ruins of war I headed for the urinal stalls along one wall, glancing over my shoulder just in time to see the horror on the faces of my sophisticated female, and male, shipmates at the realization that it was a unisex john. I had encountered much more primitive versions in Casablanca in 1944.

I took the metro to the Gare de Lyon in Paris, bought a ticket and found myself in a third class compartment on wooden seats with seven Frenchmen. I had not eaten since breakfast, and my stomach heaved as I watched them undo their cloth suitcases and ancient leather briefcases to lay out a cornucopia of dark bread, sausage, cheese and wine in unlabeled bottles.

They ate with the unselfconscious sensuality with which a

Frenchman deals with food, ripping off pieces of bread, cutting slices of sausage and cheese with ancient pocket knives and tilting the wine bottles to wash it down. Across from me an elderly woman stopped at one point and stared, suddenly spewing at me a seamless lilting sound, ending on what was clearly a question.

One of the men glanced over at me and said something to her in a curt tone. Suddenly the compartment which had been totally silent exploded in a cacophony of voices as all seven spoke at once, gesticulating wildly in what seemed to me at the time the prelude to a riot. When things quieted down a newspaper was suddenly spread across my lap and contributions from the other passengers began to fill it. The woman leaned over and smiled a snaggle-toothed smile, tapping me on the shoulder and motioning toward the food.

I ate, accepting a swig from various wine bottles, unable to refuse, gagging on the bitter *pinard*. After the food disappeared, one of the men, who looked like a farmer, extracted another unlabeled bottle of colorless liquid from his knapsack and passed it over.

"Mar," he said, encouragingly. "Mar. Bon. Bon."

I tipped it back and almost strangled to a delighted roar from the other passengers who quickly polished off the bottle. It made white lightning taste like tea. I have, in the years since, come to prefer *vieux marc* to the finest cognac, treasuring this honest unvarnished distillate of the grape above its effete and attenuated confreres, Cognac and Armagnac.

When the train arrived in Grenoble the next morning, one of the passengers took my arm and led me through the streets of the ancient town and deposited me on the steps of the university, shaking hands and tipping his hat in a gesture reminiscent of my father.

The university directed me to an ancient, unheated warren of buildings in the center of Grenoble which served as a hostel for students. My room was a cubbyhole with a bed, an iron chair and a chipped porcelain basin and pitcher. The john, a hole in the floor, and a tap of cold running water were down the hall. There was no shower or bath. A bare twenty-five watt bulb provided the only light except for the *meutriere*, a narrow window in the three-foot thick wall which had once allowed archers to shoot at attackers in relative safety.

Breakfast was a large bowl of ersatz coffee, which tasted vaguely of fish, mixed with thin blue skim milk, a chunk of dark bread made from sawdust and a minuscule pat of excellent butter and homemade jam. Lunch and dinner were mostly watery vegetable stews, with a rare sliver of unchewable gristle, accompanied by chunks of the same bread.

The French were on the verge of starvation at this point, before the Marshall Plan kicked in, but they nonetheless refused to eat the cornmeal which the United States shipped in great quantities, their newspapers accusing us of insulting their honor. Corn, in all its manifestations, was food for pigs in France.

I had arrived two months before the winter semester began, and was assigned to a class filled with Italian summer students who were already advanced French speakers. The professor, a sallow young man suffering from what seemed to be a terminal case of tuberculosis, handed me a set of books printed on wrapping paper, among which was one conjugating the eight thousand French regular verbs. One of the Italians, who spoke a little English, explained to me that the French were too arrogant to admit that there any irregular verbs in their language.

The Italians were a cheerful lot, experts in student larceny. They cheated not from necessity, since they already spoke excellent French, but as a sport. I later learned that French students were compulsive exam thieves as well, the newspapers reporting their various exploits with tolerant glee.

I bought a Petit Larousse and a weighty set of French-English, English-French dictionaries. With these I began working my way through a book which listed the six thousand most important words in French beginning with the most used. I also bought Stendahl's *La Chartreuse de Parme* on the advice of the Italians, and immersed myself in the unlikely adventures of Fabrice del Dongo, sitting for hours in cold cafes over a glass of watery beer and, filling page after page with unknown words.

And I went to the movies. *Clochemerle*, about the construction of a street urinal in a country town; *Dedee d'Anvers* with Jean Gabin and the delectable Simone Signoret; *Les Enfants de Paradis* and dozens of others, including one in which a young woman comes upon a dead body and exclaims: *Eh, beh, Merde, alors,* to my considerable shock when I later looked the word up.

In class I listened. After a week, the professor hauled in a French student and made it clear that he was studying English and would be willing to trade conversation lessons with me. His name was Louis, son of a doctor from Aix-en-Provence, and for the next two months we spent three-to-four hours a day in cafes and cheap restaurants, soon evolving a drill where one of us would read a sentence and the other would repeat it.

It was, in fact, a system not very different from that used by the Foreign Service Language Institute where, twenty years later, I agonized through forty-seven weeks, six hours a day in a room with three other people learning Polish. Three years later I repeated the same routine in Turkish.

By the time the rest of the American students arrived, I had begun to read the newspapers with relative ease and babble ungrammatical but comprehensible sentences in an impeccable Grenoblois accent. The new arrivals had almost all learned to speak by listening, not to native French speakers, but American teachers whose accents were flawed. Years later a linguist at the Foreign Service Institute explained to me that correcting such faulty pronunciation was virtually impossible. Once the mind is imprinted, it clings to the first learned response with formidable tenacity. He was right.

My conversation partner had arranged for me to move into a private house, still without heat or bath privileges, but comfortable and clean. More important he had introduced me to a hostel for homeless young women where students were allowed to eat in the dining room. The meals were invariably plates of vegetables, thrown together helter skelter, but much tastier than in the student cafeterias.

He had also discovered that I had money. By French student standards, vast amounts of money. I found myself taking him to small restaurants in back streets where a meal for two would run less than two dollars with a bottle of wine bearing a label, usually a Beaujolais, then only a cut above the cheapest Algerian wines.

One evening he suggested bringing along two of the young women from the hostel. Afterwards, we took the *teleferique* to the mountain top cafe and bar overlooking the town, the ceiling of which was decorated with Chagall-like nudes.

We left the young women, both of whom were in their late teens, at the hostel, and I had started the long trek toward the suburb of La Tronche where I lived when Louis grabbed my arm and motioned me to follow. We circled the building, a former school, and stopped by a window which rapidly opened. Inside was what had once been a classroom, now filled with bunk beds of sleeping figures.

Anne awakened me at dawn the next morning by biting my ear lobe, putting a finger to her lips. I dressed along with half a dozen other shadowy male figures and joined the line to climb out the window. About ten days later the director of the hostel discovered what was going on and shut down the nightly trysts.

I was in the habit of visiting the public baths once a week and had, on a couple of occasions, persuaded Anne to join me in the immense tubs, although she considered bathing in winter life threatening. The baths, subsidized by the state, were virtually free. Over the next six weeks we spent long afternoons in the tubs, alternating with the immense shower stalls which sprayed water from all angles with the force of a fire hose.

This sybaritic existence rapidly ran down my small store of cash, and I was finally forced to borrow a few francs from my friend Berk to make it through the month until our GI checks arrived.

We received two hundred francs per dollar from the French banks, but one of the students had made a life-saving discovery. By taking the bus to Geneva just across the border in Switzerland, we could exchange our checks at five hundred

French francs to the dollar. This very nearly tripled what was already a luxury living allowance for a student.

Since bringing francs into France was illegal, there was always a chance that a search would leave us totally broke. The risk was worth it. Various strategies, none particularly clever, were evolved to foil the customs agents. In one train search a quick thinking smuggler held out his anorak, the thick wad of thousand franc notes in his hand through the fabric, while the customs officer felt the rest of the garment.

Another time Dimitri Theodopoulous had pinned his stash inside his underwear. I was behind him going through the custom lines when the safety pin gave way and thousand franc notes began to drift down his leg leaving a snail-like trail behind him. He grabbed the seat of his pants and held on while I gathered up the notes which had slipped loose. Looking back I can't remember that anybody was ever caught, and I now suspect the customs agents knew what was going on and were laughing at us.

One day, as we emerged from the baths, Anne informed me that she had been admitted to a hospital in Lyon for treatment for a calcium deficiency. She left the next day. There were other candidates to replace her, but I had become accustomed to her cat-like face and wicked sense of humor. Looking back, I suspect that much of her reaction to my clumsy lust was simulated, her undernourished, almost emaciated body going through the motions of receiving pleasure. In any event, she was now gone, and I missed her.

Our teacher in the class for English-speaking students was a dark, slender woman of about forty, with a classic Mediterranean face. Green eyes, slanted slightly, a beak of a nose and a body which, even under thick layers of clothes, seemed to promise some sort of ineffable reward. It was my first experience with the unconscious sensual calculation which seems to be innate in gallic women.

At one point, exasperated that my southern accent was interfering with my pronunciation of the French "r", she said, "Monsieur 'arper, before I can teach you French, you must first learn English."

Years later one of my classmates, Olga von Ziegesar, said that I sat like a besotted fool staring at her throughout the lessons.

"All you had to do was make a move," Olga said. "Madame Vidal was a forty-year-old widow. You were an incredible primitive animal, a troglodyte, something the French find exotic after all their intellectualized men. She would have taken you to her bed in an instant."

As the semester ended Madame Vidal invited the class to her house for a final party. I carefully searched among my books for the appropriate good-bye in French. As I left, shaking her slender hand, I bowed and said, "Madame, j'ai joui cette soiree."

Behind me the rest of the class broke up into cackles of laughter and Madame Vidal sucked back a giggle.

"You idiot," Olga told me as we walked back to town. "The verb 'jouir' means to enjoy sensually."

At about this time, the newspapers were full of the possibility of a coup d'état by Charles DeGaulle. The French people were living on the verge of starvation, the Marshall Plan was still in its formative stage and the Communist Party had obtained almost forty percent of the vote in the last elections. The only alternative to a takeover by the leftist parties seemed to be the recall of the wartime hero.

That fall DeGaulle had begun what the newspapers called a "march on Paris", following in Napoleon's footsteps when he returned from Elba. The day he arrived in Grenoble the streets filled with masses of his supporters surging toward the center of town where he was scheduled to speak. The communists quickly mobilized a counterforce. I was standing on the university steps, clad in a bow tie, yellow sweater and sporting a classic crew cut, when the two groups began streaming into the square. A young professor detached himself from the communist mass, grabbed me by an arm and threw me into the university.

"You fool. Stay out of this," he said, rejoining the roiling crowd which had now met the Gaullists in savage combat throughout the square. I watched the carnage from the second floor of the university as dozens went down, beaten with clubs and iron bars, trampled underfoot. Six people died in the riots that day.

Circling the square were lines of the Garde Mobile armed with stubby carbines, standing at parade rest, watching the battle. After what seemed like an hour, but was probably no more than five minutes, an order cracked out above the noise. The troops came to attention, carbines held at an angle across their chests, and began to advance into the crowd. It was a textbook example of how to stop a riot.

The troops moved slowly, guns slamming rhythmically into the bodies of anything in their way, avoiding heads, driving into the upper body with six-inch blows, moving the crowd toward the exits around the square. Behind them police cleaned up, swinging their capes, the bottoms of which were weighted with lead, like scythes at those who slipped through the lines, cutting them down and dragging them off to trucks parked in the side streets. It was over in no time, combatants on both sides turning and running to avoid a beating, leaving behind the crumpled bodies of the dead and wounded.

Later in Paris, I was to observe a dozen or so similar scenes as students and strikers went into the streets. The controlled, dispassionate brutality of the forces of order was always impressive. The techniques for crowd control had evolved over more than two centuries of confrontations, and they were handled with a routinized application of measured force. After all, the students seeded among the rioters were virtually all from the governing classes taking part in a rite of passage as stylized as a German dueling society. Nobody wanted to risk killing a youth who might one day be prime minister.

When the streets of the United States exploded in the sixties, the police and national guard had no such experience. Force was either brought to bear in a scattered ineffectual manner or used so massively as to be counterproductive. The panic of the guardsmen at the Kent State debacle would never have happened in France.

There was of course, a major difference between the stylized rioting in France and the United States. Street demonstrations are an accepted means of influencing French governments, which have been historically insensitive to the needs of most of the population. The mandarins of the French bureaucracy continue to rule the country with a total disregard for local concerns, despite a cosmetic decentralization which still leaves all real power in the hands of the Paris-appointed prefects, the equivalent of American state governors. These autocrats control the local bureaucracies, police and finances, throwing sops to local councils.

The U.S. riots were either outpourings of pent up fury by a downtrodden black minority, as exemplified by the unrest after the murder of Martin Luther King, or middle class student demonstrations against the draft during the Vietnam War. These soon ended, as a U.S. governmental system, much more attuned to the wishes of the populace than in France, poured massive amounts of public money into minority areas and repealed the draft, turning to a mercenary army of lower class whites and blacks to fight its wars. Student demonstrations ended abruptly with the end of drafting of the upper and upper middle classes, and, with the exception of sporadic outbreaks, the black minority has accepted what amounts to government bribes to remain passive.

Over the years, watching street violence in Europe, Africa and the United States, I have become convinced that street demonstrators alter nothing and risk destroying representative government in non-authoritarian societies. Revolts are marginally useful only in overthrowing criminal regimes totally lacking in legitimacy. And even here, the tragic result is most often nothing more than an exchange of tyrants.

DeGaulle's march on Paris fluttered to a halt after the riots in Grenoble, and France continued to be ruled for the next decade by centrist governments forced to make massive concessions to the working classes in order to pacify the powerful communist-dominated trade unions. But during my two years in France the possibility of an uprising of the proletariat was just beneath the surface. The ferment among French intellectuals, most of whom favored a revolutionary socialist regime, would dominate the eighteen months I spent in Paris.

One day, following my classes at the university, I came upon a young woman huddled on one of the benches outside, crying softly. She was a striking figure. Flaming red hair, a complexion so pale as to be almost translucent, clearly not French. I stopped and asked if I could help. Over coffee at a nearby cafe it turned out that she was from the Saar, a German province on the French border which had been annexed by France.

Its German-speaking population was forbidden to send its children to German universities, and Hildegarde had come to Grenoble. There was only one problem. Once the French discovered she was German they would not rent her a room. Since she had to show her identity documents to prospective landlords, she was in despair, living in a hotel, her money draining away.

I had by this time moved to a scruffy pension near the university. The proprietress reluctantly agreed to rent her a room when one became available. In the meantime she could share mine. I promised not to take advantage of the situation, half sincerely, but an alcoholic dinner, proximity in the narrow bed and youthful hormones rapidly overcame good intentions.

It was for me a highly satisfactory arrangement which unfortunately did not last. Hildegarde rapidly made contact with the few other German students at the university, and within the week had obtained a room in the home of a French family which had supported the pro-German Vichy regime. But before she moved out of my room, and my life, she had invited me to join some other German students in a walk through the surrounding mountains.

There were seven of us in the group, including an Arab student who for some reason spoke German. We rode to the end of a streetcar line and began walking up into the hills around the city. Years later I was to discover that Germans love only one thing more than walking. Singing. The two go together like beer and sausage.

The five young Germans in the group were all war veterans,

and they walked with the sort of disciplined grace of former soldiers. Suddenly, like spontaneous combustion, they began to sing, falling unconsciously into step. I would learn the words to these songs at my first foreign service post in Vienna when, at 2 A.M., full of wine, similar young survivors of the Russian front would burst into song.

"Wozu sind die strassen da. Zum marchieren, zum marchieren." Or it's variation *"Wozu sind die Maedchen da, zum verfuehren, zum verfuehren." "Wir fahren, wir fahren gegen Engeland."* And the ineffable old song for a dead comrade, *"Ich hatte eine Kamerade. Einen beserren findst du nie."*

French farmers leaned on their hoes and rakes as we passed, listening to the famliiar marching songs. "Why are the streets there. To march on, to march on." "Why are the girls there, to seduce, to seduce," "We're marching, we're marching against England." And, "I had a comrade. You'll never find a better."

Seven

Je suis Marxist, tendance Groucho

French student, 1949

"Hey buddy, you're American aren't you?"

He was sitting at the cafe table in front of me with a beautiful young French girl. Wearing a superbly cut Harris tweed jacket, a camel's hair overcoat thrown carelessly over a chair in front of him. The two were having trouble communicating, since she spoke no English and he no French.

"Yes."

"You speak French?" He had a New York accent overlaid with Choate and Yale.

"Yes."

"Care to join us for a drink? Do a little translating?" He had the arrogant look of a Tuscan nobleman, dark, hook-nosed, with the supreme confidence money conveys.

I had been in Paris for a week, living in a heatless, windowless room between the landings in a roach-ridden hotel in the Rue Mouffetard, around the corner from the Sorbonne. My GI Bill check was a week away, and I nursed a coffee attempting to warm up during one of the coldest Parisian winters in a hundred years. Trying to figure out how to stay alive on a hundred francs a day. Twenty cents at the illegal rate of exchange.

In late December Howard Berk and I had bought two 100 cc. French motorcycles for a hundred dollars apiece and planned a trip across northern Spain, then on north to Paris. Two hundred and thirty pounds turned out to be too much for his little machine, and he traded it for a museum piece, an immense 1932 Renault which, underway, sounded like a Tiger tank in rut.

The Rhone valley is, as I now know, a verdant paradise in spring, summer and fall. But in the winter of 1948-1949 it was shrouded in an icy fog, and the wind cut through us to the bone. We were frozen solid on arriving in Avignon and sought out a cheap hotel. The proprietor turned out to be the illegitimate son of an American soldier in the first World War. His faded picture hung on the wall of the tiny dining room.

The man was proud of his father, whom he had never seen, but who had over the years regularly sent money to his mother. He cooked us a magnificent meal and sent us on our way the next day with two immense baguette sandwiches and enough black market gas coupons to get us to the Spanish border.

By the time we reached Cerbere, the French border town, we were a villainous-looking pair, unshaven, covered with mud and grease-stained from cleaning and replacing spark plugs and repairing tires. From this point on the trip turned into a nightmare peopled by the Three Stooges.

We were held up at the Spanish border for half a day in Cerbere waiting for the French to issue our exit permits. The road to the Spanish border was barely passable. The French had told us that nobody used this crossing point, which we'd picked by looking at a map, and the Spaniards would probably not let us in. He was very nearly right.

Our first encounter was with two green-uniformed characters wearing tricorn hats and armed with rusty rifles which looked as if they dated from the Battle of Solferino. They were members of the infamous Guardia Civil which infested every corner of Spain at this time. First they waved us back toward France, but we stood our ground, unable to communicate, pointing to the Spanish visas issued us by the consul in Lyon.

Finally, shrugging, they took us down the road to a small stone building on the edge of a village which looked as if it had been built by the Romans. A customs house, my dictionary said of the faded sign over the door.

The whole place exuded a sort of nameless menace. Berk and I at this point were beginning to panic, since we had bought a fairly large bundle of pesetas in Switzerland—at an absurdly good exchange rate—and they were squirreled away in our packs. We waited with one of the tricorn hats while the other disappeared in what was clearly a deserted village. He returned in an hour with a short, fat man who looked amazingly like Franco, affecting the same odd mustache.

He spoke some French, and informed us that it was Sunday and the border was closed. Of course, he said, the border was always closed since this was not an official crossing point, and we were violating Spanish law by being in a closed military zone. We talked. A woman appeared and made superb, thick coffee. A bottle of brandy appeared. We drank a toast to Franco, choking a little on it. He, in turn, toasted our president, Franklin Roosevelt. I punched Berk to keep him from correcting the little man.

We were poor students, eager to visit the wonders of Spain. He would understand that to go back through France to the proper crossing point would take all our funds. Perhaps an exception could be made. Finally, as the sun went down, he fumbled in the dusty desk and came up with a metal stamp, took our passports and slammed it down leaving a very dim imprint. He also passed over a handful of gas coupons, waving away our offer to pay. We thanked him profusely and got the hell out of there, heading for Barcelona.

In the winter of 1948-49 the city, later to be my home for five years, could have served as a set for one of Ingmar Bergman's grimmest films. Its people were sullen zombies in tattered clothing, fear fighting with hatred on their faces as they moved along dark streets filled with pairs of tricorn-hatted Guardia Civil. We spent one night in the Hotel Cavadonga before heading out across northern Spain for Pamplona to pay homage to the Hemingway of *The Sun Also Rises*.

We never made it.

There were a couple of serious problems with our plan. First, all the bridges along the mountainous northern highways had been blown in the Civil War of 1936-39 and never repaired. Second, the mountains still harbored groups of Republican resistance fighters who crossed the wild border from France for hit-and-run raids on the Guardia Civil units which roamed the countryside. It was illegal for us even to be in the area.

By the time we discovered all this we had passed the point of no return, paying peasants with mule carts to carry our motorcycles up and down steep ravines whose bridges were tangled masses of twisted steel and concrete. The Guardia Civil, always in pairs, leaned on their pre-World War I rifles and watched us pass in silence. We stopped late one afternoon at an inn deep in the mountains east of Jaca. The low-ceilinged bar soon filled with silently staring peasants as we ate a superb lamb stew and drank the harsh local red wine. Finally two of the Guardia arrived, pushed their way through the crowd and began barking at us in Spanish, pointing their rifles at us and gesturing toward a large hunting knife Berk had strapped to his waist.

We answered in French to no effect, and it began to look as if we might be in the local slammer very shortly when the innkeeper intervened, motioning to the Guardia to sit down and supplying them an earthenware jug of wine. I raised my glass to one of them and touched his. It was a magic gesture. Spaniards, as I was later to learn during eight years in the country, were, as are most poor peoples, immensely generous to guests. Berk and I ordered more wine, which cost about three cents a liter, and invited the bar patrons to drink with us. Before the evening was over we had switched to homemade brandy, slivers of wood and leaves in the bottoms of the unlabeled bottles.

By the time the local doctor, sent for by the innkeeper, had arrived, everybody was suitably loaded. He spoke excellent French and quickly fixed things with the two Guardia who had, by this time, decided we were men of parts. Only one of the crowd, a toothless old man almost blind from cataracts, kept snarling at us in an impenetrable guttural.

"He is a veteran of the war," the doctor explained. "He doesn't like Americans."

"Oh, yeah," Berk said. "I guess he wanted the Germans to win."

The doctor looked puzzled. "The Germans? No, no. Not that war. The war of 1898 when you imperialist Americans robbed us of Cuba, Puerto Rico and the Philippines." As academic historians are so fond of saying, you have to know the context.

Next morning most of the village turned out to see us off only to be presented with an anti-climax. Berk's ancient motorcycle wouldn't start. After calling again on the good doctor for help, it was agreed that he and the machine would be taken by truck to Jaca for repairs. We split at this point, since my money was draining away, and I headed for Paris. Berk later took his ancient machine out to the end of a pier in Bordeaux and consigned it to the deep. The papers for my motorcycle, it turned out later when I tried to sell it, were a crude forgery put together by the French dealer, and I had no legal right to the machine.

"My name's Roger. This is Janine. What'll you have, buddy?"

"Ham sandwich and a beer."

"Look, buddy, what I want you to tell her is that I've got two classmates coming in tonight. Just got off the ship. I want her to rustle up two of her friends and meet us at the Hotel Scribe English Bar at seven tonight. Tell her the honor of France is at stake. They gotta be real nice babes." I bit into the sandwich, gesturing to the waiter for another, and over the next half hour set up a three-day schedule for the pair.

The girl had taken out a small pad and made notes, green eyes focused like laser beams as I translated, and the pile of saucers, left by the waiter to indicate what we had consumed, stacked higher and higher. Finally, Roger got up and extended his hand. "Thanks, buddy. You're a real sport. Listen, how about meeting us here tomorrow, same time?"

I nodded as he turned and walked toward an immaculate pre-war Citroen, a black *traction avant* famed as the French gangster car, parked illegally in front of the cafe. I never met anybody else in

France with an automobile. As he drove away I suddenly realized he hadn't paid. The stack of saucers came to six hundred and fifty francs, leaving me less than a hundred for the next seven days.

I went back to my hotel in a rage, crawled into my sleeping bag for warmth, and waited for seven o'clock. I put on a shirt and tie, dressed in my one suit, shined my shoes and walked across Paris to the Hotel Scribe. The English Bar lived up to its name, wood paneled walls decorated with hunting prints, plush leather chairs surrounding gleaming mahogany tables. Roger and his friends stood at the bar, three young men out of a Fitzgerald novel.

"Hello, Roger." He didn't recognize me immediately.

"Oh, hi buddy. Meet Irv and Sy. whatcha doin' here?"

"You owe me six hundred and fifty francs."

"Oh, shit. The drinks. I forgot to pay. Can't get used to the system here. Here, buddy. Here's a thousand. Have a drink." I motioned to the waiter, changed the thousand, tossed three hundred and fifty on the bar and left.

Paris was a small town for American students in nineteen forty-nine and fifty. We congregated in the bars and restaurants encircling the Sorbonne from the Rue Mouffetard to the Rue Monsieur le Prince. I had begun the Great American novel, a gothic tale of the south, Faulknerian in tone, Hemingway in style. Around us France suffered through the paroxysms of a nation torn apart by economic disaster, ancient feuds, battered pride and political divisions which had brought them to the verge of civil war.

When I first arrived I attended lectures at the Sorbonne and the Ecole Libre des Sciences Politiques, read voraciously and became fascinated with the endless warfare waged among French intellectuals. From the beginning I was torn between the icy Cartesian advocates of classic rationalism, such as Raymond Aron and Francois Mauriac, and Jean Paul Sartre's romantic existentialism. Their debates were the antithesis of anglo-saxon pragmatism. Everybody seemed more interested in being brilliant rather than giving in to the humble business of making sense.

Most intellectuals were hypnotized by the magnetic perversity of Sartre and his espousal of the Hegelian thesis of a forward-marching history. In their cosmology the communist regimes of the East were, by definition, creating a better world. Awful injustices were clearly taking place, but the brutal means justified the noble ends. In addition, the Soviets offered a counterbalance to the hated American capitalists who had stripped France and Europe of their rightful preeminence in the world. The underlying leitmotif of it all was a slightly addled French chauvinism.

But in the cold rooms and warm cafes of Paris, in that winter of 1948-49, I was enchanted. Surrounded by ideas, wit and intellectual passion in a city where Hemingway and Joyce had drunk the night through together in the Dome and Coupole with Gertrude and Alice just around the corner. And Scott and Zelda had danced the night away while Henry Miller wandered, randy and hungry, through the back alleys of the City of Light.

My notes of a lecture at the Ecole Libre still give me a slight chill. This nameless scholar, slim and desiccated, spoke on the theory and practice of diplomacy, taking as his text Francisco Guicciardini, a Florentine contemporary of Machiavelli. He described the Italian as ambitious, calculating, duplicitous, avaricious and power loving. He was also a superb diplomat, meeting treachery with fraud, parrying force with sleight of hand and a great realist, always crediting human nature with the basest of motives.

This secular Jesuit, dominating the hemicycle, went on to describe, admiringly, that Guicciardini would contemplate the blackest crimes with chilly enthusiasm provided they were clever and useful. He admired the diplomat's cold-blooded loyalty to masters he despised, much in the manner of Henry Kissinger's servile relationship with Richard Nixon. He lauded Guicciardini as a political pathologist, dissecting the cadavers of failed policies to avoid future errors. Contemptuous of sentimental stupidity, he seems to have considered his friend Machiavelli something of an amiable visionary.

It's difficult to exaggerate the difference of such an approach to international politics with that taught in American universities. The cognitive dissonance between our diplomats, reared in a tradition which stresses reasoned compromise and good faith, and their European counterparts imbued with an ethos of cynical self-interest based on the maximum use of the power at their disposal, is unbridgeable.

I was less taken aback than most of my American comrades by such cold-blooded realism, having been saturated with my father's similarly jaundiced view of mankind and his emphasis on always avenging yourself on your enemies. Preferably when they weren't looking and with a smile.

Although I was moderately fascinated by finding soul mates among the amoral French political theorists, it was Sartre and the tumult surrounding him and his cohort that was infinitely more seductive. The only problem I had with the Sartre cult was his blind commitment to communism and, even more, to its Soviet version. I found it hard to reconcile his immense intelligence and literary genius with his simplistic politics, heavily tinged with an almost infantile chauvinism. After all, France was a divided nation with a wrecked economy, negligible military might and no support for its grandiose third force policy.

It was only decades later, when I found myself on the periphery of an academic environment, that I realized that most intellectuals, not just the French, are offended by messy reality and seek psychic security in hermetic theories which allow them to escape the unreasoned chaos of real life.

But Sartre's *Weltanschauung* was immensely seductive to a twenty-three-year-old. God does not exist. Rationalism is myth. Every man must decide his own destiny in a moral vacuum and in an absurd and meaningless world. We are all waiting for Godot. He articulated a view of modern society which I dimly recognized as a reflection of Uncle Marvin's cracker-barrel anarchism.

Nonetheless, if one thing had congealed out of the mass of political rhetoric I had absorbed to this point, it was a suspicion of raw power. From Suetonius' *Twelve Caesars* through medieval despots to modern fascism, it was clear that once individuals or oligarchies, either of the left or right, took control of a society, that society would be ruthlessly milked to the advantage of its rulers. A cliché, but, like most clichés, a truth.

The messy, inefficient and often corrupt American system, cobbled together by that trio of sublime cynics, Jefferson, Hamilton and Madison, from Montesquieu, Hume, Hobbes, Locke, Machiavelli, Guicciardini and Thucydides, was political genius of the highest order. It resulted in a society which at least restrained man's worst instincts. While it did not establish a truly level playing field, it did offer opportunities to energy, intelligence and creativity which no previous governmental mechanism had even attempted.

Thirty-five years as a professional observer of political systems from Ghana and Nigeria to France, Germany, Poland, Spain, Austria and Turkey, as well as extensive study of the theorists, have left me unshaken in this belief. It has also convinced me that attempts to graft the American experiment onto other societies are both arrogantly ethnocentric and visionary. The United States, protected by distance and immense oceans, was given a chance no other country has enjoyed.

But life is not all politics and philosophy. If there is no God and no existential Good, then the choice seems to lie between nihilism and some sort of artificial personal code which will mediate between our logically absurd existence and the inescapable imprints which scarred our psyche before we arrived at the age of reason.

The answers of the mid-twentieth century arise from the sudden disorienting loss not only of God but of the nineteenth-century belief that pure science could and would solve all our problems. The sudden crumbling of Newtonian truths into the wild anarchy of Einsteinian relativity where space, time, mass and velocity merge, was hallucinatory. Even this cool intellectual domain was deconstructed by the Gödelian thesis that all systems contain unprovable propositions and are incomplete.

More recently the anti-humanists have attempted to ape this new science of uncertainty, reaching back to early classical philosophers to propose a world befogged by linguistic ambiguities. Thus

Wittgenstein's turbid and tortured relativism sees the world "through a glass darkly." His later acolytes, Michel Foucault, Paul DeMann and Jacques Derrida—faggot, fascist and fraud, in the words of one cynical opponent—denied the existence of any objective reality with neo-scholastic obfuscation.

At the time I listened to the debates and, possibly influenced by lassitude induced by continual undernourishment, decided the hell with it. It sounded all too similar to the circular reasoning of Anselm's proof of the existence of God, with both equally irrelevant to my experience. The key question raised by all the academic deconstructionist brouhaha may be "how many assistant professors can dance on the tip of Derrida's prick?"

It is a curious phenomenon of the twentieth century that the theories of Marx and advocates of arcane French intellectual constructs remain relevant only in the departments of history, literature and philosophy in American universities. As a French classicist, Jean Paul Rey-Coquais, told me recently, "Jacques was sitting bored in a cafe one day and, as a joke, invented deconstruction on one of those brown paper tablecloths. Which then fell into the hands of an American tourist. Who believed it."

There might not be an objective reality, but a broken nose spilling blood over my chest was all the proof I ever needed to refute this. I remain convinced that the search for absolutes is a form of arrested development, academic infantilism and onanism which ignores the warning that "perfection is the enemy of the good."

So, in Chernyshevsky's immortal question: What is to be done?

Freud's paradigm, work and love, is certainly one seductive approach, and I have more or less incorporated it into a world view which is based on an antiquated code of personal honor and a clinging to even a flawed rationality at all costs.

Facing death without the crutch of belief is hard. Facing meaninglessness is even more difficult. As I age my pessimism becomes ever more profound. The only verities seem to be sex, food, wine, a perfect backhand, a *bon mot*, a sudden blinding insight. All else is vanity.

Unfortunately, I was imprinted early with a set of primitive values which I have been unable to shake. Loyalty to friends. Giving back to society in the same measure that which one takes from it, crudely known as paying your dues. Looking cowardice in the eye and facing it down. Never calling a ball out when it touches the line. Treating women gently. Taking revenge on enemies. In short an incoherent and useless set of rules which, however, I violate at my peril.

This was, then, the atmosphere of my Paris in the late nineteen-forties. An inchoate youthful seeking after utopias and eternal verities combined with mild sexual license, quaint by today's standards, and the giddy exoticism of swimming in an intellectual soup spiced by a language and culture as hard-edged and unforgiving as a Picasso line drawing.

It was about this time that I came up with Harper's Third Law: *Genius is to take a complicated subject and break it down into understandable components. Stupidity is to take a simple topic and convert it to impenetrable complexity.* The French educational system was designed not to seek out truth but to teach the ability to defend a position or, if indefensible, to obfuscate the argument and wrap your opponent in a spaghetti of irrelevancies. Conversation was a game, played with skill and gusto. I adjusted to the ambiance effortlessly.

Each age selects its own intellectual poison. Existentialism and its post structuralism spin-off took France off the hook for its military and intellectual impotence. The French were simply unable to face their loss of any role as a world power or the relative insignificance of their cultural pretensions after the debacle of World War II.

Existentialism was also a personal cop-out, a relativist rationalization enabling the individual to distance himself from a society torn by deep political and social divisions. A third of the people had supported the fascist Vichy regime during the war and, in the postwar period, forty percent voted for a Communist Party which was the vassal of Moscow. Intellectuals invented a crutch to enable them to function.

In much the same way Marxist, deconstructionist and post structuralism theories—so popular on American university campuses today—allow isolated American academic intellectuals to validate the narcissism of the sixties, seventies and eighties and to survive the tolerant contempt of the great pragmatic human sea in which they must swim.

The irony of it all was that this scenario was played out in France against a backdrop of unremitting intellectual combat within the rigid framework of the French tradition of "unity above all" and the Cartesian syllogism. The leitmotif of the debate, just beneath the skin, was that unvarnished realism which permeates French literature from *Les Liaisons Dangereuses* to *Germinal* to *Le Petit Homme d'Archangelsk* and *Voyage au Bout de la Nuit*.

It also, more or less incidentally, enabled French intellectuals to shake off whatever guilt feelings they may have had and participate in the joys of sensuality without reserve. As a character in Simone de Beauvoir's *Les Mandarins* said, when asked why she slept with every man she went out with: *"Ca brise la glace."*

Eight

Sartre is the most instructive specimen of the intellectual's tendency to look ridiculous.

Cornelius Castoriadis

"Puligny Montrachet, monsieur," the sommelier said. I'd asked him for a wine to go with the trout. It was 1957 and I was in Paris on vacation from a job as sales manager for the Pillsbury Flour Company on the West Coast of Africa. A job I had wound up in after being forced to resign from the foreign service for marrying a Viennese. La Perouse was a three-star restaurant on the Quai des Grands Augstins I had often walked past during my student days in Paris, swearing to return and eat there when I was rich and famous.

It was hallucinatory to come back to the great city with money in my pocket, a warm Irish tweed jacket on my back and living in a hotel with heat and a bath. Eight years before when I arrived in Paris in January 1949, cold, broke, riding an illegal motorcycle, with nothing more than the clothes in my pack, I had one contact, a fellow Atlantan with whom a mutual friend had put me in contact. We had exchanged letters when I was in Grenoble. Although I had made it a point to avoid Americans, I swallowed my principles and called on him.

Alec was a character out of a Tennessee Williams play. Small, delicate, highly intelligent with a biting wit and nerves on the surface of his skin, he lived in some luxury in a huge, high-ceilinged room just down the Boulevard St. Germain from the

Cafe Flor and the Deux Magots. A graduate of Emory and a member of the Atlanta *haute bourgeoisie*, he spoke excellent French and quickly took me in hand, insisting that I register at the Ecole Libre des Sciences Politiques.

Science Po in the late forties was a finishing school for the sons and daughters of the rich. Its primary aim was to train young aristocrats for the French diplomatic service. Its major attraction for me was a program for *etudiants libres* who were not required to take exams. Since nobody had to attend classes at any French university, it was a totally free ride. For some reason the Veterans Administration in Paris put up with this situation, and I could collect my GI Bill sustenance payments and spend my time writing the Great American Novel undisturbed by the vulgar details of being a student.

It had already become clear to me that this was a nation obsessed with the concept of power. The Ecole Libre provided confirmation. The French might pay lip service to truth and beauty, but their hard-edged, elegant logic was always directed at domination. Winning at whatever cost. Years later, when I lived part of each year in France, I realized that this same attitude governed their attitude to the simplest details of daily life, from refusing to stand in line to tailgating at a hundred miles an hour on a deserted highway. Intimidation was the name of the game. For the fun of it.

This attitude is at least a partial explanation for the astonishing ability of this relatively poor, militarily insignificant country's ability to impose its self-interest on the world for the fifty years since the end of the Second World War. It has been a triumph of intelligence and will. I continue to be both repelled and fascinated by their pure elitism and unrivaled intellectual brutality.

Prenez garde de l'amour, their poet Paul Valery warned. Which translates, in a sense, as "if you seek love, you lose power." Nobody could ever accuse the French of this fatal American weakness.

The lectures at the Ecole Libre tended to concentrate exclusively on France's great diplomatic triumphs from Richelieu and Tallyerand to DeGaulle. The rest of the world circled the hexagon, as France was called, like chaotic barbarian planets around a sun radiating culture and Cartesian logic. Humiliating military defeats, revolutions, religious discord and economic irrelevancy all paled in comparison to the overriding role of France as the guardian of true civilization.

I attended lectures in the steep hemicycles more or less at random. Once Alec dragged me to one being given by the great Andre Siegfried, a short feisty little man with a spade beard and piercing blue eyes. In a previous lecture he had defined the role of the diplomat as one who "seeks out the sources of power, defines their motivations and forecasts their actions." I've never heard it said better.

On this day he was lecturing on the American Civil War, seen, as we later joked, from the standpoint of a one-eyed Martian. As nearly as I can remember, Siegfried saw the conflict as arising from the Machiavellian machinations of an England intent on separating the South and its agrarian cotton culture from the industrial north, while at the same time reducing the growing power of its recalcitrant former colony. All this, of course, solely designed to deprive France of access to southern cotton and other raw materials.

It was my first encounter with what later became Harper's Fourth Law: The Myth of the Central Position—the widespread belief of all peoples that the world circles around their navel.

Siegfried founded many of his conclusions on reports sent back to Paris by the French ambassador to Washington who, it turned out, was a great uncle. In the course of his lecture, Siegfried located the "department" of Colorado on the West bank of the Mississippi river.

"We've got to tell him he's wrong," Alec whispered to me.

"Better you than me," I said. Correcting a French professor was the equivalent of volunteering for the guillotine.

After the lecture, Alec accosted the little man with exquisite deference. Siegfried looked him up and down as if he were an insect. "Yes."

"Professor," Alec said in his best French. I am desolated to inform you that Colorado is in the western United States, not on the Mississippi river."

Siegfried drew himself up to his five feet four inches, and with a withering stare said, *"C'est un detail,"* and stalked off.

He was quintessentially French, and his lectures were peppered with one line aphorisms. "Diplomacy is the art of winning without war." "A revolution is nothing more than a change in the governing classes." "If the English can't win by the rules, they change the rules." French students picked up this habit from their professors and often concocted their own more or less humorous ones.

"Marx is God, and Ford is his prophet."

"Savages die of starvation; the civilized of indigestion."

Alex belonged to a loose-knit circle of highly self-conscious American and French student intellectuals who gathered in the cafes of St. Germain-des-Pres, acolytes of Jean Paul Sartre, Simone de Beauvoir, Maurice Merleau-Ponty and lesser lights of *Les Temps Modernes,* an influential existentialist magazine. He dragged me to the quai-side book stalls, forcing on me Flaubert's *Madame Bovary,* Zola's *Germinal,* Rimbaud's *Les Fleurs du Mal, Les Liasons* Dangereuse and especially Proust and Gide, his favorites.

My tastes differed from his. Louis Ferdinand Celine's *Voyage au Bout de la Nuit* and *Mort a Credit* and Raymond Radiguet's *Le Diable au Corps* impressed me more than the cork-lined room. I had a poetic phase, immersing myself in Mallarme, Valery, Appolinaire, Rimbaud and the ineffable nonsense of Jarry. For a while Andre Breton held me in his grip with his hymns to the primitive, hatred of sentiment and celebration of black humor, eroticism and simple madness. It was a heady time, as I bounced between the intoxication of words at St. Germain-des-Pres and the pangs of unrequited lust, during my meetings three or four times a week with Roger and Janine to sort out their complicated social life.

One evening, when Janine was down with the flu, Roger dragged me with him to a ballet done to the music of Carmen. The stars, Roland Petit and Gigi Jeanmaire, danced the most powerfully erotic performance I've ever seen. "Keep that up and they'll replace burlesque," Roger said as we left the theater.

I had also, as I've done for more than fifty years, begun to work out in a gym near the Salle Wagram, site of the boxing matches in Paris. I occasionally had a beer after workouts with the manager of two black fighters married to French women. Their manager, a light-skinned black named Jim English, bore the same name as one of my great-grandfathers and we agreed that we were probably related.

In a weak moment I agreed to spar with his middleweight, a talented fighter with all the moves and a punch to match them. The agreement was that I could go all out but Jason would pull his punches. I was still in reasonably good shape and the first few sessions were exciting, a little like being in a cage with a benevolent panther. Since I didn't have much of a punch, Jason was often careless. Once he looked up and saw his wife come through the door of the gym. Unaware of what was happening, I nailed him with a right hook delivered from the heels.

The next thing I knew, Jim English was holding up my shorts and massaging my diaphragm. "What happened?"

"He, uh, kind of landed one in your short ribs," English said.

Jason apologized profusely, but I went back to working out on the heavy bag after that.

Janine and Roger had become a couple as the French say. They were, as she told me, *bien tombe.* She was an unaffectedly mercenary young woman who was also the eternal *femelle. Une chienne,* as she once put it, grinning. He was, at the level they met, a rich young stud. He made no pretense of studying, ambling around Paris, eating in good restaurants, spending the evening in night clubs and "screwing himself blind" in his inimitable phrase.

Once, he dragged me with him to see the work of an artist somebody had recommended. We climbed the circular fourteenth-century stone staircase of a building behind the Square Viviani to a studio under the eves. It was a hot summer day and when we opened the door a young woman, sitting nude on the floor eating an apple, glanced up and rose slowly, slipping into a cotton dress. Over her shoulder the towers of Notre Dame rose close enough to touch.

The walls were covered with abstract canvasses so heavily painted as to be almost three dimensional. I wandered around the studio which also served as bedroom, living room, dining room and kitchen, as Roger looked over the man's work, eyes mostly on the girl. Finally he stopped in front of an immense painting with a vague resemblance to a city.

"What 'dya call that?" Roger asked in his Harvard-cum-Bronx accent.

The painter looked at the girl, who shrugged. "Bridge in Venice."

"Yeah? Where's the bridge?" Roger asked.

The painter pointed to a whitish slash in the middle of the canvass.

Roger haggled with him over the price for a few minutes before agreeing to a quite respectable sum. "Look," he said. "I can't handle anything that big. How about you slice out about three feet by three of it, here," he indicated the putative bridge.

The painter stared at him in despair, looking once again at the girl who picked up a straight razor and handed it to him.

Shortly thereafter, I took off for a month on a pilgrimage to a village on the west coast of Scotland. It was a grim time in Great Britain. Food was rationed, and the people looked even more tired and worn than the French. I hitch-hiked north from London, spending the nights in youth hostels, living on oatmeal breakfasts and cold canned spaghetti, the only foods not rationed. Once, outside York, I was picked up by a prosperous looking man in his fifties in a well kept pre-war Rover sedan.

"Yank, are you?"

"Yes, sir."

"In the war, were you?"

"On a carrier," I said.

"Why are you doing this?" He held up his thumb.

"Hitch-hiking? I don't have much money."

"If you don't have money, you should stay home," he said,

clamping his mouth shut and never speaking again. After about fifty miles of silence he pulled up at a pub on the edge of a village and motioned me to follow him inside. He pointed to a table and a few minutes later a waiter appeared with an immense bowl of stew, a platter of country bread and a quart of beer. I stared at the meal, appalled. I had a total of thirty pounds, a hundred and twenty dollars, to last me six weeks, and I could see a large chunk of it going down my gullet.

I ate. When I looked up the man had finished his drink and left. I stood and asked the bartender how much I owed him.

"The gent paid for your dinner, sir," he said, smiling.

My next ride was in an ancient Riley, one of the many museum pieces still on the roads of Europe at the time.

"Throw your pack in the back," the driver, a slim woman of about forty wearing the tweeds which seemed to be the uniform of the country, said. "Palmerston won't harm it." Palmerston turned out to be a small monkey who joined us in the front seat after checking out my pack. He bounced around the car like a furry ball for the ten miles she took me. When I picked up the pack from the pavement, I saw that Chesterfield had shat neatly on the top, smearing it in. It gave off a godawful odor which I was never able to eradicate.

My last ride, in a new hearse being delivered to Edinburgh, took me into Scotland. From there I took a bus north to a youth hostel just outside a place called Bonar Bridge. The hostel was in a fairy tale castle, built by a nouveau rich English industrialist in 1910, and the most comfortable place I slept in the British Isles. My destination was another youth hostel in the village of Lochinver seventy miles across the narrow neck of Scotland on the West Coast.

The hostel manager told me that every Tuesday and Thursday a fish lorry made the trip over and back, leaving at six a.m. The driver would take me with him. I had bought a rust-colored Harris tweed jacket in Edinburgh to keep from freezing to death in the July chill, and my money was getting dangerously low. I was on the road the next morning at five a.m. and by ten I began to think something had happened to the fish lorry.

I trudged on, eating some of the country bread I'd snatched at breakfast, seeing nothing on the one-lane road but sheep and thousands upon thousands of rabbits. It was a strange and haunting landscape without a tree, gorse covering the low hills, changing from dark green to blue as the sun came up. The English had driven my ancestors from these lands to turn them into hunting preserves, and here and there in the fields the stone ruins of a roofless cottage showed through the undergrowth.

I walked until about eight p.m., without seeing a car or a human being, and finally curled up beside the road wrapped in the new jacket and awaited the morning. The sun came up at three a.m., and I set off, hungry and cold. Four or five hours later I arrived at a crossroads and a cottage, half buried in the ground, and knocked on the door.

"And what might you be doing here?" the owner, wearing a jacket much like mine, but looking about two hundred years older, asked. I explained.

"Yank, are you?"

"Yes, sir," I had long since given up trying to explain that Southerners were not Yanks.

"Yanks are always looking for their people up here. Waste of time. Come in." An immense plate of oatmeal appeared and I ate it as if it were caviar. When I finished he brought out a stone jug and poured about three jiggers in a glass, pushing it toward me.

I took a sip and gagged on the raw scotch. My host grinned and poured himself one. "Good for what ails, you." he said, touching his glass to mine. "The lorry driver will be stopping in an hour or so. He was a day late this week."

Lochinver turned out to be a deserted village. The youth hostel, located in what had once been a school, was run by a student of Celtic. I was the only visitor he had had all summer. It was a lonely place, inhabited by a few fishing families and herders of the sheep on the lands of absentee English lords. My host had the key to the church and helped me go through the records. I found traces of my family in a stained parish register and one gravestone where the name had not been obliterated by time and the weather.

In the evening my host played his guitar and sang haunting Celtic lays in a high thin voice, stopping occasionally to declaim verses of Robert Burns. On the following Tuesday, before boarding the fish lorry back to Bonar Bridge, I left him all my books. A lonely fanatic in the midst of what is still the most beautiful landscape I have ever seen.

Back in France the texture of my life changed. Roger, and with him Janine, had disappeared. Alec had returned to the States, somewhat to my relief, since over time I had discovered that most of his circle of friends were homosexuals as was he. Strange as it may seem, at a time when to be "gay" has become an acceptable mainstream lifestyle and exhaustive examinations of their customs are to be found in any bookstore, I was only vaguely aware of what the terms "queer", "faggot", "pansy" and "fairy" signified. Screwing boys in the ass, as a navy friend had explained, seemed to me a thoroughly unlikely explanation, and when I thought about it all, I assumed it was simply an advanced form of effeminacy.

Until one day one of the group invited me to lunch, put his hand on my thigh and suggested that we adjourn to his room for a fuck. I must have looked stunned as I removed his hand. He wouldn't believe that I wasn't, as he put it, "one of the boys."

"You know Alec is a raving faggot, don't you?" he said.

"No."

"Jesus X Christ. You can't be that stupid. Ninety percent of us are, you dumb shit. We've all been envying him his stud." He then proceeded to unveil for me, in graphic detail, just what queers do to each other. It sounded to me then, and still does today, not only unsanitary but aesthetically revolting.

"A question of taste, no pun intended," as another homosexual friend said when I asked what the difference was between screwing a man in the ass and a woman in the vagina. "Why don't you try it sometime and find out?"

I've never had the urge to take him up on his offer, but until the AIDS epidemic came along I figured, what the hell, *chacun a son gout*. Now I'm not so sure. The hidden hand of nature may be out there protecting the propagation of the species by discouraging non-procreative sex, just as venereal disease may be its way of discouraging promiscuity.

My own sex life in Paris was a lot less lively than that reflected in the literature of the period. First, I was perpetually broke. Second, most of the French female students were from strict bourgeois households with no intention of offering themselves to poverty-stricken foreigners. Third, I lived for most of my final year in a one-room windowless ground floor cubicle warmed by a minuscule space heater. The room was so small the single bed partially blocked the entrance.

At one point the hormones began to rage so badly, I considered coupling with some of the attractive women who were, in desperation, offering themselves on the streets for a pittance. Walking down the Boulevard St. Germain one day, a beautiful woman of about thirty, with immense blue eyes, a trim athletic figure and a face full of intelligence, approached Alec and me.

"Allez ou allons?" she asked when Alec told her to bugger off, her voice cracking with the effort at wit. She was dressed in an obviously expensive black suit, shiny with age.

I would have given her every cent I had for an hour or two with her, and I told him so as she walked away.

"Men like you only get women like that in the aftermath of an awful war," he said.

For a time I was joined by a young Dutch girl I'd met in one of the *caveaux*, cellar hangouts where students gathered. The Bole was just off the Place St. Michel and featured a group of folksingers chanting bawdy 14th century songs, mostly about priests and nuns.

In right profile Julie was a pretty, if overweight, young woman. The left side of her face was deeply burned and scarred, as was much of her body, from an American incendiary bomb. She was a borderline alcoholic with a tendency to dissolve into tears after gulping glass after glass of cheap Dutch gin.

She was in Paris on a three-month grant to improve her French before taking the government examination to become a teacher. Although her English was excellent, she refused to speak it with me, explaining that if she picked up an American accent, she would fail her English exam.

She was, like most European students, a communist and violently ambivalent about the United States. Enthralled by our films, jazz, Edgar Allen Poe, Hemingway, Faulkner and what she called our "primitive innocence", she was repelled by American "capitalism, racism, imperialism and materialism."

She was also an affectionate, fun-loving young woman desperate to be loved. As she said about her scars, "at night all cows are black." She left early in December, promising to return when her exams were over. My letters went unanswered, and I never saw her again.

Vera was a Swedish Jewess, about six feet tall, towering over my five nine. She would have been a raving beauty, with coal black hair, a translucent olive skin and taut athlete's body, had one of her superb green eyes not stared over your left shoulder while the other focused on your right. She picked me up in the standing room section at a performance of Moliere's *Le Bourgeois Gentilhomme* at the Comedic Francaise.

Vera lived in some luxury in a small hotel in the Rue Cujas off the Boulevard St. Michel and was clearly not poor. One weekend she financed a bicycle tour of the Loire Valley, arranging the whole trip with frightening efficiency. But we seemed to spend most of our time in bed, not to keep warm, as I often had with Julie, but to take a shot at setting some sexual records. It was my first experience with a strung out, virtually unending, female orgasm. The modern observation, that "a man's capacity for orgasm compares to a woman's as a muzzle loading rifle to an AK 47", was all too accurate. She would first defuse me rather cold bloodedly before bringing me back to a performance level I could sustain indefinitely.

Once again, fate intervened in this idyll in the form of a determined mother who descended on Paris, apparently reacting to an injudicious letter from Vera. The lady didn't object to the sexual liaison. It was the prospect of her only daughter marrying a heathen which disturbed her. We pledged undying love, or lust anyway, before she left for Stockholm.

At the same time my GI Bill ran out. It was a fairly desperate time, since virtually everybody I knew had already gone home. Only Ward Kirchwehm and his wife remained, and they were even poorer than I was. He was the son of a Bohemian immigrant machinist and she was a beautiful willowy college girl. Tall, slim, athletic and innocent. Ward had spent most of his youth in an orphanage, escaping via a football scholarship to a small Illinois college and, after the war, through the GI Bill. He will appear periodically in these memoirs as will Howard Berk and others. But in 1950, he was no help.

I'd applied at the American Embassy for a menial job and been told by the lady personnel officer that "she wouldn't give me a job cleaning the johns." On the way out I saw a notice for the examination for the career foreign service. I filled it out, having only a vague idea of what it was.

I then made another attempt to sell the black market motorcycle and this time got my ass in a sling. I was passed up the line through a series of bureaucrats who didn't believe my disingenuous lies about how I had obtained it, until I arrived at a ministry in the Rue Vaneau around the corner from the Rodin Museum. I was ushered into a large office overlooking a garden and greeted politely by a slim, elegantly tailored man in his forties.

He listened to my story, told in what was by then rather good French, and at the end said, in excellent American-accented English, "You're lying and not very cleverly. Now tell me how you bought the motorcycle."

He listened to my confession and smiled, signed the papers allowing me to sell it and pushed them across the desk. "I sympathize with your desire to stay in France, Mr. Harper, but I really do think it is time for you to go home. I've taken the liberty of writing your father," whose name and address was in my passport, "and suggesting that he send you another ticket replacing the one you cashed in and making this one non-negotiable."

He then took me to lunch at a nearby bistro, and sang a hymn of praise to the United States and to the education in engineering he had received at Cornell twenty years before.

I went home on the DeGrasse, third class. On the way out of Le Havre, the first night's five course menu with two kinds of wine boasted of the progress French Line had made on the North Atlantic run. In 1900 it had taken twelve days to make the crossing. Now they were doing it in seven. Twelve days later, after one of the worst Atlantic storms on record, we arrived in New York.

In the meantime, only about sixty of the three hundred passengers in third class showed up regularly for meals. A group of returning students, almost all of us navy veterans, collected wine from the other tables as the waiters, many themselves seasick unto death, ignored us, and stayed blitzed for the entire crossing.

Nine

Sliding down the razor blade of life.

Tom Lehrer

"What's your biggest problem?"

She thought for a while, an acne scarred young woman and born again Christian who was a social worker in Spartanburg, North Carolina. I wasn't interested in her problem. But mine was getting laid, and she seemed the likeliest prospect, so I listened attentively.

"Well," she said, in the deep southern drawl of these mountains, "I guess it's getting the little negra boys out of bed with their sisters when they get to be ten years old."

I was a reporter on the Spartanberg Herald, the only paper that answered of the hundred or so I'd applied to when I got back from France. It was a great job. I covered the courthouse, city police, sheriff's office, State Patrol and hospitals, working from about noon to midnight for forty dollars a week.

I lived first at the YMCA, which was run by a religious fanatic who was also a mighty hunter of anything that moved. We often went after quail in fields illegally seeded with corn, his two pointers ranging among the stubble, suddenly frozen, tails straight out, right paw lifted in the classic point, every muscle quivering until he gave the almost imperceptible signal to flush the quarry. He never missed. We often came back with forty or so of the small birds, which he grilled for breakfast for the traveling salesmen and penniless wanderers who inhabited his rooms.

Spartanburg boasted at the time the flyweight boxing champion of the world, a wizened little man named Pappy Gault. He trained at the YMCA gym and, inevitably, invited me to spar with him. I had no idea who he was and agreed, intending to go through the motions and humor the little man. Hell, he weighed a hundred and twelve pounds soaking wet and I was up to a hundred and fifty-five. I should have realized something was up when a small crowd of weight lifters gathered around the makeshift ring.

Boxing Pappy was a little like chasing a wisp of smoke. He moved like a ghost or a shadow, occasionally flicking a gentle straight left into my face, snapping a skinny arm in a blur. At one point he feinted to the left, back right, then left, turning me almost in a circle, and playfully slapped me in the ribs with an open glove.

Later I realized what I'd escaped when I watched him pound the heavy bag, rattling the chains holding it to the ceiling in repeated three, four and five-punch combinations too fast to follow.

Pappy had bad luck. One night, long after I had left Spartanburg and when he was no longer champion, a reformed murderer who had "come to Christ" lost his religion momentarily and shot Pappy dead after a poker game argument.

I later moved to a classic boarding house, a large clapboard structure in what had once been the town's elite neighborhood. Five men—two retail clerks, a mechanic, a bank teller and I—shared one bath. Breakfast, supper and the room rent came to a hundred dollars a month. Entertaining female guests in your room led to automatic expulsion by the slender, gray-haired tyrant who ran the place.

Small southern towns of the era were in a time wrap, their life patterns reflecting more a somnolent pre-World War I America rather than the jostling, dynamic, aggressive country which came through the second World War no longer an immense backwater but a dominant world power.

The social worker was just beginning to come around, lust and the prospect of luring me into marriage overcoming Christ, when I went to war with the culvert and wound up convalescing and having my broken teeth rebuilt in Atlanta for the next six weeks. The job didn't wait for me.

Will Davenport and I painted slum houses during the day, and at night I drank beer with old college friends in the taverns of the time. One night Alec, my friend from Paris, and I went to a particularly scruffy one called Tom and Jerry's. We toured the horizon of world problems, talked about Paris and his inability to find work because he was so obviously queer. I noticed the two men in the next booth turning to look at us, overhearing Alec's high-pitched lament and snickering.

There was a hint of violence in the air. Being overtly queer was a red flag to the bar's lower middle class clientele. But Alec was oblivious, railing against the bigotry of the redneck masses and his fate. When we stood to go, the two in the next booth stared at us with an all-too-familiar swaggering insolence. I returned the stare, preparing for the inevitable.

The shock of recognition hit all three of us at once. The two men were the friends of my youth, Harold Anderson and Linwood. They turned, confused, to their beers, and Alec and I left.

I spent a fair amount of time in my father's office which he shared with a partner who financed many of his shady deals. Junius Ogelsby was an elegant upper class southerner of about eighty. He had never really held a job, living off a rich and tolerant wife. Ogelsby, a graduate of Princeton, was a wispy little man, impeccably dressed in hand tailored suits and British shoes.

He was a throwback to the early nineteenth century. One afternoon he expatiated at length on the tragedy of the civil war which had cost his family most of its land and money.

"Totally senseless war, Edward," he said. He and my mother were the only people who used my full name. "Only Lincoln's monumental ego and those fanatical New England puritans expiating their guilt over the origins of their fortunes, which came from the slave trade, could have perpetrated that criminal war."

I protested that Lincoln was universally revered and admired as an idealist and one of the truly good men of his time.

"The winners write history, my boy," he said. "Six hundred thousand men died in that war which was nothing more than a pointless power struggle between the industrial north and an agrarian south. There was no idealism involved. Lincoln had no intention of freeing the slaves when it started. He referred to them as 'niggers' and had repeatedly recommended that they be shipped back to Africa in his campaign speeches. And, of course, during the war he violated the constitution repeatedly, suspending habeas corpus, running a nasty little dictatorship. He was an ignorant, uneducated, power hungry demagogue with a flair for mesmerizing rhetoric. Sound and fury signifying nothing more than an obsessive hunger for power."

"But dividing the country would have led to disaster," I protested.

"Nonsense," Ogelsby said, drawing on one of the fine Cuban Portugas cigars he bought during semiannual visits to the Havana fleshpots. "What would have happened if the South had seceded? First, the North would have annexed Canada and we would have taken Cuba and Mexico, both of which were sparsely populated at the time. The slaves would have been freed within fifteen years against fair compensation to the owners. Our natural affinity with the Negroes would have led to much better race relations than we now have."

He blew a few smoke rings toward the ceiling and continued. "The South would have developed a Mediterranean style, elegant and corrupt, while the Northerners would have imploded into the puritanical messianic fanaticism in which they reveled."

And Ogelsby may well have been right. Was the Union worth the hundred years of vengeance and hatred which succeeded what he called The War of Northern Aggression? Are the blacks better off for having been forcibly freed only to suffer under the tyranny of the southern whites taking vengeance on them as surrogates for the northerners who had first defeated and then tormented them?

Brazil freed its slaves in 1888. The result is, although imperfect, an infinitely more integrated and racially tolerant society than that in the United States. It seems unlikely that the South would not have done the same, paying compensation to the owners to end a system everybody agreed was not only immoral but inefficient.

Oddly, Lincoln's saintly reputation is undergoing some cautious revision as historians chip away at the myth. His comment in the Lincoln-Douglas debates, that "there is a physical difference between the white and black races which I believe will forever forbid the two living together on terms of social and political equality", sounds like a modern Ku Klux Klan bigot in full flight. The time may well be at hand for a critical biography of the man, warts and all.

At the time I found Ogelsby's fulminations bizarre but amusing. As I write this, however, with the spectacle of Russian repression of its minorities, the senseless massacres in the former Yugoslavia, India's unwillingness to free a Moslem Kashmir, the Tamils of Sri Lanka and the tribal chaos of Africa, I wonder about the sacredness of the American Union. Was preserving it really worth more than half a million dead, a hundred years of hatred and vengeance from the repressed semi-colonial south and, tragically, a repression of the blacks not much better than slavery?

What would happen today if California decided to secede? Or New England? Or the eleven states of the Confederacy? Would we risk a bloody war to prevent it? I somehow doubt it.

My next hundred letters seeking a job brought a reply from The Sanford Florida Herald, a five-day-a-week paper in a somnolent central Florida town of twenty thousand a few miles north of Orlando, which advertised itself as the "celery capital of the world."

The paper was barely making it, and I was asked to check in at eight-thirty every day on the time clock, although I got in at seven, and check out at five-thirty. I seldom left before eight.

It was the best job I ever had.

I converted the front page from a rather chaotic artifact into a pristine balanced format modeled on the *New York Times,* using the excellent techniques taught at the University of Georgia School of Journalism. The society editor, a zaftig newly married redhead, had coincidentally also gone to the journalism school at Georgia, and between us we made it into a prize-winning newspaper, somewhat to the bemusement of Roland Dean.

I had carte blanche in my daily sports column, *Straight from the Horse's Mouth,* where I did a fair imitation of Red Smith, the premier sports columnist of his day. Once, having listened in the local saloon to the fishermen brag about the huge catfish they'd caught in the alligator-infested lake which bordered the town, I offered five dollars to anybody who would deliver a hundred pound catfish to the Herald.

The office was deserted the next morning when I arrived, and I headed out to the back alley where everybody was gathered. Lined up were half a dozen ancient pickup trucks each containing one of the biggest and ugliest catfish I'd ever seen. Their great gaping mouths, scarred from the many hooks they had thrown, were surrounded by obscene growths, and they were beginning to smell.

Half a dozen grinning blacks were standing around expectantly. I turned to Roland who smiled and handed me a wad of five dollar bills which I passed out to the winners. In the course of the morning four more turned up. The final cost to me was sixty dollars. Roland magnanimously agreed to take it out of my salary at five dollars a week.

The paper's advertising salesman, Tom Doyle—a puckish Irishman with a fine voice and a repertory of tenor roles from Italian opera—Mike Siriani, the lifeguard at the local tourist hotel, and I formed the core of a tennis group. On weekends we would gather around the hotel pool trying to figure out some way to make more than the forty dollars a week each of us was drawing.

One Saturday, Mike, who was from Boston, hauled us off into a corner away from the pool and offered a proposition.

"Listen, guys. I gotta sure thing. You know the bug operation over in Orlando?"

The "bug" was a numbers game run by a small time Italian gang in Orlando, twenty miles from Sanford.

We agreed that the "bug" existed.

"Yeah. Well what you don't know is that the head guy, Guido, don't trust nobody. He brings the take over here to the bank every day at midnight and drops it in the night deposit machine."

"How do you know that?" Doyle asked.

"I seen him do it. I was out with Eve last night, and coming home I saw him with this big canvas bag stuffing it into the night deposit box."

"Christ, Mike, you can't break into a night deposit box. You'd need ten pounds of dynamite and wake every cop in central Florida."

"We don't break into the box. We club him when he gets out of the car and take the sack."

Doyle and I exchanged glances. Mike kept a tape-wrapped club under the front seat of his 1932 Chevrolet convertible "in case of emergencies." The only emergency I'd ever seen him get into was having a wheel come off the car one evening, when we were coming back from Orlando, and go rolling gaily past us down the highway as we skidded off the road on the axle.

We didn't rob the bug man, although, years later in a Christmas card from Doyle, I learned that Mike had become one of the bank's tellers. At least he got to touch the stuff.

At this distance in time my year-and-a-half in Sanford has receded into the shadows. It did, however, lead to the publication of my first free-lance article. This resulted from a call from a local black mortician informing Roland that a respected black lady of the community wasn't a lady after all, but a man. She had lived as a woman, for reasons known only to her, for fifty years, married and died a respected member of her church.

We carried a feature on this bizarre story, the Associated Press picked it up and a few days later *Ebony Magazine* called. They commissioned an article on the lady which appeared in their July 6, 1951 edition. A fifty dollar check arrived in the mail a couple of weeks later.

Except for a few hurricanes it was an uneventful period, until the last few weeks before my departure for Washington to go into a foreign service indoctrination course. Among the members of the ruling class in Sanford was a character named Brailey Odum who ran the local Oldsmobile dealership.

Brailey was a classic car salesman, big, handsome in a fleshy kind of way, he had a virtually endless chain of meaningless chatter which soothed most people into a kind of dazed somnolence. He wasn't, however, stupid. Underneath the act was a shrewd businessman and a feral intelligence. He often came by the office after the paper was put to bed, around two in the afternoon, and talked politics with Roland. Occasionally he would stop off at my desk and let the charm roll. A month or so after I'd received my appointment, as a third secretary and vice consul in the career diplomatic service, he stopped me after a late baseball game and led me to a bench overlooking the lake.

"Ed, I'm gonna run for senator," he said. I'd heard rumors of this without paying much attention. "I got most of the car dealers in the state backing me and the funeral guys are gonna come around soon. Money won't be a problem. And I got a gimmick which is gonna win the election."

"What's that?"

"I'm gonna walk across the state from one end to the other." He grinned his wide, innocent grin. "I'll get more coverage than all the other candidates put together. Free. Ain't nobody with a big name runnin' next year. All one of us gotta do is get recognition and we win."

"Sounds good Brailey." I couldn't figure out why he was talking to me.

"Listen to me, boy. I'm offering you the chance of a lifetime. I want you to run my campaign. Write my speeches. Handle the press. I been watching you for a year now. You write real good. And you're organized. Got that goddamn mess of a paper running like grease. Hell, Roland says he woulda given you a ten dollar raise if it would have kept you." He laughed his big booming phony laugh, and it sailed out across the water toward the other shore.

"What you gonna be making in the guvamint?"

"Eighty a week."

"I'll give you a hundred and expenses, starting January 1. When I win you'll be my office manager. Down the line we'll go to Washington together. Play your cards right, someday you could get elected representative from a safe district. What do you say, boy?"

I said no, but I've often wondered what would have happened if I'd gone with him. He came within a hair of winning with a totally disorganized campaign and an incoherent program.

I sold my car, a nineteen-forty Chevrolet coupe, for two hundred dollars a few weeks later, and headed for Washington where the entering foreign service class of twenty-six men and one woman would spend three months in training. It was a heady time. I was one of twenty-seven out of more than two thousand who had taken the exam. All my classmates came from elite universities. Most had graduate degrees. They ranged from twenty-four to late-thirties, about half veterans of the war. A third would eventually become ambassadors.

We were part of a small, elite corps of eight hundred career diplomats, a majority with some independent means. Diplomacy was then, and remains to this day, mired in the eighteenth century when most business was conducted, not in offices, but over dinner or in the salons of the powerful. To succeed you need to entertain. To entertain you needed money. The pay was low, although I had doubled my newspaper salary, and the allowances pitiful.

The diplomatic services of all Europeans countries were then staffed, and still are, by highly trained young men from aristocratic or *haut bourgeois* families. Their selection processes were designed to form a corps of like-minded men from the same class and caste who could communicate with people of similar background from other nations. French was still the major language of diplomatic communication, although English was rapidly replacing it. My Ivy League colleagues, most to the manor born, fit into this neat little elite with only minor adjustments, usually aided by at least a year of study abroad.

This comfortable atmosphere had already begun to suffer some severe shocks when our class went into training. First, and most important, a large chunk of the globe was in the hands of former violent revolutionaries. While many of the Soviet diplomats were intellectuals, only a few of the old aristocratic class had survived, usually tolerated for their technical expertise. Similarly, China and the emerging third world countries were governed by people totally unfamiliar with European conventions and usually contemptuous of them.

The American foreign service had, very reluctantly, begun to change, expanding its secretive recruiting policies to a much wider range of the population and, in the mid-nineteen fifties, amalgamating what had once been service personnel with the hard core of consular, political and economic reporting officers. The result was that highly motivated, shrewd and hard charging members of this group rapidly manipulated the promotion system to the bewilderment of the old boy network.

Within a decade ambassadors were being appointed whose major expertise was in shipping household goods, renting apartments and keeping the plumbing working. Their resentment of those who had entered by taking the examination was ferocious, and a minor war raged between the "old FSOs" and the upstart mustangs.

The worst result of this—aside from the intellectual shortcomings of some of the mustangs—was a sudden and complete bureaucratization of the organization, making "management" the main criterion for promotion to the senior foreign service rather than that creative intelligence capable of penetrating the mysteries of other cultures, and, in Andre Siegfried's phrase, "defining the motivations of their leaders and forecasting their actions" while recommending realistic options to Washington.

A sort of intellectual arteriosclerosis set in. Creative reporting was dangerous reporting. Daring leaps into the unknown were frowned upon. Safety was all. The days when men with independent incomes could and did discreetly defy the system, secure in their knowledge that they wouldn't starve, were over.

Caution and toeing the line were the watchwords for career advancement.

But this was mostly in the future at the time of my appointment. Before leaving Washington, the class had been taken to a cut-rate clothing store in Baltimore called Schwarz's. Here we were discreetly guided toward charcoal gray suits and black wingtips. The dinner jackets were fashionable and cheap. More important, Schwarz sold on credit to entering foreign service officers.

Part of our training involved a trip to New York where we were put up at the Seamen's Institute, a hostel for sailors with whom, as vice consuls, we would have much to do if we were stationed in port cities. One of the many parties to which we were invited over our three month course, to introduce us to suitable wives as one of the class realists observed, was held at the Colony Club.

I asked my Grenoble friend, Olga von Ziegesar, to join me for the evening, picking her up at her home on One Gracey Square. The doorman at the Colony Club greeted her by name as did all the flunkies. Olga later married an impecunious German aristocrat descended from Teutonic knights, Fabian Kalau vom Hofe, who, without a high school degree, wound up a senior vice president of Morgan Guaranty Trust Company.

That night, however, our maximum leader—a career failure—pickled in alcohol, who was assigned to shepherd us through the course—was taken aback at his southern kulak's contacts. My stock rose.

In those days even third secretaries traveled first class. The plane to Europe was a Stratocruiser, a propeller-driven monster with a lower deck given over to a bar and card tables. The flight took sixteen hours. About half way across, the party in the bar got lively. A handsome, if slightly overweight German blonde dripping diamonds, joined the fun, quickly learning both the words and music to a variety of American songs. She had a voice the texture of honey.

We gave her a royal, and alcoholic, sendoff at the London

stopover as she was met at the bottom of the gangway by half a dozen people bearing bouquets of flowers. We idly speculated who Hilde could be.

I had a day's layover in Frankfurt, and I spent it walking the streets of the gutted city, searching for one undamaged house. Mile after mile of ruins stretched into the distance, bricks stacked in neat piles in front of each smashed apartment house or store. Grim, pale faced women worked in groups around the scattered houses, cleaning and stacking the bricks.

Night falls quickly during northern European winters, and when we landed in Vienna at five p.m. in early December it was already dark. An embassy car met me and another passenger, a middle-aged man with a stiff left leg, the result of a war wound, at the airport which lay in the Russian Zone outside the limits of the city itself. Vienna was then controlled by a commission of the Allied Powers, the United States, Britain, France and the Soviet Union. Each month one of them took charge of the central city, and the change of command was marked by a parade and cocktail party. Joint patrols by soldiers of the four powers were famous as four men in a jeep.

Suddenly, as we drove through the Soviet zone, a Russian armored car pulled alongside and motioned to our Austrian driver to follow. My companion, sitting in front to allow him to stretch his stiff leg, leaned over and carefully stashed his briefcase under the front seat. We followed the Russians off the main road into a village and pulled up at an official looking building. A Russian officer met us at the door and escorted us into a room bare of all decoration, except for a picture of Josef Stalin on one wall and a rickety table covered with a green felt cloth.

I started to speak, when my companion put a finger to his lips and shook his head. We sat in silence for an hour and a half in the empty room before the officer returned and led us back to our car.

"They found it," my companion said, feeling under the seat for his briefcase.

"How do you know?"

"I wedged it at an angle. It was straight when I pulled it out."

"What's in it?" He was rapidly inventorying the contents of the battered leather case.

"Information on uranium deposits in Czechoslovakia," he said.

We were dropped off at the Bristol Hotel on the Ringstrasse across the Kaerntnerstrasse from the Opera House. It, along with the Sacher and the Imperial, was one of the city's great prewar hotels. The Russians had taken over the Imperial and the Brits had the Sacher. The American occupation forces used the Bristol as a temporary billet for field grade officers and above in transit and high level visitors. It was still staffed by the original personnel, more used to serving the Prince of Wales than middle western colonels and generals.

Still unnerved by the detention, eager to explore, I left the hotel and walked through the dark and gloomy place for hours, crossing the Danube into the grim workers; suburbs of what was essentially a nineteenth century city. Lost, I tried my few German sentences on passersby. A crowd gathered.

"Wo ist die Oper, bitte?" I asked. Only it came out "Where is the waiter?" *Oper*, opera, and *Ober*, waiter, being indistinguishable in my rudimentary German. Finally, a rather elegant man spoke to me in English. I explained my problem, and he led me to a streetcar.

"This is the Russian Zone. You must get out immediately," he said, lifting his hat.

The Bristol's dining room still served off Augarten China and silver cutlery, the staff done up in dinner jackets with white ties, an affectation insisted on by some earlier commandant and still adhered to in my time.

Franz, the concierge, was a famous personage in pre and postwar Vienna. If he liked you he could and did get unobtainable tickets to the Opera and Burg theater, tables at the best restaurants and—rumor had it—for general officers, the favors of expensive Hungarian courtesans. The hotel's English Bar served the best dry martini in Europe east of the Paris Ritz, and its marble-topped tables, ancient leather sofas and Thonet chairs matched the eighteenth century hunting prints.

Over the years I continued on every trip to Vienna to visit the bar and sample its famous martini. Then, sometime in the seventies, the hotel was renovated and the prints moved to a much larger bar with expensive mahogany tables and a piano in one corner. The antique bartender had retired, and the martinis had lost their inimitable touch. I went back only once, many years later.

Vienna was ruled from 1945 until the signing of the State Treaty in 1955 by a joint commission of the four occupying allied powers, each of whom controlled a chunk of Austrian territory. The French got the mountains near the French border, the Russians the plain next to Hungary, the Americans the dreary industrialized central area and the British the magnificent Carinthian alps and lakes.

Vienna, the capital, was embedded in the midst of the Russian Zone as was Berlin in Germany and occupied jointly by the allies. It was a situation ripe for disaster once the Cold War had begun. But for some reason, probably the relative unimportance of Austria in the larger scheme of things, the system worked. Each month, at the change of command, the troops of the two powers exchanging control paraded past the Palace of Justice and a reviewing stand containing all four commanding generals and the high commissioners of the allied powers.

The Russians, superbly disciplined and uniformed, altered their marching gait to a goose-step as they approached the reviewing stand, heavy boots pounding the pavement, armament jangling as in old German newsreels. The French Chasseurs Alpins raced by at the run, their band throwing French horns in the air and catching them. The British Black Watch, kilts flaring in the sun, marched stolidly past with their peculiar splay-footed parade step, pipes screeling out the classic call to battle. And then there were the Americans, a military police detachment, all six feet tall but slovenly, often out of step, their rifles held at perilous angles, some surreptitiously chewing gum and grinning.

As a career officer, despite my less than exalted rank, I was invited to the cocktail parties which followed the changing of the guard. It was the only point of contact among the four allies, already deeply embedded in the Cold War. The era was romanticized at the time in films such as *The Third Man*, and it was an exciting place. The Viennese, a melange of the detritus of a great empire, mixing émigré Slavs from Czechoslovakia, Slovenia and Croatia with Hungarians, Rumanians and Poles and a Germanic element long ago corrupted by the great cosmopolitan city.

The city's culture was still deeply permeated by the impact of its former Jewish minority which had approached three hundred thousand before the war. Yiddish words were threaded through the everyday dialect of the Viennese, and the literature of the dead empire had been dominated by names such as Kraus, Schnitzler and Freud. But, despite the fact that there were virtually no Jews left in the city, a virulent anti-semitism prevailed.

One of the brilliant remnants of this disappeared culture was a cabaret, *The Sempel,* whose director and principal actor was a hooknosed caricature of the Jew. Already in his seventies, Karl Farkas was, despite the prevailing climate, one of the most beloved figures in the city. His biting commentaries from the miniature basement stage spared no one. Not the Viennese, the Germans, the allies and especially the Russians, whose monument to their conquest of the city, an immense infantryman, was known among the populace as "the unknown rapist." One of the stars of his revue, Cissy Kraner, epitomized a certain Viennese type. Blonde, overweight, lower middle class, second generation Slav, both innocent and corrupt, funny and tragic, the eternal survivor, singing satirical songs in an innocently lascivious little girl voice that seemed to sum up much of the city.

My first job was as passport and visa officer in the consulate, a classic old building located behind the nineteenth century Gothic Rathaus. It was my task to renew expired passports, perform notarial services for citizens, arrange for their legal representation if jailed and ship home their bodies when they died. And I issued visas to Austrians wishing to immigrate or travel to America.

My predecessor, Robert Weltzien, an American aristocrat in the old foreign service mold of Choate and Princeton, was an elegant young man in the throes of an affair with a recklessly gay, beautiful young British woman, Marie Norton, who later became his wife. He pointed to the desk one day and said: "You have to realize, Harper, it folds down into a bed." And it was true that a visa to America, in the grim days of 1952, was worth virtually any sacrifice to the Viennese whose pragmatic sophistication was tinged with cynical corruption.

One of my tasks was interviewing prospective brides of our occupation forces to see if they qualified for visas. The troops, as with all garrison forces in conquered lands, were very nearly out of control. Their access to the goodies of the PX—cigarettes, silk stocking, booze of all kinds, plus the everyday luxuries of America which were then exotic artifacts to Europeans—gave them carte blanche with the working class girls of the city.

And there were one hundred and forty women for every hundred men in a country where the male population of breeding age had been virtually wiped out in the war. Everywhere you looked grim, beaten figures missing a leg or an arm, black patches over blinded eyes, trudged through the dark and dilapidated streets of a city known as the "water head" by non-Viennese. A great and glittering capital before World War I, Vienna had deteriorated into a bloated provincial backwater in the twenties and thirties.

Liaisons between the soldiers and the local women were inevitable. And in many cases this meant prostitutes. In theory moral turpitude was grounds for not issuing a visa in those days. However, the law in its wisdom assumed that marriage wiped the slate clean. Our soldiers were curiously indifferent to the background of their prospective brides, many of whom were in fact beautiful young women, on the street because there was very little alternative.

I would sit in judgment with the visa file of a prospective bride open before me, uncomfortable young soldier sitting next to his intended. Fifteen arrests for soliciting, three forced treatments for gonorrhea. The lists were endless. In one case I looked at the drop dead beautiful young blonde sitting across from me, superb legs crossed strategically, and the black soldier from southern Alabama who stared at her as if she were an ice cream cone.

On a wild day a few months previously, she had accompanied him and three of his friends to the American Zone. This entailed driving through the Russian Zone for several hours. The drill was simple. You signed out at an American checkpoint on leaving Vienna, passed through the Russian controls and signed in at the other end as you entered the Zone. If you exceeded the fifty-mile an hour speed limit, you were fined. Stopping, except for emergencies, was forbidden.

On this day the four soldiers had raced through the countryside at speeds up ninety miles an hour, pulling off at intervals to drink beer and share the favors, in turn, of the young woman across from me. They were arrested for drunkenness at the Zonal checkpoint, and a routine check revealed that the young woman was infected with gonorrhea. It later developed that she had succeeded in the course of two hours in infecting all four of her companions.

I broke the rules that day and asked her to leave the room. I pushed the file across to the young soldier and suggested he read it.

"I know all about her," he said. "But she's changed. She's a good girl now."

"Are you planning to take her back to Alabama?"

He grinned across the table. "You mean I'd be lynched in about two hours? Naw. We goin' to Chicago. I got a brother there."

I issued the visa.

Other problems were less tractable. U.S. law in 1952 stated that any naturalized U.S. citizen who returned to the country of his birth and resided there for more than three years was presumed to have become a citizen under fraudulent conditions and his citizenship was voided. This law had been passed because large numbers of immigrants in the late nineteenth and early twentieth centuries had come to the United States, become citizens and returned to their native lands, there to establish families, the children of which had a right to American citizenship. In the economic and political turbulence of the thirties and the beginning of the war, large numbers of these people—often third generation, speaking no English and having no contact with America other than a grandfather—stormed our consulates throughout Europe seeking passports.

The Jews who had managed to escape the Holocaust and emigrate to America were unintended victims of this law. Many were from well-to-do families who had been forced to sell their businesses and homes at bargain rates after the Nazi takeover of Austria in 1938, in order to obtain the precious exit visas which saved their lives. Following the war, Austrian laws, passed under allied pressure, returned these assets to surviving Jews.

A fairly large number were older people who had adjusted badly to the American environment and were often living in poverty. In Austria they were, if not wealthy, able to live comfortably on their assets. They returned, unaware of the law which lifted their American citizenship after three years. I arrived on the scene just as they began to come into the consulate to renew their passports.

The sight of these people, whose suffering often included the loss of most of their family and friends, practically kneeling in supplication before me was more than I could take. They were terrified of losing the piece of paper which could save their lives in the event of a future pogrom. In an unpleasant session with the Consul General I forced him to allow me to write a despatch, as they were then called, to the State Department pointing out that the law was unconstitutional on the grounds that it discriminated against citizens not born in America.

I never received an answer to that despatch, although in 1959 the Supreme Court agreed with my thesis and the law was erased from the books.

In the meantime, to the horror of my Viennese assistant, Countess Thierry, I issued passports to all the people who applied and stashed their files in a locked cabinet in my office.

The incompetence of the bureaucracy being what it was, nobody ever noticed. When I was later transferred to the political section, I had the file cabinet transported to the cellar, locked it and threw away the keys.

Genius being the ability to hold two contradictory thoughts in your head at the same time, I believe that the foreign service is a paramilitary organization and that, if you take the king's shilling, you sing the king's song. However, in this one instance I am proud of my calculated violation of the law and discipline.

Ten

Civilization carries with it the price of repression which can be moderated but not abolished.

Sigmund Freud

He met me at the door of the Foreign Ministry, an elegant eighteenth century building located in the Ballhausplatz across from the imperial palace, the Hofburg. Tall, slender, with a great beak of a nose, Kurt Waldheim was at the time chief of personnel of the Austrian foreign office. I had been sent by Walter Dowling, the deputy chief of mission of the U.S. Embassy, to sound him out on who would be appointed as the next Austrian ambassador to the Soviet Union. It was the odd and arrogant act of a conquering nation to its vassal, for I was a third secretary calling on a first, a major breach of diplomatic etiquette and probably, as I look back, deliberate, since the Austrians had been evading higher level probes.

The Foreign Ministry was located in a building where, on July 25, 1935, 150 Nazi thugs murdered Austrian chancellor Dollfuss in an abortive coup aimed at taking over the country. During the coup Hitler, aware of the attempt, was attending a performance of Wagner's *Das Rheingold* at the composer's shrine in Bayreuth.

Waldheim, as I was to learn, was an anomaly in the Austria diplomatic corps which was larded with counts and barons, titles somewhat denatured since they were inherited by all descendants. His family was barely middle class, and he rose through the ranks by utilizing a thick skin and a willingness to be endlessly servile to his superiors while trampling on subordinates—a classic Central European habit pattern.

He put me off about the ambassadorial appointment but accepted an invitation to dinner at my modest apartment at Linkewienseile 127. The furnished flat consisted of a living room with a sofa which folded down into a bed and a dining room decorated in *Baurernstube,* country tavern, style. An immaculate, if out of tune, Bechstein baby grand occupied a living room dominated by Biedermeier antiques and the bibelots of three generations of owners. Given the number of pianos in German-speaking households, being a piano teacher must be one of their most secure professions.

The young woman with whom I was having an increasingly heavy affair agreed to prepare a typical Austrian menu of *leberknoedelsuppe, Wiener Schnitzel, gemischten Salat* and a Sacher Torte—liver dumpling soup, breaded veal cutlet, mixed salad and chocolate cake. The evening turned out to be a great success. After a year of total immersion in the country, my German was fluent if ungrammatical, and the Waldheims quickly relaxed under the influence of an American foreign service secret weapon—the dehydrated martini.

This concoction consisted of dry martinis mixed of Bombay gin and Noilly Prat vermouth at seven-to-one and placed in the freezer compartment of my antique refrigerator. The impurities, which rose to the top and froze, were carefully scraped off and what was left was served in frosted glasses. Europeans, arrogant in all things but particularly alcohol, tended to drain this nuclear warhead, tastebuds paralyzed by the cold, in unwise quantities.

Alcohol loosens not only the garter straps of young women but also diplomatic tongues. Waldheim had three big ones, about a liter of an excellent, Durnstein wine and had made a dent in a bottle of Remy Martin Imperial Reserve from the ambassador's private stock which he had graciously allowed his staff to share. Or, as his secretary whispered, he was broke and couldn't afford to pick up the shipment.

It turned out to be a fairly gay evening as diplomatic dinners go. The martinis loosened some of Waldheim's stiffness and he told a series of deprecating jokes about the Austrians.

"The Hungarian coachman," he said as his wife rolled her eyes in despair at what must have been one of his favorite stories, "was driving the carriage through the Count Esterhazy's estate one day grumbling to himself. 'My father was a count, my son is a count, and I'm still a coachman'." I laughed politely although it took me a while to get the point.

"You know, we Austrians in 1912 had the most beautiful army in the world. The uniforms were glorious. The household cavalry, all six feet tall, rode splendid horses. When the troops paraded on the emperor's birthday there were regiments from all over the empire. Poles, Hungarians, Croats, Czechs, Ruthenes. And do you know what the fools did?"

I admitted I did not.

"They sent them off to war." I could have sworn I saw tears in his slightly drunken eyes. He then rattled off a series of jokes about Graf Bobby, a standard figure of Viennese fun for a hundred years.

"Graf Bobby was sitting in the Sacher cafe, head in his hands moaning. His friend Baron Feistritz came by and asked what was the matter."

"I am ruined socially, Feistritz. Ruined."

"My God, Bobby. What have you done?"

"Last night I was at Graf Schoenborn's for dinner. I got a little drunk, and I went outside to piss. And I wrote my name in the snow."

"But, Bobby, that's not so bad. People will only laugh."

"You don't understand. It was in Graefin Schoenborn's handwriting."

By the time he got to the cognac, Waldheim was totally unbuttoned, babbling incoherently, eager to impress his deferential young American counterpart. I led him into a discussion of the Soviet Union, and at one point he leaned across the cluttered cocktail table and, in a stage whisper, muttered the name of the new ambassador to Russia. His wife, sober and appalled, rose abruptly and dragged him out of my apartment.

Next morning I asked to see Dowling, a fellow Georgian and later ambassador and high commissioner to Germany.

"Yes, Harper. What is it?"

I related the events of the previous evening, and Dowling waved them away with his usual imperiousness. "Nonsense, Harper. He was misleading you. We know the man who's being appointed," and dismissed me.

Three days later the man Waldheim had given me was named to the post.

The tyranny of the hierarchy had already begun to oppress me as it became increasingly apparent that the foreign service was a paramilitary organization where following orders—*Kadaver Gehorsamkeit*, the obedience of a corpse—and total commitment of time and energy to the job were the *sine qua non* of success.

Here and there, however, a sense of humor appeared among the younger cohort. Once, over lunch, several of us had an hilarious discussion, watered by a good bit of wine, over a question our superiors had to answer on our performance rating. "Does the subject have a penchant for petty intrigue?" We split down the middle, half maintaining this characteristic was absolutely indispensable in a diplomat and the other half defending the contrary.

Weltzien's departure had left a hole in my social life. Unlike most of the Ivy Leaguers in the foreign service, who were determined straight arrows, he affected a persona more in the style of *The Great Gatsby*. No mannered Updike hero he. Inserting his monocle, and staring imperiously from his six feet three inches with the bearing of a Prussian aristocrat, he could command a room until an irreverent giggle destroyed the illusion.

One day he came by the consulate and dragged me down the Ringstrasse to the *Kunstshistorisches Museum*, repository of a great many of the world's finest art works. Weltzien stopped before an immense Titian, inserted the monocle, hands behind his back, and approached, his nose within inches of the painting. An anxious guard started towards us as my friend turned on his heel and let the monocle drop to dangle from a black ribbon, shouting as he did so "Falsch!"

We turned and left the museum with deliberate haste.

I had spent my first six months in Vienna in a daze. For the first time in my life I had more money than I could spend. I had bought a small French Renault, made of tin and pasteboard, from a soldier, and it possessed a diplomatic license plate with the number W204. The Viennese would kill for a number under a thousand. The embassy garage had white CD signs front and back, suitable for the large American cars driven by most of my compatriots. Police at every intersection came to attention, as I passed in this absurd apparition, and saluted me.

In a country where, even in normal times, the sexual mores were at the very least relaxed—fifty-six percent of the live births in the province of Carinthia in 1939 were illegitimate—and a large percentage of the breeding male population was killed during the war, Vienna was a sort of sexual paradise for single male diplomats.

There were, however, unforeseen cultural problems. One evening a handsome young woman struck up a conversation with me in a cafe, and after we had consumed an immense meal at one of the city's elegant restaurants, the Stadtkrug, we adjourned to my room at the Bristol. Following a token resistance, her hand strayed to my fly. And stopped abruptly.

"Where are the buttons?" she asked, frowning in bewilderment. Zippers had not yet made their way to the tailor shops of Vienna.

On another evening, in similar circumstances, a young woman arched her eyebrows as she stared down at me and said, "but you don't look Jewish." In vain I explained that all men of my generation in America were circumcised. She clearly did not believe me. Fortunately lust overcame racism, and she did not allow it to interfere with the project at hand.

It was most unusual to be turned down, and when I met a striking, raven-haired young woman at a dinner party given by an Austrian government official to whom I had issued a visa, I was taken aback at her decidedly chilly reception of my attentions.

However, the party dragged on, as they tended to do, and it was past two a.m. when we descended to the street. I was the only one among the guests with a car, and I offered to drive the young woman home. She glanced at the vehicle, which still had an army license plate on it, and shook her head.

"I don't intend to disgrace myself by getting into a car with a military number," she said and began to stride away. I followed, and we walked through the deserted streets for more than an hour until we reached her family's apartment.

Once the CDs appeared on the car, her reluctance to be seen with me rapidly disappeared. Some weeks into the affair, Lisl announced that she was going on vacation to climb the Gross Glockner, Austria's highest mountain.

"I tried last year, but one of the climbers was wounded in the war and became dizzy during the final few hundred meters and the guide had to break off the climb. This year I'm going to make it."

She finally agreed, most reluctantly, to allow me to accompany her. I outfitted myself with German war surplus boots and other climbing paraphernalia, totally unaware of what lay ahead. The guide, a former member of the Austrian alpine troops, spent the first night telling us the plan for the climb, interspersing it with tales of how his unit slaughtered large numbers of the American Tenth Mountain Division during a battle in Italy.

"First, planes come. Bomb, bomb, bomb. Then artillery. Boom, boom, boom. Then machine guns. Ratatatatat. Then one Ami stick head out. We shoot one bullet. He duck. Then planes. Artillery, Machine guns." At this point he would laugh uproariously and down another slug of the white lightning the peasants made out of apples and cherries and whatever other fruit came to hand.

I refrained from asking him if he knew who had won the war.

We left the next morning at four a.m. It was the fourth of July and broad daylight. We climbed all day across glaciers, up ice faces and vertical stone walls. Our guide was a short wiry man with small feet, and the steps he cut in the ice faces were too small for my oversized boots. I clawed my way up the mountain, and by the end of the day the tips of my woolen gloves were worn through and bloody.

We spent the night just below the summit in a hut, the *Adlersruhe,* the Eagles Nest. The guide threaded his way through about thirty members of the French mountain division, bivouacked in a large heatless outer room eating iron rations, and led us into a warm and spacious kitchen full of German and Austrian climbers.

One of these men, a German, was already slightly plastered, and I was fascinated by the large dent in the middle of his forehead. He proclaimed that he would not climb the next day, since he had a tendency to become dizzy because of his war wound. Then he discovered that my companion, the only woman on the mountain, intended to go. I watched his ego swell, and he turned to his guide, another taciturn Austrian mountaineer. "I will climb," he said. "I will not be humiliated by a mere woman."

His guide nodded, hardly glancing up from the large chunk of smoked pig fat he was carving onto slices of black bread and stuffing into his mouth, washing it down with water glasses full of white lightning, better known to the Austrian ski teachers as *Kurvengeist* or the Spirit of the Curve. Then the singing began. Folk, tunes quickly turned to the war songs I remembered from my walk in the mountains near Grenoble. Outside, the French army, aroused, began their own chauvinistic chanting. It felt as if we were on the edge of the Third World War.

We got to bed around three a.m. and were awakened by Hans, the guide, at five. The peak was not far away, but the mountain was swarming with climbers. The French had left early, and we met them coming down, but ahead of us were the dozen or so Germans and Austrians. Now, the Glockner is not in a class with the north face of the Eiger, but not only had I never climbed a mountain, I had also rarely seen snow before.

The Glockner is really two peaks. The Kleinglockner just below the Gross Glockner. The two are joined by a narrow stone ridge, to the left and right of which are about a thousand meters of nothing. Hans casually walked out toward the middle of this ridge and my companion followed him unhesitatingly. They stood on this narrow strip of stone as I watched the rope tighten in disbelief. There was no way to belay it, since it was too short to span the bridge. Lisl yanked on the rope in irritation, and I unslung the rope and walked, terrified, out onto the ridge, trying not to look down.

We were soon on the other side, at which point I tapped Hans on the shoulder, as we waited for the two Germans ahead of us to scale the vertical stone and ice wall to the final summit.

"What," I asked, "would you have done if one of us had fallen?"

"Jumped off the other side," he said as if it were the most self-evident thing in the world. At this point Lisl's left *steigeisern*, spiked metal attachments to our boots, came loose. Hans handed me his ice axe, leaned over clinging to the cliff with one ungloved hand, and rewrapped the ancient leather thongs. As he finished, one of the German climbers just to the right of him screamed in agony and let go his hold, beginning to fall away from the vertical face of the mountain.

Hans, moving with incredible quickness, was at his side instantly, gripping him by the back of his jacket, slamming him against the mountain.

"Ach," the German said, turning an agonized face toward Lisl, "excuse me, fraulein, but I was wounded in the war and my shoulder occasionally dislocates. I am a doctor and will fix it immediately," He then gripped the offending shoulder, wrenched it brutally, uttering a scream of pain, and patted it with what seemed like affection. "I am alright now," he said to Hans, who let him go to continue his climb.

We arrived at the top without more drama to find the place packed with Germans taking each others pictures. Aside from hiking, singing and drinking, the thing Germans like to do most is take each others pictures. Among them was the man with the hole in his head. At the sight of Lisl, he bowed deeply from the waist and kissed her hand. "Thank you a thousand times," he said. "Without your being here, fraulein, I would never have made the climb."

We spent the second week of the vacation at the Pension Meisl in Poertschach-am-Woerthersee, a picture book Austrian town on a stunning lake girdled by the sombre Karawanken mountains. In those days it was still a nineteenth-century place, the old mansions of the aristocracy transformed into rambling bed and breakfast hotels. We went there often over the next two years, to sail, play tennis and make love in light, airy rooms overlooking the lake.

The first few days were idyllic. Late breakfasts of crisp *Semmel* slathered with sweet country butter and homemade jams, and endless cups of thick dark coffee made with the beans I contributed on each trip. Then one day my future wife announced another test. She would swim to a fairy tale village across the lake, Maria Woerth, while I rowed the ancient boat—and she would row back while I swam. I shrugged. I'd been a lifeguard one summer. It didn't look all that far. And anyway, she swam a sort of exaggerated dog paddle. I didn't think she'd make it.

She did. And I did as well, but only after giving up my elegant crawl after the first three hundred yards and lapsing into a breast stroke remarkably like a dog paddle.

Some fifteen years later, while stationed in Poland, we returned to the scene of our early love, embedded in a marriage already fraying around the edges. In exploring the valleys and lakes of the region, we came across an old wooden farm house with a hectare of land around it for sale at an absurdly low price. The peasants were leaving the uneconomic farms in the high meadows for rapidly industrializing small cities.

For the next dozen years as we moved from Poland to Turkey to Spain to East Berlin, my wife and children spent idyllic summers at this farm, swimming in the icy waters of the Weissensee at the end of the narrow valley. The boys, clad in leather pants, helped the neighboring farmer's son herd the cows and chop wood for winter and climbed the surrounding peaks with him.

After a year slogging through the routine of the consulate in Vienna I was transferred to the political section, a bloated entity with twelve highly intelligent, ferociously ambitious career officers fighting for a piece of rather small turf. I was made biographic reporting officer, a training ground similar to writing obituaries on a newspaper.

My quick and dirty style contrasted badly with the slow, thoughtful and lazy rhythms of the foreign service. Soon my reports began to pile up on the desk of the chief of the section, Arthur Compton, scion of a famous scientific family. Arthur was so laid back he was virtually catatonic and seemed to conceive of his job as a bottleneck allowing no reports to leave his desk.

I soon began spending a fairly large part of my time reading German history and political philosophy. Dowling had been replaced by a new DCM, a slender, elegant low-keyed man who occasionally wandered the halls of the cavernous embassy building, once the home of the Austrian diplomatic academy.

He came upon me one day, feet on my desk, deeply immersed in Oswald Spengler's *Der Untergang des Abendlandes.* Next to it lay Clausewitz's *Vom Kriege*. Good southerner that I was, I leapt to me feet. He picked up the books and glanced at the titles, suppressing a smile. "Excellent choices, Harper. Keep reading." And turned and left. It was a foreign service of gentlemen which was soon to die.

Vienna at this time was a vital place. Austria sat on a sliver of highly strategic real estate surrounded on the east and north by a dozen or so Russian armored divisions poised to slash across central Europe at the underbelly of Germany, outflanking our forces to the north. In a war, Italy would have been isolated and conquered within days, and there is little doubt that the Soviet army would have been on the Rhine within weeks and the channel shortly thereafter.

U.S., allied and French armies in Europe had been cut to the bone as we relied almost totally on the deterrent value of atomic arms. With the first successful Russian nuclear test, this defense was no longer credible, and we had begun to rearm Germany as the only buffer to defend Europe.

The Austrians, consummate cynics—as all border peoples seem to be—watched in bemusement. At the interminable parties with Lisl's friends, mostly of my generation or a little older, all the men veterans of long years at the front, the moment of truth usually came well after midnight when a half dozen two-liter bottles of wine had been emptied and the war songs sung.

"Why didn't you fight with us against the Russians?" was the inevitable question. And it was hard to answer as we rearmed them six short years after the war had ended. I at first tried honesty. Hitler was a monster. The Jews were being massacred. Innocent peoples overrun and brutalized. We feared Hitler's ambition to dominate the world.

They would have none of this. Innate anti-semitism was so virulent in Vienna and Central Europe that nobody accepted that we might really have cared about the Jews. Citing morality nearly always brought up our repression of the blacks, slaughter of the Indians and clearly repressive capitalist system.

By this time I had become enamored not only of the young woman, who had wrapped me neatly around her axle, but also of the corrupt charm of the city. It had none of the hard edge of France, which still fascinated me, but there was about it a whiff of degeneracy which reminded me in disconcerting ways of my own South. And it was fun. The young Austrians who had survived the war were determined to enjoy themselves before another conflagration enveloped them. There was an air of no tomorrow about the place which sucked you in.

Add to this the beauty of the city and the countryside, and an exchange rate which enabled the occupiers to live in a princely fashion, and you had an atmosphere of almost frenetic hedonism. I had no desire to throw any offal into this pleasant punchbowl. So I invented a rationale for the United States entering the Second World War. One that shamelessly pandered to their preconceived ideas.

It went, stripped of the academic jargon, something like this:

The United States, a primitive and naive country, always followed the British lead in its international politics. And, of course, we all know what the Brits did for centuries. Confronted with two enemies they invariably allied themselves with the weaker of the two against the stronger. After the defeat of this threat, they would then change sides, supporting the defeated enemy against their former ally.

We had simply done the same thing. First aiding Russia against Germany until it was defeated and then changing sides. The success of this ploy depended very largely on a curious trait among all Central Europeans, but especially the German speakers. There is a wistful admiration for the British which borders on adulation. The shriveled empire's diplomats are dressed by Huntsman and shod by Lobb and bear themselves with a stuttering arrogance encased in elegant manners. It's a hard act to counter. Their shrewd ruthlessness, lack of sentimentalism and unvarnished realism, though toothless, still command immense respect on the continent.

My explanation was accepted, and we moved on to what really absorbed them—how many goodies I could supply them from the PX without losing my privileges.

It was in Vienna that I first became aware of the virulence of anti-semitism. In the South of my time Jews were regarded as a strange, somewhat exotic, folk who kept to themselves, and were occasionally preached against in primitive churches as the killers of Christ. But by and large, being white, they were co-opted into the ruling class. The fact that they tended to be small shopkeepers, rather than powerful bankers or great economic forces in the community, cut down on the hatreds which evolve from envy.

In Vienna, and later in Poland, I ran into a kind of deep-seated, cultural animosity toward Jews which seemed at times to be almost genetic. It was an antipathy which permeated all the states of Central Europe and made comprehensible the ease with which the Germans exterminated six million people. They had help.

As a dedicated rationalist, I accept the role irrationality plays in this manmade world. Nonetheless, I persist in believing that bringing high intelligence and goodwill to bear on problems can result in that understanding which leads to their solution. I cling to this belief despite the fact that high intelligence and goodwill have generally been in short supply while chaos, death and destruction are more likely than peaceful solutions. I confess, however, to some puzzlement at the continuing virulence of anti-semitism.

There are certain obvious problems associated with races which are difficult to assimilate, or who resist giving up their unique cultures to blend in with the main stream. Clearly Jews, believing themselves to be a people chosen of God, fight losing their identity. Despite this, assimilation in Germany and Austria was more advanced than in any other country in Europe, and the congruence of German and Jewish cultural values and characteristics was remarkable. The Jew was more at home in Germany than anywhere else.

My father's theorem—people envy them, boy—undoubtedly contributed to some of the antipathy. Once public institutions were opened to Jews in the nineteenth century, cultural life in central Europe saw a flowering of creativity. The proportion of university students was disproportionately Jewish, and writers such as Kafka, Kraus and Schnitzler combined with such towering figures as Freud and Marx to give this obscure people a very high profile.

However, the one country in Europe where the Jew's cultural impact was minimal was France. And it was, in some ways, the most anti-Semitic. What is perhaps most puzzling to the rationalist is the case of Poland, which between the wars had the largest Jewish population in Europe. More than three million Jews, many emigrants from repression in Czarist Russia, were pervasive at all levels of society, from peasants to intellectuals.

The Poles stood by, unmoved and often lending a helping hand, in the pogroms committed by the Germans. The same was true in the Baltic states, the Ukraine and virtually all the nations of Eastern Europe.

When I arrived in Poland in 1969 there were fewer than 30,000 Jews living there. Yet the previous year a campaign of rare virulence had forced them out of important government jobs and driven many in the cultural community to emigrate. Poles I questioned about this outbreak of mindless prejudice shrugged or pointed out that the secret police apparatus which followed on the heels of the Soviet Army in 1945 was composed largely of Jews as was the prewar communist party.

While there is a certain coarse logic to such arguments, these men had in fact long since been purged by later, more liberal, Polish communist regimes and no Jews occupied high profile positions in the country.

The same was true of Austria in 1951. With the exception of Bruno Kreisky, a Jew so assimilated he was often accused of anti-semitism, there were virtually no Jews in positions either of power or profile in the country. Yet a pervasive paranoia infected the society.

The case of Freud is instructive. He is perhaps the best known Austrian of the last century, and despite the criticism his theories are now undergoing, he was certainly the most influential philosopher of the human psyche of the past hundred years.

In Vienna he was regarded as a rather laughable charlatan who practiced among the neurotic young women of the Jewish community, guarded and repressed while their male counterparts were free to roam the fleshpots of the *goyim*. A small, rather shabby museum in his old apartment in the Berggasse was his only monument.

The Viennese view of the Russians was another psychological curiosity that can only be called schizoid. Given the rapine and pillage which accompanied the Russian conquest of Vienna in the spring of 1945, the Austrian attitude toward them was oddly ambivalent. My wife's mother told the story of her father, an elderly man in 1945, being accosted on the street by a soldier who took his gold pocket watch. A Russian officer saw the scene and beat the soldier to the ground with his pistol butt, returning the watch to the old man with a bow.

The jokes, told about them drinking ink and staring at flush toilets in wonderment, became part of the occupation legend. There were also the very Russian jokes. One of my favorites went like this:

A Russian scientist attends a conference in Paris. After listening to his confreres outline their recent discoveries in medicine and physics the Russian gets up to address the group.

"We Russians," he began, "have made great discovery." Holding out his large hands palm up he continued. "We take flea and put flea in left hand. Jump, flea we say and flea jump to right hand. Then we rip legs off flea. Jump flea, we say, but flea does not jump. Discovery: rip legs off flea, flea cannot hear."

But the Russians were a relatively minor problem for American diplomats at this time. In the United States an obscure Wisconsin senator named Joseph McCarthy had begun a vicious campaign to discredit the State Department in general, and the career service in particular, by accusing them of being homosexuals with communist sympathies. At the same time an unknown congressman from California, Richard Nixon, had zeroed in on a high ranking civil servant named Alger Hiss.

The Hiss case became a litmus test for my generation. If you believed his inelegant, jowly accuser, Whitaker Chambers, a confessed former communist, Hiss had been a Soviet agent for fifteen years as he moved in the rarefied circles of American diplomacy. Another high ranking civil servant, Harry Dexter White, was similarly accused. If you did not believe the accusers you yourself were suspected of communist sympathies.

The cold war had begun in the late forties, and the drama of the Berlin blockade with its airlift and heroes had dramatized the Soviet-American conflict. The Korean War brought it home in an even more brutal fashion. As in all mass democracies, conflicts of principle tend to become demonized. During the depths of the depression of the nineteen-thirties, many among the American left began to see in Soviet Communism the only force combating the rise of fascism and as a solution to the seemingly chronic economic problems of a capitalist economy.

Many intellectuals, actors, academics and generally disgruntled people joined the Communist party. As the nation turned to the right, electing the war hero Eisenhower as president, a witch hunt began to ferret out these traitors. Both Senator Joseph McCarthy and the House Un-American Activities committee publicly savaged Hollywood actors and directors and reduced them to public groveling to save their careers. Those who refused were blackballed.

In one of the curious anomalies of American politics, a man who was to become an icon of the left, Robert Kennedy, sat at McCarthy's side throughout these hearings, feeding him questions and directing investigations conducted by his staff. As late as 1962, in an interview in *Esquire Magazine*, Kennedy defended McCarthy, only to emerge from this reactionary chrysalis following his brother's assassination.

Career civil servants—particularly a band of China specialists, for the most part sons of American missionaries in China before the war, who had forecast the victory of the Chinese Communists—were pilloried as communist sympathizers who had "lost" China. The culmination of this hysteria was the conviction and execution of a pair of supposed Soviet agents, the Rosenbergs, for revealing atomic secrets to the Soviet Union.

At that time, and until the revelations which have surfaced from Soviet archives following the collapse of the communist regime in Russia, I was convinced that most of the hysteria of this period was criminally perverse. I began to doubt only after reading Allen Weinstein's book, *Perjury,* on the Hiss case. This writer, with impeccable liberal credentials, set out to exonerate Hiss and wound up convinced of his guilt. Soviet intelligence files have now confirmed that Alger Hiss and Harry Dexter White were indeed Soviet agents and the Rosenbergs unquestionably betrayed atomic secrets to the Russians.

And, although the "Old China hands" in the State Department were not Soviet agents, their sympathies certainly lay in large measure with a Communist regime which became deified over the next few decades as a miraculously progressive force in dragging a medieval China into the modern world. Some of this myth may have substance, but the most recent dispassionate research indicates that the cost of this "progress" was probably in excess of fifty million people starved and killed by one of the most repressive and brutal regimes ever recorded by history.

Looking back, the seductions of communist ideology for the intellectual are easy to understand. In a messy and chaotic world, full of anomalies, and with no solution visible to the continuation of war, chaos and destruction, it offered what seemed to be a way out. The sacrifice of some personal freedoms appeared to be a negligible price to pay for economic progress and political serenity.

Today, once again suffering through an age of uncertainty, many people in Eastern Europe are turning to the same leaders who oppressed them, seeking the comforting cocoon of the all-powerful state to combat the confusing anarchy of democracy. There are clearly situations in which the idealized concept of representative government loses its force when confronted by perverse anarchy.

Such is the case over much of the world today, particularly in Africa and parts of Asia where the people have turned to often corrupt authoritarian regimes to control the chaos surrounding their daily lives. Americans are probably going to have to realize that the propagation of a form of Jeffersonian democracy, which has worked so well in our protected environment, may not be a feasible transplant. Or even a desirable one.

In Vienna, in the summer of 1952, we received an announcement of the imminent arrival of two investigators from Senator McCarthy's staff. Their names were Roy Cohn and David Shine, both young men in their twenties and already notorious for seeking out homosexuals in government. Homosexuality was then regarded as a reason for dismissal because of the likelihood of blackmail, turning otherwise loyal citizens into security risks.

Cohn and Shine were in many ways incompetent clowns. But the wave of terror which flooded through the foreign service was palpable. While I have no idea of the percentage of homosexuals in the career service at this time, it was undoubtedly higher than in the population at large. A closed club of civilized, tolerant individuals sharing the same values and background is a haven for aberrant groups.

One suspected homosexual in Vienna, a man who married a rather unattractive secretary as camouflage and later became an ambassador to a minor Middle Eastern country, came to my office to commiserate with me when my request to marry was rejected and, winking, said: "Boys always were out and now girls are too."

Although my politics were then, and continue to be, a mild form of conservative social democracy, I was enraged as only the young can be by the unfairness of the witch hunts. In a meeting with Ambassador Thompson, called to warn career officers to lie low when Cohn and Shine arrived in Vienna, I rose to say that if either of them showed the slightest rudeness to me I would break their jaws.

Two days later Thompson called me into his office and told me I was being sent to Salzburg to help out in the consulate during the busy summer festival season, thus avoiding the visit of Cohn and Shine.

My future wife, an opera buff as were virtually all Viennese, was ecstatic. I had access to free tickets to any performance I cared to attend, and she came down each weekend on a late train, returning to her job in Vienna on Sunday evening. I lived in a pension on the outskirts of Salzburg run by a former opera singer.

She had been the mistress of a famous Nazi era sculptor who had validated the myth of Teutonic Aryans via massive realistic statues of buxom women and muscled men. Many of his works graced her garden. Outside my modest room rose a nude eight-foot tall iron maiden, right hand delicately fingering her right breast. Across from her a massive marble swan copulated with a clearly ecstatic Leda.

I had very little to do that summer, working mostly on weekends. One Saturday I spent strolling the streets of the town with two charming young American women who had parked their car and were unable to remember where. We finally found it tucked away in a medieval alley.

Another day a high ranking member of our Marshall Plan Mission in Paris came in on a Sunday to report an accident. The Austrian police had confiscated his car and passport and had apparently threatened to jail him despite his diplomatic status. I accompanied him to the police station where a man whose face was crisscrossed with dueling scars bent over a stack of forms, ignoring us.

After clearing my throat a couple of times I called out to him in a fairly loud voice. He snapped out of his chair, a lean and menacing figure dressed in a police uniform which closely resembled that of a Second World War German army officer. He approached us, red faced and hectoring, demanding to know what we wanted. I introduced myself and asked for the keys to my senior colleague's car and his passport, pointing out that as an American official the Austrian police had no jurisdiction over him.

The man, face congested, began to scream at me at the top of his lungs, eyes bulging. I was stunned. In general, Austrian officials were obsequious bordering on the servile when dealing with Americans. His rage finally triggered a similar response from me. When he paused for breath, I pounded on the ancient oak countertop and shouted at him that either the car keys and passport would be forthcoming within one minute or I would return with a platoon of American occupation troops and take them from him.

A look of intense hatred crossed the man's face. But he ripped open a drawer and flung the documents and keys across the counter.

I led my colleague out into the courtyard and handed him his papers. "What did you tell him?" he asked.

I repeated what I'd told the Austrian.

"You're not allowed to do that are you?"

"No," I said, pushing him into the car. "And you'd better get the hell across the border before he realizes it."

Eleven

Whoever said life was fair.

John Fitzgerald Kennedy on appointing
his brother, Robert, Attorney General

Kurt Fisher and I were contemporaries. He had seen action in an anti-aircraft youth battalion at the end of the war, finished the university and entered the Austrian diplomatic service. We met early in my tour, at one of the interminable cocktail parties which were the twentieth century equivalent of the salons where diplomatic business had been conducted for hundreds of years.

I invited him to lunch at the Franciskaner, Vienna's most elegant restaurant, and he reciprocated by taking me to Stiedl's, a simple, inexpensive traditional Viennese restaurant in the Steindlgasse. It soon became a joke between us that I, the rich American, would host regular lunches at some elegant eatery, and he would take me to typical Viennese *Kneipe*. I had much the better deal.

On the first day we began a dialog which was to continue until the end of my tour in Vienna. It was also, in many ways, a paradigm for similar relationships with other Europeans over the years. We met to talk politics and to interpret the inexplicable vagaries of each other's countries and cultures.

Fisher, who finished his career as Austrian ambassador to the United Nations, pointed out from the beginning that all Austrian foreign policy was designed to achieve one goal: the end to the country's occupation. Unlike Germany, regarded by all Europeans as a rogue power best kept under control by the joint

Russian, French, British and American occupations, Austria was looked upon as a slightly comic opera place, whose only importance lay in its strategic geography.

In addition, following the war, the Austrians had skillfully managed to portray themselves as Hitler's victim, forced into the *Anchluss* against their will. It was a point of view hard to take seriously if one viewed the massive crowds which greeted his entry into Vienna after German troops marched in unopposed in March 1938. But it was a useful fiction for all the conquering powers. In diplomacy, as in life, reality always gives way to necessity.

Even more important, the country's political leaders had managed to keep a truly national government in being, kowtowing as necessary to the allies in each of the four occupation zones. The central sector of the capital, Vienna, changed hands among the Russians, Americans, British and French each month in a remarkable example of pragmatic politics as the Cold War deepened in all other areas.

Austrian leaders of the period danced a skillful waltz among the occupying powers, playing them off against each other, persuading the Russians to make minor concessions of authority, then running to the western allies and demanding the same privileges and powers from them. They walked a diplomatic tightrope, using essentially two different sets of envoys, one specializing in the Russians and the other in dealing with the allies.

Late in 1953 Fisher sat across from me, about to be transferred, and lifted a glass of the excellent Wachau wine he always ordered. "To the peace treaty freeing my country."

I touched glasses with him and drank the toast. "You're kidding, aren't you?" The end of the occupation had always been a central topic of our conversations, but neither of us had ever taken the possibility seriously.

"No. Stalin is dead. The Russians are eager to make a deal neutralizing West Germany. If we play our cards right we can convince them to offer up Austria as a trial of the concept."

"We would never agree," I said. The real estate was too strategic for us to give up. It stuck like a spear into the Russian area of influence, outflanking Czechoslovakia and barring the route to Italy.

"My dear friend," Fisher said, grinning. "You already have."

"How so?" Negotiations over a treaty freeing Austria from occupation had been going nowhere for almost a decade, each of the victorious powers offering small concessions to keep the natives happy but with no serious intention of agreeing to leave.

"When you get back to the embassy, read the recent protocols carefully. You will find that you and the Russians are in essential agreement on virtually every topic. There are no more real differences to settle. If the political will existed, we could sign the treaty tomorrow."

"Yeah. But nobody wants to leave. Not us, the Brits or the French. And certainly not the Russians."

Fisher shook his head. "The Russians are ready. And you will not be able to deny us a treaty if they agree." He turned out to be right. Distracted by internal upheavals following the old dictator's death, the new Russian government sought above all else to neutralize a resurgent Germany, now recovering rapidly from the ravages of war and building a formidable armed force. Austria was the bonbon they offered to entice the western Allies into such negotiations.

Fisher was right. A year after I left Vienna the State Treaty was signed by the Soviet Union and the three Western Allies establishing a neutralized Austria. With classic perversion the Viennese immediately bewailed their luck. The departure of the foreign troops had deprived the old city of its one claim to fame—as a hotbed of intrigue and spies. Instead of an exotic meeting ground between East and West, it had become once again the bloated capital of a small, unimportant country in a backwater of Europe.

But that all came later. My last year in Vienna went by in a blur. Lisl had begun to pressure me to make some sort of commitment to marry her. There was only one problem. Foreign Service regulations stipulated that any career officer planning to marry had to submit his resignation along with his stated intention to wed a non-American. A board then considered his request and either accepted the resignation or approved the marriage.

It was an elegant solution, since it avoided forcing the officer to ask permission to marry, something patently illegal. As I agonized over this decision, life continued in a swirl of parties, both within the diplomatic corps and among Lisl's friends.

One evening she dragged me along to an immense apartment near the Hochhaus, a modernist skyscraper built in the nineteen twenties. The host, a slender, balding man named Pfeiffer, did business in scrap copper with Lisl's firm. At one point in the evening I found myself one-on-one with Pfeiffer and asked idly about his business. He then told the following story.

"I run a copper wire factory for the Russians," he said, ignoring the startled look on my face. If the Embassy found out I was frequenting the parties of civilian functionaries of the Russian occupation, I was in for a serious security investigation.

Ignoring my consternation, Pfeiffer continued. "It belonged to my wife's family before 1938," he said, "but she's Jewish, and when the Germans invaded on March 13, 1938, she, her parents and our children left for Venezuela. It was agreed that I would stay and try to salvage something, since I'm not Jewish.

"The Nazis confiscated the factory but kept me on as a manager, since I'd divorced my wife by then."

"How did you become manager for the Soviets?"

Pfeiffer shrugged. "They confiscated the factory in 1945 and moved the wire-making machinery out onto a rail siding to take it to Russia. It sat there in the rain for a month, and we finally moved it back in and began converting scrap from the ruins into usable copper wire. After a while the Russians gave up the idea of shipping the equipment to Russia and retained me as their manager, putting in a Russian commissar over me."

He grinned. "A few nylons, some French cognac and a modest bank account in Switzerland made dealing with him relatively easy. But he wasn't cautious. Some envious superiors caught on, and he wound up in Siberia. Now we get a new commissar every year or so. They generally leave me alone."

"And your wife and children?"

He nodded toward a slender dark-haired woman across the room. "Her parents both died in Venezuela. She came home in 1946 and we remarried."

I got out of the party as quickly as possible, hoping that one of the city's innumerable double agents had not reported my name back to one of our intelligence organizations.

In 1959, on vacation from Nigeria, I ran into Pfeiffer on the Kaertnerstrasse and we stopped at a cafe for a glass of wine.

"What happened to the factory after the Russians left?"

"My wife instituted legal proceedings, and the factory was returned to her."

"How is she?" I asked out of politeness.

"Fine. We're divorced now, so I don't see much of her."

"And the factory?"

"Oh, I still run it for her," he said, sipping the wine and smiling at me over the rim of the glass.

If Pfeiffer was the musical comedy side of Vienna, Oskar, the husband of one of my wife's friends, was the darker side. A tailor before the war, he had spent three years on the Russian front. Toward the end he found himself shot through the lung on a train blocked in the Warsaw railway yard, the Russians across the Vistula preparing to attack a city left in ruins by the failed uprising of the Polish Home Army.

Oskar left the train and headed south on foot, ditching his uniform, picking up on the way a farm wagon, a horse and a peasant woman trying to escape the oncoming Russians. Like many Viennese Oskar was of Czech extraction and spoke the language fluently. When Russian patrols caught up with them on the highway, he passed himself off as a Czech slave laborer just trying to get home. The Russians spared him and cheerfully raped the peasant woman one after another before moving on.

It was a scenario repeated over and over before they managed to cross the untended Czech border. Oskar made his way to Prague and caught a train from there to Vienna, his lung dripping blood throughout the trip.

Among the many harrowing tales he told was one about the capture of some 300,000 Russian soldiers in an encircling movement as the battle for Kursk began. The prisoners were herded into a shallow bowl awaiting transport from the front, when word came of the Soviet breakthrough. The whole German front was imploding. There was no way to get the prisoners behind the German lines. The order came to lower the muzzles of the German 88s encircling the encampment, load them with shrapnel and systematically slaughter every man in it.

Since he had been a clandestine member of the communist party before the war, the Russians recruited him into the police in 1945. He was thrown out in 1947 when the Austrians finally took control of the city's government. The father of Oskar's wife, Hedi, had been a police detective when the Nazis took over the country and was co-opted into the Gestapo after the invasion. He continued to work as a simple policeman until the end of the war when he was executed by a Russian firing squad.

Then there was Foreman, a clerk in the embassy whose pretty sister was the mistress, serially, of half a dozen high-ranking American military officers. Foreman, whom I met at one of Weltzien's parties, had joined the Waffen SS, the fighting unit of this notorious Nazi organization, at eighteen, eager to right the wrongs done Germany at Versailles.

He rose quickly to Sturmbahnfuehrer on the Russian front, winning the Iron Cross with Oak Leaves. On leave he and his childhood sweetheart, who was pregnant, decided to marry. As an SS officer, Foreman, in order to marry, had to prove his impeccable Aryan heritage going back 200 years. He set in motion the bureaucracy, and, after another tour at the Russian front, came home to be confronted by a board of SS senior officers.

One of his great-grandfathers on his mother's side, it turned out, was a Jew. Foreman was stripped of his SS uniform, the SS tattoo under his arm was surgically excised and he spent the rest of the war in a work battalion which, as Weltzien was fond of pointing out, almost certainly saved his life.

The Austrian educational system was similar to what I had

come up against in France. The Austrian who had done his equivalent of the French baccalaureate, the abitur, had his head stuffed with information and was trained to reason syllogistically. The more formidable had studied with the Jesuits. In order to gain any respect it was necessary to meet and beat them on their own turf.

Unable to duplicate their Eurocentric education, I decided to immerse myself in the 1919-1939 period of Austrian history and back this up with an encyclopedic knowledge of Oswald Spengler's *The Decline of the West*. I had bought, before leaving the states, a two-volume, 1906-page work on this period by Charles A. Gulick published by the University of California Press. Entitled *Austria: From Habsburg to Hitler*, it gave a minute chronology of the time, following events on virtually a day-to-day basis.

In the late nineteen-twenties a priest, Ignaz Seipel, allied with the non-Nazi, right-wing, semi-fascist parties in Austria, became chancellor. Gulick detailed his career in excruciating detail. At any point where I felt cornered by the brilliantly educated young Austrians I would shift the conversation to Seipel and his cohort. Confident that they were far more expert on Austrian history than I, they more often than not fell into my trap.

Once I'd wiped them out with my knowledge of this obscure man and his period, they were hesitant to take me on in other areas. Another ploy I used shamelessly was attributing my own *Weltanschauung* to Spengler. It was often possible to throw off an opponent's carefully constructed syllogisms by a cryptic quotation, made up out of whole cloth, along the lines of: *Eine Macht die nicht benuetzt wird verkummert*—a power unused, atrophies. It's a rather meaningless phrase but possesses the obscure pomposity so beloved of all Germanic peoples.

One evening, worn down by attacks on American foreign policy, treatment of its blacks, the massacre of the Indians and half a dozen other sins, I stared at a bottle of white wine on the table. It bore the label Dornbirn. I looked around the table and solemnly reminded the gathering of the eighteenth century political scientist, Helmut von und zu Dornbirn's axiom: Ruthlessness in pursuit of virtue is not a sin. They had all read Dornbirn, *nicht wahr?*

Of course they had all read my fictional philosopher. And my made up variation of "the ends justify the means" was guaranteed to deflect the discussion from America onto the knotty philosophical problem then confronting all European intellectuals: was the Soviet Union's massive repression, brutality and mass murder justified in order to carry out the destruction of the evil capitalist system?

At the time the European intellectual of any nationality tended to be totally enamored of the socialist experiment. The wars, political chaos and social upheavals which had accompanied the advent of the industrial revolution were all attributed to capitalism. The breakdown of the old order and the disruption of cultural traditions had unanchored much of Central Europe.

The monotheistic God, invented by obscure Middle Eastern priests to explain the inexplicable, and who later became the instrument of non-priestly rulers in controlling the ignorant masses, had died in the trenches of World War I. The Great God Marx had taken his place.

But I had another, more urgent, problem than philosophical discussions. My tour in Vienna was due to end in January. In August, Lisl demanded to know whether I intended to marry her. It was not a decision I wanted to face. My resignation was almost certain to be accepted, since virtually nobody had been allowed to marry citizens of countries controlled, even partially, by the Soviet Union. Blackmail through the wife's family was always a possibility.

The long lasting affair had, for me, been a relief. I'd discovered early on that being a Don Juan was not my metier. Fulfilling the massive hormonal demands of youth was an absolute priority, but the amount of time and effort it entailed was irritating. Our liaison had been a fine solution for me, and for her it was an entry into the superficially dramatic and exotic world of diplomacy.

The ties that bound us over eighteen months had, however,

subtly changed. Our interests coincided along many lines. She had grown up in an environment of constant danger. Her family were conservative Catholics who resented the intrusion of the Nazi state into their affairs. Half Hungarian, half Czech, she had the classic Magyar features and dark coloring.

The war had left indelible scars. When the Russians declared Vienna an open city in the spring of 1945, rapine and pillage were the order of the day. She spent several weeks sleeping on the roof of their apartment building to escape being raped by marauding soldiers. There was little food and not much hope.

Her father, an engineer, died working up to his neck in a bombed airplane factory late in the war. Her grandfather, with a plate in his head from a war wound in World War I, died in a fall from a ladder shortly after the war ended.

She somehow had managed to complete her education and was the main support of her mother and grandmother when I met her. She was, in many ways, a product of her time. Cynical, worldly, with an eye for the main chance which was clearly me. But she was also imbued with an almost Spartan sense of honor. And very tough.

In the end I submitted my resignation along with a request to marry. It would take some months to go through the diplomatic mill, and she was no longer eligible for a visitor's visa after having stated her intention to marry me. In a catch-22 situation, she could not on the other hand get an immigration visa until we married.

A Canadian colleague, sympathetic to my problem, arranged for an immigration visa for her to Canada and she departed in September 1953. She told me much later that she never really expected to see me again. And she very nearly didn't.

Within a few days after she left I found myself in bed with my language teacher, a medical student who had worked on my German with typical Teutonic ferocity for eighteen months. I have known three women over a long life who were genuine, ferocious sensualists. Elisabeth was one of them.

We normally spent an hour each evening in my small apartment over my German lesson. Sudden sexual deprivation, familiarity and opportunity coalesced one evening in an encounter that left me dazed. In the vulgar Franglais of a friend from my Paris days, she was a *machine a screwer*.

For the next six weeks we did little else. The State Department had acted with alacrity on my resignation, and I was due to leave in January. I left the office at all hours to rendezvous with Elisabeth with a lust that refused satiety. One night, lying next to her in my narrow bed, I told her I wanted to marry her.

She leaned on one elbow and stared at me. "You must be joking. You are marrying Lisl." She had become quite friendly with my fiancé over the past two years.

"I'll call it off."

She ran a finger over my face, smiling. "You Americans really are children, you know. I can't marry you. I don't want to marry you. My father is a doctor. I plan to enter his practice. I will almost certainly marry a doctor, have two children and live in Graz for the rest of my life. There is no place for you in my life."

At that moment I resolved never, ever, to have anything further to do with a female doctor.

She broke off the affair amiably, and I spent the next week or so trying to sort out my emotions and taking a vow of chastity.

It was not to be. Lisl's friends continued to include me in their parties, and at one such evening I met a spectacular young woman who turned out to have been one of the country's finest swimmers until an appendicitis operation had forced her to give up training. She looked it. Broad shouldered with a muscular body which moved beneath a black knit dress with the leonine confidence of the natural athlete.

Mona, who had studied at a high school specializing in French, was clearly fascinated by the American diplomat. She spoke excellent unaccented French. As the party ended she asked me for a ride home and, once in the car, suggested we go by my apartment for a brandy.

Even in the Vienna of the time, it was a direct approach, and I couldn't think of a gentlemanly way to get out of it. My resolution of chastity dissolved rapidly.

From the beginning she combined the false sophistication of the young with something distinctly, and disconcertingly, child-like. She would show up, skis on her shoulder, outside my door and drag me off to the slopes on the outskirts of Vienna. Or come over before breakfast with warm sweet rolls from the baker down the street.

One day, contemplating her as she wandered nude around the apartment, I noticed that there was no appendicitis scar on her side.

She looked at me and grinned. "It wasn't appendicitis. I had an abortion. My coach took me up to his apartment one day after training and gave me three scotches." She shrugged. "I was only fourteen. It was the first time I'd ever had scotch."

"Your sister said you had the operation last year."

"So?"

"You mean you're only fifteen?"

Twelve

The place where optimism most flourishes is the lunatic asylum.

Havelock Ellis in *The Dance of Life*

Lisl and I were married in Toronto. She had, within three months, worked Viennese charm, intelligence and a talent for recognizing and pursuing her self interest into an office manager's job and a growing circle of admirers. In retrospect, she would probably have been better off if I had not kept my commitment.

She wanted, above all, a secure bourgeois existence in a new world suburb. A docile hard working husband, children, eventually an interesting job, and a quiet old age. *Klein und Bescheiden*, she said, an untranslatable German phrase whose closest meaning is: a sensible and unnoticed life. What she got was instability and drama in obscure corners of the world with an unpredictable and restless man.

Before leaving Vienna I had followed my tried and true method of finding a job, and had written more than a hundred letters to major U.S. newspapers. Two answered offering interviews. The *Minneapolis Tribune* and a paper in Bangor, Maine. I flipped a coin and went to Minneapolis. The Tribune in early 1954 was superb newspaper, written and edited with the precision of a book by a staff which included columnist Carl Rowan and Charles Bailey, later co-author of the best selling novel *Seven Days in May*.

Paul Veblen, a nephew of the famous economist, ran the

news desk aided by a talented Latvian émigré named Dan Hafrey. These two had hired me to give the copy desk some needed international expertise in an attempt to lift the foreign coverage to a level comparable to that of the *New York Times.* The Cowles family, owners of both the morning *Tribune* and evening *Star*, possessed a cash cow and were willing, with the *noblesse oblige* of the very rich, to invest some of their immense profits in making the *Tribune* a prestige newspaper.

Agence France Press, Reuters and the *New York Times* services all flowed across the copy desk along with the Associated Press and United Press wires. A story on a new French government, the fall of Dien Bien Phu or the negotiations in Korea would be edited from all these sources and usually carried on the front page. But the paper was located in the heart of the midwest, and interest in worldwide news was limited to a small elite.

In the nature of things, the paper carried large numbers of stories with headlines such as:

Tractor Tips

Kills Driver

There were weekly citations for the best headline, which I often won with such eccentric gems as:

"Thieves who came to dine now must serve."

"British private eyes must have clean monocles."

I was a quick and dirty editor. My experience came from my days on the Sanford Florida Herald, when I barely had time to breathe deeply in the seven or eight hours it took to put the twelve-page daily together virtually alone. The *Tribune* copy desk was run by a growling tyrant named Lou Green, who seemed to have patterned himself after a movie caricature of the genre. He was a superb editor at certain levels. Levels prized by the paper's culture.

He never misspelled a word. He could instantly spot a headline that didn't count to the letter. And his command of capitalization—our copy came in all caps, and one of our routine tasks was to underline the capitals—was uncanny. My priorities and skills were alien to his nature. He found my knowledge of French and use of AFP and Reuters a strange aberration, possibly a threat to his tyranny. My spelling, learned—or not learned—in twelve different schools in five different cities, was a personal affront. Mostly, however, he realized that I could not be broken on the wheel of his massive ego. Nonetheless, my incompetence was more or less accepted by Veblen, Hafrey and even Green, since my special skills were moderately useful.

I soon realized that there was no future on the copy desk, and I came to dread the three-to-midnight stint each day. Lisl and I rarely saw each other, since she worked as an archivist in the paper's morgue on an-eight-to-five schedule with weekends free. I worked every Saturday and Sunday as low man on the desk.

In desperation to escape the copy desk, I soon began to contribute articles to the paper. Features for the Sunday section were accepted with alacrity. Travel articles researched in the city's excellent public library were gratefully received. And I became a regular book reviewer which was the beginning of my final downfall.

Toward the end of my first year on the paper, I reviewed a book by a German film writer and novelist named Ernest von Salomon. Von Salomon was a creature of his time. In June 1922 he drove the car for a group of right-wing assassins who killed the German Foreign minister, Walter Rathenau, a Jew and a German patriot who was hoodwinking the Allied reparations authorities. Unfortunately, his subtle policy also fooled the extreme nationalists who killed him. Von Salomon was arrested and sent to prison for six years. By the time he was released in the late twenties in an amnesty of political prisoners, the right-wing movement had all coalesced around the Nazi Party which this young aristocrat found offensive, primarily for aesthetic reasons but also because of its anti-semitism.

He moved to San Jean de Luz in southern France for several years, making his living as a screenwriter, returning to Germany just before the war with his Jewish lover. Both survived the war, she by concealing her identity, he by laying low. In 1945 both were arrested and imprisoned by Allied war crimes courts because of his participation in the murder of von Rathenau. He describes with vivid bitterness the mistreatment both suffered at the hands of what he called American "concentration" camps. Both were eventually cleared of any collaboration with the Nazis and freed.

The book, written as if in answer to a questionnaire the Allies required all Germans to fill out, was a wide-ranging view of the intra-war years, often perverse but full of arresting insights. Von Salomon fit no pattern and neither did his book, which I had read in German in Vienna. His insights were those of a cultivated intellectual and minor nobleman who bemoaned the death of a monarchist, Bizmarckian Germany. Not very sensible, perhaps, but hardly criminal.

He was published by the Rohwolt Verlag, a liberal press later destroyed by the Nazis, and quotes with wry wit an exchange between Rohwolt and his wife. Rohwolt: "Did you know my dear that lions copulate thirty-six times a day?" Mrs. Rohwolt: "Rohwolt, you're no lion."

My review attempted to reflect the book for what it was—an honest, if often perverse, attempt at assessing a murderous period in world history. I did not then, and still do not today, after spending some ten years in Germany and Austria, feel much empathy for the country or its people. Stereotypes are invidious but, like clichés, they exist because within them is a core of truth.

The Germans combine a truly fierce sense of righteousness and discipline with a maudlin sentimentality. The result is often insufferably pompous and patronizing. This virtually universal character trait is summed up in the self-mocking phrase *Besser Wisser* which translates—badly—as know-it-all. Von Salomon was refreshingly lacking in any of this.

Lou Green read, or misread, my review and was immediately convinced that I was pro-German and, therefore, a violent anti-Semite and set out to eradicate me from the paper. It didn't take long. Veblen and Hafrey, who was also Jewish and thought my review brilliant, were unable to protect me. Everybody on the copy desk wanted out. To allow the junior member to escape would have caused a massive revolt.

Veblen, a gracious and civilized man, suggested I might look for another job. Soon. The next day I scanned the help wanted columns of both papers and came across a singular advertisement. Wanted, it said, French speaking trainee for overseas position with major international company.

I called and was invited to an interview with The Pillsbury Company, a large flour manufacturer whose owners, the Pillsbury family, were among the movers and shakers in Minneapolis. It was a simpler time. There were no batteries of tests, my college transcript was examined in a cursory way, and all of a sudden I found myself in the office of the vice president for overseas operations, William Sparboe, known to one and all as Shang. He had won this nickname in the intra-war years by making many a perilous sales trip to the Pacific on freighters carrying the company's flour, often winding up in Shanghai.

Shang had with him a fireplug of a man with a broken nose and a scarred face marked by perpetual hostility and anger. Sparboe introduced him as the manager of Pillsbury's Portland, Oregon export office. His name was Vince Miller. The two men interviewed me in some puzzlement. My resume bore no resemblance to anything they had ever seen. I finally realized Miller was staring at my nose.

"How'd you get the broken nose?" he asked.

"Boxing."

"Forgot to duck, huh? How many fights you have?"

"Forty or so."

He started down at my resume and back up at me, incredulous. "Where?"

"Golden Gloves. Navy. University of Georgia. Smokers."

"Sumbitch, Shang," he said, grinning, turning to the vice president. "He can't be all bad. I'll take him."

It was agreed that I would move to Portland at Pillsbury's expense and train there for a year. After which I would be transferred to the New York office. The company's overseas division had suddenly become an unexpectedly profitable part of its operations, as the United States began to feed most of the world, sending shiploads of flour to dozens of obscure countries, thus keeping American farmers from drowning in grain by subsidizing its export. Africa was a huge market, and a large chunk of it spoke French.

Selling flour in 1954 required very little skill. Most of the world was on the verge of starvation. The Pillsbury office in Portland watched over a conveyor belt as agents throughout Asia flooded its mills with orders. The agents were mostly Chinese, parts of close knit communities scattered throughout the area between India and Japan. Their commission accounts often amounted to millions of dollars, left at minimal interest in Pillsbury's care in the event that another of the periodic pogroms against the Chinese broke out.

Occasionally one of these men would visit our offices. Leon Ah Why, our Indonesian agent, in a way summed them up. When his commission account reached a million dollars he took passage on a Dutch ship to Portland to, as he put it in pidgin English, "look at his money."

He was about five-feet-two inches tall, in his mid-forties. His suit was two sizes too large, a fedora rode on his ears with the front brim curled upwards and he never removed a heavy overcoat although it was summer. He wore no socks and had no upper front teeth.

He could barely communicate in English, but his small eyes never quit moving, and mirrored a quick intelligence. He was turned over to me. I took him on sightseeing trips to the great dams of the Columbia river, Mount Hood, through the immense wasteland of the Tillamook Burn and to the spectacular Oregon coast.

He seemed most interested in American lifestyles, contrasting the large house of Vince Miller with my small apartment, fascinated by the streams of traffic. "Where are the workers?" he kept asking. "Everybody rich?"

His English improved rapidly over the two weeks he spent

with me, and toward the end he became more the guide than I did, taking me to an obscure Chinese restaurant in the port area, where the waiters bowed to the floor and feasts were served in private rooms by the owners. A Moslem, he had four wives and fifteen children, he said. Each wife had a house for bird's nests so that when he visited them he could have the soup made from their saliva encrusted on the nests.

At the other end of the scale was an American-born Chinese in San Francisco who, in a moment of rage with me over some foul up on a shipment, screamed that I should come down to San Francisco with a bushel basket of hundred dollar bills and we would go out on the Golden Gate Bridge and throw them over one at a time until one of us was broke.

He laughed until he almost choked when I informed him that I didn't have enough money to make the first throw. On my next trip to San Francisco he took me to the best French restaurant in town and offered me a job.

"I need a front man," he said. "I have an MBA from Stanford's business school, but everybody thinks I'm a coolie." I declined politely. He seemed likely to be even less tolerant of my lack of dedication than either Lou Green or Vince Miller.

The Pillsbury office in Portland was located in a warehouse. Two glass boxes for the two managers and a small pit for the secretaries and me. It soon became obvious that my training was a joke. The number two in the office, Barney Skille, spent most of his time processing orders and entering on them the arcane code which was stamped on each bag indicating its owner and destination.

Skille, whose father, in his seventies, still took a one-man boat out to sea to fish for salmon for a living, was Norwegian. Laconic to the point of being mute while sober, Barney never shut up after a couple of drinks. He was regularly invited to lunch by the three representatives of bag manufacturers, who included me in these invitations much to Skille's distress. It seemed obvious to them that I was being groomed to take over from him and have the power to allocate the millions of bags used to ship the flour spewing from the company's mills.

Vince was an American paradox. Underneath his roughneck exterior there was a shrewd intelligence with that touch for penetrating another's weaknesses which is the mark of a great salesman. Another Miller has nailed the type indelibly in *Death of a Salesman*. Vince was also an alcoholic, who had received an ultimatum from the company to go on the wagon and never joined us at these lunches, but he drank heavily at private parties. He was an aggressive and insufferable drunk, married to a cringing pitiable woman whom he treated with utter contempt. He had taken one look at Lisl and gone into rut. She handled him with the careless contempt European women seem to be born with, insisting that I leave the problem to her.

Shortly after arriving in Portland, we met on the ski slopes of Mount Hood a French couple, Georges and Katie Cassarno. He was struggling to start a timber business and she ran the ballet school at the local cultural center. We were quickly folded into a group of frustrated artists and provincial intellectuals who gathered around them. The town was becoming a city, and the head of the cultural center, a talented Russian émigré pianist, crippled in his youth by polio, named Ariel Rubstein had managed to get enough money together to put on an opera. He chose Aida.

Katie Cassarno, who had danced in the Paris ballet company, choreographed the ballet scenes using students in her classes. Lisl played piano for the rehearsals. I was dragooned into doing the publicity. Most of the cast were local but Ariel had contracted for Daniza Ilitsch, long past her prime, but once a well known soprano, as Aida and a second rate tenor, Rudolf Petrak, as Rhadames.

The opening performance was a total disaster. At one point the orchestra lost total cohesion, Madame Ilitsch stood stage center, tears of frustration running down her cheeks, as Ariel hummed the orchestra back on the beat. Fortunately most of the audience didn't notice.

My participation in this production was a final straw in Vince Miller's assessment of me. It convinced him that I was a useless, limp-wristed wimp, unworthy of the virile business of peddling flour. My participation in the routine of the office was reduced to zero, and the ax was clearly, once again, approaching my neck. At thirty, my work resume was beginning to look like a streetcar schedule.

It was at this point that I was forced to attend the smoker of one of the local businessmen's clubs. Vince wanted his whole staff—Barney, me and the office manager—in attendance. This was the mid-fifties. Most of the men were war veterans who had grown up in the sexually repressive atmosphere of the times, coarsened by the one-night stands in army camp towns and occupation armies, mired in marriages where sex was more duty than pleasure. This was their big night out.

The final act of a bawdy review was a striptease by a skinny, large breasted woman who wore a look of weary desperation during most of her act, which culminated in a nude bump and grind among the tables while the men stuffed bills into her genitals, stroking her in the process.

Vince, drunk and beside himself with lust, turned to me as she passed where we were standing and said, "You're a jerk, Harper. You don't deserve that wife of yours. I'd be a lot better in bed with her than you are."

I backed away from him, got set and landed a right on his jaw, which caved in two knuckles and knocked him across the dance floor into a table full of glasses and bottles. Drunk or not, he took a good punch. He was on his feet and coming after me when a half dozen laughing men intervened, one pushing me toward the door, the others holding Miller back.

It was Saturday night, and when I got home I sat down at my little Olivetti portable, where my second novel was taking shape, and wrote a letter to Shang Sparboe outlining what had happened and telling him I was going into the office on Monday morning to demand an apology. If I didn't get it, I intended to deck Miller again. I mailed the letter Sunday morning, as Lisl and I contemplated our financial condition, which consisted of a twenty-five-dollar bank balance and her job as a secretary which barely paid our rent.

On Monday I got in early. When Vince arrived I headed into his office, trailed by Skille and the office manager.

"You owe me and my wife an apology, Vince. Either I get it or we go out in the warehouse and settle this."

His reaction amazed me. This genuinely tough middle-aged man, who certainly had no fear of me, writhed and cringed in his chair, growling and whining at the same time, barely containing his rage, but clearly consumed by panic. His job was on the line. He was desperate. He finally choked out an apology.

I walked out a little dazed, remembering my letter to Sparboe. Two days later one of the secretaries motioned toward the phone, eyes wide. A call for me from the vice president, Shang Sparboe. They all, of course, knew of the incident and were expecting me to be fired. So was I.

"What happened, Harper?" Sparboe asked. "You deck the sumbitch?"

"No, Shang. He apologized."

"Oh, shit. I was hoping you'd decked him. We been tryin' to fire the bastard for two years."

Sparboe arrived the next day and, after several hours of closed door sessions with Miller, came out to announce that Vince would go on three months sick leave and Skille would take over the office. I would be transferred immediately to the New York office. It was a lesson I was never to forget and Harper's Fifth Law was born.

In confrontational situations, the man willing to go the last inch will win ninety percent of the time.

Thirteen

Vulgar of Manner, overfed
Overdressed and underbred
Heartless, godless, hell's delight
Rude by day, lewd by night

Byron Rufus Newton on New York City

Charles N. Koons sat behind a desk the size of a dining room table. The city was spread out like a carpet unrolled under the window of his immense office in Rockefeller Center. A painting of his yacht, the size of an eighteenth century frigate, dominated the wall behind him. He was a middle-aged man, with a mane of white hair and hard little light blue blue eyes buried in reddish suet.

"Let me get this straight, Mr. Harper. Your company," he glanced at a sheet of paper in front of him, "Pillsbury Mills, has received an offer from the United States government to bid on a shipload of flour to Paraguay."

"Yes. It's part of the export subsidy program. The tender offer goes to every flour mill in America. The low bidder gets the contract."

He nodded. "Yeah. Overpay the farmers to overproduce and then pay starving foreigners to take it off our hands. Why did you call me on this?"

"I buy and sell forward foreign exchange contracts for Pillsbury. I called around to find out who was big in Paraguay and the guy at First Boston said you were a major player."

"And your company plans to bid on the shipload?" He glanced again at the paper. "Twenty thousand metric tons."

I hesitated. I was in way over my head all of a sudden. I'd been in the New York office for a year, sharing a cubbyhole with one of the two traders who bought and sold thousand-ton lots of flour from small mills around the country without the infrastructure and expertise to handle exports. They usually held the contracts as the government export subsidy fluctuated, applying for it when the subsidy rose, taking small profits but making large amounts of money on huge volume.

It was a mini-operation within the Pillsbury export office in New York, which covered the world outside the orient. But the pressure was intense. If the subsidy nose dived, leaving the traders with millions of dollars in uncovered contracts, the losses could be immense. So could the profits when the subsidy rose.

The New York office was run by Bill Spoor, a former Dartmouth football player who later became chairman of the board of Pillsbury. He had designed and run the export subsidy operation which had become an impressive cash cow. Looking back, and remembering the cryptic conversations my office mate had with the government officials in the subsidy division, it seems clear that some form of bribery was in operation. We always seemed to know which way the subsidy was going, cashing in the contracts at the most profitable moment.

By the time I arrived in New York, the word had gone out that I'd decked Vince Miller which gave me a certain cachet in the macho business environment of the time. The level of racism in the office was rampant. We had customers in eighty third world nations, all of whom created problems. Africa one of the most profitable markets, caused the most trouble. The scatological humor reflected the frustration. When a cabinet head in the Eisenhower administration, in his cups on an airplane flight, told a newsman sitting next to him that "all blacks wanted was loose shoes, a tight pussy and a warm place to shit," the assistant sales managers erupted with glee.

Normally the internal competition among this group was vicious, particularly so in the little speculative pressure cooker. The two traders cut me out of the core of the operation, leaving me to deal with the dregs. In addition to handling foreign exchange, I worked a few small accounts, mostly staring at the wall waiting for the day to end, and trying to figure out how to get a decent job. My assignment to Africa was clearly on hold.

Spoor, who used his size and athleticism to develop a menacing presence, had clearly been amused by my one-punch fight with Vince. Over the course of the next year, he must have noticed my inability to break into the speculation operation, and I had the feeling my days on the edge of the executive suite were numbered. Effective aggressiveness was the name of the game for him, and my passivity, a reflection of my boredom, was evident. He came in one morning and tossed a piece of paper on my desk. "Let's see what you can do, Harper. Sell us a shipload of flour. Earn your pay."

My office mate grabbed the paper off my desk as Spoor left, alarm etched in his jowls. He glanced at it and started to laugh. "We can't compete on that. The Texas mills will underbid us by a nickel. Bill's jerking your chain."

With nothing else to do I'd called around, gotten Koons name and asked for an appointment. He was clearly taking me seriously.

"We plan to bid," I lied, "but our competitors in Texas will probably undercut us."

"Mr. Harper, I have to tell you that I owe you one on this. Your friend at First Boston is right. My company, a family organization, occupies an important niche in Paraguay. Your call was the first indication of this flour offer. I don't mind telling you my people in Asuncion got a rocket from me about letting this slip through the cracks. The minister of agriculture is going to be here on Friday, to explain why I wasn't informed, at which time we'll arrange the details of this bid."

He leaned across his desk smiling. "I like your initiative, Mr. Harper. We're a very discreet operation here. Avoid publicity. Play down our influence. However, as I said, I owe you one, and in return I can guarantee you the undertaker's look on this contract."

It was lunchtime when I left Koons, and I stopped off at a White Rose bar and sat for a while with a beer and one of their superb hot pastrami sandwiches. Somehow I'd fallen into a possible coup. As Gielgud's television advertisement quotes Shakespeare: "There comes a time in the affairs of men which, taken at the flood, leads on to fortune." The trick was to avoid being drowned.

I walked across the street to our offices on 47th Street, not sure what I had heard, having no idea what the "undertaker's look" was. Outside the executive area was something we called the "pit", where the freight forwarders and other underlings toiled away. My predecessor in the speculation office had been relegated to it when I arrived. It seemed likely to be my fate as well.

I stopped at a couple of desks to chat and casually brought up the undertaker's look. One of the older forwarders glanced up. "Means they'll give you a look at all the other bids before you submit yours. You can't lose."

I went into Spoor's office and tossed the bid on his desk. "I just sold a shipload of flour, Bill." He looked up, taking the heavily chewed cigar he affected out of his mouth and staring at me in disbelief.

"Yeah? Speak."

I told him about Koons and ended with the undertaker's look. It was clear from his expression that he, too, had no idea what it meant. There was a time I'd have let him hang, savoring the moment, but by this time I'd learned it never pays to upstage the power, so I explained what the phrase meant without seeming to.

"When are you seeing Koons again?"

"Friday at ten. With the agriculture minister."

"Harry will go with you," he said, naming the senior of the two speculators. "Fix it with Koons."

Harry and I went together to the Friday meeting. A thoroughly chastened agriculture minister, in a chalk-striped suit and yellow pointed shoes, sat in respectful silence while Koons outlined how the bid would be handled.

I was effectively cut out of the deal at this point. Harry saw to that. On the evening of the bids we held a death watch in the office for the call from Koons. As the bids came in, the agriculture minister somehow had managed to transmit the amounts to him as they were opened in the government office. Ours went in a few minutes before the deadline, a penny a bag below the low Texas mill, and we had the contract. Next day, Spoor contracted with the Texas company which had tendered the next lowest bid. Their mill was running and the flour was piling up. Markets were glutted. He bought a shipload of bulk flour with a profit ten cents a bag in it for us. One hundred thousand dollars for half a days work.

A week later Shang Sparboe came to town, and he and Spoor took me to lunch. They informed me I was going to Africa as Pillsbury's first resident overseas representative. I wasn't being given the title of assistant sales manager, but if I handled the job well, I'd be promoted after a two-year tour. I got a four-thousand-dollar a year raise, from ten thousand dollars to fourteen. I was a little dazed. In five years I'd gone from a job I loved at two thousand dollars a year to one I hated at fourteen. I was trapped.

Time in New York outside the office was a blur. We were quickly folded into the circle of Marie and Bob Weltzien, now married. He worked as an account executive for an advertising firm, and he and Marie ran a floating cocktail party in their Fifth Avenue apartment. The guests included many of his old Choate and Princeton friends, now rising steadily through the ranks of law and business. And here and there some original he had picked up, such as an elderly Ukrainian named Valery Koussarenko-Koussarevitch, who had been a cabinet minister in the short-lived Ukrainian government following the Russian revolution. He was now a janitor at an apartment house on Staten Island.

One night, exiting the Weltzien's apartment with him in the midst of a snow storm, he took my wife's hand, peeled her glove forward and kissed her hand in a gesture full of ineffable grace. He then turned toward the subway entrance and headed for Staten Island and his basement apartment.

Or Leila Meredith, wife of a Standard Oil executive, and a

genuine Russian princess, born in New Jersey. She had the waif-like beauty of a ballet dancer, combined with a presence which transcended arrogance. I once asked her why the Russian generals were all short and stubby.

"We bred them that way," she said without missing a beat. Years later, in Malaga, she sat in a portside restaurant and fed shrimp, an expensive delicacy in a Spain racked by poverty, to scruffy cats, oblivious to a circle of emaciated children watching impassively.

Weltzien's friends were young American aristocrats on the make, with slim, highly educated, mink-clad wives, their paths smoothed by family connections and money. Bright liberal, facile and articulate, they engaged in an unending game of one-upsmanship. Their education seemed to have programmed into them a streak of civilized cruelty.

What struck my wife, a classic European, was the undertone of viciousness between the men and women. "They're emasculating their men," she said, shaking her head. "How stupid."

Once when, embedded in a political discussion, I had asked Lisl to bring me a drink, one of the women grasped her arm as she turned to comply. "Tell him to get his own fucking drink. This is America, darling. The men can't order you around the way they do in Europe. It's fifty-fifty here."

"Why should I give up forty percent?" Lisl said, smiling and going for the drink.

Another time, during a discussion involving a subordinate of President Eisenhower named Sherman Adams who was enveloped in controversy, she turned to one of the young tigers and asked: "Is Sherman Adams good or bad?"

He turned to the group. "Did you hear that? I don't believe my ears. A woman has actually asked my opinion on something."

Looking back, the dissonance between American men and women at these parties, reflected earlier in Thurber's cartoons and much of the popular culture, was a prelude to the more serious gender warfare permeating America today. Bored, vaguely disgruntled, these young women were on the edge of beginning families, moving to the suburbs and becoming part of a culture they instinctively knew would make no use of their excellent education and talent. A very few escaped. Most did not. They are today an embittered, usually divorced or widowed, lonely and confused minority engulfed in what to them seems the paradise of women's liberation. This failed dream of their generation shadows the lives and ambitions of their daughters and granddaughters who want it all.

Bob and Marie weathered it all. He later became, for a brief period, president of the Timex Watch Corporation, commuting by helicopter from Hamden, Connecticut where he lived in the house of the former president of Yale. He often retired to his room at conferences to practice Chinese calligraphy and work on his translation of Nietsche's *Thus Spake Zarathustra*. She mothered five children without losing either her intellectual force of wry British sense of humor.

Then there were Olga von Ziegesar, my friend of Grenoble days, and her husband, Fabian Kalau vom Hofe, the descendant of Prussian noblemen. A high school dropout, Fabian looked like an idealized German officer. He was, at this point, unemployed and remained so for almost a decade, before going to work for the Morgan Guaranty Trust Company after faking a resume and using the influence of Olga's family.

Fabian was a child of his time. The son of an aristocratic Dutch mother and a German father descended from the Teutonic knights, he had grown up with his aunts in Northern Italy. He spoke five languages and was the paradigm of a European nobleman. In 1945, drafted into one of the youth corps to man anti-aircraft guns, he and a friend deserted. Fabian found his way between the lines and surrendered to a French army division which was commanded by one of his cousins. He was soon free, acting as the man's orderly.

He later became a senior vice president of Morgan and director of the bank's branch in Paris, in the Place Vendome across from the Ritz Hotel. The bank was a tomb, it's eighteenth century building protected as a national monument. Fabian had a good act, but he hadn't really changed much. He had lunch sent in from some three-star restaurant, apologizing for not leaving the office.

"My staff are mostly Americans who were born in France. Third generation Morgan employees. When I took over the place was run like a private club. Three hour lunches, golf in the afternoon. It had to change. So I set the tone." Underneath he was still a great hedonist, but he'd discovered the seductions of power and was enjoying it immensely.

In 1980 he was conned by the Polish government, which played on his guilt as a German, into loaning them three hundred million dollars. The loan was never repaid and cost him his chance to become chairman of Morgan. He now divides his time between a manor house in France, a chalet in Switzerland and an apartment in England, a renaissance man in a post industrial world, attempting to create the civilized aristocratic environment of his youth. Kind to his servants and friends, a man without a country.

One of the Pillsbury assistant sales managers also befriended me. Henry Klingman was the son of German immigrants, a veteran of the Tenth Mountain Division's fighting in Italy and a former member of the youth corps of the German American Bund, America's Nazi party. When he discovered I spoke German, he took me under his wing in the office, bringing me along to the nightly drinking sessions of the assistant managers and easing my way.

Drinking and whoring with Arab and Latin American customers were major elements in the office's sales success. Virtually all the sales managers returned from lunch glassy eyed and blitzed. After a memorable cable went out to a Saudi customer, offering a hundred thousand tons of flour at a price a dollar a bag below its cost, Spoor mandated that no more offers would be sent out after lunch. The Saudi had a sense of humor and did not hold us to the price.

Affairs with the secretaries were commonplace, as they joined us after work in the mid-town bars. This was another time and place, and the young women from working class families were dazed by these young men who traveled the world first class and dealt in millions of dollars.

A favorite story, relayed to me by Klingman, dealt with my office mate who had led one of the secretaries back to the office after a drinking session and was pumping away with her on the office floor when three or four others came back, took in the scene and cheered.

Klingman and I played tennis on Sunday morning on Staten Island, with me making the long trek down Manhattan on the subway from our one-room apartment on 105th Street west to the ferry. Staten Island was then a bucolic place full of parks and open spaces. Another world from the city across the harbor.

Klingman was an American phenomenon. The working class immigrant's son, rough-edged, coarse, bright and hopelessly envious of the Ivy League Spoor who, recognizing his frustration, provoked him with amused cruelty. The result was an explosive, embittered man who had no friends in the office and turned to me. I was later to misjudge the friendship which developed. He would betray me most grievously.

Our neighborhood at a hundred and fifth was on the edge of a very rough part of New York, even then. One evening, having no television set, and desperate to see Archie Moore fight Rocky Marciano for the heavyweight championship, I walked up Broadway until I found a quiet bar. It was packed. An integrated crowd was on the raw edge from an explosive combination of alcohol and anticipated violence. I slipped into a seat at the bar next to an immense black man with arms the size of logs. The fight started well. Moore, a natural light heavyweight, boxing with the finesse and intelligence which informed his every move, ducked a Marciano left hook and crossed his right, feet planted, flush on Marciano's jaw. The champion went down. I was on my feet yelling with encouragement. It looked like a knockout punch for an instant. Skill and smarts had finally triumphed over brute force and bloody ignorance.

But it was not to be. Marciano shook his head and bounced to his feet, punching mercilessly. My neighbor turned to me between the second and third rounds and asked, face impassive, "White boy, how come you rootin' for that nigger?"

It was a delicate moment. I looked him in the eye and said. "He's an intelligent boxer, an artist. The other guy is a stupid brute." A grin spread across the man's face and he waved to the bartender.

"Bring my friend here a beer." When Marciano knocked Archie out in the fifth round, I slid out as quickly as I could, first ordering a payback beer for my companion.

Klingman came to our hotel room on Lexington Avenue, the night before we left for Africa, along with Marie and Bob Weltzien. The two were divided by an unbridgeable cultural chasm. Klingman, the German worker's son, former member of an American Nazi organization; Weltzien, the descendant of cultivated, atheistic Jews who had immigrated to America in the wake of the 1848 revolution. His family were part of the New York aristocracy. The one thing they had in common was fluency in German. It wasn't enough.

In the course of the alcoholic farewell celebration, Weltzien at one point sang both the soprano and tenor parts of a section of Lohengrin, his falsetto a piece of incomparable comedy. Klingman, who had become increasingly aggressive and had begun to make veiled anti-Semitic remarks as the evening progressed and the alcohol flowed, rose to dance and sing a Nazi song to a *Schuhplatler* rhythm. Weltzien, trying to defuse an explosive situation, then sang the affecting seventeenth century German war song *Ich hatte eine Kamerade* and Klingman was reduced to sentimental blubbering.

My wife and Marie, who had watched the two men at each other's throats with detached European contempt, broke up the party, and we headed for Ghana the next morning nursing massive hangovers.

Fourteen

Those who serve a revolution plow the seas.

Simon Bolivar

The Nigerian minister of finance, Okitie Iboe, a product of a centuries long line of chiefs and the best British schools, was resplendent in a white linen robe and a soft fez decorated with threads of gold. A fan turned lazily above his head. Shang Sparboe's seersucker jacket was soaked under the armpits, and his black cotton pants had crawled up his crotch and lost their crease.

"Mr. Minister, your experts have been examining our proposal to build a flour mill for a year now. I'm here prepared to complete the deal." It wasn't the Nigerian way of doing business. But Okitie Iboe had become accustomed to blunt, rough-edged Americans as Nigerian independence approached. The country was awash in oil. There was money to be made. And the industrial nations' sharks were in a feeding frenzy.

Our proposal to build a flour mill was in competition not only with British, German and French companies, but also with those of a local Greek businessman, George Leventis, whose interests formed an interlocking web across the spectrum of the Nigerian economy.

There was a major problem with anybody building the mill. A third of the process of converting wheat to flour is feedstuff. The tsetse fly made growing cattle impossible in Southern Nigeria. Distance and expense obviated shipping the feed north to the semi-desert grazing regions. In addition, Nigeria's climate made wheat growing impossible. The raw material had to be imported. Our calculations indicated that the price of flour milled locally would be double that of imported. The Nigerians had already agreed to impose a prohibitive protective tariff. As Shang had said "the consumer be damned. Industrialize at any cost."

Okitie Iboe tented his fingers and leaned back in his new swivel chair covered with fake tiger skin, a present from the United Africa Company, the most powerful company in Nigeria. "Mr. Sparboe, your offer is indeed of interest to us. Your flour, Pillsbury's Best, is by far the preferred brand in my country. In fact your agents," he glanced at me and smiled, "control about ninety percent of the market. Obviously we would prefer to deal with old friends such as yourselves."

Sparboe waited.

Iboe cleared his throat and shuffled some papers on his desk. "Of course, the offer of Mr. Leventis is also of some interest to us. He, too, is an old friend of Nigeria's and must be given every consideration."

"He's offering to dismantle an obsolete mill in Greece and ship it here," Shang protested. "The machinery is worn out and will break down four or five times a year. The technology is outmoded. It requires almost a hundred people to keep it running. Our offer is of a new, state of the art, flour mill. Fewer than twenty skilled technicians can keep it operating. There's no comparison between the two offers."

Iboe smiled. "By your standards that's true, Mr. Sparboe, but we look upon these ventures as training grounds for our backward people. Leventis has guaranteed employment and training for two hundred of them. How many will you need?"

Sparboe looked uncomfortable. "Well, I'll be frank, Mr. Minister. Our millers are men who have taken twenty years to learn their trade. We can't just put people in a training program and turn out flour millers. Doesn't work that way. It's an art, milling flour. You can't learn it overnight. We'll take on five apprentice millers, however, and, as I say, bring in twenty trained technicians to run the mill. We would probably need another twenty or so for menial jobs. Cleaning up, stuff like that."

"So, you would employ only twenty-five or so Nigerians and the Greek will hire two hundred," Iboe said. I had explained the Nigerian attitude to Shang before coming into Iboe's office. Nigerian wages were pitifully low. He understood that we would have to take on dozens of them to sweeten the pot, but the prospects of profit, and of losing the market entirely if we didn't get the mill contract, were worth the extra, useless, expense.

Shang agreed to hire more workers and outlined our plan, giving production schedules, guaranteed completion dates, projected prices and, most important of all, how we would handle the sale of residual feedstuff. It would have to be exported to a glutted market. Pillsbury had the connections to sell the feed which none of our competitors could match.

Iboe already knew all this, having been thoroughly briefed by the permanent British colonial service officer who really ran the ministry. "Yes, I think that will be satisfactory, Mr. Sparboe. There is, of course, one final point to settle."

"What's that?" Sparboe asked, the picture of innocence.

"My participation," Iboe said.

Sparboe's face lit up. "I like dealing with a man like you, Mr. Minister. No beating about the bush. Right up front. Well, I have here in my pocket," he reached in and laid an envelope on the table, "the keys and papers for a Cadillac Fleetwood, the finest car made in America."

"Yes? Very nice of you, I'm sure Mr. Sparboe. But I already own two Rolls Royces and a Mercedes. I was, in fact, thinking along the lines of thirty percent."

Sparboe turned to me frowning. "What's he mean?" he said in a stage whisper.

"Just what he said. He wants thirty percent of the mill. Probably in the name of one of his wives or some relative."

"Thirty percent," Sparboe said, voice rising. "Jesus that's highway robbery. Not even the Haitians asked for that."

Iboe smiled broadly and spread his hands out in an expansive gesture. Pillsbury had been prepared to go as high as ten percent, but in an hour of haggling Shang couldn't budge the minister an inch.

Some years later, in one of the many coup d'état in Nigeria, Iboe was cornered by a group of mutinous soldiers, and died reaching into his robe and throwing handfuls of five pound notes at them begging for his life.

My four years in Africa were coming to an end when Shang made his offer to build the flour mill. They had started in Ghana a few days after that country's independence celebrations. We were met at the airport, leaving the clean, air conditioned confines of Pan American Airways for a journey back into the nineteenth century.

Pillsbury's agent was one Edward Patrick Doolin, known universally as Paddy, a tall emaciated man with a mop of unruly black hair, hook nose, skin tanned the color of aged leather and piercing violet eyes. He had been a fighter pilot in the war, a motorcycle racer afterwards and had wandered down to Africa as what the Brits called a "bagman", a commercial traveler with a bag of samples peddling his wares. Pillsbury had hired him as its agent some years before, and he had become a great favorite of the New York office because of his encyclopedic knowledge of expensive London brothels and nightclubs.

The flour trade had exploded just as he became agent, and he spent his earnings with abandon during trips to England to meet with our New York executives. Incredibly, no Pillsbury representative had ever visited Africa in the ten years following the war, although it was one of our most profitable markets, absorbing some eighty million dollars worth of flour a year.

Our entry into the market was guaranteed by a secret agreement with the United Africa Company, known as UAC, whereby this immensely powerful subsidiary of Unilever received a ten cent override on every bag of flour we sold. With this locked up Pillsbury was guaranteed a dominant share of the market in every British colony south of the Sahara, where UAC was king of the mountain. It was a delicate arrangement, since none of their managers were aware of the override and often tried to circumvent it. My job wasn't to sell flour but to stroke the UAC people, keep them happy and report on what was likely to happen as these countries became independent.

Pillsbury, its Pillsbury's Best brand almost an icon among the Africans, as its empty canvas bags were converted into clothing across the continent, had been riding an incredible cash cow until disaster struck.

It was a classic example of the Law of Unintended Consequences at work. One of the company's itinerant bakers had visited the market a year before and suggested a change in the makeup of the flour we shipped. Until that point it had been a very high protein blend, a difficult flour for bakers to work with. His advice was routinely followed. And chaos resulted in every African bakery from the Cameroons to The Gambia.

Pillsbury had sent along with the new shipments detailed instructions on how to alter, very slightly, the baking methods. Unfortunately, the African bakers were not only illiterate but stubborn, wedded to their hard-earned trade which was one of the rare areas where natives had replaced expatriates.

Suddenly, overnight, their bread wouldn't rise, or it exploded. Panic ensued. Hundreds of thousands of bags of flour rotted in the warehouses. The company immediately reinstated its previous flour formula and paid compensation, but the damage was done. A half century of trust had been betrayed, and our competitors had gained a foothold in the market.

This was the situation when Paddy Doolin met us at the airport. The first impression on arriving in West Africa is the heat. An oppressive, humid, leaden heat. There were two seasons. Rain and no rain. The local languages had no words for time in any western sense of the term. In the dry season the sky was a pale milky blue. In the wet season the rains came every afternoon, torrents of water cascading off rooftops and flooding the streets.

The gutters in British colonies were six-foot deep ditches

filled with sewage, garbage and detritus. Dry, they became noisome cesspools. Wet, they were raging torrents often overflowing the cement banks and befouling the streets. The narrow lanes were clogged with ancient cars and Mammy Wagons—small trucks fitted with benches—each bearing a painted sign on its tailgate. These substituted for buses, often packed to the point where the built up springs dragged the ground.

Their drivers were raving maniacs, weaving among cars, pushcarts and people with a fatalistic abandon, one leg cocked out the window, ready to jump as one once told me, the other periodically moving from gas pedal to brake, foul fumes rising from the tailpipes.

They drove on the left hand side of the road, in theory, but in reality everybody fought for the center lane. Head-on collisions were common. When the two Cameroons, one British and one French, were later joined at independence, the minister of transport was asked what he planned to do about the different driving regulations, the British holding to the left and the French to the right.

"We'll change to right hand drive, but not too drastically," he said. "We'll begin with the trucks." It probably wouldn't have made much difference in the accident rate if they had followed his plan.

Paddy drove us from the airport through a neighborhood of modest bungalows with gardens and fences, with here and there a more imposing house which would have fit into an American suburb.

"This looks rather nice," my wife commented, breaking into Paddy's unending Irish hustle.

"Nah," he said. "You don't want to live here. Bunch of lower middle class British twits. What you want is the real Africa. That's what Americans want. That's what Bill Spoor said he wanted you to do. Get to know the natives. They're going to be running the place. Got to live like them to know them. Not get involved with these damned expatriates." We were later often invited to his imposing mansion built in the same neighborhood.

He drove with the reckless abandon of an ex-motorcycle racer, bullying, screaming, sitting on the horn, ignoring the impotent police in wool shorts and shirts and long socks as we weaved through chaos. He pulled up finally at a decaying villa, painted a vile orange, its garden overgrown with weeds.

"This is it," Doolin said, glancing at me sideways. "Actually, I used to live here. Very comfortable. Nice neighbors," he said, indicating a growing collection of the black faces staring over the high walls on either side. "Don't want to encourage them, though. Pain in the arse they are, fucking Africans. Too bloody friendly."

"Sam," Doolin bellowed and a slender young Ghanaian came bounding down the stairs. He was the color of ebony, muscles etched on the body of a Greek athlete. An open handsome face, now contorted with fear of Doolin who cuffed him affectionately. "Get the effing bags, Sam. Say hello to your new master."

Sam performed something between a bow and a genuflection. "Welcome, Massah."

Behind me Lisl began to giggle. "You've finally made it back to pre-Civil War days," she whispered. I tried for four years to break Sam of "massah" without success. We became, in the truest sense of the word, friends. He woke me every morning with a glass of tea and a slice of pineapple on a plate, pulling back the mosquito netting and nudging me gently. Dragging me from bed if necessary. Massahs who didn't get up didn't last long, Sam had learned.

When I traveled up and down the coast, he brought his pallet into the house and slept before my wife's door, a wicked looking machete at his side. He cooked and cleaned. His young wife, who kept a stand in one of the city's open air markets, washed and ironed our clothes. They lived in a spotless small house at the back of the compound, and their greatest tragedy was in not having children. His wife was sterile we discovered, after persuading them both to go to a British doctor.

At the many dinners we were forced to give, he served as he'd been taught, with simple elegance. And he educated us, gently, with immense tact and great sensitivity. When snakes occasionally appeared in the house, he would explain which were harmless and which were the Black Mamba, whose bite meant instant death. He led my wife through the native markets, took us to the beaches where the waves were less treacherous, and explained the tribal complexities and taboos of his people.

He would not go with me into the north, the territory of the feared Ashanti, a warlike people, tall with aquiline features and the haughty bearing of a warrior class. For centuries they had moved south in the dry season to collect slaves among the peaceful coastal peoples. When the Portuguese arrived, they sold their prey to the European slave traders. They had fought the British successfully for decades before finally being defeated. Sam was sure he would be eaten by them if he went north, and he adamantly refused.

It soon became clear that Doolin was terrified of me. With reason. He was beyond being incompetent. He had, the previous year, persuaded Bill Spoor to allow him to consign 300,000 bags of flour, worth about a million dollars, to a local Lebanese merchant named Zakour. Normal payment for all shipments was upon collection of the shipment at portside. Zakour was allowed to take possession of the flour on signature of a ninety-day note. That note had remained unpaid for six months. My first job was to get the money.

"He'll pay," Doolin said. "One of my best customers. You'll not be wanting to harass the poor man, now. He's having a bit of a problem, he is. But he'll pay."

We called on Zakour, who inhabited a hole-in-the-wall bakery in an alley off one of Accra's main streets. He was a fat, oily man wearing dirty khaki shorts and a singlet. He and Doolin embraced, and he served us sweet tea. After fifteen minutes I brought up his unpaid debt. He waved a soiled hand.

"One hundred thousand pounds," he said. "I paid two days ago. Do not worry, young man. I will pay. Zakour is an honorable man. Zakour will pay."

"See," Doolin said. "He's paying. Quit worrying. Let's go by the club for a drink." The club was a rambling wooden building, dominating an eighteen-hole golf course with sand greens. It had a view of the ocean and the only restaurant in town. Paddy was the snooker champion and one of its best golfers, which was not surprising since he spent most of his time there.

I had a beer with him and afterwards went to Barclay's Bank which held Zakour's note. After some delay I was taken in to one of the officers, a slender, balding fortyish man with shifty, watery, pale blue eyes.

"Oh, yes. Mr. Zakour. One of our most valued customers, don't you know."

"He owes us about a million dollars, and he says he paid a hundred thousand pounds of it this morning. Can you check and let me know if that's true."

"Oh, I say, old boy. You're not questioning his veracity?" He looked shocked. He was a good actor.

"Can you check, please."

He disappeared and returned with a wire basket full of disorganized paper. "In here somewhere, don't you know," he said, smiling. "Oh, yes, Here we are. Three hundred and fifty thousand pounds. Rather a lot, eh?"

"Yes. Has he paid any of it?"

"Well it may not be registered yet. Why don't you come back next week, old boy? Wouldn't want to waste your time. We'll have it sorted out by then." The man's eyes were shifting like ping pong balls and his sunburned face was pale. Sweat had popped out on his forehead.

"I'll wait here while you find out."

Fifteen minutes later the banker came back and sat down. "I'm afraid there's been no payment."

"Has he got any money on deposit with you?"

"Oh, I say old boy, we couldn't possibly tell you that. Not ethical, don't you know."

"How much business do we do with your bank in a year? In the millions, no? Be a pity if we transferred it to another bank, wouldn't it?"

He had long, slender bony hands and they were knotted

together now. "Well, as a matter of fact, he's transferred most of his funds to the Lebanon. "There's virtually nothing in his account."

"When?"

"Some months ago."

"Just after he sold the flour?"

The banker nodded. There was no point in asking why he hadn't warned us. He was clearly in Zakour's pay. The question was whether Paddy was, too.

At Doolin's hole-in-the wall office I found him practicing on his dart board. "We need a lawyer, Paddy. We've got to attach any assets Zakour has before he can liquidate."

For once Paddy looked me in the eye. "He's on his way to the airport, sport. Everything he's got has been sold to his relatives. We've been royally screwed. He betrayed my friendship."

I called Spoor that night, and he arrived two days later. A million dollar loss on a credit sale he had approved could easily cost him his job. At the least it would be a stain on his brilliant career. Bad judgment.

I picked him up at the airport with Paddy. We spent the next ten hours with bankers and another set of Lebanese customers, the Aschkar clan, who were mortal enemies of the Zakours.

"Can't do nothing," Edward Aschkar said. "Fucking lost your stupid money, Bill. How you be so stupid, loaning a million to a Lebanese? You never loan me nothing. Doolin, you stupid or you a crook," he said, turning to Paddy.

Spoor asked what we could do.

Aschkar shrugged. "Kill him. Cost maybe five thousand dollars. I can handle for you. But you no get money back."

"How about suing him in Lebanon?"

Ashkar, who had the predatory face of an unshaven hawk, cackled with glee. "Suing Lebanese. In Lebanon? How many years you got, Bill? Fifty, a hundred. Anyway, he don't got nothing in his name. All buried. Gold coins. Or in sons' names. You fucked good, Bill."

We worked out a plan. I would write a series of reports

explaining that Zakour was good for the money but having liquidity difficulties. He was a good customer. Paddy would order flour in his name, sell it to other people and transmit small payments against the debt, keeping it active on the books. Spoor would arrange to write it off in segments over the years so the loss would not appear so large. And that's what we did.

Everybody survived. Paddy kept his agency. Spoor's reputation was saved, and I got another thousand dollar raise. More important, Spoor took a look around and asked me how long I thought I could stand it.

"The Brits get two months vacation a year."

"Two months?" He was incredulous.

"Yeah. Ask UAC."

Six weeks later I got a call from him approving two months vacation a year and, much more important, the veiled right to pad my expense account to the limit.

By the time Spoor agreed to my terms, life in the Gold Coast, now Ghana, had begun to take on a surrealist edge. One morning Doolin came into the office with a small overnight bag. "We're going north for a couple of days, sport. Our agent up there has invited us. We'll stop by your house to pick up some clothes."

I'd become accustomed to his abrupt and irrational decisions, but I wanted to see the Ashanti region, home of the warrior tribe which had successfully resisted British conquest for a hundred years. They had ruled the West African coast for centuries, haughty ebony aristocrats, slave traders, vicious enemies and, once conquered, fast friends.

Our agent, A Swiss timber dealer named Karl Maerz, was married to one of the daughters of the Asantehene, the Ashanti king. He was immensely rich even in defeat and controlled large tracts of timber, mostly mahogany which Maerz was ruthlessly clearcutting.

Vicki, the king's daughter, was British educated and a breathtaking beauty, the color of dark chocolate, slender as a reed, with the finely chiseled features of the tribe. A black Nefertiti. She met us at their home, an immense Swiss chalet built of mahogany on the center of Maerz's timber yard.

Vicki yelped with joy at the sight of Doolin, who was, if nothing else, an amusing addition to what was to turn into a lost weekend of booze, gorging and promiscuity as Maerz closed down his operation and invited his half dozen Swiss co-workers and their Ashanti mistresses to a bacchanal. We started with what I thought was beer in fluted glasses but turned out to be Piper Heidseck Brut and continued on wine, beer, scotch and various exotic Swiss liqueurs, as relays of waiters served platters of ham and cheese alternating with steaming cauldrons of groundnut chop.

Vicki, an aficionado of Louis Armstrong, played record after record from a massive jazz collection covering one wall, sitting with me alternately crying and laughing at her fate as the wife of the gross Maerz, a man with no visible redeeming features as he filled his belly and pinched any woman whose behind came within reach.

Late in the evening one of the Swiss stopped behind Vicki and reached inside her kenti cloth, slipping his fingers down her back and pulling back her brassiere strap to let it snap forward. She screamed in pain and scrambled out of the room to roars of Swiss laughter.

A few minutes later, as I sat dazed from what must have been several liters of champagne, Vicki crept back into the room, stalking her tormentor who stood, rocking from heel to toe, before a table filled with bottles and half eaten plates of food. As he rocked back she gripped one buttock between her hands and bit down on a large chunk of the flesh beneath the cloth of his shorts. Amidst raucous laughter Vicki escaped and the local British doctor, weaving and laughing, spread the wounded Swiss on a cocktail table and swabbed scotch on the wound.

"Need to have those hemorrhoids looked at old chap, what?" he said.

I had now begun to travel up and down the coast of West Africa from Gambia to Nigeria, not trying to sell anything, but seeking information on what conditions would be like as independence came to the British and French colonies which circled like pearls down from Senegal and around the Gulf of Guinea.

My territory ran in theory from South Africa to Morocco, but the French excluded us from their markets and the Belgians had a monopoly in the Congo. In effect I covered Gambia, Sierra Leone, Liberia, Ghana and Nigeria with occasional pro forma visits to the French colonies of Guinea, the Ivory Coast, Togo, Dahomey, the French Cameroon, Gabon and the French Congo. Spain's Equatorial Guinea was unreachable except by ship.

The only airline serving this route was West African Airways, a joint venture of several of the British colonies which operated a rickety fleet of DC-3s which rumor had it had been purchased from Paraguay. It was a paradigm for the wry witticism summed up by the initials WAWA—West African Wins Again. Schedules were meaningless. Maintenance seemed to consist of changing the oil and patching ancient tires.

The pilots were, however, superb. A collection of ex-Royal Air Force officers and Polish pilots who had escaped to fight in British units in the Second World War, they tended to be heavy drinkers, maintaining handsome African mulatto girlfriends in every port of call and subsisting on the black humor of fatalism. Crashes were surprisingly few but breakdowns endemic.

On one memorable trip I flew for almost a month to the Ivory Coast, Liberia, Sierra Leone, French Guinea and the Gambia. Abidjan, capital of the Ivory Coast, was known as the Paris of West Africa, a slight exaggeration. Although there were good hotels and excellent restaurants—as in all the French colonies—and the French African elites, known as *evoluees,* were generally much better educated than their British counterparts, these countries, too, functioned at a level of chaos difficult to imagine.

The transition from Abidjan to Monrovia, capital of Liberia, was mildly traumatic. It was as if one had traveled in a couple of hours from a bad imitation of provincial France to the black ghetto of Americus, Georgia, in about 1910. Suddenly you moved from limpid, singsong French, to a city where people spoke in the deepest of southern accents, and the police swaggered through the streets armed with rusty army surplus .45s on their hips, dressed like American policemen.

Liberia was founded by The American Colonization Society, an organization established in 1816 whose mission was to ship all blacks back to Africa. Congress appropriated one hundred thousand dollars to finance the project. After an abortive attempt to found a colony on Sherbro Island off the coast of Sierra Leone, an expedition commanded by Lieutenant Matthew Perry, later to become famous for opening Japan to American traders, bought land in what is now Monrovia for twenty thousand dollars. Free Southern blacks began to move in. The colony survived attacks by the hostile local Kru tribesmen with U.S. military help, and the unlikely project became a success of a sort.

The ramshackle wooden houses, unknown in the rest of Africa where voracious termites feasted on wood, sat on brick pylons as they did throughout the American south. The presidential palace dominated the center of the city, its garden filled with cement elephants, lions, tigers and giraffes. More often than not the single guard sat on the steps of the entrance dozing with his head resting on the tip of his American 1903 Springfield, a weapon so rust-encrusted it would have been equivalent to suicide to fire it.

Across the street a faded sign hung at a perilous angle, proclaiming the wooden building to be the Ministry of Commerce. Although I'd booked a room at the one local hotel weeks before, there was no record of it, and I was politely shown the door. After passing over several American dollars, the currency of the country, a taxi driver took me along back alleys to a rambling mansion overlooking the harbor.

Inside I was greeted by a large white woman with an uncanny resemblance to the German concentration camp guard, Ilse Koch. Wearing no make up, hair pulled back in a bun, she was a formidable presence.

"Wot you want," she said in a stage German accent.

"A room."

She started to laugh. "This not hotel. This whore house."

Behind her an anxious looking black man with a fringe of gray hair stuck his head out from behind a curtain. Desperate, I dropped into German, explaining that I needed a place to sleep, not a woman.

The black man, who turned out to be Hannah's husband, for that was her name, immediately poured forth a torrent of virtually unaccented German, pulling me into the bar, offering me a drink. He had been, he said, a steward on the German-America line for twenty years. His wife was one of the cooks, until the war stranded them in Liberia.

Pillsbury did virtually no business with Liberia, which was the most poverty stricken, primitive country on the West Coast, but I always stopped off for two days on my trips to renew what became a near-friendship with these two exiled 20th century Pilgrims.

I met the whores that evening over dinner, a collection of worn aging women of every European nationality playing out their string at the end of the line. They were patronized by high ranking Liberian government officials and some of the few American expatriates in the country.

There was one other tenant in the hotel. A slender Frenchman in his fifties who traveled the coast for one of the French trading companies. We shared a table.

"You know," he said over a bottle of excellent German Mosel, "I came out here more than thirty years ago. I was the only Frenchman in Liberia. You see that pipe sticking out of the harbor?"

A badly rusted cast-iron pipe rose out of the befouled harbor waters.

"I'll tell you how it got there. One day, the President called me into his office and showed me a tattered French magazine. Must have dated back to around nineteen-ten. There was a picture of a steam roller. A beautiful thing. Decorated with iron carvings. Painted scarlet. He said he wanted that steam engine. The roads in Liberia needed repairing."

He poured the last of the Mosel and ordered another bottle. "Well, he was right about the roads, and he wouldn't listen when I told him the steam roller was a little out of date. It had to be that very machine."

He sipped a touch of wine from the new bottle and gestured to the waiter to pour it. "So I cut out the ad and sent it to my headquarters. You have to remember, I was twenty years old. Mostly I sold razor blades, soap, cheap perfume and undrinkable brandy. This was the chance of a lifetime.

"It took months, but I finally got back a letter saying they had located one of the ancient machines and were putting it in shape. The president called in one of his many generals and ordered him to France to learn to drive it." He paused, staring into his glass.

"The big day came. The ship arrived with the machine sitting on the foredeck. And you know what happened?"

I shook my head.

"I suddenly realized that there was no way to unload it. Monrovia had no port facilities at the time. Cargoes were unloaded into canoes and rafts out in the open sea." Accra was another port without a harbor. In one of the more baroque incidents of my African experience, I was invited to dine on one of the ships handling our flour. A sedan chair waited on the beach. Four crewmen cheerfully lifted it and carried me out to a canoe waiting in the surf, depositing me dry-footed in the large dugout vessel.

"What did you do?"

"What could I do?" he asked with a Gaelic shrug. "I got six canoes, planked them over with heavy boards, closed my eyes and had them lift the damn thing off the deck and lower it very, very gently."

"And it sank?"

He shook his head. "No. It was a miracle. The sea was very, very calm. The boys did a superb job. They tied it down and brought it in to the little jetty. I arranged for planks to be laid and we pulled it up with ropes. The president was there with the general in his splendid uniform with all his decorations and a red sash. It had been some months since he had taken his driving course, and he was understandably nervous. The boiler was fired up and he engaged the gears."

"And?"

"He put it into reverse and drove it off the pier into the harbor. Voila," he said, pointing to the pipe. "There she rests for the archeologists of the twenty-fifty century. Of course, the president had the general shot."

His story reminded me of the French company representative in New York who said he had survived the summers in Ouagadougou by immersing himself in a barrel of water and sipping wine through a rubber tube attached to a keg.

I had already decided that the most realistic books on Africa were two nineteen-thirties novels by Evelyn Waugh, *Scoop* and *Black Mischief*. His wildest satire often turned out to be true.

Since the tribal groups cut across the arbitrary colonial boundaries, there was a certain sameness to the British and French West African colonies except that the plumbing tended to work in the British areas and the food was incomparably better in the French. I often drove from Nigeria to Ghana and back through the French colonies of Dahomey and Togo. In the British colonies crisp businesslike border guards wore wool shirts and shorts, long white socks and heavy British army shoes. Their cousins in the French areas were dressed in sandals, none-too-clean khaki shirts and shorts, kepis at a rakish angle and a Gauloise hanging from their upper lips.

At a lakeside restaurant in Togo one evening, my wife and I attracted the attention of four elderly Togolese at the next table. Finally, one of them rose and approached us, bowing formally, and spoke to us in impeccable German.

"My friends and I heard you speaking German. We all studied in your great country, and we would like to invite you to join us for champagne and desert." Togo had, of course, been a German colony until the end of World War I. We spent a pleasant two hours with the men, two doctors, an engineer and a school teacher. Their nostalgia for Germany belied the West African saying that the natives came into the presence of their British masters bowing, on their knees to the French and on their bellies to the Germans.

From Liberia I headed up the coast for Freetown, Sierra Leone, site of the finest protected harbor in West Africa. It was one of those anomalies of the colonial culture of West Africa. In the early nineteenth century, after Britain had outlawed the slave trade, it became a dumping ground for the cargoes of captured slave ships, since the British men of war were stationed there. Hence the name Freetown.

At about the same time reformers in England began sweeping the slums of London and the cities of the industrial midlands of prostitutes and transporting them to the colonies. Most went to Australia, but a fair number were dumped on the beach in Freetown. They intermarried with the freed slaves and their mulatto offspring became the ruling elite.

Freetown was also the site of Graham Greene's most famous novel, *The Heart of the Matter.* On my first trip there with Paddy Doolin we stayed at the famous City Hotel, a nineteenth-century building circling an inner courtyard. Handsome mulatto prostitutes promenaded on the covered walkways on all five floors.

The hotel was famous along the coast for its curious bar, made of some yellow metal which, when wet, would stain anyone who leaned on it. This mark was virtually impossible to wash clean. It was something of a badge of honor, and anyone you encountered along the coast with yellow elbows was one of the select few.

On that first trip Paddy and I, three if not four sheets to the wind at Saturday noon, had settled in for lunch when a roar of irritation rose from the diners. "Chicken curry, Severini," the assorted peddlers, oil drillers, diamond smugglers and ships' officers yelled. "There's no goddamn chicken in this curry."

Severini, straggled into the dining room to placate them, dragging his badly crippled left leg, a relic of the Italian army's war in the African desert, behind him. He was a great friend of Paddy's, and he alternated servility with snarls as he circled among the tables.

Meanwhile Paddy had disappeared. I glanced through the window and saw him circling behind the wall surrounding the hotel which was topped with broken glass. Among the shards stood a line of black vultures. I watched him approach one of the birds with a large stick of firewood and clout the unsuspecting animal on the head, grabbing it by the feet and throwing it through the open window into the dining room.

"Here's your fucking chicken," he yelled as the poor stunned bird's sphincter failed and it emptied its guts onto the dining room floor. The odor was so powerful strong men almost fainted as we staggered toward the exit.

On another trip I was scheduled to accompany our agent, a squat Brit named Robbie Robinson, to the opening of a new bakery upcountry. The governor general was going to preside, since the bakery was the property of a prominent Mendi chieftain. We started out very early one morning, the leading vehicle a Landrover carrying four bodyguards, followed by the governor general's 1933 Rolls Royce and finally Robbie in his Mercedes.

The governor general was resplendent in a white uniform, green sash, World War II medals, a sword and plumed helmet. He looked like a human peacock. It took six hours to negotiate a hundred and fifty miles into the deepest bush, before we arrived at the chief's principal village. He turned out to be an immense man who had attended Eton, as had the governor general, and Balliol. The bakery was probably the greatest thing that had happened in the village since the slave raids of the eighteenth century ended.

The chief's palace was an immense four-story mud hut, although he lived in a modern bungalow two miles from the village. Several thousand villagers were milling around the courtyard where great iron cauldrons of the ubiquitous groundnut chop, a sort of West African stew built on a base of peanut oil, bubbled away. It was enriched with giant black snails, lizards, fish, pork and anything else that moved. The snails, carriers of a deadly liver fluke, had to be marinated in lye for several days before being eaten.

The director of the feast was a short plump Englishwoman, the chief's chef. She emerged from a large iron-barred cage embedded in the palace wall, herding bearers with barrels of the local beer, carefully locking the cage behind her.

The chief and the governor general retired for a private lunch before the opening ceremony, and the Englishwoman, whose name was Grace, fed us an excellent omelet washed down with beer in her kitchen at the back of the iron provisions cage. Outside, the gathering was gorging on groundnut chop and beer, arranging impromptu dances and generally having a jolly time.

The chief and the governor general finally emerged, and the beplumbed representative of the queen disengaged his sword and whacked a ribbon leading to the bakery. The crowd surged in and began looting the shelves of bread. The governor general retreated to his Rolls and sped out of town as the chief, surrounded by burly guards headed down the road toward his house, leaving behind a milling crowd suddenly grown surly as the beer and food began to give out.

Suddenly half a dozen menacing looking tribesmen appeared before the open iron grill of the provisions area and began demanding the beer stacked in cases behind us.

"Oh, dear. This could be rather serious," Grace said. "Would you mind closing the iron gate, Robbie? I'll snap the lock on." Easier said than done. As Robbie tried to slam shut the grill, several of the tribesmen pushed against it. Suddenly the squat Brit exploded, landing a right to the chin of the biggest of the Africans and knocking him back into the crowd.

"Belt the bastards laddie while I close the gate. Otherwise we'll wind up in the pot." I landed a couple of punches on the slightly nonplused and very drunk Africans, and Robbie got the gate closed and locked. Suddenly the enraged multitude attacked. It was clear that the cage wasn't going to hold. I had visions of being impaled through the grill.

Behind us Grace began passing forward beer bottles and canned goods from the chief's treasure house. Robbie and I slipped them between the bars to outstretched hands. The crowd's mood changed instantaneously as the beer bottles were opened. Laughter and dancing began again as we emptied the storehouse.

"I think it's time you boys got underway, dearie," Grace said as the provisions gave out. "They're happy now but when they sober up a bit, they'll get surly again."

"Come with us, Grace," Robbie said.

"Ah, they won't bother me," she said, smiling. "They're like children, you know. I deliver their babies and nurse them and their wives. They'll go home and sleep it off."

The last stop on my tour was always the Gambia, a sliver of land along the Gambia River, the meat in a geographic sandwich with Senegal the bread. It was a pleasant place, sleepy, gentle, clean. A small hotel on the beach was the best accommodation in British West Africa and even the food was edible.

West African Airways flew into and out of the Gambia only once a week, so I was forced to spend six days there at the end of my trips. I swam, played tennis at the local club and was, over the years, drafted on the local cricket team patronized by our Lebanese agent.

On this trip I arrived at the hotel at the same time as a taxi dropped off a fat nondescript little man wearing thick glasses and carrying two very large suitcases. Jaroslav Krupa was Czech, and he spoke no English. At the hotel desk he tried in vain to make himself understood, finally asking if anybody spoke German. I agreed to translate, and he, in gratitude, insisted on buying me a series of beers which segued into wine with dinner, later shifting to his personal supply of Asbach Uralt.

Krupa, like most Central Europeans I have known, was a man with a fatalistic view of life tempered by a sense of humor which winkled amusement and simple pleasures out of the chaos of life. He was a mine of the black jokes I was later to encounter in Warsaw.

"I tell Russian story," he said that first night.

"A small bird is flying across the snow-covered Siberian steppe, cold, hungry and at the end of his rope. Finally, he falls to the ground and is gradually covered with snow. A cow comes along at this point and defecates on top of him. Revived by the warmth of the manure, the little bird sticks his head up through the pile, sees that the snow has stopped and begins to sing. At this point a wolf happens by, hears the bird singing and eats it.

"There are three morals to this story. First, because somebody shits on you doesn't mean they are your enemy. Second, just because somebody shows an interest in you doesn't mean they are your friend. And third, when somebody shits on you, it is never a reason to sing."

"What are you doing in Africa?" I asked as the second bottle of Beaujolais went down.

"I am toy salesman," he said, looking at me with a bemused smile. "And you?"

"I sell flour." His smile expanded into a wide grin.

"Herr Colleague," he said extending his hand. "We are in the same business." I thought no more about this rather strange remark until, two days and six meals later, Krupa suggested I come with him on an outing the next day, a Sunday.

We left quite early, picked up by a Lebanese in a Volkswagen bug, his small son riding next to him in the front seat cradling an automatic shotgun. The Gambia was a peaceful place, and I'd heard nothing in half a dozen trips about danger.

We headed out of town on the colony's one road, a twenty mile stretch to nowhere. After about three miles the driver, a silent surly man, suddenly brought the car to a wild stop, grabbed the shotgun from the child, leapt from the car and began firing into the trees which lined the road.

I ducked at the first shot expecting a horde of spear-wielding savages out of a Hollywood movie to slaughter us on the spot. As our driver stopped to reload I peeked over the rim of the window and saw the bodies of three monkeys, two still alive and writhing, on the ground under the trees. What looked like hundreds of others were escaping in a wild cacophony.

"Monkeys eat peanut crop," our driver explained, climbing back in. "Shoot, motherfuckers." A few miles further on, he again braked wildly and grabbed for the gun, this time firing into a group of white egrets peacefully standing on one leg in a stream which ran under the road, leaving a mass of bloody feathers floating on the muddy water.

The road came to an end at the gates to some sort of mining complex, an immense skeletal structure rising along the riverbed. Two typical West African guards in woolen socks, shorts and shirts, wearing little red fezzes and carrying long staves stood guard. Our driver parlayed with them briefly and several one pound notes changed hands. We were waved through the gates and the Lebanese drove us toward a small one-story cement block building.

He snapped the lock with a quick twist of a crowbar and Krupa and I entered. It was some sort of geological laboratory, walls covered with sample bottles bearing names such as Zircon and Aluminite. Krupa immediately pulled out a handful of small envelopes and began taking samples. He glanced over at me.

"You don't have envelopes? Here, take some of mine." I followed him dutifully through the bottles taking a pinch of each and writing what it was.

"Pictures," he said. "I need pictures, Herr colleague, but I am too fat to climb into that structure. You will please be kind enough to take them? I will send you copies since you do not have camera." I climbed through the spidery structure, following his directions, and snapped off three rolls of film.

We parted the following day at the airport, he taking a small French plane north toward Dakar and I heading south on West African Airways and home. I have before me now his card which he gave me as he left, admonishing me to look him up in Prague. I wonder how the toy business is there these days.

It was a twelve-hour flight home with stops in Guinea, Sierra Leone and Liberia before arriving in Ghana. Our pilot was one of the interchangeable Polish former military pilots, all known by the generic "Ski." He flew the ancient DC-3 with the same panache he'd used in the Hurricanes over London. We came down in Sierra Leone in an exquisite three-point landing and we were joined by a half dozen other West African traveling salesmen and civil servants.

One, Luke Lukehardt, who worked for the Goodyear Tire Company, was a noted wit. As we took off he yelled across the aisle. "Hey, Harper. The left engine is on fire."

"Yeah, sure Luke," I said, trying to curl up into a ball and sleep. The plane's sudden lurch yanked me awake. Black smoke was belching from the engine as Ski hauled away at the controls, turning it back toward the runway as we lost altitude at the speed of a falling rock. Somehow he got the old plane straightened out and headed back toward the airport behind us.

The wind always blew from the same direction. We'd taken off into it, of course, and were now headed downwind toward the immense bay. The tires locked and blew, skewing the plane to the left as we stopped about five feet short of the water.

Ski emerged from the cabin followed by his African copilot, one long white sock down around an ankle, sweat dripping from his bearded face. "Well, gentlemen, we made it once again. Let's go get drunk."

Unfortunately, we were the last flight of the day, and, when our wheels had lifted, the airport manager and his crew had bolted for town, leaving the tin-roofed concrete hut which served as a terminal locked. We trudged across the runway, a dozen forlorn men in sweat-soaked clothes, and watched as Ski used a length of pipe to break into the terminal.

He called Freetown and explained our problem as we gathered at the small bar. Ski poured a water glass full of warm vodka and stared at it morosely as a pimply-faced young British assistant district officer stood next to him, trying to hold a beer with two shaking hands.

"Where'd you learn to fly, Ski?" he asked.

"Polish Air Force."

"What sort of planes did you fly?"

"Spad."

"What did you do during the war?"

"Germans invade. We attack."

"What happened then?"

"Machine gun jam."

"What did you do then, Ski?"

"Pull saber and attack," the Pole said, lifting the glass and downing about a quarter of a liter of vodka in one long gulp.

Some months later a thick packet arrived in Accra with a Prague postmark. Inside were pictures of the Gambian mining complex and a note wishing me a *Froehliche Weinachten.*

Fifteen

A man who sells a worthless product at a high price for many years...himself.

The flour peddler's definition of genius.

Juan W. Barleycorn Jones met the ship as we docked at the port of Santa Isabel on the island of Fernando Po. How we got there is a convoluted tale. Pillsbury Mills had transferred me from the relative comfort of Accra to the teeming chaos of Lagos, Nigeria, after my first year in Africa. The course the new Ghanaian government chose after independence was crucial to what followed as the rest of black Africa gained its freedom from colonialism. Its leader, Kwame Nkrumah, studied for many years at black colleges in America, absorbing not only much of the philosophy of W.E. Du Bois and Marcus Garvey but also becoming a convinced Marxist.

He took over a peaceful small nation, a major producer of cocoa, rich in mineral wealth including gold. Its tribal problems pitting the coastal peoples against the Ashanti in the north had been brought under control by the British. A small, efficient army and police force assured public safety. A rosier scenario would be hard to imagine.

Nonetheless, between nineteen fifty-seven, when Nkrumah took over the country, and 1966, when he died in embittered exile, the country had gone through a decade of economic and political trauma which dissipated its fiscal surplus and alienated most of the people. A disastrous attempt to impose what Nkrumah called scientific socialism deteriorated into economic chaos and official corruption and left the economy in ruins as capital fled and the expatriate advisors to the inexperienced ministers were ejected.

Over the past thirty years the country has been wracked by a succession of military coups and financial disasters which have left the population in penury. In Ghana's wake, and accepting much of Nkrumah's Marxist rhetoric, the rest of Africa plunged into similar experiments in socialism, often as in the former French colony of Guinea, with extensive Soviet aid and similarly disastrous results.

I left Africa in 1960 and have had no further first hand experience there. However, it seems clear that the continent may well become, as Howard D. Kaplan says in his book, *The Coming Anarchy*, "the symbol of worldwide demographic, environmental and society stress, in which criminal anarchy emerges as the real strategic danger."

But all that came later. In the late nineteen-fifties, Nigeria was by far the most important country in my territory, its population of between eighty and a hundred million dwarfing the rest of the miniature countries about to become independent. In addition it sat on a huge reservoir of oil under the Ibo tribal region centered on Port Harcourt.

A series of disparate events led to my transfer. First, half the world away in Haiti, a son of our agent there, Gabo Khawly, had been very nearly killed by the dictator Duvalier's thugs, the Ton Ton Macoutes. Gabo and his four brothers had been assigned to support different political factions and his group had lost. In exile and at loose ends, Gabo had asked Pillsbury to find an agency for him.

At the same time I had been forced to fire our agent in Nigeria, a wizened alcoholic lecher named George Allen, at the insistence of our Godfather, the United Africa Company. George was simply too scruffy and too lazy for them to tolerate. The market was triple that of the rest of West Coast combined, and Bill Spoor had called me to New York to make me an offer I couldn't refuse: Become, with Gabo Khawly, the Pillsbury agent in

Nigeria while continuing to supervise the rest of the area. We would split the commission on sales of hundreds of thousands of bags of flour. Spoor set the commission at a level, which would give me an income virtually double my modest salary. It was clear they were willing to do almost anything to keep me in place. Nobody else wanted to go to Africa at any price.

Gabo, about my age with a masters degree in business administration from Georgetown, was a short, fat, unwashed character who spoke a kind of pidgin English overlaid with a heavy French accent. His French, however, was elegant, the result of a decade under the tutelage of French Jesuits.

I pointed out to Spoor and Gabo that Lebanese were anathema to the British. They were barred from the clubs which were only now, with independence looming, accepting token Africans with Oxbridge educations. Gabo shrugged. He had read the numbers and instinctively knew we were looking at a potential gold mine.

The deal was done. Using blackmail ruthlessly I managed to shake loose two apartments and office space from one of the shipping lines in the British enclave of Ikoyi and, with the United Africa Company's discreet pressure, was allowed to join the exclusive Ikoyi Club. This was a major concession since the lower middle class Brits who staffed the commercial companies and the public school boys of the colonial service shared an abiding hatred of the Americans who were blamed for dismantling their empire. They especially mourned the Paradise Lost of India.

I was eventually to be accepted into another, even more exclusive shrine to snobbery, the Lagos Yacht Club, when one of the members could find no other buyer for his little Hornet racing sailboat. Gabo, meanwhile, took an African mistress and submerged contentedly into the Lebanese community.

The partnership had perfect symbiosis. I was the outside man, doing the selling to the big British companies, giving lavish parties, stroking the British provisions managers and losing golf balls by the score to their buyers. Gabo kept the books and handled sales to the Lebanese and Africans. Between us, in a very short time, we had doubled, then tripled sales. Our commissions piled up at an impressive rate.

Before the first year was over, Bill Spoor convoked us to London for a meeting. Over a genial alcoholic lunch at Wheeler's he was effusively complimentary of our success.

"There is, however, fellas, just one problem."

We listened.

"You're making too much money."

"Huh?" Gabo asked, beady black eyes narrowing to slits in the yellow tallow of is cheeks. "What the fuck you mean, we making too much money, Beel? We work asses off in that hell hole. We earn every fucking nickel."

"Yeah, but you're both going to clear more than my salary this year. You gotta understand. We made a mistake when we agreed to that commission set up. You're gonna have to take a fifty percent cut, fellas. Hell, you'll still be rich."

I saw a budding dream of financial independence and retirement to southern Spain going up in smoke. Not Gabo, however. His usually servile demeanor toward Spoor had undergone a metamorphosis. His face was congested with rage. His voice rose into a hysterical soprano.

"You listen, you sumbitch, Beel. My father and grandfather your agents for sixty years. My father, he know old man Pillsbury. You try to fuck with my commission, he go to Minneapolis and he screw you like a chicken. You hear me Beel Spoor?" His voice rose to a semi-scream in the elegant confines of the restaurant. "You fuck with me, he have you keeled."

Spoor, six feet four of pure muscle, stared at the paunchy little man in disbelief. He paid the check and escorted us out, threading through the tables of disapproving stares, Gabo yapping at his heels in increasingly incoherent rage. I was horrified. Even with only half the commissions, we were going to make out like bandits. I could see Spoor terminating the agreement and my income cut back to a miserable salary. But Gabo wasn't to be denied. In the end Spoor backed off. Still another example of Harper's Second Law at work.

The following year we once again tripled sales. My income had gone from fifteen thousand dollars a year to close to fifty, a princely sum in 1958. Our expenses, by mutual agreement, were minimal. Since our money was held in New York accounts, we paid a miniscule tax in Nigeria. And since I was not a U.S. resident, I paid no American income tax. It was, in my father's inimitable phrase, a license to steal.

The price, however, was high. Gabo was right. We earned our pay. Lagos was a tropical hell hole, teeming with masses of diseased beggars, thieves and starving peasants thronging in from the country. The place was summed up by an exchange between the Duke of Windsor and the Governor General during a visit by the duke in the nineteen-twenties.

"I say," said the Duke. "Place is the asshole of the universe, wot?"

"Yes, your highness," the Governor General replied, "and Ibadan is twenty miles up."

My two-month vacations diminished to one as, in addition to the Nigerian agency, I continued the hair raising trips up and down the coast. A German friend suggested taking a couple of leisurely weeks off on one of their freighters which called at Lagos. Which is how we met Juan W. Barleycorn Jones, a native of Sierra Leone, who spoke fluent German, French, Spanish and English and was a leading businessman on the island of Fernando Po. The W. stood for Wilberforce, the nineteenth century Englishman who had helped abolish the slave trade.

He met each ship as it docked on the island with a sort of minivan and offered tours, not as he put it, for the money, but to escape the stultifying provinciality of the local Spanish colons. The island itself was an improbable sight, rising ten thousand feet out of the empty sea, a great green pimple covered with plantations on its fertile slopes.

The port of Santa Isabel was an Andalusian village transported to the Equator. A clean, somnolent, whitewashed garrison town of modest villas and squares dominated by small churches.

"The Spaniards are ignorant peasants," Jones, his name

pronounced "Hohn-nes" in the Spanish manner, said. "I studied law in Seville, and they all live in the twelfth century." His great-grandfather had owned a small coastal sailing vessel, an itinerant trader descended from prostitutes and freed slaves. Over the years he and his family had established trading posts up and down the coast. The Joneses were the Hanseatic traders of West Africa.

"This is where the Nigerians contract laborers live," he said gesturing toward rows of neat, conical, windowless, mushroom-shaped cement huts. "The local natives, the Bubis, won't work. Life is too easy. They fish a little. Pick bananas off the trees and breed. So we import the Nigerians. Only the men. And send them home after their two-year contracts are up."

As we climbed out of the banana and coffee plantations, the fauna changed to palm oil trees, then to fields of tomatoes, corn and, further up, wheat. Near the top, in the cool of ten thousand feet, orchards of pears, peaches and apples appeared. It was a simple paradise, neatly ordered, somnolent and gentle.

We had a superb Spanish style dinner of shrimp grilled in garlic, spiced rice and flan at Jones' villa. He drove us to the ship and stood with us on the bridge for a moment, staring out at the magic island. "It will all disappear in chaos and agony when independence comes," he said.

Jones and I exchanged letters over the years, until the early seventies when we lost contact. I read here and there of the bloody independence which came to Equatorial Guinea and Fernando Po, including a bizarre tale of homosexual love and murder at the American consulate in Santa Isabel.

Then, returning one day from my job as press attaché at the U.S. Embassy in Madrid in 1978, I found three black men sitting on my sofa. They were, it turned out, members of the Bubi government-in-exile of Fernando Po. The foreign minister, the defense minister and the commanding general of their resistance movement. Jones, killed in a revolt, had given them my address.

"He said you would help us, senor," the foreign minister said, speaking elegant educated Spanish. "We, the Bubis, are being massacred by the Fangs from the mainland. They have driven my people into the hills, burned the plantations and ravaged the island. No one will help us. You Americans must come to our aid."

It was a cry I was to hear many times over the years, always impotent to answer it. America, the land of unlimited opportunity, savior of the world's oppressed, had in reality become a large bag of idealistic flatulence. We talked into the night as my wife cooked a Viennese meal and the men told their tales of horror and slaughter. Next day I turned them over to the head spook at the Embassy and never saw them again. But all that was much later.

Meanwhile Nigeria headed for independence. Leventis had won the contract for a flour mill and the Harper-Khawly flour agency was headed for dissolution. I had made plans to leave a few days before the fateful day, having been warned by a Nigerian friend in the ministry of finance, Olu Omololu, that both Gabo and I were targets for prosecution for nonpayment of taxes.

I had met Olu on a French ship, the *General Mangin*, on which my wife and I had returned from a European vacation. We had spent two halcyon weeks aboard this vessel, which we boarded in Casablanca, drifting down the coast in a haze of Puligny Montrachet and Piper Heidsieck. Olu, who spoke no French, was returning home from sixteen years in English public schools and at Trinity College in Ireland without having seen his homeland. The only African on board, he was, with that careless xenophobic cruelty of the French, placed at a table by himself.

After two days my wife and I introduced ourselves and asked him to join us. He turned out to be a remarkable man, the son of a principal chief, a natural gentleman with all the graces of the Yoruba aristocracy combined with the manners of an upper class English education. His tolerance of British and French racism was a phenomenon which never ceased to astonish me. It was as if he simply did not notice.

We saw each other often and became close friends over the next year in Lagos, so I was not surprised one day when the president of the yacht club approached me with a curious proposition. After two years I was more or less accepted in this club. It happened because of an early sailing race which my crewman, a French nobleman of dubious sexual orientation, Andre de Margerie, and I had almost won. My little yawl, a racing machine, was equipped with a sliding board on which the crew sat to maintain it upright.

As we turned the last buoy, with an unbeatable lead over a catamaran, Andre moved to the very outermost edges of the board, perched there like a bird. At which point the wood, weakened by inner rot, gave way, dumping him into the water. By some miracle I brought the boat head on into the wind without tipping, with Andre, clinging to the railing and the jib sheet, half in the water, screaming at me at the top of his lungs. *"Vas y, Edward! Vas y! On peut toujours gagner!"*

We lost, of course, but our gallantry, or idiocy, won the reluctant admiration of the club members who gave us a standing ovation as we steered into the hard.

It was shortly before independence when the president, a high-ranking civil servant in the finance ministry, approached me. "I say, old boy. Omololu. Splendid fellow, don't you know."

I agreed.

"Friend of yours, no?"

"Yes."

"I wonder if you might," he hesitated, "you might approach him about becoming a member of the club."

I barely stifled the laughter which welled up within me. The yacht club occupied some of the choicest real estate on the harbor and was a prime candidate for confiscation. It had no African members. It needed protection.

"I don't think he's into sailing."

The president waved a languid hand. "Oh, I say, old boy. We wouldn't expect him to participate. Just be a member."

I broached the matter with Olu at the predominantly African club of which we were both members. He smiled and put his arm around my shoulder. "Of course, I'll do it. We plan to preserve the yacht club in any case, but sooner or later they're going to have to let in some Nigerians. Tell him I'd be delighted."

I arranged to bring Olu down for a turn around the bay. The nervous little boat was not easy to sail in the best of circumstances, and with a totally inexperienced and clearly terrified crew I almost turned it over several times. On the beach, Olu turned to me. "Look, I'll join this club. But please don't ever ask me to sail again. I can't swim, and that harbor is full of barracuda."

There were other reasons, aside from a prospective jail sentence, to leave. Our first son had been born in a low forceps delivery without anesthesia, my wife screaming at the top of her lungs, in a filthy British clinic run by a fat red-faced unhygenic butcher. With her normal stubborn courage she had refused to go to her mother in Vienna for the birth. But even she agreed that Nigeria, with its miserable heat and endemic diseases, was no place for young children. It was at this point that my first novel, *The Assassin*, was accepted by Berkeley.

My father had by this time invested a large chunk of my ill gotten gains in a filling station and three stores in a respectable lower middle class neighborhood of Atlanta. The complex was managed by one of my myriad first cousins and brought in, net, about eight hundred dollars a month.

On our last vacation from Nigeria we had toured Spain winding up in the dusty little tourist town of Torremolinos on the Costa del Sol. We were looking for a village house to buy. The owner of the Bar Central, an American named Sugarman who had amassed some capital while working on the American naval base at Rota, suggested I contact a former co-worker named Milton Epps at an even smaller and dustier town down he coast.

We drove down to Los Boliches one day after lunch and knocked on Milton Epps' door. He stuck an obviously sleepy head out and thus began what my wife came to call our Spanish Period. Milton, who Sugarman had neglected to mention was black, suggested we return at a more civilized hour, and when we showed up at four p.m. he met us turned out in impeccable khaki shorts and Spanish fisherman's sandals. With him was a lovely young woman, blonde with immense violet eyes and what turned out to be a Rumanian accent

She had, Milton told me as he mixed gin and tonics in his kitchen, been the mistress of a Rumanian count who had deserted her on the Tangier ferry. Milton had taken her in as, I later discovered, he was likely to do to any stray who showed up on his doorstep.

It was to the little stone house he bought and renovated for us that we came after leaving Nigeria. We took ship on a British freighter headed for the Canary Islands one day before independence was declared. There we transferred onto a Spanish vessel which put us ashore in Malaga.

In the summer of 1960 we and Milton were the only foreign inhabitants of Los Boliches, although Fuengirola, a kilometer up the road, had a budding foreign colony of self-conscious non-painting painters and non-writing writers. They talked in short, convoluted Hemingwayesque sentences, smiled rarely and cultivated a *Weltschmerz*, well watered with the local wine which sold for about a nickel a liter at the illegal exchange rate.

Over the next year the Costa del Sol began what was to be an incredible metamorphosis from a sleepy backwater of medieval villages to, within a decade, a fair clone of Miami Beach. Milton tried in vain to convince me to buy large chunks of coastal land, but I was not stupid. There were several hundred kilometers of pristine beach, true, but no water and no electricity. I did not buy.

The two villages, Los Boliches and Fuengirola, sat at the foot of a corniche rising up through terraced fields to Mijas, a village which had been discovered by the Scandinavians and the English some years before. Their tasteful villas were scattered among the parasol pines which covered the slopes.

Within weeks of our arrival, the first foreign bar, the Delphin, opened in Los Boliches. Others followed. A Swede bought a chunk of beach down the road and each week planeloads of blonde young women, rarely a man among them, would descend to lie semi-nude on the beaches as the young men of the villages gathered like flies to honey. The sight of some short, wiry fisherman with the features of a Saracen pirate, swaggering down the street with a six-foot-tall blonde Swedish amazon on his arm was common.

Ever a sensualist, I developed the habit of having the local barber, Ermenegildo, shave me at noon in his little shop across from the church. He charged three pesetas, less than ten cents. Ermenegildo was probably about forty-five, totally lacking in upper teeth. He had been crippled when the net of his fishing boat snagged on a submerged rock and mangled his leg. His sons still fished the sea for the pitifully few fish left.

One, Pepe, came in one day with a dazed, exhausted look on his face.

"Where were you last night, Pepe?" his father asked.

"With the Suecas," his son said.

His father paused, razor a quarter of an inch from my throat, a look of ineffable envy on his worn features. "And what did you do?"

"You know the little wooden house they have built on the beach?" the boy asked.

"Yes."

"Well, Papa, we stripped off all our clothes and went inside." I felt the slight nick of the razor on my chin as the barber stood transfixed.

"And?"

"There was a fire, Papa. A fire hot as the embers of hell. And rocks on the fire. They threw water on the rocks and the steam rose up to burn our faces. And then," the boy now had a wild look on his face, "they beat each other and us with branches from the fruit trees. Afterwards, we left the hut and jumped into the sea."

"In January? In January you jumped into the sea." Only the crazy Scandinavians swam in the frigid Mediterranean waters in winter.

"It was cold, Papa. God, it was cold. But," his eyes glittered at the memory, "they took us up to the hotel and warmed us in their beds."

"Juanita will kill you."

The boy shrugged. "Who will tell her? And, anyway, she would not believe them if they did. Who would believe such a story?"

We remained in Los Boliches less than a year. Our second son was born in Malaga, and we faced the reality that there were no schools worthy of the name. Even worse, the little towns were filling up with foreigners, remittance men and bums mostly, with some sort of artistic pretense.

There was also a large homosexual community, among them a mildly famous painter named Maurice Grosser. He was a contemporary of Hemingway and Fitzgerald, a graduate of Harvard whose father had owned a department store in Montgomery, Alabama. Maurice was a painter, describing himself as the maker of the best Corots since the master himself. He had, in his youth, traveled through the south painting portraits of young black boys, still his favorites.

His book, *The Painter's Eye*, still strikes me as one of the most perceptive introductions to the mysteries of painting extant. Utterly without cant, and written in plain English, it explains the visual as best one can with words. His contempt for the totally unreferential abstract art which had begun to dominate the art world was immense.

"Wallpaper," he would mutter at a reproduction of Jackson Pollack. "Man couldn't paint a hand if his life depended on it."

One evening I stood at the Delphin Bar, sipping a Manzanilla at the expense of a wealthy British homosexual whose Rolls was parked out front, when Milton blew in and surveyed the scene.

"Well, Edward, I see you're the only man here tonight," he said.

I think that may have sealed my decision to leave the little nirvana of Los Boliches. For me there was tennis, sailing and interesting companions, but my wife was from a great city and missed the cafes, theater, opera and restaurants it offered.

We were, in addition, a bourgeois household encased in an ambiance increasingly bohemian. I shut myself into a small attic room each morning for a five-hour stint on my current book. Nobody was allowed to interrupt. The afternoons were given over to tennis, sailing and sitting in the cafe in Fuengirola's main square, drinking Manzanilla, eating the magnificent olives of the region and watching the clones of Hemingway and Fitzgerald talk about their great novels and verse which never seemed to materialize.

Although I was the only published writer, my pitiful suspense novel was regarded with contempt as were my conservative winning ways at the floating poker games. One morning, my wife came up the winding staircase in mid-morning with Milton in tow.

"I have to see you, Ed," he said dropping into a cross-legged posture on the floor with the grace of the dancer he had been, staring up at me with the innocent, guileless stare he affected.

"What's up Milton?"

"You know Jeff and Judy?"

Jeff and Judy were two rich Australians who lived in a large villa on the winding road to Mijas. They gave lavish parties and seemed to spend all their time in cafes and the budding nightclubs of Torremolinos, while a covey of Spanish servants ran their house and cared for their two children. Jeff was handsome in a fey way, and Judy was a thoroughly homely overweight blonde who giggled a lot.

"Well," Milton said, "a week or so ago Judy came home and found Jeff in bed with the houseboy."

I started to laugh.

"It's not funny, Harper," Milton said. "She threw him out of the house. He came down the mountain and asked me to put him up. He hasn't got a pot to piss in, you know. The money is all hers. So I did, but he got worried about her up there alone with all the gigolos around, and he asked me to go up and sort of take care of her. Hold her hand." I'd seen Milton driving Judy around in her little MG convertible and thought nothing of it.

"So?"

He stared up at me, half smiling, half embarrassed.

"You're kidding," I said. "You didn't sleep with her?"

"Well, yes. My first time with a woman." He laughed his high-pitched laugh. "Wasn't all that bad, really."

"Congratulations, Milton."

"What do you mean, congratulations? Jeff denounced me to the governor general for adultery. I've slept with every boy in the village and nobody ever said a word. I sleep with a woman, and the governor gives me twenty-four hours to leave the country."

I accompanied Milton to the local notary where he signed over to me the hundreds of acres of land and house he owned. "Otherwise they'll think of some way to steal it," He said. And I drove him down to Gibraltar and waved good-bye as he took the ferry to Tangier.

It was to be five years before I saw him again. By that time the Costa del Sol had exploded in a frenzy of development. Milton's land was worth several million dollars.

Sixteen

Long live death!

Battle cry of the Spanish Falange

I read George Orwell's *Homage to Catalonia* somewhere to the west of Kwajalein atoll one day in the fall of 1945. A thousand or so soldiers with enough points for discharge occupied the hangar deck, allowed up once a day in groups of one hundred to the flight deck. I had participated in one of the boxing smokers staged to break the monotony the night before, and my left eye was still swollen almost shut. I thought then, and still do, that it is one of the most evocative memoirs every written, and I decided, one way or another, to visit Barcelona some day. I was to live there for five of the most pleasant years of my life.

We arrived in the port, a wife, two babies in diapers and an English bull terrier, Grisbi, who looked for all the world like a white pig, all crammed into the bouncing box of a Citroen 2 CV, its springs virutally dragging the ground.

These were halcyon years. Our income was enough to live in modest luxury amidst the poverty of a Spain just beginning to emerge from the destruction of the Civil War. Within days we had found an apartment in what had once been a separate village, Sarria, at the base of the mountain towering over the city. Tibidabo.

Sarria, with its covered market, medieval square, cafes, bodegas where you brought your own bottle to be filled with superb Rioja at a nickel a liter, was to be the center of our existence. Within a month we had bought a one-time summer house far up an unpaved road with a twenty percent grade. The road followed the right of way of a narrow gauge railway, long since torn up and used to make weapons in the war.

Casa Omphaloskepcito, whose address was: Torre del Bosque, Fon del Mon, Barriada Ideal de Vallvidrera—the House in the Wood, at the End of the Mountain in the Ideal Valley of the Glass Blowers—sat on the edge of a great parasol pine forest overlooking a panoramic view of Barcelona. It had been condemned to destruction a decade earlier by a city planning commission which intended to extend the forest throughout the semicircle of the mountains ringing the city.

As was often the case in Spain, nothing had come of the plan, and the *barriada*, or neighborhood, of some fifty small summer houses was left in peaceful limbo. We bought the three-bedroom house for five thousand dollars, and for another five installed central heating, furnished it and opened up an unused cistern on the upper lot to make a swimming pool. A German engineer married to a Catalan and I, over a period of two years, persuaded most of the other members of the little community to contribute to buying a new pump to replace the fifty-year-old machine which lifted water to a common cistern at the top of the mountain. It was their first experience with democracy in action, and only the urgent need for water managed to submerge their natural anarchy. This hilarious experience made me wonder at the time if Spain would ever manage to become a successful representative democracy. As usual, I was wrong.

The barriada was a sort of scruffy paradise. A young woman, Rosa, soon appeared who offered to work as a maid for ten dollars a month. And I made a call on a Catalan businessman whose name had been given to me by one of my tennis partners in Torremolinos. Miguel Lerin was then in his mid-fifties. His reddish blond hair, blue eyes and ruddy skin marked him as a Catalan type.

"My ancestors were Visigoths," he once said, only half joking. He dressed in handmade suits and Lobb shoes and spoke an impeccable British-accented English. Lerin worked in the family business which occupied a warren of cubby holes in an eighteenth century building in the Calle Fernando just off the Ramblas. His eighty-year-old father ran the customs brokerage with an iron hand, and Miguel had very little to do.

He became, over the years, a close friend despite an immense gulf in our perceptions of the modern world. Miguel lived in the late nineteenth century, a bourgeois sybarite, a former officer in the fascist army during the civil war and, paradoxically, a passionate Catalan nationalist despite Franco's brutal suppression of the region's language and culture.

If genius is the ability to hold two contradictory thoughts in your head at the same time, then Miguel was certainly one. As with most of the Catalans I came to know, he had a wicked sense of humor and among friends would ridicule the "old man", Franco. He and his class nonetheless lived in deadly fear of his death, expecting a revolutionary outbreak at least as brutal as the civil war of the thirties.

Memories of that war impregnated virtually every situation in Spain in these years. It had ended two decades earlier but the memory of its brutality was as fresh as newly spilled blood. I learned Spanish reading *Don Quixote* and three novels about the war by a Catalan writer, Jose Maria Gironella: *Los Cipreses Creen en Dios, Un Million de Muertos* and *Ha Estallado La Paz.*

Although written from the perspective of a conservative Catholic, the books were in many ways an apolitical scream of agony at what the country had suffered. The excesses of both sides, as Orwell documents so eloquently on the left, and the superb war reporting of Hemingway and others detailing the atrocities of the right, make the rebuilding of a modern democratic Spain all the more remarkable.

Gironella's novels, in the grand sweeping tradition of nineteenth century European literature, lay bare the social fabric of an essentially feudal society torn up by its roots and replanted in the mid-twentieth century. It was a plant watered with blood.

The tennis club into which Miguel Lerin introduced us was

the first and most exclusive in Spain. Barcelona 1899. Twenty superb clay courts, two large swimming pools—until the year before segregated by sex—and a sixteenth century clubhouse of understated elegance. I bought a family membership for one hundred and fifty dollars and sold it ten years late for fifteen hundred. The last price I heard for such an "action" was twenty thousand which is one measure of the vast distance this country and its proud, talented people have traveled in the last quarter century.

Lerin owned a mansion at the top of the mountain above our little cottage. His plaything, he called it. A retreat from his immense apartment in town where his wife was queen. After four children, he explained to me, she had informed him that she wanted no more sexual relations. Since she was a devout Catholic, contraception of any kind was out of the question. Miguel had shrugged and accommodated himself, as most Spanish men did in any case, with a series of mistresses, usually widowed middle class women, secretaries or high class courtesans.

He would often walk down the winding path through parasol pines to join us for afternoon tea, a bizarre figure in a superbly cut business suit, highly polished shoes and, in winter, a homburg. One day in the spring of 1962 he brought with him a handsome young French girl, the daughter of a business acquaintance who had come to Barcelona to learn Spanish.

He called me aside in our small garden as Lisl and the young woman set a table for tea. "I have done something wholly dishonorable, Eduardo," he said. I waited.

"Jacqueline has been staying with my wife and me in town until her little apartment is painted. She is a fascinating young woman, unlike any Spanish or British woman I have known." He had spent two years in London many years before.

I agreed that she seemed highly intelligent and well educated.

"Yes. But she is more than that. She is open, joyous, genuinely sensual," and he dropped into Spanish, something he rarely did with me, to achieve the poetic intensity he sought.

I almost laughed, thinking back to Milton and Los Boliches.

Maybe I should buy myself a soutane. "You didn't Miguel," I said.

"Yes. Well, Eduardo, I'm really not sure how it happened."

I glanced across at the young woman who seemed to wink at me across the small garden.

"Hopefully, she was not a virgin," I said.

Lerin looked stricken. "Dios, mio. I never thought of that." He was fifty-five and she twenty-one. When he died in 1990 at eighty-three they were still together.

Through Lerin and membership in his exclusive club we were accepted into Catalan bourgeois society. Despite a rather rigid social hierarchy, dominated by the old nobility, the club, a mirror of Spain's contradictions, was curiously egalitarian. Its members were mostly Franco supporters but there was a minority which had fought on the Republican side in the Civil War. It was a totally taboo topic, never discussed.

Years later, when I had returned to Spain as press attaché at the embassy in Madrid, Juan Cebrian, editor of *El Pais,* attempted to explain Spain's egalitarianism.

"Eduardo, you know the expression *'hidalgo'*."

I nodded. "It means a petty nobleman."

"Literally," Cebrian said, "it means *'hijo de algo'*, the 'son of somebody.' For centuries when Spain was chasing out the Arabs and uniting itself, any man who could afford a sword, a horse, a wide hat and a cloak, could call himself that and be accepted. It is still a tradition here."

Lerin himself occasionally told stories, usually bitterly humorous, about the war which he had spent on the southern front. As a Catalan he was immune to much of the fanaticism of the Andalusian and Extremadura extremists who reflected the harsh realities of their regions. Catalonia was, after all, the richest part of the nation, its best educated, the closest to that Europe which derided Spain as "Africa beginning at the Pyrenees."

One summer in Andalusia during the war, when the heat was a hundred degrees in the shade, Lerin related, the German officer who was attached to his unit protested the agreed habit of the fascist and republican troops to stop fighting from noon to five to avoid the worst heat of the day.

"We will attack," the German said, "at three o'clock after lunch when they are all asleep."

"I protested," Lerin said. "The front was a stalemate. Nobody could advance without unacceptable losses, so we sat where we were and let the crazies in the north fight their suicidal battles. But if we attacked at noon they would have to retaliate. Think of the discomfort!"

"What did you do?"

Lerin shrugged. "We found him a very appetizing whore who got him drunk every day at noon and made immense demands on him until the sun went down."

Lerin was an infamous dandy, a nineteenth century boulevardier and dilettante, regarded even by his friends as a figure of ridicule. His name had entered the vocabulary of the Catalans as the epitome of "cursi", affected and pompous. At a formal dinner one night he so irritated his table mate, a gentleman from Gerona, that the man burst out, *"Eres mas cursi que Lerin!!"*

"I *am* Lerin," Miguel said, indignantly.

In the many years I knew him, I found him a witty, intelligent, tolerant, generous friend, and I still mourn his death.

In addition to the political differences of the Spanish members of the tennis club, there were two other, even more hostile, subgroups. These were first the Jews who had fled Germany and been given asylum by Franco between 1938 and 1945. One rumor, which I have never been able to confirm, had Franco being descended from one of the Jewish families which converted in 1492 rather than be driven into the Sephardic diaspora. These families, known as Marranos, Christians for five hundred years, still occupy a separate niche in Spanish society. Whatever his reasons, there is no question that no Jew in Spain was ever shipped back to Germany and none were refused asylum. Tens of thousands transited the peninsula to safety and many remained.

Then there were the Nazis. As World War II wound down hundreds, if not thousands, of middle echelon party members made their way across the Pyrenees bearing portable wealth. Others escaped after the surrender. Among them was Otto Skorzeny, the rescuer of Mussolini, who became a successful Madrid business figure.

The hatred of the two groups was unbridgeable, but hormones and youth occasionally took over.

The beautiful blonde daughter of one of the prominent Nazis fell madly in love with the heir to the Loewe leather company, a Spanish Jewish family with a long pedigree. They looked like twins as he, too, was blond and blue-eyed and could have posed for an SS recruiting poster. The young people eventually won and were married in what must have been a very stiff ceremony.

I wrote and sold two more novels in Barcelona, *Janine,* which Berkeley brought out as a paperback and *No Damn for Hantha,* a serious political novel about Ghana. Again Berkeley bought the paperback rights but, unable to find a hardcover publisher, did not bring it out.

My hubris had, however, been aroused by the sale of *No Dam for Hantha.* Instead of continuing to write about my shady hero who took on difficult and dangerous jobs and lived on his sailboat, long before John D. Macdonald's McGhee and his houseboat, I turned to serious fiction. Nothing sold. In order to bring in a little more money, I began at this time to translate a series of abstruse Catholic religious textbooks, by a father Augustin George, from French to English for Fides Publishing in South Bend, Indiana. Aside from being admonished for using the King James Bible instead of the Catholic version, I faked being a Catholic layman fairly well.

It was an odd job for an atheist, but they paid $750.00 for each volume which took me about six weeks to do. This financed our periodic voyages to Vienna and the overnight trips to Perpignan we made to avoid having to get a permanent residence visa.

It was during my translation of the *Life of Paul* that I realized the remarkable similarity between Karl Marx's thought processes and those of this founder of the church. And, of course, Paul was the first tent preacher, promising the Corinthians everlasting life, passing the plate and heading for Thessalonika with the same message before they could start to die. His epiphany on the road to Damascus served as paradigms for other religious hustlers from Joseph Smith to Oral Roberts.

We were living a sybaritic existence. Our two young children were placed at age three in the *ecole maternelle* of the local French *lycee*, thanks to the intercession of the French consul general, one of my tennis partners. There they were cared for from 9:00 a.m. until 5:30, fed a four-course meal and taught impeccable French. Looking back it must have been a confusing time for them since their mother always spoke to them in German, I in English, the school in French and their school friends either in Castillian Spanish, or, more likely, Catalan. It's probably a miracle they didn't wind up mutes, and at one point the school's director ordered my wife to stop speaking German with them as it "was confusing."

A season ticket at the opera for ten performances of second echelon companies from around Europe was fifty dollars. The average theater ticket was a dollar. One could eat a five course meal at the Finisterre, then the best restaurant in town, with champagne, superb Spanish wines and fifty-year-old brandy for ten dollars for two.

Each winter we took our two infants and maid with us to the Catalan resort at La Molina in the Pyrenees for three weeks of skiing.

All this on the income from a two-pump filling station and three stores in a lower middle class section of Atlanta.

It was a paradoxical life, however. Our Spanish friends found it quaint that I, an American, would live in what to them must have seemed a hovel. Most seemed to attribute it to some sort of artistic perversity. Writers, painters, artists of any kind were treated with a kind of respect and tolerance reserved for the half-witted in some primitive societies.

Although the Civil War shadowed every aspect of life in Spain in the nineteen-sixties, there was almost no overt evidence of repression except for the ubiquitous presence of the Guardia civil with their tricorn hats and insolent strut. The population, cowed and exhausted by one of the bloodiest revolts in modern European history, was sullen but obedient. And the upper classes lived in a kind of repressed terror of what seemed to be the inevitable renewal of hostilities when Franco died.

When a fanatical, and typically quixotic, Communist activist named Julian Grimau was arrested in Barcelona and subsequently either jumped or was thrown to his death from a window in the city's police headquarters, the Spanish establishment was embarrassed. Nobody had been killed for political reasons in a decade. They were finally becoming mildly respected.

I have no idea what really happened, but Lerin insisted that, according to his sources, Grimau, terrified of the torture he thought awaiting him, in fact did jump.

"He was a silly romantic," Lerin said with a shrug. "We knew every member of the cell he was visiting. He would have been escorted to the French border, secretly, and pushed over had he not jumped. As it is, we have once more aroused all the leftist fanatics and given them ammunition to attack us." I didn't altogether believe him, but there is a certain logic to what he said.

My mason, an illiterate anarchist who had fought throughout the war and spent years in a detention camp, was a man of immense dignity and wit. He agreed that Grimau was a fool. The communists had never had much real support in Catalonia, and after their betrayal and slaughter of the anarchists, by far the largest revolutionary party in the region, they had none.

I asked him what it was like after the war. In the beginning, he said, the guards in the prison camp had attempted to break the prisoners' spirit but had soon ceased. Life was hard but not impossible.

"They were Spaniards like us," he said, shrugging. "Cruel but human." He reminded me of a school teacher I had met near Almunecar, a town east of Malaga, when we were looking for our first house. This man, a known political activist in the Communist Party, had lost a leg in the war and had been exiled to a village tucked away up in one of the remote valleys leading down to the sea. He spoke French and agreed to help us look for a house. At one point he had said, with great wistfulness, that he would like to see a bullfight once again.

I arranged to go with him to a corrida in Malaga where Ordonez, one of the greatest matadors of all time, was fighting. I'd never seen a bullfight, and my friend explained its intricacies as well as the philosophical underpinnings of the spectacle. It was a bad day for the fights. The wind flicked the capes capriciously and even the great Ordonez chose caution over bravado. The picadors enraged the crowd as they weakened the bulls excessively and the matadors cut short their more flamboyant, and dangerous, turns.

Then, in his final fight, Ordonez seemed unable to take the whistles and jeers of the crowd. He stood like a statue and dared the bull, cape fluttering in the wind, controlling the animal superbly until a gust flicked up the cape, giving the animal a clear view of his tormentor. A horn went into Ordonez thigh, lifting him high in the air. It was, however, a superficial wound, and the great man waved away his entourage and made the kill, blood seeping through his suit of lights.

The crowd and my school teacher friend went wild with delight, forgiving him and his companions everything. He was awarded the tail and ears by the judges, who might otherwise have been lynched, and paraded around the ring with them before collapsing.

While all the drama was unfolding I noticed at one point a half dozen men in blue coveralls who seemed to be the janitorial crew. They cleared away the dead animals, leveled the arena between fights and generally did the scut work of the spectacle. They seemed utterly oblivious to the bulls, joking, smoking cigarettes, drifting casually out of the way as the animals banged their frustrated skulls into protective barriers.

One, after a bullfighter was unable to put away a bull that had sunk to his knees, blood spurting from his mouth, took a large hammer and chisel and calmly walked over to the animal, placed the chisel against the base of his skull, whacked it with the hammer and watched the bull topple over. I've seen the same thing happen with other bulls, standing and swaying, their heads hanging low, after the matador had repeatedly jammed the sword home without succeeding in making the kill.

I was forced to watch many more fights over the years with friends visiting Spain and, as press attaché later in Madrid, with journalists looking for spectacle. I was never able to penetrate the mystique which so fascinated Hemingway. The sacrifice of the bull, for that is essentially what is taking place, is clearly some sort of antique virility rite. As with all violence, it has an erotic quality which is reflected in the faces of the spectators, particularly the women. It was one of the few aspects of Spanish culture and society which left me cold.

I reread Orwell's *Homage to Catalonia* after some months in Barcelona, once again struck by the vividness of his experiences at the front. He at one point crouched in a trench above the town of Huesca, whose lights flickered in the distance, and promised himself he would return for a coffee there once the war was over.

I took a weekend off and followed in his footsteps to the grange from which he observed Huesca, and in which he was later wounded, intending to write an article "A Coffee in Huesca." It was an absorbing journey through a landscape of semi-deserted villages and towns devastated by war. Sietamo, where Orwell was treated in a hospital, was a ruin, its people ragged, undernourished and sullen.

As I looked down on Huesca from the grange, I lost heart at the tragedy of it all, cut short my expedition and headed my Rosinante, the little Citroen Deux Chevaux, south toward Zaragoza through a landscape out of *Don Quixote*. One ancient medieval town after another, all dominated by immense churches devastated during the Civil War, goats and children entering through broken doors, roofs caved in, priceless murals unprotected on their walls.

After some three years in Barcelona our financial situation began subtly to degenerate. The area of my modest real estate investments had begun to change. As the lower middle class white population drifted toward the suburbs, their small houses were taken over by black families. The tenants in the stores became black. The Jewish merchant who ran a grocery store across from my little complex first put up iron grilles, then hired an armed guard and finally sold his shop.

My redneck cousin, who ran the filling station for me, was very nearly killed in a holdup and refused to return. My father urged me to sell while I could, but it was hard for me to believe that, simply because the neighborhood had become black law, and order would not in the end prevail. These people were, after all, of the same class as the whites who had left.

My father then hired Will Davenport, my onetime surrogate father and painting companion, to run the station. Will had gone on the wagon some years before, and although now an aging and gentle giant, he was a menacing figure, face and shaved head covered with razor scars, souvenirs from his many drunken Saturday night binges and brawls. He lasted six weeks. Three young men came into his station one night, killed his dog and beat him into submission with crowbars. His hospital bills were larger than those I paid for my cousin.

It was neither the first nor the last time that I allowed ideology to overcome common sense, and by 1964 I was forced to lease the property to a black taxi company which was run by the local franchise owner of the illegal lottery concession, the famous "bug." The station was never robbed again. The Spanish idyll was coming to an end. I began to look for a job somewhere in Europe.

Seventeen

The history of nations active in international politics shows them continuously preparing for, actively involved in, or recovering from organized violence in the form of war.

Politics Among Nations
Hans J. Morganthau

I got there at seven-thirty a.m. It was a Saturday. The Champs Elysees was deserted, except for a few Algerians who had turned on the fire hydrants and were sweeping the streets with brooms made of twigs. The concierge watched suspiciously as I walked up to the second floor and found a room marked Radio Free Europe.

I settled down on the floor and opened the International Herald Tribune. The advertisement for a writer-editor had stipulated nine a.m. I was the first one there. By eight o'clock another half dozen people were in line. By nine the number had swelled to fifty and wound around the hall and down the stairwell.

At 9:30 a tall, lanky character in an ancient tweed jacket, unpressed chinos and unshined shoes, tie hanging limp from an unbuttoned collar, appeared and unlocked the door with trembling hand and closed it behind him. Ten minutes later, coatless, he opened the door and motioned me inside.

"Coffee," he said, waving vaguely toward a percolator. I poured a cup and sat down across from him. His desk was piled high with letters.

"Name?"

I told him and he began sorting through the pile aimlessly until I reached across and plucked mine from among the mass of paper. He smiled faintly and settled back on his spine, feet on the desk, to read it.

We talked. For an hour. Two. Three. About politics, women, our war, the Soviet Union, the Cold War, Vietnam, French versus German wine, the South—he was from Tennessee—and God knows what else. His name was Lucien Agniel. He had gone ashore in Normandy and fought all the way to Germany. Working for one American organization after another, he'd managed to stay in Europe for the next twenty years. An international bum, much like me.

He was now the deputy programming director of Radio Free Europe, an ostensibly private but CIA financed radio complex with headquarters in Munich. It broadcast to Poland, Rumania, Czechoslovakia, Hungary and Bulgaria in their native languages. The job up for grabs was editor-writer in Special Events, a subsection of the news department, but independent of it, which recorded world leaders voices and wrapped news stories around their words. The theory of this technique was that, since large numbers of Eastern European intellectuals spoke German, French and English, they would find our broadcasts more credible if we included the original words of the leaders.

As he probed through my background, raising his eyebrows slightly at my two published novels, Agniel began to confide in me. The station was a rat's nest of intrigue, he said. Everybody was at each other's throat. The émigrés who did the broadcasting hated each other, particularly the Hungarians and Rumanians, but all the others had centuries old grievances against each other as well.

There were several waves of emigrants which made for dissension within the different branches as well as between them. Fascists and monarchists dominated the first waves. Apostate communists, usually idealists who saw in socialism the holy grail, were the next wave, purged as the Eastern European countries had been taken over by apparatchiks slavishly loyal to the Soviet Union. Internecine strife among our target countries later produced periodic infusions of ideologically incompatible younger recruits. RFE was a comedy, wrapped in a tragedy, surrounded by idiocy.

"Worst thing is the Americans," Agniel said, refilling his cup with coffee the strength of a small atomic reactor, drinking it black. "They get infected by the émigrés and start their own intrigues. Only they're amateurs at the game. Right now the programming section is in a war with the newsroom which sort of works for us but really is independent. What we're doing is using Special Events to make them look bad. We've got seven people in the SE, and they've got about a hundred in the newsroom. They're ponderous and slow. We're quick and dirty. If we can convince the émigrés to use our stuff with the quotes in the original languages, we'll make the newsroom look incompetent, and we can take it over in reality as well as in name."

"And whoever takes this job is going to be the tip of your lance."

He grinned over the coffee cup. "You got it, son. Think you can handle it?"

"Sure." That was the last thing I was, but I also had nothing to lose.

"Okay," he said, sweeping all the letters on his desk into a heap on the floor. "Let's get the hell out of here and have a drink."

He paused in the hall and stared at the army of hopefuls waiting. "Sorry, folks. The job's been filled."

Over lunch in a workers bistro in the Rue de la Boetie Agniel explained that the present head of Special Events, a bearded Englishman named Michael Morden, was about to be fired. If I worked out over the first three months, I could move into his slot. My salary would be about ten thousand a year with a housing allowance.

Within two weeks we had arrived in Munich and been assigned a transient apartment. It was very much like the foreign service. The government's hidden hand was everywhere visible. While only the top executives were officially "witting"—that is, knowing of the CIA involvement—everybody was aware that the millions being spent in the low slung buildings abutting the Englishcher Garten were not financed by the nickels and dimes of the school children of America as one poster would have it.

We were told to go out on the local economy and rent our own housing within the allowance stipulated for my job. "At your grade you'll have to settle for a small apartment," the Bavarian in charge of such matters said. "This is the agency we use. It's run by my brother-in-law. He'll fix you up."

Like all Austrians, my wife held the Bavarians in contempt, considering them coarse, ignorant, beer drinking louts. Nothing like stereotypes to simplify life and add a little zest. After one session with the brother-in-law she began to look on her own. Within days she had found a small house in a newly-built subdivision, Bogenhausen, just within our allowance.

We now met the first of the many intrigues which infested the organization. The housing manager, enraged that Lisl had gone to someone other than his brother-in-law, informed her that we were not entitled to have a house, but an apartment, despite the fact that the price was the same. It would not be good for morale. He was taking the house, he said, and assigning it to the head of the Bulgarian station manager who outranked me. We could have one of the brother-in-law's apartments.

Lisl shrugged and said there was no problem. She could arrange another, bigger, house in the same suburb for the Bulgarian. But the house she had found was hers, and if he tried to take it away from her she would point out to his American superior that he was not only incompetent and incapable of finding decent housing she had located within days of arriving but probably corrupt as well. She smiled as she said it.

The man, used to dealing with hungry, cringing exiles, caved. The story was soon common knowledge, and the head of the Hungarian desk, a charming old aristocrat, made a point of congratulating my half-Hungarian wife on her genetic courage as he kissed her hand.

Within a couple of months the bearded Brit was eased out, and the campaign to destroy the newsroom's reputation being waged by Agniel and his chief, a former Westinghouse Broadcasting executive named Gordon Davis, began in earnest. Had Lou and I realized that Davis was a blustering pusillanimous ass, we might have conducted the campaign differently. As it was we attacked.

It is in the nature of a bureaucracy to be slow, and RFE had over the years developed a culture of easygoing inefficiency. The cafeteria was open twenty-four hours a day and at any time it was half full of employees, usually sitting and chatting over schnapps or the preferred poison of each of the émigré nations. Polish vodka, Wyborowa, was the favorite.

This laziness of the exiles was essential to Special Events' campaign, since our stories were short and crisp, ideal for radio and easy to translate. Thirty seconds of DeGaulle in French, eviscerating the current British prime minister, preceded and followed by four paragraphs summing up the event. We took DeGaulle live off the air and wrote the story from the Agence France Press wire, making five copies of the audio and script and running it by hand to each of the émigré stations within minutes.

The newsroom was staffed largely by former newspapermen, many cynical Australians escaping from their dreary continent to the fleshpots of Europe. Politically they tended to be part of the nutty left fringes then popular in Europe. And they were, to a man, ferociously contemptuous of their American bosses.

Their copy tended to be long and involved, harder to translate than the short crisp sentences I'd brought with me from my days on the United Press radio desk. By monitoring radio stations around Europe and the United States, Special Events was soon able to score "beats" time after time. The fact that the newsroom chief editor, Gene Mater, was cordially hated by all the exiles for his abrasive arrogance helped in this backstairs war.

Obviously, our work was peripheral since it hinged on being able to capture the voice or some other usable sound to hang our story on. Nonetheless, it provided a potent weapon in the interminable intrigues which swirled around the confused old retired general who ran the place.

Agniel also branched out. One of his more bizarre gambits was to send me along with a mad, alcoholic half-Czech, half-Yugoslav writer on the Czech station on a tour of Yugoslavia. RFE didn't broadcast to Yugoslavia, but Tito's successful defiance of the Soviet Union was envied and admired by our audiences. My companion and I were to travel across the country accumulating interview tapes which would later be broadcast with translations.

It was, to put it mildly, an insane scheme. We went without journalistic visas to a country which, though much less oppressive than the Soviet Bloc satellites, was nonetheless a solid tyranny, controlled by the omnipresent police. To this day I have no idea why we weren't immediately arrested as we crossed the border. Possibly our spooks had explained our trip to their Jug counterparts and gotten tacit acceptance.

More likely the Yugloslavs were simply stunned by our audacity. Or maybe they didn't even notice us among the mass of tourists beginning to descend on the country. In any event we crisscrossed the place in my ancient Opel for three weeks from Dubrovnik to Zagreb, interviewing with increasing confidence everybody we met from waiters to hotel managers to people in cafes. We finally cornered a couple of policemen and spent two hours with them in a cafe talking about crime.

At one point I looked at a map and traced what looked like a short cut across the rugged Bosnian mountains. The road, never good, grew more and more narrow until we emerged into a clearing where a young boy played a hand-carved flute to his flock of goats. A haunting scene, probably not much different from ancient Illyria. We became mired in mud, and, as if from nowhere, a group of Yugoslav mountaineers surrounded us. Wordlessly, they disappeared and returned with four mules, dragging us out of the swamp and turning the car around, pointing back the way we had come.

Our last night we wound up in Banja Luka, a grim industrial city, in a dilapidated hotel. We ate and drank at the communal table. My companion, in many ways a typical Eastern European intellectual, had spent the trip terrified of being arrested. Now, fortified by wine and slivovitz and on his way out, he became increasingly aggressive. I understood nothing of the discussion, but it was clear that he was being more and more patronizing and insulting the drunker he got. Suddenly things turned ugly, and one of the ham-handed local workers rose and reached for my friend's throat. I intervened, and we were saved from mayhem by an English speaking school teacher. I dragged my blitzed collaborator off to bed.

Next day he told me he had been pushing for the return of King Peter to the throne. I headed for the border by the shortest route.

Good personal relations with the various émigré desks were crucial in our combat with the newsroom, since they were the vital element in the station's success or failure. Lisl's Hungarian connection was useful. I had the good fortune to win the station's men's doubles tennis tournament with a young Polish announcer, Joe Petacek, upsetting the Czech dominance of several years. The celebration that followed still gives me a headache in retrospect. And the Bulgarian, our neighbor in Bogenhausen and a charming gentleman of the old school, was aware that Lisl had obtained his house for him and was appropriately grateful. So much for political philosophy and substance in the real world of petty intrigue.

The exiles ran uncannily to stereotype. The Rumanian chief, Bunescu, was held in universal contempt by the other émigré station managers. His servility to the American management was summed up by the following exchange:

General: "What time is it, Bunescu?"

Bunescu: "What time would you like it to be, General?"

Many of the Rumanians were monarchists who had served in the degenerate King Carol's army in the thirties, an army whose officers were more famed for their corsets and lipstick than for warlike qualities.

Jan Nowak, the head of the Polish station, was his antithesis. He had repeatedly parachuted into Poland during the war, carrying messages to the resistance, and was a man of immense physical and moral courage. He fought a brutal battle to increase his margin of independence from the station's American policy makers who imposed ideological content on the broadcasts.

The Hungarians were circumspect without being servile. In one notorious incident, the son of one of the senior commentators had begun to interpose the word "heroic" before any mention of the Vietnamese Communist Viet Cong in his news broadcast. Controls over content were handled by a separate organization of native speakers who monitored all the broadcasts. It was, however, in the nature of the organization that these "controllers" were often related or even married to the broadcasters. The young Hungarian was undone only because a Hungarian-speaking member of the American embassy in Budapest happened to hear one of the broadcasts and bring it to the attention of the General.

The babble of languages led to endless misunderstandings and not a few bitter jokes. One described a man "who can speak twelve languages and can't think in any of them." Another lampooned the character who announced, "I am spiking twelfth lenguagis, zee best of wich is being Inglish."

The exiles were also adept at what I've come to call the Eisenhower Gambit. During his presidency, the General was accustomed to make statements which were often so elliptical and foggy as to defy understanding. He was universally regarded, by the verbally adept press, as a second-rate mind who spent most of his time on the golf course.

Recent memoirs have painted a somewhat different portrait. He played golf in the afternoon but stayed up until midnight reading reports and documents. Unlike the benighted Nixon, who protected fools, he cut the throat of any subordinate who caught a breath of scandal with the quiet ruthlessness of a Tuscan assassin. When confronted by his press attaché, Jim Hagerty, with embarrassing questions from the press, he grinned and said, "don't worry, Jim. I'll go out and confuse them." Which he did.

On one memorable occasion he instructed Hagerty to go out and tell a bald-faced lie. "They'll catch me at it, Mr. President," he said, appalled. At which point Eisenhower, putting an arm around his shoulder with that genial grin he affected, said: "Better you than me, Jim."

As Guicciardini put it so well: duplicity is the essence of government. It was understood that alliances in the RFE environment were based on pure, immediate self-interest, and treachery was normal behavior.

Before my arrival at RFE the biggest event in the station's history was the Hungarian uprising in 1956 which was ultimately put down with much loss of life by the Soviet Army. It tended to mark and inhibit the station's actions until the fall of the Berlin Wall, since REE's broadcasts were blamed for raising false hopes among the Hungarian freedom fighters that the United States would intervene in their favor.

In retrospect, and with a little caution, Lou and I could probably have stood off the newsroom and possibly had Gene Mater's scalp in the end. Hubris got the better of us. Mater's enforcer was a hulking giant named Koch who swaggered through the halls like an SS *Obersturmbahnfuehrer*, intimidating by his size and a deep-throated growl. He terrified my staff of four German women and two writers and generally was a disrupting influence.

When one of the writers resigned in the face of the pressure, I hired as his replacement a six-foot-four-inch Irishman named Jack Farrel. He was a gentle character, red-haired, with the lean long-muscled body of a natural athlete. His only journalistic experience was as a copy boy with the *New York Times*. He came from a family of cops and would have made a good one himself. But somewhere along the line he had conceived the idea of becoming a newspaperman. He'd left the army in Europe and was kicking around on the verge of starvation when he came aboard. Jack was barely adequate as a writer, but I didn't hire him for that. During his interview I'd asked him why he hadn't become a cop.

"I don't like violence," he said. "When I was growing up I was always the biggest kid around. Anytime a bully was giving the other kids trouble, they'd make me fight him. Later on, I'd be the one in the bar to take on anybody who started picking on my buddies." He shrugged. "I was pretty good. Quick hands," he said looking down rather sadly at his scarred paws the size of hams. "Finally I just got real sick of it." He reminded me of a character in a Eugene O'Neill play.

I hired Jack for the same reason his friends had dragged him to bars. On his first day at work, Koch came over to Special Events with some cooked up complaint, and I took him out to introduce him to Jack who stood up to shake hands. They were about the same size, but Jack was a slab of muscle and Koch was mostly lard. He was a blustering bully but also an intelligent man. There was something serious about Jack. A sort of quiet strength. Koch began to avoid Special Events after Jack came on board.

It wasn't long before we all realized that our quiet giant had a serious problem. He was an alcoholic. A nonaggressive but hopeless case. He was also regarded with great affection not only by all of the Special Events staff but by the exiles, many of whom were borderline alcoholics. We carried and protected him when he was on a bender which happened about once every two weeks. My staff was now a more and more beleaguered group, but morale soared as we gave the newsroom fits.

At the weekly general staff meetings, Agniel and I began to stick it to Mater, unsubtly underlining our coups and their gaffes. It was a mistake. Gene Mater was a part of the bureaucratic web of the place, a ruthless infighter in the internecine wars. Lou's hubris made him overreach. Mater mobilized the gray little men who ran the administration, the head spook and the Rumanian and Czech station heads, in a campaign to get Lou.

He suddenly found himself isolated, deserted by the treacherous Gordon Davis who lacked the courage to stand up to the power. Lou finally resigned to take a job at *U.S. News and World Report*.

I was suddenly all alone. Gordon Davis had disappeared off the scope, scrambling to save his job by servility, as Mater pressed his campaign to take over Special Events. He sat down with me one day and made an offer which I should have accepted. If I would recommend that Special Events be joined with the newsroom, he'd guarantee me my job. I was good, he said and he'd let bygones be bygones. Otherwise it was open warfare.

Out of the foolish pride which has often guided my actions, and because I despised and distrusted Mater, I refused. From then on the knives were out. Special Events received virtually no support. Our access to the international wires was impeded, the newsroom set up its own quick reaction group and staffed it twenty-four hours a day, and, most important, all the émigrés realized that Special Events was in a war it couldn't win. Their support evaporated.

The end came swiftly. On a Saturday, Jack had interviewed Averell Harriman at the airport on some conference he'd attended during a stopover at the Munich Airport and, in editing the tape had inadvertently reversed it in resplicing it, a simple error and one anybody used to working with tape would have caught instantly.

We routinely handed over our tapes to the newsroom after writing out stories, and on this weekend the deputy news editor, Tom Bodin, a tall, wispy young man with an Ivy League arrogance, called me at home and peremptorily ordered me into the office. I'd had a martini and was mellowing out, so instead of telling him to perform pederasty on himself, I went.

He played the tape and began screaming at me, face inches from mine, about the incompetence of me and my staff, a bunch of drunken half-wits as he put it. I hit him in the gut, really leaning into the punch, and for a minute I thought I might really have hurt him, since he folded up like an accordion and writhed on the floor gasping for breath. You have to be careful with a gut punch with people who are out of shape.

He gradually began to breathe normally and got to his feet, sidling past me out of the newsroom. A few hours later Gordon Davis came by my house and told me the general was going to fire me summarily. I should go into the office and talk to the head spook, a man named Kaufmann, who really ran the place. I did, but before seeing Kaufmann I placed a phone call from my office to the chief correspondent of *Der Spiegel* magazine, which had been calling for Radio Free Europe to be dismantled, and offered to spill my guts about the organization. Before I hung up I heard the telltale click of the listening device we all knew were wired to our phones.

Kaufmann, a typical spook, well tailored, mild mannered, self-effacing, the very model of an accountant, offered me a coffee and leaned back in his chair. "You realize you can't go around belting people?" he said.

"Yeah."

He tented his hands and looked me in the eye. "The general realizes you must have been provoked," he said. "So we're willing to give you generous severance. Six weeks. Does that sound fair?"

"No. I've got a two year contract with six months to run. I want it paid out. Plus you pay the way for me and my family back to the States."

"And if we don't meet your terms?"

I grinned. He'd heard the tape of my phone call.

Two days later Kaufmann gave me a check for the rest of my contract and the equivalent of tickets to the United States. "This payment is being made on the assumption that you keep your mouth shut," he said.

"Is all this going into my security file?"

It was Kaufmann's turn to smile. "The Agency doesn't operate that way, Harper. As far as we're concerned you're not a security risk. Just impetuous." He came around the desk and shook hands. "You provided a little entertainment in a very dull job. Sorry I couldn't save your ass. Good luck." For some reason, I always got along well with the spooks.

Four days later we opened the little house in Barcelona, and I faced a bleak future. I was forty years old with a checkered career behind me, no prospects and very little money.

Miguel Lerin who, over the years had become a close friend, realized our predicament. He invited me to lunch one day after one of our tennis matches, none of which I'd ever managed to win, despite the fact he was twenty years older, and made a suggestion.

"The American Chamber of Commerce in Spain is just about to replace its Secretary General," he said. "He's a Catalan with American citizenship, and we've discovered many irregularities during his tenure. In fact, the Chamber is in very bad organizational shape. We need a real American to run it. The pay is modest, eight thousand dollars a year," an excellent if not princely salary in Spain at the time.

I took the job of course, after meeting with the board in Madrid. The ten men around the table represented some of the most important companies in Spain, among them a Domecq from the wine and brandy empire, the head of the Ford Motor Company and the chairmen of several banks. The meeting was followed by a three-hour lunch, and I headed back to Barcelona, the chamber's headquarters.

The offices were located on the top floor of one of the magnificent nineteenth century buildings on the Ramblas, overlooking what had once been the hotel which had housed the *POUM*, the anarchist group for which George Orwell fought. Some fifteen people worked in an environment resembling a scene from Dickens. Several antique Underwood typewriters represented the only modern note. There was one telephone on the desk of the deputy director, Martinez, who sat in solitary splendor outside my immense office.

Papers were strewn across the desks, but nobody seemed to be doing anything. Coffee cups and trays of pastries were seeded among them, along with the small, thick bar brandy glasses. It was ten o'clock in the morning.

Martinez, whom I had met earlier, introduced me to the staff, about half of whom were out of the office on various errands which I later realized meant sitting in the cafes which line the Ramblas.

The next eight months were in many ways a comedy only Spain can produce.

The purpose of the American Chamber of Commerce in Spain was to supply information on import and export opportunities to American and Spanish firms which were members. Martinez had explained that he went through the correspondence and handed out the routine inquiries, saving the most important for me. He had established a habit of inviting me down for a coffee and brandy, morning and afternoon. One day he was late and I encountered the postman with a large bundle of correspondence which he deposited on Martinez's desk.

Two senior clerks pounced on it. I took it out of their hands, virtually by force, and dumped the contents on my desk. There were dozens of letters requesting information on a myriad of topics from wine purchases to the sale of fertilizer. Half an hour later Martinez marched in to my office and began gathering up the letters, apologizing profusely for causing me a problem.

I told him that henceforth I would look through the mail first. He started to protest, then shrugged and agreed. That afternoon about ten inquiries appeared on my desk. The next morning a half dozen. We had another talk.

"Senor," he said. "You can't possibly want to see all the mail."

I did and I would. Nothing happened. For several days a dribble came across my desk. The mailman never seemed to come to the office. Finally, I stationed myself outside the entrance to the building, stopped him as he entered and accompanied him up the ancient elevator. At the top floor the senior clerk awaited him. I took the bundle of mail and invited the mailman into the large office which housed the staff.

We had our first staff meeting. In my distinct, slightly ungrammatical, Spanish I informed one and all that the mail would be brought to my office each day and that nobody was to touch it before I had looked through it. I would dismiss any employee who disregarded my orders, an empty threat since nobody could be fired in Franco's Spain short of an attack on the boss with an axe. I then took the mailman into my office and gave him a hundred peseta note, a fair chunk of his weekly wage, and told him he was to give nobody the mail but me. A regular tip would be forthcoming if he did as he was told. I left an unstated menace in the air if he refused.

Martinez was enraged, his dignity and authority fatally wounded. Plus which, he probably was going to lose a very lucrative part of his income which, I had already figured out, came from selling the import-export information to members and nonmembers of the Chamber. He would, he said, protest my highhanded measures to the board of directors.

I handed him the phone and suggested he call the president. One of the things I'd been hired to do was stop the sale of information by the previous secretary general to favored clients. When he was fired Martinez had simply picked up the scam. In the end, Martinez, a consummate realist, accepted the situation, knowing that he would be there long after I was gone.

Our offices covered virtually the entire floor of the building and had been there for some seventy years since the founding of the organization. Ancient files, piles of books and the general detritus of more than half a century were stuffed in various nooks and crannies. I closed the office for two days and we went through the mass of paper, obsolete office equipment and books in the dusty, oak-paneled library which were long since out of date. Martinez then sold off most of the junk, and with the proceeds the entire office descended on one of the beach restaurants and spent an alcoholic afternoon gorging on excellent Spanish champagne, lobster and paella.

Among the things to be sold was a 1911 edition of the Encyclopedia Britannica in mint condition, bound in velum and printed on onionskin. I paid ten dollars for it, rationalizing my guilt with relative ease. Corruption was infectious. It now sits before me in a handmade bookcase with a second edition of Webster's Unabridged Dictionary open on its slated top, retrieved from the garbage dump when USIA replaced it with its vastly inferior successor.

One of my first tasks—after cleaning up the office, repairing broken furniture and instilling as much discipline as any Spaniard was likely to accept—was to visit the six branch offices of the Chamber in Burgos, Valencia, Sevilla, Granada, Madrid and Malaga.

I chose Valencia first, sending a letter announcing my arrival to the local secretary general since I had not been able to reach him by telephone. I arrived in that beautiful city in mid-morning. The offices, much as in Barcelona, were located in an ancient building of stunning beauty. The concierge, upon being told who I was, led me to Chamber's suite.

Office hours were from ten to one, the ancient brass plaque proclaimed, but the concierge said that, in fact, the offices were never open to the public. He would, if I liked, telephone the secretary general, he said, opening the immense oak door with a key the size of a small shovel. Inside was an elegant, impeccable set of rooms lightly covered with dust. An outer office with four antique desks, another of the ubiquitous Underwoods—which probably dated from 1910—a large library furnished with leather bound books and beyond this the suite of the secretary general with a superb view of the harbor.

A half an hour later this worthy arrived. Short, fat, bearing, as did many Spaniards, a striking resemblance to El Caudillo. I'd already found my letter among the neat piles of unopened correspondence on his desk.

"My apologies, Senior Secretario," he said, wiping perspiration from his face. "If I had known you were coming I would have set up a board meeting. As it is, we will meet them tonight for dinner at my club. Now, you must allow me to invite you for lunch."

He took me to one of the port side bistros where he ordered a Lucullan feast. Into the second bottle of a local white wine, as fine as any I've ever had in France, I leaned across the table and asked him an indelicate question. Why did he have no staff? Why was the office unmanned? Valencia had one of the largest memberships of any regional office. How did he maintain his membership without any visible means of giving help to members?

He looked puzzled. "Are you not aware, senior, why we join the American Chamber of Commerce?" I admitted that it was beginning to puzzle me why four thousand businessmen would pay the rather hefty membership fee each year for what amounted to a nonexistent service.

"But senior, we join because we know that when the revolution comes again, as it assuredly will, your gunboats will come into our ports and rescue us and our families."

Back in Barcelona I asked Martinez to set up a lunch meeting with my predecessor, the Catalan who had acquired American citizenship and been fired for peculation. He turned out to be a man of immense charm. Intelligent, subtle and clearly amused by the invitation. He knew from Martinez all of my reforms.

I asked about the gunboats. He laughed. "One of my predecessors came up with that one. It works better every year as Franco ages.

"Harper," he said. "It will be interesting to watch you evolve. You will start as all Americans in this country. Energetic, organized, addicted to efficiency. Faithful to their wives. And gradually, over the years, you will be overcome by lassitude. Your priorities will change. You will relax. Your blood pressure will diminish. You will take a mistress."

"I couldn't support one on what they're paying me."

He shrugged and spread his hands out, palm upwards. "The correspondence can be very profitable. Let me tell you a tale about one of our compatriots. Some years ago one of the large American glass factories, recognizing that Spain would soon recover from the civil war, bought a controlling interest in a local manufacturer of bottles. A small company, run by a family, which had fallen on hard times because its bottles were consistently flawed.

"The American company sent over a manager who had been taught Spanish. Unfortunately he knew nothing of the country and soon had antagonized not only the company president, elder son of the family, but the workers as well. The major glass kiln continued to turn out flawed bottles. Sales were in a precipitous drop. Finally the manager, who had begun as an engineer, shut down the kiln and imported from the United States all the material to refinish the inside of the kiln. It was mid-summer, my friend, a hundred degrees in the shade.

"This man, short, stocky, red-haired and with a crew cut, stripped to his shorts and entered the kiln. For ten days he worked, bringing in helpers in relays, carefully refinishing the clay lining of the kiln. Nobody had ever seen anything like it. A manager, an engineer, working with his hands like a peasant. The president was horrified. His father and grandfather, now a very old man, came to remonstrate with the American who listened politely and continued to work."

"So what happened?"

The Catalan smiled. "The story has a happy ending. The factory began to produce good glass. The workers, strangely, had ceased to laugh. They began to admire this strange man. They even began to work a little harder for him.

"He has been here ten years now. His wife has left him, and had has married his mistress. There are rumors that he is living beyond his means and has been skimming profits. The Spanish owners are tolerant. He is not greedy. The factory has quintupled production, making them rich. It is understandable that this man, with a modest salary, should take a little for himself. But the Americans will audit him soon. If they are good, they will find out, fire him and replace him with another fanatic. And Spain will have to begin to teach him all over again."

I visited all the other regional offices with similar results, except in Sevilla where one of the Domecq family was president. The Domecqs are descendants of a Scottish trader, who began in the sherry trade, and over the centuries they have become the most important wine and brandy producers in Spain.

The story told in Spain is that when Henry Ford spent some time at the Domecq estates, he turned to his host upon leaving and said: "Well, Jose, I may have more money than you do, but you live better."

As he entered the Domecq Rolls, his host is supposed to have turned to a Spanish friend with a smile and said: "Well, Henry is half right."

The Domecqs had no need of the chamber. Their commercial tentacles had for years understood and exploited the American market. Tio Pepe was synonymous with sherry, and their Fundador brandy was giving the French a run for their money. He agreed to be president of the board as a favor to the American ambassador. And he used my visit as an excuse to give an immense black tie dinner for more than a hundred people on his estate. I have before me the embossed invitation which convoked this gathering.

The eight months I spent as secretary general were a fascinating time, and my Catalan predecessor was probably right. I was popular among the Spanish members. My Castillian had improved significantly. My southern manner and manners were more attuned to theirs than most Americans. I would, indeed, have relaxed, played tennis daily at my club, taken a siesta after a two-hour lunch, and begun, discreetly, to tap into the cornucopia of corruption open to me. And, in order to conform to the mores of the nation, have taken a mistress.

Helas, as the French say, I chose another path.

Eighteen

What we hold is, to speak frankly, a despotism; perhaps it was wrong to take it, but to let it go is unsafe.

Pericles
Quoted by Thucydides in
The History of the Peloponnesian War.

"Are you willing to serve in Vietnam?"

"Yes."

I was once more facing a foreign service panel, this time for the United States Information Agency, the propaganda arm of our government. A friend from my Paris days was now a senior officer in this adjunct to the Department of State. The United States Information Agency was at the time, 1967, deeply involved in an attempt to "win the hearts and minds" of the South Vietnamese people. There were two schools of thought on how this could best be done. One held that, with time, skill and patience, we could convince them to accept the tenets of American democracy. The other, crudely put, stated that "if you grab 'em by the balls their hearts and minds will follow."

As the war escalated in violence, USIA began having trouble recruiting people to serve on its propaganda teams in that unfortunate country. My marriage had begun to come unraveled over the past couple of years as my Viennese wife wished, with ever more desperation, to come to America and begin a life as a suburban housewife. She was then, and has remained, one of the great American patriots, embracing the country with uncritical eyes and open arms. She had become increasingly unwilling to accept my risk taking and addiction to personal honor at the expense of a little practical servility. She was, in short, a classic central European survivor locked in the embrace of a southern Cyrano.

My joining USIA and going to Vietnam, where wives were not allowed, would give her some breathing room in her beloved America and both of us a chance to reevaluate our marriage. I was looking forward to it. My theoretical training in diplomacy in France had taught me that war was indeed, as Clausewitz postulated, diplomacy by other means. The judicious use of force went with the turf of being an imperial power.

Although I had been overseas during the years when our involvement began, the geopolitical logic of the Kennedy and Johnson administrations, led by such moderate liberals as Dean Rusk, Robert MacNamara and McGeorge Bundy, seemed impeccable. The North Vietnamese, supported by Russia and China, seemed poised to take over not only South Vietnam, Cambodia and Laos, but also the revolution-ridden Malaysia and a defenseless and corrupt Thailand. The Philippines were fighting an increasingly effective Hukbalahap rebellion.

A Soviet takeover of this string of countries would have put them athwart the Strait of Malacca between Singapore and Indonesia, cutting the Japanese supply line to Middle East oil supplies. It would also have left the fragile regime in Indonesia, a country with more than one hundred million people with oil and mineral resources essential to an exponentially expanding Japanese economy, at their mercy. In 1965 a communist coup had come within an inch of taking over this country.

It was Japan's occupation of Indochina in 1941, with the tacit agreement of the French Vichy government, as a prelude to invading Indonesia, that led to the U.S. oil and scrap metal embargo. And it was this embargo, designed to strangle Japan economically and force it to cease its campaign to dominate southeast Asia, which caused them to attack Pearl Harbor. All this flowed from the need to control the key to naval supremacy in Southeast Asia, which lay in Cam Ranh Bay in Southern

Vietnam, the finest deep water harbor of the region. Unfortunately, complicated interlocking scenarios such as these are difficult to convey to the population of a mass democracy, just as the dangers of Nazi expansion in Central Europe could not be explained in the late nineteen-thirties.

American diplomats and military strategists, looking at the map—and confronted with continuing Soviet adventures, such as the emplacement of atomic missiles in Cuba in 1962, and the brutal suppression of the Prague Spring in 1968—felt it was necessary to confront what seemed to be another expansionist thrust into an area vital to the interests of America and its allies.

Had we known then of the growing tension between Russia and China, or that the North Vietnamese were, in fact, as wary of Chinese domination as of the United States, our policy in Southeast Asia would have been different.

But we knew none of these things. Prudence dictated denying strategic dominance of the region to a surrogate of the Soviet Union. Thus throughout the Kennedy-Johnson presidencies, and well into the Nixon-Kissinger years, our leaders pursued a strategy designed to block North Vietnamese expansion to the south.

Nixon's prescient article in *Foreign Affairs* in 1968, suggesting that—in contradiction of all his previous virulent campaigns against communism—now was the time to seek an accommodation with the Chinese empire, was our first recognition that we might be able to drive a wedge between the two giant Marxist powers. Nixon—never a true ideologue, always an opportunist in the mold of a Talleyrand, Palmerston or Bismarck—was fortunately the one American leader who could bring off this about-face.

Little did we know then that Russia and China had been drifting ever more rapidly apart since 1959, when Khruschev refused to share atomic secrets with his ally. The Chinese were ripe for an open break. But all this was in the future when the USIA recruiters routinely approved my application for a mid-level position.

My guru in the Agency, Ward Kirchwehm, was a senior

counselor and head of policy in the film production unit. Kirchwehm had begun his career as a local employee in the American Embassy in Paris in 1952, entered the career service, and clawed his way to a rank one notch below the grade from which most ambassadors were chosen. The USIA film unit was headed by George Stevens junior, son of the famed Hollywood director, and a man with no other qualifications than the name he inherited from his father.

Kirchwehm arranged for me to take over as policy officer for Africa while I presumably awaited assignment to Vietnam. Stevens, who was a rich, laid-back, socially prominent dilettante wired into the democratic part establishment, was later replaced by Bruce Hershensohn, producer of the film on John Kennedy's funeral, *Years of Lightning, Day of Drums.* This powerful documentary contributed mightily to the myth of Camelot.

Hershensohn, who later ran unsuccessfully for the U.S. senate in California, was a political animal considerably to the right of Ashurbanipal. He was also an utterly charming naïf who took over the film program with the intention of doing battle with the evil empire of Moscow wherever he could find it. In pursuit of his aim to use films as a dagger in its heart, he set up a chart with all the countries of the world listed in a column on the left and across the top a line of numbers from one to ten.

Kirchwehm and his five regional policy directors were convoked into Hershensohn's office for a meeting. Bruce was one of the most ingratiating and persuasive men I've ever met. He was stoop shouldered, slender bordering on the emaciated, and with a face so much the caricature of a Jew he could have played Shylock without makeup.

He showed us his chart and indicated that the numbers represented the degree of risk of each country "going communist", with one being the least risk and ten indicating that it was in the Soviet Union's pocket. We were then asked to rate the countries in our region on his scale. This, Bruce informed us, would allow us to target our attacks on those countries most important to us and most at risk.

Something between panic and stifled hysterical laughter greeted this statement. It was an approach which, taken in isolation, had a certain mad abstract logic, although far removed from any practical application. But Bruce was deadly serious. My colleagues, seasoned public servants all, had long since learned to humor the eccentricities of political appointees. We worked our way down the hundred and fifty or so countries, calling out "five", "seven", "three" or whatever as Bruce entered our considered judgments on his chart.

I recall trying to remember where some of the newly-named African countries for which I was responsible were located as I called out a series of "twos" and "threes". In those days everything in Africa was engulfed by a fashion for some sort of third world socialism, often covertly financed by the Soviet Union in a mind-boggling waste of resources. The United States generally ignored the area unless some vital economic interest was at stake, as it was in Angola and the former Belgian Congo, now Zaire. Anything, however improbable, could and *did* happen on the Dark Continent.

At the time, I put down Hershensohn's chart to the naiveté of a political amateur. But as I look back, it was a precursor to many another unintentional act in what was to become an ongoing international comedy masquerading as diplomacy. Murphy's Law—anything that can go wrong, will—was a leitmotif of this drama, but the actors, playing on a stage the backdrop of which was a nuclear holocaust, often seemed to be unconscious standup comedians.

If there was a red thread which was woven through this tapestry of absurdity, it was ego. It overpowered both the rigid satanic logic of the geopoliticians and the bleeding hearts who believed that good will and wanting something badly enough would make it happen.

USIA was an organization made to order for a former idealist turned cynic. Its task was to present the United States to the world as a model democracy with an enlightened government dedicated to world peace, representative government and economic prosperity. Done right this image would convince the rest of the world to support our aims and ambitions.

It was a concept of breathtaking naiveté, utterly lacking in any understanding of the real world of ethnic hatreds, simmering desires for vengeance, centuries old geopolitical conflicts, opposing economic interests and, most of all, a lack of any understanding of what representative government entailed. Elections, sure. And, of course, once in power any sensible leader would subvert the system to insure that he was re-elected until senility, assassination or a violent coup d'état removed him.

The looting of government coffers by the ruling class, not unheard of even in that sanctimonious paradigm of virtue, America, was standard practice in most of the world outside a few countries occupying the European peninsular.

Having said that, there was no question that the United States for decades held a fascination bordering on awe even among our enemies. Looking back I'm convinced that very often, when our government made some decision or demarche which was so patently counter to its self-interest as to defy belief, as when we barred our businesses from using bribery to obtain overseas contracts, our adversaries stood transfixed. What could be behind such an absurdly stupid act? Obviously there was some Machiavellian hidden strategy. The result was that our enemies were often transfixed by indecision and we lucked out.

The bribery law was merely one of many silly actions taken in the name of idealism. It cost our companies as few pennies to hire agents of dubious virtue, often expatriate Chinese, Lebanese or Greeks, as middlemen who paid the bribes after taking a generous cut themselves. Nothing changed except the rhetoric.

The American belief in the evident superiority of our culture, governmental mechanisms and economic practices, and our proselytizing for them, was a much more serious problem. Even today, faced with decades of fierce resistance, most Americans stubbornly believe that everybody else should follow our path. Any major world power will be accused of ambitions to dominate. We nurtured this belief with our messianistic campaigns for "democracy", "human rights" and "free trade", none of which had much resonance even among our allies.

Free trade, particularly, was no more than an invitation to enemies and allies alike to indulge in blatant surreptitious mercantilism at which the Japanese were the most adept. With the largest market in the world, and a basically autarchic economy, we have rolled over and played dead time after time in economic negotiations which have kept our market open while the Japanese have kept theirs hermetically closed. No wonder they view us with contempt as political cretins. As Oswald Spengler so aptly put it, "a power unused atrophies."

In other cases our actions reflected a breathtaking arrogance. Do we really expect a nation such as the Chinese, with a history of six thousand years of high culture and with one fourth of the population of the globe, to knuckle under to our concept of "human rights?" What believable sanctions can we bring to bear on this behemoth of a nation? What is the point in trying? What business is it of ours how the Chinese run their country?

Diplomacy should, to repeat Andre Siegfried's dictum, be targeted toward isolating the centers of power of a nation, defining their motivations, forecasting their actions and, wherever possible, persuading them that their self-interest is served by support for U.S. policies. All done behind the scenes. USIA should have directed its resources to the final point.

Instead it dissipated its energies in "programs" so dear to the bureaucratic soul, spending vast amounts of money pushing American culture which was already pervading every nook and cranny of the world to a point where it often enraged not only our enemies but such allies as France and Britain. It was left to the CIA to bribe newspaper editors and writers to present our hard-edged political viewpoint and support our policies, always a risky business since the recipient immediately becomes a potential blackmailer.

But none of this was clear to me in the months I spent in the film department. Our efforts were harmless attempts to "relate" to the Africans. We sent films on African-American successes in business and culture such as the Alvin Ailey dance troop and the publisher of *Ebony Magazine*. Expensive glossy magazines proliferated, targeted at individual countries, almost exclusively designed to present the United States as a benevolent power. Unfortunately all but an infinitesimal percentage of our audience was illiterate.

What came across to the Africans, living in abject poverty, often ingesting fewer than the minimum caloric level to survive, was a dreamland with which they had nothing in common. Worse, such messages presented fertile ground for rulers who preached that the industrial world was looting Africa of its riches to live high on the hog themselves.

Thus the Law of Unintended Consequences undermined these high-minded efforts. Fortunately, the Soviet Union was as inept as we were, sending them snowplows, automobiles designed for Arctic conditions and unsuitable for the tropics, outdated machinery and unconsciously racist and arrogant "advisors". They also sent guns to insurgents, turning the continent into a nightmare of violence and anarchy which has still not subsided.

Watching all this unfold, I decided that USIA was probably a total waste of money. We, the most powerful nation on earth, were never going to be loved. Feared maybe, but not loved. And so I evolved Harper's Sixth Law: any job not worth doing was worth doing badly. Henceforth I looked upon my "career" as a grant to write my novels.

Immediately, I had a piece of luck,

The film officer responsible for Eastern Europe was transferred unexpectedly. Waiting for a replacement, Kirchwehm added it to my little empire. At the time the one country in the area where we were able to operate with a modicum of success was Poland. The USIA Eastern European area office was a tightly knit little group, many the sons and daughters of émigrés who had emigrated to escape the Holocaust. They had learned the difficult languages, Czech, Polish, Hungarian, Rumanian, Bulgarian, as children. As a result of my experience at Radio Free Europe and my long years in Europe, I developed a rapport with this cabal, and when an opening occurred for a press attaché in Poland I was offered the job.

I was ambivalent. By this time Vietnam had begun to fascinate me. But our policy there was beginning to come unraveled. The national consensus was being eroded by campus demonstrations against the draft, and a lot of people were dying in far away rice paddies for reasons the population could not understand. It was where the action was, but it was also a career morass, engulfing officers and spitting them out, their task an impossible one.

I finally opted for Poland. After forty-seven weeks of Polish language training, cooped up for six hours a day in a room with three other students and a mad countess, our instructor, I received a fluency rating and we were off to Warsaw.

It was the beginning of a great adventure.

Nineteen

Say yes to everything and do nothing.

Polish proverb on how to deal with tyrants

In the fall of 1972, the man destined to become the last Communist prime minister of Poland, Mieczyslaw Rakowski, called me from Dulles Airport. Earlier that year, at a farewell reception at the residence of the American ambassador in Warsaw, I had extended him an invitation to spend a few days at my home in Reston, Virginia. Rakowski was then the editor of *Polityka,* a weekly journal of opinion targeted on the Polish intelligentsia. During my three-year tour as press attaché at the Warsaw embassy, we had engaged in an intense dialogue covering every aspect of East-West relations and developed a wary friendship. As required by State Department regulations, I documented the dialogue in several dozen memoranda of conversation—memcons in the jargon of the trade.

Rakowski was one of a dozen Polish journalists who were cleared for unlimited contact with westerners. Sophisticated, well read, fluent in English and one or more of the Western European languages, they were point men in the Polish communist party's effort to gain a sympathetic hearing for their country. Warsaw was a way station for American journalists on their way to and from Moscow, and my apartment at Mianowskiego 16 became the site of a continual exchange of views between Polish and western journalists.

Rakowski at this time was in his early forties, a former

resistance fighter and respected party intellectual. He and his journal had not only survived a brutal attempt at its destruction by Interior Minister and candidate Politburo member, Mieczyslaw Moczar, during the communist party crisis in 1968, but he had protected the Jewish members of his staff from the vicious anti-Semitic campaign which drove two-thirds of Poland's 30,000 Jews into exile.

On April 20, 1968, after seven weeks of brutal attacks by the Moczar faction against "Zionists and revisionist intellectuals," Rakowski finally fought back. *Polityka* had been accused in a commentary in *Trybuna Ludu,* the party newspaper, of elitism and exaggerating the importance of the managerial class at the expense of the workers. The article, by Wieslaw Mysiek, a Moczar supporter, went on to accuse him of "making light of the heroism of World War II resistance fighters."

Rakowski replied in an elegantly moderate article in which he described the Moczarist concept of primitive egalitarianism as utopian and impossible to implement in the real world. After conceding that *Polityka* was aimed at the intelligentsia, he wrote that "real equality means providing citizens with equal opportunity to develop their talents, not an enforced and artificial egalitarianism which deadens initiative and penalizes the gifted."

He went on to answer accusations that *Polityka* was a proponent of modern capitalist management techniques by asking if it should espouse "old technology and outdated administrative practices." Rakowski at the same time refused to dismiss his Jewish staffers or to take part in the anti-Zionist campaign. He did more, sending several of them on assignments abroad during the worst of the Moczarist anti-Semitic tirades.

When I first met Rakowski a year later at the home of my predecessor, John Trattner, later to become State Department press spokesman, the power of the Moczarist element had receded, and the anti-Zionist campaign wound down. But the bitter enmities within the party elites, and particularly among its intellectuals, were only papered over. Rakowski questioned me at length about the new Nixon administration's foreign policy goals. He seemed fascinated with the possibility of an American rapprochement with China which he said would increase Soviet paranoia and make Nixon's attempt to reach an understanding with the Russians difficult if not impossible.

Rakowski was astounded, as were most Poles, that American diplomats could speak Polish, however haltingly. I explained the agonizing language program and, in a backhanded compliment, he said my Polish reminded him of a dog walking on front paws: I didn't do it very well but doing it at all was remarkable. When I mentioned that we had also been given heavy doses of Marxism-Leninism he threw up his hands in a gesture of mock despair.

"If you want to discuss Marx we should take a room at the Europejski Hotel, buy a case of vodka and spend a week at it." He was right. In three and a half years in Poland I at some point was confronted on virtually every major political, literary and philosophical movement from Thucydides, Aristotle and Machiavelli to existentialism, Lacan, Derrida and post-structuralism. Neither Marx, Lenin nor communism was ever mentioned and for good reason. In Poland they had ceased even then to be relevant.

Three years before, Poland had celebrated its thousandth anniversary as a nation, dating from the baptism of King Mieszko I in 966. For most of that thousand years it had been caught between the twin millstones of Prussian and Great Russian imperialist ambitions. During much of the period the Poles were their own worst enemy. After a brief blaze of glory in the fifteenth and early sixteenth centuries, when its frontiers extended from Smolensk to the environs of Berlin, the nation entered a period of permanent decline. In one of the earliest manifestations of its national will to suicide, the Polish nobility evolved an extraordinary institution called the *Liberum Veto* which allowed a single member of the aristocratic assembly to veto any legislation.

The nation's kings, elected in tumultuous mass assemblies on a great meadow outside Warsaw, were denied an army and reduced to impotence by the anarchic power of the nobles.

Centuries of chaos saw Poland's powerful neighbors, Russia, Prussia and the Hapsburg Empire, chip away at its borders, finally absorbing it in a series of partitions in 1772, 1793 and 1795.

The modern Polish political psyche was formed during two centuries of national resistance to this dismemberment. In bloody and despairing revolts in 1794, 1830-31, 1863-64 and 1905, Polish patriots were slaughtered by Russian Cossacks, each rebellion adding to the romantic legend of the Heroic Pole going down to defeat against overwhelming odds.

The most recent examples of quixotic despair were the Polish cavalry charges against German tanks during the Second World War and the two-month uprising of the Home Army in Warsaw during July and August 1944. With Soviet divisions in sight of the city, the non-communist resistance gambled on being able to drive the Nazi occupiers out of Warsaw and gain control of the capital before the arrival of Soviet-backed Polish troops. Such a victory would have established the legitimacy of the Polish government in exile in London and given it bargaining chips with the Russians.

The Soviets refused to play the game. They halted their armies across the Vistula for two months and waited for crack German Waffen SS units to bring down the Home Army and, in the process, destroy ninety-five percent of the city. When the remnants of the resistance surrendered, the Soviet forces quickly overwhelmed the sea of rubble which was Warsaw.

In one of my earliest conversations with Rakowski, I mentioned the story of the Polish lancers attacking German tanks and received a blast of indignation which I recorded in a memcon.

"The stories were fabrications of British and French propagandists," he said. "No Polish cavalryman would have been so stupid as to attack a tank with a spear. It is just such romantic nonsense that leads us to destruction." I remembered this outburst two years later in the spring of 1971 when Senator Mike Mansfield had begun a campaign in the U.S. Senate to reduce the American military presence in Europe by half, bringing home 150,000 troops.

In early May, Chalmers Roberts, diplomatic correspondent

for the *Washington Post*, was on a tour of Europe. He arrived in Warsaw shortly before the so-called Mansfield amendment was due to be voted on in the Senate. As a matter of course I invited Rakowski and another Polish journalist of reputedly liberal leanings, Wieslaw Gornicki, to lunch. Late in 1981, following the declaration of martial law in Poland, when I was Counselor of Public Affairs at the U.S. Embassy in East Germany, I was astonished to see Gornicki appear on television in full uniform as the spokesman for the Jaruzelski government which came to power in February 1981.

By that time Rakowski had reluctantly agreed to become prime minister, since he was one of the few members of the Polish elite trusted to negotiate in good faith by the solidarity leaders. He accepted the post in order to calm down the country and stave off a Soviet bloody invasion similar to those in Hungary and Czechoslovakia.

Jaruzelski and Rakowski were vilified in the western press at the time, but, in one of those ironies which are so typical of Poland, by 1991 fifty-three percent of Poles thought Jaruzelski was justified in imposing martial law, finally recognizing that Soviets might indeed have intervened had he not. And, in an even greater irony, one of Rakowski's closest protégés in the tumultuous nineteen-eighties, Alexander Kwasnisewski, was elected president of Poland late in 1995, defeating the Solidarity leader Lech Walesa.

Twenty years earlier, however, both Rakowski and Gornicki were regarded as representatives of the sane and sensible "liberal" wing of the Party establishment, seeking a more open and less repressive society. Polish journalists are formidable drinkers and their preferred poison is vodka. A chilled, rapidly depleted, bottle of Wyborova stood next to the untouched wine over lunch as the conversation with Roberts ranged over the landscape of East-West relations.

The Poles listened, fascinated, as the American, a passionate supporter of Mansfield's ideas, sketched his hopes for developing détente between the Soviet Union and the United States. Only

Kissinger and Nixon's pessimism and paranoia stood between a breakthrough which could end the Cold War and the dangerous confrontation in Europe, Roberts said. An American gesture reducing troops would force the Soviets into reciprocal action. The momentum of such acts of good faith would lead to increased confidence and set the stage for a genuine condominium of East-West interests.

We adjourned to my living room and a second bottle of vodka fresh from the freezer. My memcon of the meeting indicates that Rakowski, with exquisite tact, began to probe the premises behind the Mansfield proposal, pointing out that the Soviet Union was notoriously conservative in its approach to any European initiatives and, confronted with radical choices, always seemed to prefer the status quo to uncertain adventures. He noted that things had not gone badly for the Russians since 1945 and voiced doubts that they would look with favor on a U.S. withdrawal from a West Germany already beginning to flex its economic muscle. He wondered if the Soviets were not just as happy to have U.S. troops holding down German hubris indefinitely, since they posed no threat to the Soviet Union. The Russians, he said, had suffered twenty million casualties at the hands of the Germans. They were a known and formidable enemy. The United States was a distant and nebulous threat.

Roberts said this was news to him. He and Mansfield had always assumed the Soviets would be delighted to see the United States leave Europe. Had that not been their foreign policy objective since 1945?

Rakowski, exchanging a glance with Gornicki, agreed that this was their stated aim and had probably been their genuine one in the immediate postwar period when Stalin's imperialist ambitions were at their zenith. But things were different now. The Russians had their hands full governing unruly allies in the East. Western Europe was no longer tottering on the brink of chaos as it had been in 1945. The Germans were positioned to dominate the expanding Common Market and use it as a vehicle for reunifying their country and recovering the lost lands to the

East which were now an integral part of Poland. France and Britain might not have the will or the power to restrain this new German giant. The U.S. would. From the Soviet standpoint it was better not to take any chances.

Rakowski then asked Roberts if he had ever given any thought to what it would mean to Poland and all Eastern European countries if the Americans left Europe? Roberts admitted he did not see any connection.

"Without your troops in Germany," Rakowski said, "we will become the seventeenth province of the Soviet Union. As long as your forces are in place, we are important to them. We lie across their lines of communication to East Germany. We have leverage. Once you are gone, they can afford to ignore us."

Roberts was first stunned, then annoyed, at this unexpected turn in the conversation, and the lunch broke up almost immediately.

As Rakowski left, I pointed to the ornate ceramic chandelier which hung over the scarred Bechstein with a cracked sounding board which dominated my small living room. "That thing must be bugged. You may be in serious trouble for what you said today."

Rakowski laughed and said, "they are my brothers."

My first months in Poland were overshadowed by the convulsions of 1968 which had, it became clear in retrospect, torn the fabric of Polish society irreparably. The so-called March events were triggered by the patriotic play *Forefather's Eve*, by Adam Mickiewicz, dealing with Poland's nineteenth-century struggle against Czarist oppression. When audiences reacted, seeing a veiled comparison between Czarist and Soviet oppression, "as if a bomb had gone off," in the words of the country's most famous actor, Gustav Holoubeck, who played the leading role, the authorities panicked and closed down the production on January 31. Police broke up a student protest, but Warsaw University continued to seethe.

On March 8, students began rioting in Warsaw, and the protests rapidly spread across the country. The church protested brutal police repression, but the workers, long alienated from Polish intellectuals, refused to participate, Polish leaders were looking over their shoulders in panic at the "Prague Spring" in neighboring Czechoslovakia, hoping to avoid a spread of the infection. Their reaction was complicated by an internal struggle within the party. A triangular battle for power was developing between an aging Gomulka, isolated from the nation by his reclusive personality and long years in power, Edward Gierek, a technocrat who had spent his formative years as a miner in France, and Mieczyslaw Moczar, a leader of the internal resistance in World War II who espoused Polish nationalism, anti-Semitism and resistance to Soviet domination.

Chaos descended on the nation as the Moczarist faction instituted an anti-Semitic campaign of unparalleled ferocity, appealing to the worst instincts of the Polish populace. Although Poland's prewar population of three million Jews had been reduced by the Holocaust to fewer than 30,000 a quirk of history had placed large numbers of Jews in positions of power in the Communist Party.

In 1939 a large minority of the Polish party was Jewish. Sensibly, they fled into the Soviet occupation zone after the Nazi-Soviet partition of the country with the result that a high percentage of the surviving leaders of the party in 1945 were Jewish. They were referred to with contempt by the internal resistance, the Partisans, as the "Muscovites." Their return to Poland in the wake of the Soviet armies and their predominance in the security services of the party between 1945 and 1956, when repression of dissent was at its most brutal, led to a resurgence of the ever present visceral anti-Semitism of the average Pole.

Since paradox is the norm in the Polish political spectrum, many of the leaders of the student revolts which began in March 1968 were the sons and daughters of this Jewish party elite. The Moczarist faction mobilized its supporters within the propaganda apparat to institute a purge of Jews from positions of authority in all areas of Polish society—the Party itself, academia, journalism and the economic sector. On a daily basis,

Party media announced the forced resignation of prominent Jewish intellectuals.

In times of crisis, the Poles turn to humor to survive. During the anti-Semitic campaign, the following story made the rounds. Israel Kowalksi calls his friend Jacek Jaworski:

"Is that you Jaworski? This is Kowalski."

"Which Kowalski? I know dozens."

"Israel Kowalski. The one you hid in your closet during the Nazi times."

"Oh, yes. How are you, Israel? Haven't heard from you in years."

"Let's cut this short, Jacek. Tell me. Do you still have the closet?"

Moczar's attempt to use the campaign to force Gomulka from office and take his place was thwarted in the end by the Soviets. They were well aware of his anti-Russian stance and were unwilling to have another Ceaucescu in power across their vital lines of communication to East Germany.

Two years later, in the summer of 1970 at a reception in my house for Arthur Ochs "Punch" Sulzberger, publisher of the *New York Times*, and columnist Tom Wicker, Sulzberger asked a Polish journalist, Zygmunt Szymanski, why the Poles had driven out the remnants of their Jewish population. Szymanski glanced around the room and told Sulzberger that half the journalists present were Jewish, himself included.

Sulzberger, taken aback, asked why they stayed. Among the group around him was a brilliant young journalist, Daniel Passent, one of Rakowski's *Polityka* protégés. Passent had been thrown over the wall of the ghetto when he was three years old and reared by a Polish family. He had recently returned to Poland after a year at Princeton on a Parvin Fellowship. He now interrupted Sulzberger to say that the people present were Poles first and then Jews. As to why they stayed, in his case it was because he found English a primitive instrument of communication and that he could only find an outlet rich enough to express himself in the immense variety and subtlety of the Polish language.

Later in my stay in Poland he wrote a satirical *feuilleton* for *Polityka* describing the humiliation of the American press attaché in the finals of the diplomatic tennis tournament by the local Pan American representative, Eugene Kucha.

Passent wrote in part: "Mr. Harper showed a decidedly better service but a completely shattered nervous system. He avoided prolonged rallies and aimed at a quick victory, which is characteristic of gunboat diplomacy. As these tactics did not bring any success on the Agrycola courts, the otherwise likable diplomat lost his self-control, called himself everything under the sun and, as he still retained some shreds of *savoir vivre,* at intervals hurled a few compliments to his adversary between clenched teeth, but nobody believed him, which is normal for American diplomacy."

Wit and *joie de vivre* were never in short supply in Poland. The contrast between the grim monotonous existence of the average Pole and the lifestyle of the diplomatic colony led to ferocious competition for invitations to Embassy parties. One of the more lavish hosts, Nicholas Henderson, the British ambassador, was condemned to live in an immense poured concrete mansion which resembled a snail's shell, a tribute to the degeneracy of late modernism. This weighty circular blob was situated in the midst of high-rise apartment buildings whose miniature balconies overlooked its spacious garden.

Henderson, a mediocre but determined tennis player, had a grass court installed on its lawn and often invited my nemesis, Gene Kucha, and his nephew, Michael Packenham, a third secretary in the Embassy, and me to make up a doubles. These matches were invariably followed by tea and cucumber sandwiches served by white-gloved Polish waiters. We played and ate to the silent audience of dozens of half clad Poles watching from their balconies. During one match a magnificently endowed young woman in scanty lingerie met my eyes each time I lifted my racket to serve.

Niko, who was later ambassador to Bonn, Paris and Washington, was of another age. Six-feet-three-inches tall, in perpetual studied dishevelment, he wandered across the Polish scene like an aristocratic crow, cackling with delight at the amusements the world offered. Behind the facade of an English eccentric was a steely, slightly cruel, mind leavened by a marvelous sense of humor. He once consulted me on the guest list for a proposed lunch for leading Polish journalists, a feast which soon entered the legends of the city. More than fifty showed up to be seated at tables gleaming with fine linen, Irish crystal and antique silver. I can no longer remember the seven courses served, but the taste of the Manzanilla from his private vineyard near Seville remains vivid. After the third or fourth course, his dogs, an English bull terrier and assorted retrievers, were loosed among the tables. I half expected him to pick up a joint and fling it over his shoulder in imitation of Henry the Eighth.

The Poles loved and hungered for the good life. Some loved it too much. In October 1969 I began what turned into a three-year pilgrimage to visit editors of newspapers and magazines in provincial Poland, something all my predecessors and colleagues assured me was impossible. My first stop was Katowice, the fief of Edward Gierek, even then regarded as the eventual successor to the aging Gomulka. The second most influential newspaper in Poland, *Trybuna Robotnicza,* was published in this soot-stained industrial city in the heart of former German Silesia.

Following the war, the Poles had dedicated all their energies and resources to rebuilding Warsaw as it had existed in 1939, using the drawings Canaletto had made in the eighteenth century to recreate the old town. As a result the rest of Poland was short-changed, mile upon mile of minimalist apartments rising out of the appalling destruction of the war.

Katowice was, in addition, covered with a patina of grime from the heavy industries based on coal which surrounded it. Calling for appointments with Polish provincial media leaders was, I knew, hopeless. I had therefore decided to arrive unannounced at their offices hoping that their innate courtesy and natural curiosity would get me a hearing.

Trybuna Robotnicza was edited by Maciej Szczepanski, who was totally unknown to the embassy, although a member of both the Central Committee and parliament. I walked to the Press

Building around the corner from my hotel, followed without much pretense of concealment by two secret policemen, climbed aboard the Pater Noster, one of the potentially fatal open moving boxes which serve as elevators throughout Eastern Europe, stepped off at the sixth floor and walked down the usual drab, stained hallway to the offices of the paper.

Inside it was another world. Light, clean offices leading off a corridor decorated with haunting black and white photographs of industrial scenes and, at the end of the hall, through glass doors, the bamboo-lined reception room of the chief editor. His secretary, a striking blonde who could have walked out of the pages of *Vogue*, gave me a chilly stare and held my card as if it bore an infection.

She disappeared through the bamboo doors, returning in about thirty seconds with a gleaming smile, to usher me into a large office decked out with slickly modern imitation Danish furniture, all black leather and chrome. The view of the city through a picture window was spectacular. Scattered on his cocktail table were copies of *Der Spiegel, Frankfurter Algemeine Zeitung* and *Neue Zuericher Zeitung* along with *Pravda*. Szczepanski, a tall slim man in a black turtleneck and sports jacket, peered out from glasses as thick as the bottoms of coke bottles. He held out his hand and apologized for not speaking English which he said he was studying.

Within seconds the door opened and another attractive young woman appeared bearing a tray heaped with bread, sliced him, sausage, cheese and the inevitable bottle of vodka. Over the next hour and a half, as the vodka bottle emptied, we toured the political horizon touching on everything from U.S.-Soviet relations, the problem of China, inner German problems, the prospects for Polish-West German rapprochement and anti-Semitism in Poland.

Szczepanski became impatient with my halting Polish and suggested we shift into German which he spoke virtually without an accent. He first sketched the problems facing the region. Coal and minerals were the building blocks of Polish prosperity. Unfortunately iron ore had to be brought in from the Soviet

Union, which occasionally created problems of a reliable supply. Oil was an even greater difficulty, since the cost of importing it drained off capital needed for reinvestment.

He then hammered at a point which became a leitmotif of this and later conversations. Poland's future lay to the East with the Soviet Union. His country's fate was inextricably linked to Russia by unbreakable ties of ideology and the logic of economics.

He then turned to internal problems. Polish workers were, he said, well paid by Eastern European standards. Their diet, for example, contained a higher percentage of meat than that of the average Frenchman. But Poles were anarchic and never satisfied, the most difficult workers in the East bloc to keep happy. Housing continued to be a problem, but it could not be overcome immediately. Resources must go into rapid industrialization, not into consumer goods.

The ethnic German problem was, he acknowledged, extremely difficult. The region had belonged to Germany for a hundred and fifty years, and their policy of Germanizing the population had been partially successful. Large numbers of ethnic Poles regarded themselves as Germans and were demanding repatriation. Since they were the most disciplined and energetic members of the work force, to allow them to depart would be a crippling blow. The most important question vis-a-vis West Germany, however, was its unwillingness to recognize the Oder-Neisse frontier between East Germany and Poland. Until this was resolved very little could be accomplished. He did not believe German internal politics would allow them to do this.

Szczepanski was wrong. A year later, On December 7, 1970, West German Chancellor Willy Brandt came to Warsaw and signed an agreement implicitly recognizing the border. He then, in a gesture requiring immense courage from a German statesman, visited the site of the Warsaw ghetto and dropped to his knees before the monument to the three million Polish Jews who died in the Holocaust. It was the beginning of West Germany's *Ostpolitik*, the precursor of détente and Foreign Minister Genscher's "opening to the East."

I asked Szczepanski what impact the anti-Semitic campaign of 1968 had had in Silesia. He poured us another vodka and waved off the question impatiently. There were virtually no Jews left in the region. Few had returned after the war and none had occupied important party positions. In addition, the local party leader Edward Gierek, had refused to participate in the campaign. Throughout the meeting Szczepanski, unlike most Warsaw journalists who delighted in gossip and backbiting, refused to discuss personalities, saying only that there were differences among the Polish leadership as there were in any country.

He described a recent tip to the Soviet Union, citing a vast new oil discovery in the Tyumen region and described in detail the immense industrialization projects underway in Central Asia. This investment in raw material extraction would begin to pay off within a decade. He seemed genuinely overwhelmed by what he had seen, pointing out the absurdity of orienting Poland's economy toward Germany, a tiny corner of the European continent, whereas the Soviet Union was a quarter of the world.

Clearly left wing American intellectuals were not the only ones taken in by the Soviet experiment.

Turning to U.S.-Soviet relations, Szczepanski said he saw trouble ahead if the U.S. tried to play its "China card", since the Soviet Union was rightly concerned about the orientation of its neighbor to the East. Any attempt to exploit the divisions between China and the Soviet Union was an extremely dangerous game. Otherwise he foresaw the possibility of a gradual amelioration of relations between the superpowers but warned that the Soviet Union would, in the end, triumph since Socialism was the wave of the future. Although his ideas were conventional Communist dogma, Szczepanski was personally the antithesis of a Party apparatchik. His dynamism, willingness to discuss any topic, thirst for information and a certain rough charm could have made him at home among the tough-minded young men around John Kennedy.

Following the overthrow of Gomulka and his replacement by Gierek in 1970, Szczepanski rose quickly, becoming a full member of the Central Committee and taking over the powerful position as head of Polish television. His orthodox pro-Russian stance and authoritarian methods, verging on brutality, quickly alienated the more cosmopolitan Warsaw journalists. And he used his powers to finance a lifestyle even more luxurious than that of most members of the *nomenklatura*. His ouster for corruption on August 24, 1980, was a signal that his protector, Gierek, would soon follow.

But in late 1969 and early 1970, Gierek and his team of technocrats were regarded as the potential saviors of Poland. Although the political crisis of 1968 had receded, economic problems continued to worsen. Food subsidies, particularly for meat, were causing a crisis in agriculture with farmers refusing to deliver produce at the depressed prices being offered by the government. Prices in the free markets in every city and town went through the roof. Bizarre economic dislocations resulted in such phenomena as the "tomato millionaires," owners of glass houses who grew and sold tomatoes on the free market for five dollars a pound.

American journalists in Europe, sensing a new crisis, came in hordes. The Polish Foreign Ministry Press Office was soon overwhelmed. Its chief, Andrzej Konopacki, looked like an NFL middle linebacker gone to seed. He had served five years in the Polish Embassy in Washington and had a sophisticated understanding of how to manipulate the American media. We habitually lunched each week at the *Spatif,* a club for actors, serving the finest food in Warsaw, in order to plan the schedules of the arriving newsmen.

The club's manager, scion of an old aristocratic family, the Kinski's, had furnished the dining room with oil paintings of his ancestors and one of the family's baby grand pianos. He had also arranged a trade with the Russian actors' club in Moscow, sending them Wyborova vodka, a snob drink among the Russians, for case upon case of caviar.

After several lunches I asked the manager if it would be possible to join the club. He glanced at Konopacki who grinned and said he had to say hello to some friends, leaving me alone with the elegantly degenerate manager. He leaned across the table in a classic conspiratorial mode and said, more or less, that it was of course impossible for me to become a member. I waited. He then began to talk about the bar. It was a real pity, he continued, that the club was unable to serve scotch, which the members loved. No hard currency. He wondered if I had any idea how it could be obtained? I suggested that I had occasionally seen a case, unclaimed, in my driveway at Mianowskiego 16, and that if someone arrived at six P.M. the next day he might find it there.

At my next lunch with Konopacki, the manager presented me with a "special membership" card. For the next three years I was the envy of the diplomatic corps, inviting my colleagues for lunches which consisted of a small crystal jug of vodka in a bed of ice, a quarter pound tin of caviar and superb Polish bread fried in butter.

During one such lunch shortly after Gierek came to power, Konopacki seemed more than usually preoccupied, telling me abruptly to have a drink. He had spent several days with a correspondent for the Baltimore Sun, Joe Sterne, a hard digging old style reporter who bored in with unrelenting ferocity on the Polish journalists who met with him. Sterne, in one memorable exchange with Karol Szyndzielorz of *Zycie Warszawy,* the second most important paper in the city, asked what had happened to Gomulka? Did he, for example, have a job?

Szyndzielorz, who had spent several years at Stanford and spoke accentless English, said he was retired on a pension of 6,000 zlotys a month. Sterne protested that this hardly seemed enough to live on.

"He has a heart condition and can't eat meat." Szyndzielorz said, unsmiling, "so it should be enough." When you fell in Poland, you fell hard.

After drinking our first vodka, Konopacki, sweat breaking out on his face beneath a classic crew cut, announced that Joe Sterne was under arrest at the airport for having in his possession forbidden materials from Radio Free Europe. He had been trying for two hours to persuade the Ministry of the Interior to let him go, still without success.

I asked where Sterne was, and Konopacki, looking pained, hesitated: "The Black Hole." This was the name we all used to refer to two sparsely furnished, windowless police detainment rooms in a cellar located in the no man's land beyond the customs and passport controls. There was a whiff of medieval dungeon about it. I had to go to the airport, Konopacki said, and calm Sterne down while he arranged for his release. The Hungarian Maalev airliner was being held at the airport for him on various pretexts.

I checked into the Embassy, asking a political officer to intercede at the Foreign Ministry, and raced to the airport. In Poland, as in all Eastern Europe, diplomats are treated as favored members of the regime. A small red pass gave me instant entry to all areas of the airport. I headed for the "Black Hole", waved through by the guards. Konopacki had, however, finally prevailed, and Sterne stood in a state of near hysteria in front of a stack of papers on the luggage counter arguing heatedly with a police major.

I asked Joe what the problem was.

"He's trying to make me take the damned Radio Free Europe material. It's a setup. They're trying to get me arrested when I get to Budapest. I won't touch it."

The policeman, whom I knew from innumerable visits to the airport, turned to me and said. "You take it then. He can't just leave it here."

I grinned, shaking my head. "You'll arrest me if I do." Whereupon Sterne headed for his plane, I turned back through the airport and the policeman shrugged and walked away, leaving the offending material on the luggage counter.

It was, in a way, what the Poles did throughout 1970 as the economy crumbled. In the fall, there was suddenly a shortage of coffee. None was to be had at any price. Through a statistical error, all the coffee scheduled to be used in a year had been sold in nine months. There was no hard currency to buy more. Coffee in Poland is more than a beverage. It serves an almost metaphysical function, allowing the Poles in their cafes to vent their frustrations in a congenial atmosphere outside their claustrophobic apartments, to conduct public love affairs and talk endless politics and scandal.

The Poles and everyone else were momentarily distracted by a bizarre sideshow on the world diplomatic stage which took place in Warsaw about this time. By some quirk of Cold War diplomacy, Warsaw had once been the site of sporadic informal talks between the U.S. and China. The meetings had been broken off some years before and the contact allowed to lapse. With the advent of the Nixon administration, Washington began a discreet campaign for rapprochement with the Chinese. In late 1969, the National Security Advisor, Henry Kissinger, sent an eyes-only cable to the U.S. Ambassador in Warsaw, Walter Stoessel, requesting him to approach the Chinese ambassador at a social event and suggest that the talks be reopened. Stoessel was told that the approach should be made in the greatest secrecy.

The ambassador had a problem. He and the Chinese did not normally attend the same social functions and, since Kissinger was clearly in no mood to brook delay, some way had to be found to see the Chinese in such a way as not to arouse the suspicions of the Poles and through them the Soviets. He called in a young political officer, Tom Simons, later himself to become ambassador to Poland, and me, as the officers who spoke the best Polish and had the widest circle of contacts in Warsaw.

We explored the possibilities and settled on a Yugoslav fashion show scheduled to be held in the cellar nightclub of the Warsaw Palace of Culture, a monstrous building constructed shortly after the war as a Soviet gift to the Polish people. I occasionally played tennis with a Yugoslav diplomat and was able to obtain tickets for Stoessel, Simons and myself by explaining that the ambassador's wife was fascinated by Yugoslav fashions.

It was late January, and a mass of snow fell during the course of the afternoon. Stoessel was conspicuous by his presence, since he was virtually the only Western diplomat in attendance. Our plan was that, at the conclusion of the fashion show, Stoessel would unobtrusively approach the Chinese as they picked up their coats. He would then discreetly ask for a meeting, with either Simons or I translating his message to the young Polish-speaking Chinese who accompanied him.

It didn't quite work out as we had anticipated. Stoessel, in his haste, overturned a chair. The Chinese watched terrified as the American threaded his way through the crowd toward him, and bolted, not stopping at the coat room but bounding up the steps toward the exit to the parking lot. Simons and I raced after Stoessel who, abandoning all pretense of diplomatic dignity, pursued the Chinese out into the cold. There, standing in a foot of snow, he delivered his statement and Simon translated it to the Polish-speaking aide.

We waited several days before the Chinese sent a message suggesting that Stoessel come to their Embassy late in the evening of the following day. The Chinese chancellery was located on the edge of Dzerzhinsky Square, named after the first Soviet secret police chief, standing alone in an open field. Stoessel's car, a large American Chrysler driven by a Marine guard, entered the covered porte-cochere of the building and promptly became wedged in the narrow space. Stoessel entered the building as the driver and Embassy staff members hovering nearby worked frantically to free the car. The Polish guards on duty before all foreign embassies joined in the fun, and eventually the driver backed it out, scratched but otherwise none the worse for wear.

Incredibly, none of the resident American correspondents picked up the story until Simons' wife let it slip at the American Club bar while sitting next to the Associated Press Correspondent, Marty Zucker. Zucker had a beat and played it for all it was worth. Within hours a horde of newsmen and television correspondents flooded Warsaw. When the Chinese ambassador arrived to return Stoessel's meeting, the U.S. Embassy lobby was crammed with some of America's most distinguished journalists led by the legendary Charles Collingwood.

The Embassy elevator was supposed to have been preprogrammed to start down just as the Chinese limousine arrived at the front entrance. Stoessel would then emerge from the elevator to greet the Chinese as he entered, providing an elegant solution to the protocol issue of who would wait for whom. Murphy's Law was in operation however, and some tense young administrative assistant punched the up button instead of the down. As the Chinese entered and approached the elevator, the little red buttons indicated it was headed up instead of down. He turned toward me, where I stood attempting to control the crush of newsmen, and I began to explain the delay to his Polish-speaking aide. Visibly put out, perhaps thinking this was a deliberate insult, the Chinese half turned to leave when Stoessel finally emerged from the elevator. The assembled press applauded ironically with their usual irreverent lack of respect.

Over the next few days, insolent, self-important young men from Washington arrived on the scene to handle the delicate negotiations which led to the dramatic visit of Henry Kissinger to Peking later in the year. But the China talks hardly interrupted my alcoholic odyssey through the labyrinth of the Polish media. Warsaw, always a favorite stopover for newsmen, had become even more popular.

Dan Morgan, the Eastern European correspondent for the *Washington Post* and an old friend, had become fascinated by Poland at this time, developing close working relationships with a variety of Polish journalists. One of the most original of this weird crew was Jan Zakrzewski, who, with Wieslaw Gornicki of *Zycie Warszawy,* hosted a popular Sunday radio show called *Periscope.* Zakrzewski had spent eight months in training at the Fort Monmouth Signal Corps School during World War II and had fond memories of the United States. He and his wife, Eva Krasnodebska, a leading stage actress, lived in a lovely small house in a quiet upper-class neighborhood.

Zakrzewski was something of an oddball. Gornicki said that for a time nobody would go near him. He had bought a huge German shepherd and had hired a sergeant in the paramilitary police to school the animal. For months, the sergeant, in full uniform, marched up and down in front of Zakrzewski's house training the dog, terrifying the neighbors and any friends who happened by.

In the fall of 1970, shortly before Gomulka's ouster, Dan

Morgan and I were invited to Zakrzewski's house for lunch. We sat drinking mead, a sort of fermented honey, while our host raged about the production of *Coriolanus* done by the Berliner Ensemble which we had all attended the night before. It was a modern dress version, full of whips and chains and a cast clad in motorcycle leathers. Zakrzewski maintained that the Germans were incapable of doing anything without investing it with militarism and heroic Teutonic symbolism. Why else, he asked, would anybody choose to stage one of Shakespeare's most obscure plays except to use it as a vehicle for their suppressed Prussian arrogance?

He then told a series of jokes.

A party member in a provincial city gets up at a cell meeting and tells of a dream:

Party member: I dreamed I saw God sitting on a mountain of coffee last night.

Party secretary: Comrade, you must not say such things. You know God does not exist.

Party member: And coffee?

In another story Gomulka is kidnapped. A million zloty ransom is asked. The kidnappers say if the ransom is not paid they will release him.

And finally he told the quintessential Polish nihilist joke.

Gomulka is walking in the mountains and falls. As he is about to go over a cliff, he is stopped by a cross with a figure of Christ on it.

"Thank you, Christ, for saving my life," Gomulka said, crossing himself.

"Don't thank me, Gomulka, " the Christ said. "Thank those Jews who nailed my feet to the cross, otherwise I would have kicked you over."

Morgan, appalled at the joke, asked if the anti-Semitic campaign had definitely ended, and Zakrzewski said it had but the residue of bitterness was poisoning many relationships. I mentioned having met Machejek, the editor of *Zycie Literacke,* in Krakow, and that he was a rabid anti-Semite. Zakrzewski then told the following tale:

Machejek had led a delegation of Polish writers to Moscow during the summer. During the course of an official dinner offered by the Russian writers he got very drunk and pointed to an obviously Jewish face, remarking that he was surprised that the Russians "still had such filthy types around." At this point a prominent Soviet critic rose and said, "My name is Akcionnov but my mother's name was Ginzburg," and slapped Machejek's face. At which point Yevtushenko came to the table and also slapped Machejek, who was forced to leave the dinner and sent home in disgrace.

Morgan said that, nonetheless, Daniel Passent of Polityka was having problems, partly because he was Jewish. Zakrzewski shrugged and said Passent had criticized the police for searching people for vodka before they went to soccer matches and had been attacked by the legal journal, *Prawo y Zycie*. Passent was an admirable fellow, but he had a little too much Don Quixote in him. Attacking the police was still one of the taboos.

My memcon on the meeting expresses amazement at the openness of the conversation, which ranged widely across all outstanding East-West issues, and also at the jokes about Gomulka. It seemed clear to us at the time that Gomulka's days were numbered, although the success of his foreign policy in obtaining a tacit West German recognition of Poland's Oder-Neisse frontier in the West was a major accomplishment.

The pictures of Willy Brandt on his knees before the Warsaw Ghetto monument asking for forgiveness were front-page news for days. However, the ability of Polish communist regimes to shoot themselves in the foot soon came into play. On December 12, five days later, Warsaw Radio announced sudden price increases of 16 percent for flour, 14 percent for sugar and 17 percent for meat. As Daniel Lulinski, diplomatic correspondent for *Trybuna Ludu*, put it during a dinner with Kenneth Huszar, Vienna Correspondent of *Newsweek*, the following January: "Only stupidity could have dictated such a move two weeks before Christmas."

The consequences were predictable. On the Monday following

the increase, the workers struck and occupied the Lenin and Paris Commune shipyards in Gdansk. Attempts to force them to leave degenerated into a riot, and the police opened fire, killing an undetermined number of strikers. A Polish flag was soaked in the blood of one of the dead, and the workers marched on the Party headquarters, sacking and burning it. The strike quickly spread along the Baltic coast to Elblag, Slupsk and Szczecin.

Gomulka's support in the Politburo began to evaporate. Moczar, sensing disaster, went to ground and took no part in the crisis. According to Lulinski, General Wojciech Jaruzelski, the defense minister, told Gomulka that he would not allow regular army troops to be used against the strikers. Then, on December 17, the morning shift of the Paris Commune shipyard poured off their trains and were met by a hail of gunfire. Thirteen died. The same day there was bloody fighting in Szczecin. By the weekend a general strike was spreading across the country. On Sunday December 20, Gomulka was replaced by Edward Gierek.

In an amazingly frank summary of behind-the-scene events, Daniel Lulinski told *Newsweek's* Huszar, during a tense dinner at my house, that Gomulka had telephoned Moscow for support as the crisis deepened. He received a latter from Brezhnev which proclaimed Soviet neutrality, but he did not show it to the Politiburo for two days. When the others found out the Soviet position, Gomulka was finished.

Lulinski then described the background to one of the more bizarre events which occurred during the crisis. Poland's most famous journalist, Karol Malcuzynski, Polish television's Walter Cronkite, was the anchor of the evening news show "Monitor". He was an immensely popular man, famous for his integrity and reputedly a personal friend of half the Politburo although not a Party member. At the height of the crisis, when it was clear that Gomulka was finished, he wrote a passionate editorial in *Trybuna Ludu* in defense of the old man. He did it, Lulinski said, out of a sense of loyalty to the man who had supported him for a decade and a half. The gesture destroyed his career.

I asked Rakowski about the incident sometime later, and he

shrugged: "Karol has a very old-fashioned concept of honor." Although a friend and admirer of Malcuzynski, Rakowski clearly thought it a senseless act in the tradition of Poland's suicidal romanticism.

The optimism which had initially greeted Gierek's assumption of power dissipated rapidly. He reduced food prices and promised a close dialog with the workers, but it soon became clear that little had changed.

The Warsaw diplomatic corps wined and dined Polish journalists continually over the next few months in an attempt to discover what direction the new Gierek regime would take. In a memcon of January 21, I describe a lunch at the home of the Italian Charge, Gian Luigi Valenza. He had invited a French-speaking Polish journalist, Zygmunt Szymanski, of *Zycie Warszawy*, Baron Philippe Guillaume of the Belgian Embassy and Bernard Marguerite, the *Le Monde* correspondent.

The conversation revolved around the Polish-German talks and the Poles' insistence that West Germany officially recognize the Oder-Neisse frontier. Szymanski insisted that only unconditional recognition of the frontier would enable the Polish government to move toward reconciliation, pointing out the numberless horrors the Nazis had committed in Poland.

Guillaume, with the pedantic legalism European diplomats love, asked if the Poles would also demand a guarantee of their Eastern frontier since this problem was not judicially settled. Szymanski looked genuinely startled and a little amused that someone would bring this up. He assured the Belgian that this was a technicality that might be resolved but that he doubted that it was a serious issue.

Marguerite pressed him on the Sino-Soviet talks then in progress. The Chinese were asking for border rectifications in Siberia. Szymanski said it was most unlikely that the Soviets would make concessions. The original treaties ceding the territory were probably invalid, he said, but occupation of territory for sixty-five years constitutes a form of *de jure* rights under international law. In any event, it was unrealistic to expect the Soviets to return territory.

Guillaume noted with a smile that under that interpretation Poland only had to hang onto its Eastern Territories another forty years.

On the following day I had lunch at the home of Count Lars Bergquist, first secretary of the Swedish Embassy, with Wieslaw Gornicki, also of *Zycie Warszawy*. As I walked in the door Gornicki demanded to know why I had invited *Zycie Warszawy's* Moscow correspondent to lunch with him and Rakowski the week before. Gornicki said Kubicki, whom I had met during a visit to Moscow the previous year, was a secret agent in the pay of the Soviet Union and the paper had absolutely no control over him. Such were the hidden subtleties of Poland.

My memcon notes that "I was struck by Gornicki's apparent fearlessness in expressing opinions which border on treason at gatherings of foreign diplomats. His actions were even more strange given his ability to write for virtually any publication in Poland and the fact that he is clearly well wired to the leadership."

Sometime later, Gornicki invited Bergquist, Jerzy Jaruzelski—one of his colleagues at *Zycie Warszawy*—and me to dinner, a rarity in Poland in 1971. Jaruzelski had just returned from a visit to the United States and expatiated at length on how well the United States was dealing with the "black problem." He had been surprised at the extent of the black middle class and at how many blacks were indifferent or hostile to being integrated into the white society.

Jaruzelski then described "the total breakdown of discipline among the sons and daughters of America's upper and middle classes." He said elitist universities such as Stanford were in much more trouble than the state universities where the students were sacrificing and working part time to get an education. However he said he thought the U.S. media vastly exaggerated the seriousness of the problem.

He spoke admiringly of the openness of American society and the "terrible" repression in the Soviet Union. Both Gornicki, who had spent five years in America, and Jaruzelski sang hymns of praise to the United States, believing it to be moving toward a more "progressive" society. Gornicki played old Tom Lehrer and Bob Newhart records. My comment at the end of the memcon marvels once again how much more open and "western" the ambiance at Polish social gatherings had become.

Some of the diplomatic lunches of the period were caricatures of the genre. The best table was set by Henri de la Coste, the French political officer, whose favorite source was Janusz Stefanowicz of *Slowo Powszechne,* organ of *Pax*, the communist-sponsored alternative Catholic organization. Stefanowicz, who spoke excellent French, was good copy. On this day the Austrian deputy chief of mission, a descendant of the Hapsburg emperors, Valenza and I were present.

Poland, Stefanowicz said, was rather like an aging woman who has had many lovers. She expects less from each succeeding one, but she never stops hoping. Thus it is with Gierek. People understand he is a good and strong fellow but they realize there is little he can change. Moczar, he said, had emerged with increased power, but he could advance no further, since the Russians found him unacceptable.

At some point the Italian and the Austrian, apropos of the Polish-German frontier question, became embroiled in an arcane discussion of Austro-Italian relations. The Austrian mentioned that one of his ancestors, Admiral Tegethoff, had commanded the Austrian fleet at the battle of Lissa in 1866, a naval encounter in which an aging, rust-covered Austrian fleet had emerged from a fog bank to take the modern Italian fleet on the flank and win a notable victory. Valenza, it turned out, had relatives among the officers of the Italian fleet. Both were convinced that the battle was more momentous than Trafalgar.

Stefanowicz came up with the latest jokes. Two Poles meet on the street. One says to the other: *"Zapalimy?"* a word in Polish with a double meaning, either to "light up" or "burn up." His friend looks around before asking "Where is the nearest party headquarters."

In another, Lenin wakes up in the Moscow Mausoleum and looks over to see Stalin beside him. He grumbles, closes his eyes and forgets about it. A few years later he wakes up, sees Stalin is gone and assumes that there have been some changes. A few more years pass, and he opens his eyes and Stalin is back. Finally, still later, he opens them to find Brezhnev lying beside him and shouts: "What is this place? A mausoleum or a hotel?"

President Nixon's whirlwind visit to Warsaw in the spring of 1972, en route home from the Moscow summit, left the city stunned. I had been assigned to run press centers on Nixon's visits to Bucharest and Belgrade, so the massive influx of journalists and arrogant White House minions was no surprise. As the columnist Joe Kraft had said to me, following a run in with some minor press functionary who stalked about talking into a radio, "Give a fool a walkie-talkie and he thinks he's God."

The visit, which lasted a few minutes over twenty-four hours, was prepared by several advance teams. I was detailed to translate for an army Signal Corps colonel in charge of communications. After obtaining the immobilization of most of the telexes in the capital for the benefit of the American press corps, he demanded an array of radio bands for the use of the Secret Service. The Poles refused, pointing out that all radio bands were reserved for the Polish state.

The colonel was adamant. We finally wound up across the table from a major general in the Polish army who told the colonel in no uncertain terms that he had no intention of making the radio bands available. Even the Russians did not make such outrageous demands. The colonel, paunchy, mild-mannered, wearing rimless glasses, asked me to tell the general that he either got the radio bands or the President would not land in Warsaw. He then closed his massive briefing book, saluted to the general and we left.

When I reported to the ambassador, he immediately got on the phone to the State Department. Sometime later a call came in confirming that the colonel had full authority to cancel the visit if he could not supply adequate communications backup for the secret service. The ambassador headed for the foreign ministry. Two days later the colonel and I were back in the massive headquarters of the Posts, Telegraph and Telephone confronting a chastened major general who conceded every demand with a wave of his hand.

This is but one example of the arrogance bordering on insolence of the people surrounding American presidents when they travel. They are usually young operators from the previous campaign, already professional politicians polishing their resumes, utterly ignorant of and indifferent to the countries the president is visiting. They are masters of the "process", that obnoxious word which has come to provide cover for anyone wishing to ignore substance. They trailed in their wake a river of anti-Americanism and often left carefully cultivated Embassy contacts in shreds.

The Nixon trip itself was primarily designed to nail down the Polish vote in the upcoming U.S. election. Virtually nothing of note happened other than the mouthing of pious platitudes about increased trade and working for peace. Nixon expressed his satisfaction at the Polish-German treaty, guaranteeing Poland's western frontier, and both sides were effusive in support of superpower détente.

But all was not politics and vodka in the Poland of the late sixties and early seventies. Mostly a rather wacky, alcohol soaked, chaos reigned. And the Americans were infected by it.

Twenty

Wit is the last resort of the powerless.

Charles Maurice de Talleyrand-Perigord

Yevgeny Bogumolov leaned across the lunch table at East Berlin's Monopol Hotel Restaurant, gray eyes hard as agates. "One man with machine gun can control one hundred without. If he willing to use it and they know he willing to use it."

It was January 1981, and we sat amid the detritus of our monthly lunch discussing the threat of anarchy and civil war in Poland. I had asked Bogumolov how the Soviet Union had managed to control warrior peoples, such as the Poles and Hungarians, while the British and French had been unable to repress their rebellious colonies.

Ironically, his analysis fits nicely with what happened in the late nineteen-eighties in the Soviet Union. The leadership lost its nerve and the will to use the power it possessed.

Bogumolov was one of the dozens of KGB agents assigned to the immense Soviet Embassy in East Berlin. I had met him at a West German reception within weeks of arriving at the Embassy, and we'd arranged a lunch meeting. It quickly became a regular affair. It was customary for the Soviets to assign one of their intelligence officers to senior American diplomats. Bogumolov was my shadow.

A few weeks earlier, driving back from opening a modest cultural exhibit in the opera house of the provincial city of Gera, I had watched masses of Soviet tanks rumbling over the autobahn bridges toward the Polish border to the East. There was an overcast that day, and our satellites were blinded. I crossed into West Berlin and reported the sightings to the American Military Liaison Group which, in an anachronism of the Second World War, had permission to move freely through East Germany. Its Soviet counterpart had the same right of free access to West Germany.

The massing of Soviet troops on the Polish border was confirmed, and for several days we expected an invasion. Then the Russians stood down and returned to their casernes. Looking back, the hesitation of the Soviet leaders to crush the Solidarity movement in Poland, as they had other revolts in Hungary and Czechoslovakia, signaled the first crack in the iron will which had maintained their control over Eastern Europe.

The world was changing. Just as the British and French had flinched before the cost of maintaining their colonial empires in the postwar period, and the United States had waffled in Vietnam, so the Soviets were unwilling to face the blood-bath which would have awaited them in Poland.

Their Eastern European satellites, masters for centuries at exploiting a tyrant's weakness, undoubtedly marked the moment. But a decade earlier in Warsaw there was no evidence of political degeneracy in the Soviet bloc. All was effervescence and optimism in Poland as Gierek took over from Gomulka. The Poles celebrated and the diplomatic corps along with them.

At a dinner party for the Austrian ambassador, Rakowski, Malcuzynski and several other journalistic cronies, I had poured the *eau de vie* on the *banane flambee* and lit it with a flourish. A little too much of one as it turned out. The flames roared upward and somehow set fire to the curtain behind me. The Austrian, with decisive, if not very intelligent, zeal flung the contents of a champagne bottle on the blaze, adding to its fury.

Fortunately my wife raced into the kitchen and returned with a large jar of flour with which she doused the flames. In a sense it was just another day at the office. In the hermetic societies of

Eastern Europe, the diplomatic corps entertained incessantly. The same local journalists and diplomats turned up at every party, parroting the party line. Suffocating boredom was the result.

There were, however, compensations. The arrival by private plane of Edgar Bronfman, later chairman of the board of Seagrams, and a motley crew of hangers on which included a drop dead beautiful English girl whom they referred to as his fiancee. She was supposedly lady-something-or-other, but her accent and manners were pure Soho. I never really understood the purpose of Bronfman's visit nor, I think, did he. Nonetheless the ambassador hosted a dinner party for the group, inviting a Polish deputy prime minister and other notables.

Bronfman drank heavily and, toward the end of the evening, turned to the ambassador's wife and posed a question with an alcoholic leer.

"What's round and wet and surrounded by hair?"

She looked puzzled.

"Pussy," he cackled, waiting for her to react.

On a level playing field Mary Ann Stoessel would have left Bronfman speaking in a high voice. But, a total pro, on this night she gave him a glacial stare and turned toward her other dinner companion.

Mary Ann had paid her dues for thirty years as Walter Stoessel made his way through the State Department labyrinth to become an ambassador, kissing ass egregiously, a master of petty intrigue. She expected the same servile dedication of all embassy wives. And got it most of the time.

There were exceptions, however, and my wife was one.

At the Fourth of July party that year Mary Ann served hot dogs, hamburgers and beer to the stunned amazement of the rest of the diplomatic corps. The French, as usual, laid on a feast of pate, caviar and champagne on Bastille Day. The Brits were lavish with strawberries and cream on the Queen's birthday.

Short of servants, Mary Ann handed out trays for the officers wives to pass around. Lisl stared at the tray presented to her and, turning her back, said, "I'm not your maid, Mrs. Stoessel."

The normal, slightly diseased courtier atmosphere of embassies was similar to that of a small eighteenth century German mini-state. Our embassies were everywhere bloated, and frantic efforts to think up useless tasks still left a lot of free time. This was doubly the case in Eastern Europe where normal diplomatic contacts were limited.

Thus when Stoessel built a paddle tennis court behind the embassy and contributed a sterling silver championship cup, the annual tournament became a center of diplomatic activity for weeks. Since Stoessel was the only one who had ever played the game and he teamed with the embassy's best natural athlete, the DCM David Boster, everybody assumed they would win the tournament.

It was not to be. My partner, Nick Andrews, the head of the political section and an excellent tennis player, learned the game quickly. We defeated the ambassador and DCM in the doubles final—no singles were played—and my wife and I went on to win the mixed doubles against the Stoessel's to the consternation of the courtiers. My crowning moment came in the so-called scrambles when the best male player was teamed with the worst lady. My partner was a placid two-hundred-pound secretary who, unexpectedly, turned out to have excellent reflexes. We won.

My wife and her partner would have defeated Mary Ann and hers but Vern Penner, the lady's husband, whispered through the wire enclosure for her to lose after they had won the first set. *Helas,* fame was ephemeral. Young tigers came in, learned the game and dethroned us all the following year.

Midway through my tour a diminutive woman named Irene Jaffe, a key figure on the Department of State's Polish desk, arrived for a visit. An émigré, native speaker of Polish, she was a direct, no-nonsense little woman. The political section, terrified, treated her with deference.

After some days in Warsaw she came to a staff meeting to tell us her needs. "We read papers. No need to summarize. Also, no need opinions. Opinions, useless." She stopped abruptly and stared down at her notes. "Who Edward Harper? This man who write memcons."

She looked at me with a beady stare. "Why your memcons say one thing in first paragraph and contradict in last?"

"I write what I hear. The Poles lie in the beginning when they're sober, get drunk and tell the truth in the end."

She cackled gleefully. "Your memcons only thing we read on desk, Harper. Very funny. Very, how you say, illuminating."

I slumped in my chair, bemused. Often I would return to the office blitzed out of my mind and write impressionistic reports, combining what my interlocutors had told me mixed with other bits and pieces I'd picked up. It had never occurred to me that anybody ever read these mandated reports.

Her comment was immensely unfair to the political section. It's leader, Nick Andrews, was a brilliantly subtle political analyst, conscientious and exacting. The product of a marriage between an American oil man and a Rumanian noblewoman, he combined an intimate knowledge of the complexities of the Eastern European psyche with the chilly logic of the Anglo Saxon. He was, however, forced by the anally retentive State Department traditions to be supernally cautious.

The memcon, on the other hand, was an invitation to analytical anarchy. A free flowing report of what somebody said, and as such the only report which could leave the embassy without bearing the footprints of the political counselor, deputy chief of mission and the ambassador. The form gave free reign to an unscrupulous cynic such as I.

In the beginning, when we first arrived in Warsaw, my sons, seven and eight, were often pelted with rocks by the local children, envious of their bikes, clothes and obvious wealth. But over the years they were accepted into the local gang. Once, after a lunch at my house, Rakowski had walked behind them as they talked to a Polish boy.

"Harper," he told me, "your sons speak Polish to each other. When the Polish boy left, they continued to speak Polish." When I broached this with them, they looked a little blank. Anyone who had spent years in a school shifting from English to German to French to Spanish to Catalan must have found one more language a less than overwhelming problem. My younger son, a career foreign service officer now a consul in La Paz, having served in Croatia and Milan, is fluent in both Croatian and Italian as well.

The maximum leader of USIA in Warsaw when I arrived was one Wilson Dizard, a large, paunchy, disheveled figure who seemed perpetually disoriented. Highly intelligent, he had the contradictory instincts of an intellectual and a street huckster, trailing in his wake not only his shirttail but organizational disarray.

When it became obvious that the Apollo 11 moon landing would be the biggest propaganda coup since the end of World War II, Dizard entered into a frenzy of planning. USIA had mobilized every asset at its disposal, and we were inundated with films, photos, glossy books, exhibits and all the other paraphernalia needed to publicize the landing.

Among other things Wilson had ordered 100,000 Apollo 11 buttons, about the size of a quarter, which we planned to distribute. Nobody gave the idea much thought at the time. A harmless eccentricity on the part of a man who sometimes acted as if he had just escaped from a home for the bewildered.

The centerpiece of the Apollo campaign was a large plastic mock-up of the spaceship we mounted in front of the Embassy. On the day of the landing one of the Polish employees placed a platter of buttons in front of the mock-up. Within minutes all hell broke loose as word spread throughout the city. Masses of people soon jammed the Embassy driveway and lawn demanding buttons. We quickly mobilized the staff and moved among them handing out the little blue objects.

It was soon impossible to move. I was driven back against the plate glass windows in front of the Embassy which began to vibrate under the pressure of the crowd. Faced with the possibility of being impaled on a sliver of glass, I threw my remaining buttons high in the air and retreated into the Embassy.

We quickly set up a system of passing buttons through

windows and continued handing them out for two days until the supply was exhausted. At one point, one of the Polish employees said a con man had set up a small table in front of the space ship and was selling trips to the moon to passing peasants.

The Poles were mesmerized by the space program. When the astronauts later returned with moon rocks, embassies around the world received samples mounted in little plastic bubbles. I volunteered to deliver our specimen to provincial museums around Poland once it had been displayed in Warsaw, using the occasion to call on small town newspaper editors and directors of the small quarterly intellectual journals in each province. For some reason this sliver of what looked like coal had magical properties. Wherever I went, usually in my battered Volkswagen, the community notables turned out en masse to greet me and the rock.

Everybody in Poland seemed to have a relative in America, and the warmth and affection this nation felt for the United States was startling at a time when virulent anti-Americanism reigned in Western Europe, Asia and Latin America. It seemed, in fact, that Eastern Europe was the only place we were unreservedly admired.

"The enemy of my enemy is my friend," Gornicki said, sardonically, when I pointed this out to him. He went on to make a passionate case for our defeating the Viet Cong in Vietnam. "Otherwise, the Russians will think they have defeated you and try even more dangerous adventures."

There were other diversions. For some reason the ambassador and his wife decided to repeat their marriage vows on their twenty-fifth anniversary, and invited most of the diplomatic corps to the ceremony. Niko Henderson's wicked sense of humor was triggered. He mobilized the British Embassy staff, rented one of the ubiquitous Polish farm wagons and they all arrived sitting on straw in top hats, cutaways and striped pants. It was a typical piece of cruel British wit.

Midway in my tour, Wilson Dizard was transferred, to be replaced by a young hotshot, John "Jock" Shirley. Jock and his wife, also a foreign service officer, was one of the rising stars of

USIA. He boasted a bizarre history. His father, an American remittance man of distinguished Maryland lineage, was sailing his boat around the Mediterranean in 1939 when war broke out. He parked the yacht in Yugoslavia and moved to Budapest and was trapped there for the entire war, placing Jock in a famous Hungarian private school.

Six years later Jock, fluent in Hungarian, French and German, led his father out of Hungary to Prague just ahead of the Russian advance. Jock parlayed hard work, his knowledge of languages, slight British accent, intelligence and charm into rapid promotions. He had one priceless advantage. Under the facade of an upper class American was the soul of a Hungarian magnate. He was willing, while uncannily maintaining his dignity, to bear any humiliation, perform any servility for his hierarchical superiors—and demand much the same thing from his minions.

On one memorable morning he literally dressed a hungover and disoriented Duke Ellington in order to get him and his band to a plane to Budapest on time. He catered to the ambassador's every whim with finesse and dignity. And he was the most effective USIA officer I ever met, a man totally dedicated to performing a clearly useless and hopeless task—making the United States and its policies palatable to an envious, resentful world—with energy and enthusiasm. Moreover, he did this in the full knowledge that seeking love and understanding was an absurd task and that all we could rationally expect was fear and respect.

Jock was obsessive to the point of hilarity. Presidential visits were choreographed to the second. He was also, rare in such personalities, willing to listen. Never having run a presidential visit, Jock grilled me endlessly on the Rumanian debacle.

The Rumanians had expected about one hundred and fifty newsmen for the Nixon visit. Nine hundred showed up. Their press office was miles from the center of town, and as a result our modest operation in the Athenee Palace, designed solely for the two hundred journalists accompanying Nixon, was inundated.

Telexes were vital for the press. There were only twenty in all Rumania. In the end we got everyone, but only after egregious blackmail. Desks were delivered on the last day. Telephone lines installed as the plane landed.

The Rumanian press chief, a six-foot-six-inch, three-hundred-pound intelligence officer, with no experience other than terrifying his own press which groveled and slavishly obeyed his every order, was stunned at the mass of European newsmen screaming imprecations at him day and night. Finally, in a gesture of total defeat, he arrived on the day of Nixon's arrival at our press center in the hotel's main ballroom and handed me four wicker baskets full of credentials.

"You will distribute them," he said.

In a scene out of a Groucho Marx comedy I stood on top of a desk and called out the names of Spanish, Italian, French, Scandinavian and third world press representatives, tossing the slivers of plastic across the room to outstretched hands. The Secret Service stood dazed on the sidelines, watching potential assassins scramble for the documents. Nixon's advance team had, sensibly, simply disappeared. I discovered Harper's Seventh Law of the bureaucracy, a corollary to Caesar's advice: When in doubt, hide.

The planeload of newsmen accompanying Nixon were dazed by his popularity in Bucharest. Although the regime had put out an official map of the route from the airport to the city which was totally erroneous, everybody in the city knew the real route and 800,000 wildly cheering Rumanians lined it. One of the reporters, Joe Kraft, a noted Nixon hater, sat transfixed before a television set in our press center watching him halt the caravan and descend into the crowd.

"The son-of-a-bitch is campaigning," Kraft said, incredulous.

"Yeah," another correspondent said. "And if there were an election he'd win." Which was true. It sometimes seemed as if Eastern Europe was the only place in the world where we were not hated as a nation.

Warsaw was not Bucharest, however. We had experience and advance warning, and the trip went off without a hitch. Not so still another presidential visit, this time to Yugoslavia. By now I was an expert in these strange events, which were similar in many ways to the voyage the Spanish king made every decade or so to Catalonia to collect the taxes the Catalans refused to pay except to his person. The two-year trip left a devastated countryside and impoverished nobility in its wake. American presidential visits were equally traumatizing.

The president's entourage for these trips had increased to seven large Boeing airplanes bearing food, dishes, and, on occasion, military musicians, in addition to the press corps and a mass of hangers on from the White House staff. To accompany the president was a perquisite and proof of status without price, and vast numbers of irrelevant senior people and their staffs crowded onto the planes.

I was later sent to Yugoslavia to help set up the press center for another Nixon visit. The disorganization and confusion was, if anything, worse than in Rumania. The press attaché invited me to his office on my first day, shook off his loafers, put his feet on his desk, opened a drawer and took out a bottle of slivovitz, downing the first belt of the day straight from the bottle. From there it was all downhill.

The Agency had learned from Rumania that sending a couple of temporary duty officers to handle one of these trips was inadequate. It's reaction was normal for the bureaucracy: overwhelm the problem with people. After organizing the press center, and working out twenty-four hour duty rosters for the masses of USIA officers arriving from all over Europe, I faded into the background and watched as my seniors fought for high profile positions.

Jock arrived and was quickly assigned as the alter ego of the president's press spokesman, Ron Ziegler. He performed superbly, as always, standing at Ziegler's elbow at all times, discreetly murmuring in his ear, avoiding gaffes, bringing his exquisite touch to bear.

I had had enough and assigned myself to put together the overnight book of press information which had to be on the president's desk at six a.m. every morning. As usual Murphy's Law intervened. I had been given a secretary with a broken ankle, the result of a ski injury. She was a tall, sensual young woman from the Kentucky mountain country, with a deep southern accent and a command of profanity which would have made a mule skinner blanch.

On the first night of the visit she didn't show up at the appointed time, two a.m. She lived, I discovered, in the staff housing next to the embassy, a common practice in Eastern Europe. I finally found her small apartment. She appeared at the door in a shorty nightgown, yawning, eyes crossed in an alcoholic stupor. Behind her a nude secret service officer was mixing a scotch and water.

I pointed out through grinding teeth that she was about to get fired and sent home on the next plane if she didn't get her ass to the office in the next ten minutes. The secret service officer, suddenly focusing, panicked, grabbed his clothes and scuttled out.

She turned up in jeans, giving off a warm, if slightly sour, odor of alcohol, sweat and semen. And typed fifty pages of absolutely faultless copy over the next four hours, at the end blowing me a kiss and winking. Over the next four days she performed with equal good nature and efficiency, earning in spades the special commendation I put in her file.

Looking back, I can find no serious reasons for Nixon's visits to Bucharest, Warsaw and Belgrade. We had no vital strategic interests in the first two, and it was inconceivable that we could interfere in their relations with the Soviet Union. The Yugoslav-Soviet feud had long since ended. Trade with all three nations was minimal.

Nixon, like all presidents, reveled in the pomp and circumstance surrounding the office, as evidenced by the ridiculous musical comedy uniforms he had designed for the White House honor guard, more appropriate for the fictional kingdom of Graustark than a puritanical republic. Foreign trips were especially satisfying. Here, as the most powerful leader on earth, he was given a princely reception. Kowtowing officials led him to lavish dinners and receptions. A great relief from his treatment in the United States where, as Truman put it with his usual earthiness, "all I do is kiss people's ass to get anything done."

As my tour in Warsaw wound down, I saw my Polish interlocutors in a final round of semi-drunken lunches. Lulinski, who was almost the only humorless Pole I knew, was, as usual, deadly serious. He was also on a roll. The Polish foreign minister, Stefan Olszowski, had been a classmate of his at Warsaw University and was now a precious asset. Lulinski was also using his expertise, gained during a five-year tour as *Trybuna Ludu's* correspondent in China, to great effect as tensions grew between China and the Soviet Union. He said censorship under Gierek was much less stringent than it had been under Gomulka.

He volunteered that Rakowski was still respected but had lost much of his influence under the new regime. Karol Malcuzynski, the star television personality, was also on his way out. He hardly worked at *Trybuna Ludu* any more and was rarely seen on television.

I traveled to Katowice for one more session with Szczepanski, on the verge of becoming the head of Polish television. He was limping from a ski injury. The Embassy had invited him to visit the United States, a trip for which he was eagerly making plans before it was aborted by his appointment to the television post. In a previous discussion I had mentioned that more contact between U.S. Embassy people and Polish party officials could lead to improved relations. He had agreed to bring this up with Gierek, and contacts had promptly improved. His confidence, power, and hubris, were clearly increasing.

I thanked him for his intervention and we settled into a long and detailed discussion of U.S. politics. He was, however, evasive about the internal situation in Poland, and I noted in my memcon that he was unlikely ever to be a good source of information since he tended to parrot the Party line on any sensitive topic. One of the problems we faced in Poland was that the people willing to talk knew very little and those who were close to the sources of power said virtually nothing.

Szczepanski did not survive the overthrow of the Gierek regime. He was tried and convicted of corruption, being accused of, among many other crimes, keeping a thoroughbred horse on his yacht. Vengeance is dear to the Polish soul, and they seldom allow logic to get in its way.

In a final relaxed lunch with Rakowski, Zakrzewski, Gornicki and Janiszewski in late March of 1972, Rakowski summed up the situation in Poland after the others had left. He stressed that a new generation of political leaders had arrived with Gierek. They lacked the "complexes" of those who had matured during and after the war. The men in charge were impatient with old stereotypes. They were, he said, well educated technocrats and, above all, pragmatists.

Ten years later their incompetence led to Solidarity, Jaruzelski, martial law and the end of communism in Poland.

Rakowski, however, did foresee the continuing détente with West Germany and greatly increased credits to aid Poland in its industrial modernization. Polish relations with the U.S. would improve at the same pace as U.S.-Soviet relations. He foresaw no return to the Cold War but rather an intensification of the great power competition in the third world. The Soviet Union was a messianistic expansionist nation just beginning to feel its strength. It could not be denied its place in the sun. Poland would have to maneuver adroitly between its powerful neighbors and hope to survive.

Rakowski, like most of us, did not foresee the sudden collapse of the Soviet Union and his actions as deputy prime minister and prime minister in the eighties, so misunderstood and condemned by the American media, continued to be guided by the necessity to fend off the two aggressive giants, Germany and Russia, on either side of his nation. He was, as many of us were, wrong. But, a Polish patriot to the core, he was not the criminal oppressor pictured in the American media.

My tour in Poland was about to end three of the most stimulating and exciting years I had ever spent.

But before I close this episode, I must speak of Cynthia.

Twenty-one

Money and poontang are what makes the world turn.
And I'm not sure in that order.

Hollywood actress from the South

There were about thirty of them. Post-doctoral students in Soviet studies, most of them from Berkeley. They were gathered for a briefing in the small auditorium of the Warsaw Embassy's annex which housed the Marine guards and support staff. During the nineteen-fifties the United States had sold Poland five hundred million dollars worth of wheat and accepted payment in blocked zlotys, the currency of the country. The gift was self-interested. We couldn't give the wheat away during a worldwide glut, and the zlotys could be used for local embassy expenses and cultural programs within Poland. The thirty post-docs were in Warsaw on such a program.

The cultural affairs officer, Mike Eisenstadt, who had emigrated from the city of Danzig in 1939 a step ahead of a concentration camp and death, was a great American patriot. He was also a sensitive man, who cringed from conflict. When he began the standard embassy briefing, pointing out that the Polish Gestapo, the *Urzad Bezpieczenstwa* or UB, would probably try to recruit the students, he was howled down by the mostly Marxist group.

He had come to my office, enraged and almost in tears, and asked me to complete the briefing. On my way across the embassy parking lot I encountered two of the marines in uniform, a small dark Hispanic and a very large blond former football player. They shared the affections of my secretary, Ronnie, a spectacular and thoroughly liberated young woman whose apartment was located behind mine in another housing enclave. One or the other could be seen emerging from her quarters every morning. She made no secret of the arrangement.

"Ronnie, you realize those two are going to kill each other one of these days."

"No, they won't," she said. "I've laid down the law. First one who gets out of hand, gets cut off." Since the Marines were allowed no contact with Polish women, this was a potent threat.

I asked them to come with me to the briefing. We entered the room, and I turned a chair around and sat down, astride, facing the group, a Marine on either side of me at parade rest. The post-docs ostentatiously ignored me, chattering away among themselves. A bearded, jeans clad, mostly male, group, they affected work shoes and other working class paraphernalia. Finally, after several minutes, curiosity got the better of cool and the noise died down.

"I'm here," I said, "to tell you where to pick up your checks every month, to register at the consul's office for your own protection and give you a briefing on what life is like in Poland." I waited for the derisive cackle to die down and amused myself examining the spectacular legs of a young woman in the front row who was wearing a black miniskirt and white blouse.

"On either side of me are two marines. Jose on the left was the First Marine Division middleweight judo champion," something I made up on the spot. "Amos was a tackle on the University of Kentucky football team. If any one of you so much as opens his mouth before this briefing is finished, one or both of them will pick you up and throw you off the embassy premises, your grant will be terminated and the Polish government will be asked to expel you from the country." This was an empty threat since I had no authority to terminate their grants.

"I'm the press attaché of this embassy, and I don't give a damn about your politics or anything else you do. I'm here because you insulted my colleague."

"Hey, man, this is fascism," one beard shouted.

"Amos," I said, turning to the very large marine who started forward like a tank on rails. The speaker immediately ducked down and faded into the crowd, which was suddenly quiet.

"Everybody shut up and listen to the man," another, older, beard suddenly said, standing up and facing them. "The Nazi bastard probably means what he says." They were, after all, serious scholars. The yearlong grants were a fabulous deal. Why take chances? They shut up. Amos returned to his post, and I gave a truncated briefing and walked out.

Four days later I sat with my feet on the desk reading the *International Herald Tribune,* and trying to decide which of the local media to call on and harass over the latest nasty stories about the United States, when the young woman with the superb legs appeared at my door accompanied by two of the beards.

I'll call her Cynthia, although that was not her name. She was a truly spectacular creature. Tall with black hair, green eyes and an oval face. A body to match the legs. I stood up and motioned her toward one of the two chairs in my tiny office. She sat down and crossed her legs, revealing a lot of nylon clad thigh. The beards stood.

"What can I do for you?"

She was the spokesman. "We're having trouble at the university."

"What kind of trouble?"

"Our rooms aren't ready. We're housed in some sort of barracks. The johns are filthy. There's no hot water in the showers. And we haven't been able to get our meal tickets which means we spend a lot of money in restaurants."

"And time," one of the beards chimed in. "The bastards stand around picking their noses and won't serve us." A common complaint in Polish restaurants. You could sit for half an hour in an empty room with twelve waiters and never be served.

"Try tipping them a dollar here and there. Gets amazing results."

"That's bribery," the beard said, outraged.

"Then starve," I said, shrugging. "You realize this isn't my turf? You ought to go see Mike Eisenstadt. The cultural affairs officer you howled down. He has connections at the university and the Ministry of Cultural Affairs. He can probably do something if you're being discriminated against."

"We're not being discriminated against," the girl said. "The Polish students are treated just as badly. They don't seem to give a damn. Anyway, all they do is drink and—," she let the sentence die. "But we're serious scholars. We're losing precious research time with all this crap. And Mr. Eisenstadt won't see us. I thought you might be willing to help."

I grinned. "So you want me to exert special American Embassy influence to get you preferred treatment?"

One of the beard's started to protest, and she gave him a look which shut him up.

"Yes," she said, smiling, uncrossing and recrossing those magnificent legs.

I called Andy Konopacki at the Polish Foreign Press Information Office and explained the situation to him. "You were at Stanford. You know what obsessive nuts American graduate students are."

He protested. "Don't I have enough trouble with your goddamned journalists without this?"

"You owe me one, Andy."

"Yeah. I know." His English was totally colloquial, virtually unaccented. "I'll see what I can do."

"He'll do what he can," I said, watching them leave. Three days later she turned up at my door again.

"I came by to say thanks," she said, sitting down without being asked. It's hard to describe the aura she projected. It was sensuality but a lot more. She was that untranslatable French term, a *femelle,* knew it and was happy with it.

I took her to the embassy cafeteria for a pizza and ice cream, both of which she devoured. "God the food's lousy in this country. It's as bad as in Russia." Over the next year she fell into the habit of coming by my office just before lunch, and I'd take her to the actor's club or one of the three or four decent private restaurants in the city where, through judicious dollar tips, I'd become a valued customer.

She told me a lot about herself. "I worked my way through Berkeley as a waitress. I was on a scholarship and teaching fellowships until the Students for a Democratic Society started causing trouble, and they cut me off. I was one of Mario's minions. It pissed the administration off so they fired me."

Mario Savio had been the leader of the SDS movement that tore American campuses apart in the late sixties and early seventies. "In graduate school I was lucky. I started screwing this Algerian, and he suggested I move in with him. He'd pay all the expenses, food and rent, and I'd do the cooking. And whatever. He was something else, that guy. He could fuck three times a night and come back for more.

"When he went home, I quit the SDS and got a fellowship that let me finish my doctorate. Got another to spend a few months in the Soviet Union. And then this came through."

"What are you going to do when the year's up?"

"I've got some money saved up. I'll travel a little. It doesn't cost much. Get a Enrailpass. Live out of a pack. Sleep in trains."

In the early summer my wife took our two sons and drove down to Austria to our mountain farm. She would be gone two months. Cynthia came by one day shortly after she left, and I suggested she go to the theater with me. They were playing MacBeth. The Poles loved Shakespeare. Afterwards we went to a private duck restaurant in the old town square and ended up at my apartment.

I'm still not sure how it happened, but we wound up in bed a few minutes later and spent the next two months there. Oh, I went to the office, and she immersed herself in Polish archives. Since I had a reputation as a ferocious workalcoholic, nobody noticed the three-hour lunches or my arrival at the office at nine-thirty instead of eight.

However, she loved the theater and concerts and it quickly became obvious to the diplomatic community what was going on. For the Europeans it was amusing to see an American imitating them. Virtually everybody was keeping one of the endless stream of beautiful available Polish girls. For us, the puritans obsessed with security, this was grounds for transfer and dismissal from the service.

But a liaison with an American? There wasn't really any way they could forbid it, especially since one of the spooks was having a torrid affair with the German wife of the wimp who was economics officer, usually conducting it in the Marines' weight room at lunch. Cynthia was American. There was silent disapproval but no overt efforts to deter us.

In any event there was a tradition in the Warsaw embassy of sexual peccadilloes. A decade earlier the writer, Mary McCarthy, had come to town to give a lecture. She started an affair with the public affairs officer whose wife refused to leave. Ms. McCarthy was established in one of the temporary housing apartments for three months until his wife finally departed. The two lovers eventually married.

Jock Shirley, in his day a noted cocksman, looked on appalled that I would risk my "career" in such fashion. But we had come to know and accept each other. I probably reminded him of rakehell father. I played the game within the limits I set. He got support and loyalty from me, and he was sensible enough not to make any attempt at real domination which would instantly have converted me into a fierce and bitter enemy. He was a highly intelligent and subtle man who prided himself on being the perfect bureaucrat, acknowledging the name with the same pride with which a German civil servant calls himself a *Beamter.*

Cynthia was a lower middle class girl who had made it the hard way. Superficially a hard-nosed cynic, ever aware of her self-interest, but also a vulnerable lover who had absorbed the mores of her generation. For the first time in my life I was presented with a smorgasbord of caresses which lifted sex to another level and made sensuality an almost unbearable joy.

We screwed ourselves out of our minds for two months.

As the time came for me to join my wife in Austria, I was torn by an agony of conflict between duty, practicality and an overwhelming, obsessive lust. We had also become friends. And we talked of spending six months in southern France which would have left me broke, unemployed and, in all probability, alone, since she would commit to no more.

I almost did it, but in the end gutlessness and practicality won out. I regretted my decision for a decade, until, miraculously, I was offered a second chance. This time I took it.

Twenty-two

Convenants without the sword are but words.

Thomas Hobbes
The Leviathan

The Turkish general put his arm around my shoulders and said: "You know we Turks love Americans. But every time we look away you have stabbed yourself in the back."

We were in the midst of the Watergate crisis. President Nixon, regarded as a genius in foreign affairs, not only by the Turks but by most European diplomats, was on his way to being impeached for listening to the telephone conversations of his opponents and lying about it.

Since virtually every world statesman with the technical means to do so had probably at one time or another done the same thing, our friends and enemies were thoroughly puzzled at what was going on in Washington.

The American tendency to make either heroes or demons of our presidents has always bewildered Europeans who know that their leaders are no more than men like them. They are enveloped in the trappings of power, but beneath the facade are human beings with the normal quota of lust, greed and vengefulness.

The Europeans left-wing press, epitomized by the French *Le Monde* and the German *Die Zeit,* considered Nixon a relatively liberal president who had enforced the civil rights laws vigorously, increased the social welfare budgets and, to general amazement, instituted price controls to protect the poor from a sudden surge in inflation. And they considered his demarche opening relations with China brilliant. Most European analysts now trace the beginning of the end of the Soviet empire to this event.

"You are tearing apart your government for a minor transgression by one of the most intelligent presidents of this century," Bernard Marguerite of *Le Monde* said at the time. "It's utterly childish behavior. Why do you wonder that we don't trust you?"

It was useless to point out the morality factor in American society, a residue of the original sin of Puritanism, which pervades much of American history. I had long shared the left's distaste for Nixon and his early political tactics, and I watched the Watergate affair with a certain detachment as the press descended on him like jackals on a wounded old lion, eager to gut their longtime enemy. The concept of *raison d'état*, which Lincoln, Roosevelt and many other presidents had used to circumvent the constitution, was not available to this lower middle class man, lacking in charm and charisma.

It is interesting in retrospect to note that one of his near contemporaries, Robert Kennedy, had early in his career been a close collaborator of Senator Joseph McCarthy, participating gleefully in a campaign to harass and often jail Americans who had once been members of the Communist Party. As late as 1962 Kennedy was quoted in *Esquire* magazine as saying that McCarthy had been right. But he was a rich, handsome, assured young man, part of a mythical dynasty. By 1968 he was the darling of the American left, a breathtaking metamorphosis. About the only parallel in this century is Francois Mitterand's magical change from Vichyite collaborator to French resistance fighter as it became clear that the Germans would lose.

Watergate was particularly serious, because, as it absorbed all Washington's attention, the crisis between the Turkish minority on Cyprus and the island's Greek majority had reached critical mass. Since the British had turned over the government of the island to its inhabitants on August 16, 1960, ethnic conflicts between Greeks and Turks had verged on civil war.

Cyprus is one of the many areas in the world where a tangled history has thrown together disparate populations unable or unwilling to assimilate. Seventy-eight percent of its inhabitants are Greek and eighteen percent Turkish. The remainder are a polyglot group of Mediterranean minorities which washed up on its shores over three millennia.

After being successively dominated throughout antiquity by Egypt, Assyria, Phoenicia, Persia, Greece and Rome, the island became part of the Byzantine empire when Rome disintegrated. For seven hundred years this essentially Greek political entity dominated the island and left an enduring legacy of the Greek language and culture imprinted on its people.

As Byzantium lost power to the encroaching Turks, Cyprus became a pawn traded back and forth among marauding Crusaders, Venetians and Saracen pirates. It fell into the hands of Venice in 1489 and was finally conquered by the Ottoman Turks in 1571. The Turks held the island until 1878 when, their own empire crumbling in turn, they ceded the strategic island to Great Britain.

After independence was granted in 1960 by a Britain weary of mediating between Turks and Greeks, Archbishop Makarios, the leader of the Greek faction and head of the government, became ever more determined to attach Cyprus to the Greek mainland. The Turks were equally adamant in demanding an equal voice in the administration of the island and insisted that it remain independent.

History again was a ruling factor in the dispute. Following the capitulation of the Byzantine Empire's capital, Constantinople, now Istanbul, in 1451, all Greece fell under Turkish domination and remained its vassal until the Turks were driven out in a war of liberation in the early nineteenth century.

Over the next hundred years Greece had managed to recover other Greek-inhabited territories, most notably the island of Crete. Cyprus, however, remained a British colony. The traditional hatred between the Greeks and Turks was exacerbated at the end of the First World War when the Ottoman Empire, an ally of Germany, was stripped of most of its remaining territories by the victorious allies.

As World War I ended, the newly-founded Turkish republic, led by a dynamic general, Kemal Ataturk, was invaded by Greek armies which advanced into central Turkey and seemed about to conquer the entire country. The Turks, led by Ataturk, rallied, counterattacked and drove the invading Greeks into the sea. The successful Turkish campaign benefited from the singular incapacity of the Greek commanding general who is said to have believed that his legs were made of glass, something of a problem for a cavalry-man.

Tens of thousands of Greeks—military and civilians—were massacred as they attempted to escape the vengeful Turkish armies. In cities such as Smyrna, now Izmir, with large Greek minorities, bodies piled up on the beaches and in the harbor as ships put to sea with people clinging to their mooring lines.

By the time I arrived in Turkey in 1973, Greek attempts to attach the island to the mainland had created a major crisis. My appointment as deputy public affairs officer was, once again, a piece of luck. During one of the periodic foreign service inspections in Warsaw, I had developed an instant personal and intellectual rapport with Ray Benson, a witty and urbane foreign service officer who was the son of two Russian Jewish communists. His parents had immigrated to the United States from Russia in the nineteen thirties, subsequently divorced, and his father had returned to the Soviet Union to die there in the nineteen sixties.

Ray, an atheist non-religious Jew, boasted about having been raised on a chicken farm and working his way through college in menial jobs. He had joined USIA as a translator in the nineteen fifties, just short of receiving his doctorate, and was now in line for one of the agency's top jobs, public affairs officer in Turkey. He needed a loyal number two. Although I had just been promoted, my rank was much too low for such a job. Ray used his clout with the Eastern European Mafia to get me as his deputy. Promotion to counselor and the rarefied atmosphere of the senior foreign service followed several years later.

Turkish language training was a requirement for the post, and I again spent eight grueling months, eight hours a day, studying a language of excruciating complexity with no discernible connection to any European tongue. Learning such languages is difficult at any time, but on the cusp of middle age, the task is virtually hopeless. When a classmate, a highly decorated air force colonel destined to be a military attaché, wound up in the hospital with a bleeding ulcer in frustration at his inability to absorb the fiendish grammar, the administrators of the course panicked. My demand that I be allowed to spend the last two months of the course on my own in the charming Turkish town of Bursa was approved.

One of my instructors provided me with an introduction to Shahap Tarzi, a businessman in the city. Shahap and his wife were graduates of the American Robert College in Istanbul. He was descended from Afghan kings who had been exiled to Turkey. With that unrivaled hospitality typical of the Middle East, this couple took me under their wing, spending virtually every evening carrying on conversations with me in Turkish from six to nine at which point we relaxed into English.

It was an excruciating experience in many ways, since I could not escape the sessions. Once accepted into a Turkish household, there was no way to avoid being a part of it. Shahap also put one of his managers at my disposal for a couple of hours of conversation a day in one of the many coffee houses of the town.

Ali was a charming and patient man who was a close friend of the mayor and chief of police of the town. I was soon included in the group during their habitual mid-morning get togethers. After several weeks the mayor broached a sensitive topic. I was alone in Bursa without my wife. I must be suffering from the deprivations this caused. He and the chief of police proposed a solution.

They explained that Turkish women convicted of crimes were often, quite unofficially, offered a choice of serving their time in the fetid jails or of becoming temporary prostitutes for the leading personalities of the locality. At first I thought they were joking, but after the morning coffee I was led to the local house of detention and allowed to examine, in intimate detail, the freshest crop of young female criminals.

They were not an appetizing lot, and in any event the proposal did not tempt me. However, the sensitivities of my hosts could be easily wounded, and I finally pointed out that my religion did not permit me such pleasures, much as I appreciated their solicitude. They were aware of the puritanical nature of non-Moslem societies and accepted my excuses.

One sidelight of this rather bizarre expedition was my discovery, during a rather detailed inspection of the ladies, that it was a Turkish custom for their women to shave their pubic hair.

After two months I joined Benson in Ankara. As deputy public affairs officer I was essentially the manager of the office, handling personnel, budget and the general garbage associated with this multicultural organization. I had never supervised more than five people and was suddenly placed in charge of more than 150 in seven cities, most of them employees of America Houses. These cultural centers, whose core function was a library, were designed to mirror American culture.

The dissonance between the press and cultural sides of the agency became more and more apparent to me over the next three years. On the one hand we were in the business of isolating the Turkish power centers, principally political leaders and the media, and persuading them to support American foreign policy initiatives. On the other, the cultural, side we were attempting to mirror American culture in all its diversity and persuade Turkish intellectuals that we were a benign, intellectually rich and generous society worthy of emulation.

While not antithetical, the two tasks demanded totally different skills. Since our officers were theoretically interchangeable, a press specialist often found himself in the uncomfortable position of pushing culture and a bewildered cultural affairs officer would suddenly be facing a hostile and sophisticated media ready to cut him to shreds.

It was during this long and tension-ridden tour that I became convinced that the United States Information Agency should be abolished, its press functions handed over to specially trained political officers and a separate, quasi-governmental, overseas cultural affairs entity be created along the lines of the Alliance Francaise and the Goethe Institute.

The French and Germans staff these entities with seasoned academics, well versed in the culture and history of their countries, who spend most of their time lecturing at the universities of their host countries. American cultural officers tend to become mired down in bureaucracy, spending more time on essentially clerical tasks than in moving among the populations to whom they are assigned and illuminating American social and cultural values. In Turkey we supplied libraries, lecturers, English teachers, theatrical troupes, musicians and a myriad of other services. In a theoretically brilliant but practically disastrous decision, the centers some years before had been encrusted with boards of local dignitaries to advise the American foreign service officer who was director of the center.

It was a prescription for conflict. The local leaders, academics, businessmen and politicians, were powerful figures in their community. The deputy directors of the centers were also Turks, individuals who often remained in their jobs for decades while the Americans came and went at four-year intervals. The result was a director more or less at their mercy. Very often the America House wound up being converted into a venue for indigenous cultural events and a club for local dignitaries with little relation to United States propaganda and cultural goals.

I spent most of my three-year tour in Turkey mediating conflicts between the American directors and their Turkish boards. My only real weapon was budgetary, and I soon learned to use it to brutal effect. The threat of closure was real, since having an America House was still a matter of great prestige in a provincial Turkish city. Turks are a proud and stubborn people who never forget that at one time they ruled a large chunk of the world. We went to the brink with them many times before recovering control of our assets.

The headquarters in Ankara and the largest branch office in Istanbul presented other problems. Ankara was a dismal provincial city, capital of the country only because Kemal Ataturk wished to cleanse the government of corruption and avoid the cosmopolitan fleshpots of Istanbul. But the city on the Bosphorus remained the intellectual and cultural center of the nation, and our office there was almost as large as the one in the capital. Traditionally it had been pretty much left alone by Ankara and was manned by a senior officer.

Ray Benson intended to change all this. After getting the America Houses under control, I was to bring Istanbul to heel. The next three years were a graduate course in the management of multinational bureaucracies and the exercise of power in an environment lacking in the brutal personnel sanctions of private business. It was virtually impossible to fire anybody, American or Turk, and, in the case of the Americans, very difficult to have them transferred.

I did, however, write their performance ratings, reviewed by Ray, and between us we managed through carefully orchestrated blackmail and brutality to retrieve a high measure of control. It was a true reign of terror in the beginning, and I was cordially hated by one and all, allowing Ray to move majestically above the conflict and on occasion soften some of my ukases. However, in substance, he backed me to the hilt. Good cop, bad cop.

All this energy and effort were in the end to no avail, since it soon became clear that our impact on this nation of thirty-six million mostly semi-literate peasants was minimal. Our military bases around the country were continual sources of conflict as the troops violated the local habits and customs, insulted and sometimes raped the women, and generally conducted themselves as an occupation army.

The hatred between Turks and Greeks, both our allies in NATO, forced us to walk a fine line between them. The Greek lobby in Washington, led by Senator Sarbanes of Maryland, was the object of periodic rage in Ankara. The Turks had no such lobby, and at one point, in a bizarre demarche, they offered the famed American novelist, Robin Moore, author of *The Green Berets* and *The French Connection,* two hundred thousand dollars to write a book about one of their generals who had fought heroically with us in Korea. Such a book, the argument went, would gain a warm spot in the hearts and minds of Americans. We were not the only naïfs in the propaganda business.

The Turks were justly feared by the North Koreans and Chinese in that war. The general chosen to personify the heroic Turks, then a lieutenant, often drove a jeep between the lines decorated with severed enemy heads mounted on spikes, daring the enemy to attack.

Moore, a charming man whose politics were somewhat to the right of Tamurlane, arrived in Turkey just as I finished another political novel, *The Chinese Ultimatum* which I wrote between five a.m. and eight a.m. each morning before going to the office. The book dealt with a war between Russia and China and, within this framework, postulated the reunification of Germany, something I, even then, believed to be inevitable and sooner rather than later.

Although Moore and I disagreed across the board on politics, we became personal friends over the three months he lived in Turkey. In the end he returned the Turks their two hundred thousand dollars and did not write the book. But, on almost his last night in Ankara, he demanded to see the manuscript of The *Chinese Ultimatum*. He took it back to his hotel—much the worse for martinis, wine and cognac after a farewell dinner at my house—and at five o'clock in the morning called to offer me a deal.

He would, for half the scratch, put his name on the book with me, guaranteeing me an advance of $25,000.00. At that time, with two sons about to enter college, this was a vast amount of money to me. Embedded in this offer was some sort of scam to sell his name as a tax break to investors who would buy a portion of the book. Fortunately for me, he insisted on having the copyright in his name, since the scheme came afoul of the Internal Revenue Service some years later, and Robin suffered heavily as a result.

At about this point, and as the Cyprus crisis heated up, Ray Benson had to leave the country for treatment of a detached retina, leaving me in charge. No sooner had he crossed the border than the Turks, enraged at Greek actions on Cyprus, invaded the island, taking more than a third of it before a truce was arranged.

With Washington in the midst of the Watergate turmoil, and Kissinger and Nixon attempting to avoid going to jail, there was no way for the United States to bring sufficient pressure to bear to stop the Turks. The result has been an open wound dividing two of our most important NATO allies for more than twenty years.

In the end we managed to commit the worst of diplomatic sins. We mortally offended both nations while obtaining no diplomatic or strategic advantage with either.

There were always, in even the most serious crises, occasional lighter notes. One of the Turkish journalists, Sinan Fishek, and several Western newsmen accompanied the Turkish invasion force. The fog of war soon enveloped the correspondents who found themselves crawling through a field of grape vines, lost.

Fishek reached up and ate a grape, turning to his companions in panic. "We've got to get back. We've moved behind the Greek lines."

"Sinan, how do you know?"

"The grapes are too plump to be Turkish."

Then there was Joseph Sisco, Kissinger's emissary, standing in his underwear in the chaos at our command post in Macomber's cavernous residence, shouting toothless, bombastic threats into the telephone at a former Turkish foreign minister who was attempting to mediate between him and the prime minister.

That prime minister, Bulent Ecevit, had studied under Kissinger at Harvard and had a sophisticated understanding of the United States governmental system. He sent in his invasion force after recognizing the paralysis of the Nixon-Kissinger regime would result in no sanctions. He was right.

Another crisis involved the so-called Yom Kippur War in 1973 among Israel, Syria and Egypt. Israeli successes in the opening battles led the Soviet Union, Syria's ally, to pour weapons into the Arab country, overflying Turkey with impunity.

Ambassador Macomber, a certified maniac, was told to approach the Turks and ask them to halt the flights. Instead of protesting to Washington, he conveyed the message. The prime minister and the chief of the Turkish general staff listened impassively. When he finished, the Turkish general asked:

"Ambassador, what do you want us to do? Shoot the Russians down?" No more was heard from the United States on the overflights which continued unhindered.

When the Arab and Israeli armies ground to a halt following a fragile, often violated, cease-fire, with Israel holding large chunks of Syrian territory, including the strategic Golan heights, Secretary of State Kissinger began a month-long effort which became known as "shuttle diplomacy", often flying in the course of the same day from Jerusalem to Syria to Cairo to Amman and Jidda in an effort to bring peace to the region.

Syria had broken diplomatic relations with the United States on June 6, 1967, citing U.S. support for Israel, and when Kissinger began his shuttle there were no American diplomats in Damascus. Since he carried with him an influential press contingent on these trips, it was essential that a press officer be assigned to Damascus. This became urgent when a young consular officer, sent quickly to Damascus, was opened up like a can of tuna by American journalists who were descending on the Arab capital. Basking in the light of their cameras, he blithely spilled his guts.

Orders came from Washington for me to fly immediately to Damascus to handle the press. There was only one problem. My diplomatic passport had an Israeli visa in it, relic of a trip I took to Jerusalem to be looked over as a possible press attaché there. Nobody with a passport containing an Israeli visa would be allowed in by the Syrians. There was no time to get a new diplomatic passport, so I was issued a regular one, stripping me of any official protection, and left for Damascus the next day.

A room had been booked for me in the Yeni Ortam Hotel. Shortly before my arrival six suspected spies had been hung from gibbets in front of this building.

Twenty-three

Although it is permitted to believe that support of political dogmas is at times an excellent auxiliary (to war), it must not be forgotten that even the Koran would win no more than a province today, for in order to effect this, shells, balls, gunpowder and muskets are necessary.

Antoine Henri Jomini in *Precis de l'art de la Guerre.*

Zuher Janaan, the Syrian minister of information, held court each morning in his office as I reclined among the cushions aligned along one wall. We had arrived at this arrangement, since I had no way of knowing when Kissinger would arrive in Damascus. Without transport of any kind and no communications, it was the only way I could be sure of arriving at the airport ahead of the great man's plane.

His newly appointed press spokesman, Robert Anderson, a career foreign service officer, was an educated fool, a category I discovered over the years to be uniquely prevalent among diplomats and academics. Rich, educated at private schools and Yale, he was a classic bully, servile to his superiors and a hectoring bully to those who worked for him.

We clashed instantly when I refused to kiss his ass. Kissinger treated him with the kind of careless contempt he had for weaklings of any kind, leaving Anderson to grovel in his wake as he acted as his own press spokesman. The traveling press was an impressive group. Among them were Bernie Gwertzman, of the *New York Times*, later its foreign editor, Marvin Kalb and Ted Koppel, all of whom went on to fame and fortune. Then there were the inevitable frauds and phonies, such as Richard

Valeriani, Barry Schweid and Marilyn Berger of the *Washington Post*, a formidable bitch, all of whom have disappeared into the mists of time.

My job was to accompany Janaan to the airport ahead of Kissinger's arrival and assist in setting up the press and television pools which covered each landing. We soon divided the task, with Janaan watching over the large middle eastern contingent and I, since I spoke French, German and Spanish, handling the Europeans. Once the pool was set up I would meet Anderson as he left the plane and ride to the official rest house with him, setting up liaison with the press confined to the hotel.

Since Kissinger did virtually all the substantive press briefings himself during flights, I was essentially a messenger, bringing back from his guest house information about schedules, briefings and other logistical garbage. Anderson should have done this, but he was new to his job and terrified of the newsmen whose contempt for his pomposity was palpable. He rarely appeared.

Janaan, to keep the newsmen amused, arranged visits for them to local sites such as schools and hospitals bombed by Israeli planes, archaeological museums, the bazaars and, for anybody interested, brothels. I knew most of the tour regulars from the three presidential trips I'd handled. We lived and ate together during their stopovers, and I eventually began acting, in Anderson's absence, as a conduit to the great man for their complaints and questions.

Koppel and Kalb were determined to visit the war zone on the Golan heights from the Syrian side. The Israelis had allowed them to take a look at the battlefield from Mount Harmon, and they wanted the view from the other side. Kissinger consistently refused to pass along their request since the cease-fire was often violated. The last thing he needed was an incident resulting in the killing of prominent American journalists.

Over the first half dozen visits I had become quite friendly with Janaan and the Syrian colonel, reputed to be head of their intelligence service, who seemed to be in charge of the Kissinger operation. They both spoke excellent French, and we often had lunch together at one or another of the superb restaurants of the city.

I had come to Damascus prepared to dislike what was clearly brutal—a dictatorship run by former murderous terrorists. Reluctantly, over the next weeks, I was seduced by the personal charm of men like Janaan and the colonel who expounded the Arab position in the conflict with Israel with a passionate logic.

One could disagree, and I mostly did, but they believed that the Israelis were European colonizers, much as the Crusaders had been, who had returned to a land that their ancestors had left two thousand years before, driven out most of the inhabitants, stolen their land and enslaved those who had remained. They pointed out, with some justification, that Jews attempting to escape Nazi Germany had been unwelcome immigrants around the world, including the United States, and had been forced on the defenseless Palestinians by fiat. We, Western Europe and the United States, were self-righteous hypocrites.

I pointed out that whatever the flawed origins of the Israeli state, it existed, it wasn't going to go away and the civilized thing to do would be to seek a livable compromise. After all, the Alawites, Shiites and Sunni were different Semitic tribes and managed to live together in peace most of the time. Druzes, Armenians and Maronite Christians were also part of the mix.

They looked at me pityingly as I made this argument, and over the years it became clear as Lebanon degenerated into chaos and the Kurds, Sunni and Shiites were at each others throats in Iraq and elsewhere, that my optimism was sadly unreal.

Nonetheless, trading on my cordial relationship with these two men, I brought up the possibility of taking the American traveling press to the Golan heights front. A couple of days later the trip materialized, much to Kissinger's chagrin. As we gathered in front of the hotel to make the short run to the front, Anderson appeared with a short, almost dwarflike, young man, Edward Gnehm, widely believed to be a spook, and announced to the Syrian colonel in impeccable French that he, not me, would accompany the group.

Needless to say, I was enraged, and my face must have showed it. the Syrian glanced at me, smiled, and told Anderson that either I accompanied the group or it would not go. Anderson began to bluster, and the colonel turned on his heel and walked away.

We arrived at the base of a hill an hour's drive from Damascus just before noon and started up the hill to a bunker at the top. I had a small portable recorder operating as we began the ascent when suddenly 155 mm shells from Mount Harmon ten miles in the distance began to land five hundred yards on either side of us. The television and still photographers were galvanized, running toward the explosions like maniacs as the rest of us raced up the hill.

Marvin Kalb, long legs churning at my side, growled in despair as we neared the bunker, captured for eternity on my tape: "Don't they know I'm Jewish?"

It later developed that the Israelis, somehow informed of the newsmen's trip to the front, had, with that sardonic sense of humor for which they are famed, arranged to bracket the bunker at a safe distance to provide the group with a photo op. I noticed as we raced up the hill in panic that the Syrian colonel was sauntering slowly behind us smoking a cigarette and grinning at the scene.

Nerves frayed as Kissinger's shuttle continued for almost a month. The Syrians were in despair. It seemed as if this man, endowed with endless *Sitzfleish,* would never stop until some sort of permanent truce was arranged. Our airport visits were now routinized. Janaan would receive a call and we would leap into his aging chauffeur-driven Chevrolet and careen along the airport road in a caravan of officials.

On one memorable occasion early in the shuttle, Janaan and I were late arriving, our car skidding to a stop a few hundred yards from the reception area. We began to run, Janaan short, balding and fat, holding my hand in his as the Arabs are accustomed to do, worry beads in the other. We arrived at the base of the airplane ramp just as Kissinger and Anderson emerged. The secretary stared at us and laughed. Anderson viewed the scene with horror as Janaan continued to grip my hand.

My attempt at an explanation was met in the car by a cold stare from Anderson's bloodshot eyes. "Harper, I don't give a shit what the Arab's customs are. You are a disgrace to the diplomatic corps, holding that fat little asshole's hand like a goddamn faggot."

The American Secret Service had persuaded the reluctant Syrians to adopt their button system, under which access to different areas was controlled by a series of different lapel pins. Janaan had reluctantly gone along with this although he regarded it as humiliating. In one of the last visits he had neglected to wear his pins, and the guards at the airport gate refused him entry, although they knew him to be a high official in the Ministry of Information.

The Syrian colonel was called. He stroked Janaan's empty lapel and said something in Arabic in his soft voice. Janaan, jumping with rage, leapt back in his car and left.

"He didn't have his button," the colonel said, smiling.

"Who's going to do the Arab press pool?" I asked.

"You, my friend," the Syrian said. "You are for today the Syrian minister of information." He smiled. "Don't worry. I'll sort out the assassins."

Returning to Ankara was something of an anti-climax after the Syrian episode. The Turks continued to be irritated by our attitude on Cyprus, and I narrowly escaped serious injury when one demonstration in front of the USIA offices in central Ankara ended in rocks coming through the windows of my office. I had the desk moved between the windows after that until iron grilles could be put in place.

My wife and I took a few days off at one of the European resorts which were opening on the Turkish Mediterranean coast, an area of breathtaking unspoiled beauty. The Turks, recognizing if not approving, strange European customs, had arranged for a nude beach in a secluded cove. The local Turks soon discovered it. One day I took a long walk along this narrow strip of sand. A dozen or so Italian ladies, suitably bareassed, lay on their towels inviting skin cancer. On the rocks above, half a dozen impassive Turks crouched on their heels like a line of crows.

Finally, a particularly appetizing young Italian woman, infuriated, turned on her back and spread her legs wide. Within seconds the other women had followed suit. The Turks stood up, stared impassively at the scene, and left.

Cross-cultural differences were a standing problem. I had adopted a group of religious fundamentalists from Palestine, Texas, who had convinced themselves that Noah's Ark was located in an inaccessible crevasse at 16,000 feet on Mount Ararat. They wanted permission to climb up to it. The mountain lies on the border between Turkey and what was then Soviet Armenia, an area so strategically sensitive that virtually nobody was allowed near it.

For years the Turkish Foreign Ministry had turned down all attempts by the religious group to climb it. As Semih Akbil, the most Westernized and pro-American of our official contacts, said, "Who are you kidding? This crowd has got to be part of your CIA. Even an idiot knows that the flood, if it happened at all, was a localized event in the Euphrates Valley. If Mount Ararat had been flooded up to sixteen thousand feet the whole world would have been miles underwater."

Semih was later transferred to Rome where he was shot to death by an Armenian assassin. He was a compassionate, intelligent and witty friend. I mourn his passing.

After meeting with the group, Akbil was forced to admit that they were extremely unlikely to be CIA agents. Rather, they were dangerous fanatics. We never managed to obtain Turkish permission for these likable, earnest people to make the climb. Which was just as well, since their whole world would have crumbled when they found out that the ark was not there. Better a dream unrealized than a dream destroyed.

Business as usual meant arranging for visits from American journalists to six imprisoned Americans caught by the Turks trying to smuggle six hundred pounds of marijuana from Syria to Europe via Turkey. The pot was stashed in the walls of a van. In normal times, the van would have been confiscated, the youths fined and sent on their way.

But the United States had been for years harassing the Turks to end the growing of opium poppies which supplied a large part of the heroin entering the United States. After endless procrastination, the Turkish government, beholden to the United States for its security against the Soviet menace on its borders, finally caved in, causing serious dislocation in the economy.

After the marijuana shipment was discovered, a Turkish judge sentenced the occupants to twenty years in jail, an unheard of sentence. When Macomber protested at the severity, he was told: "You told us to stop drugs and that's what we're doing."

The prisoners were treated quite well by the Turks and allowed special privileges. The three young women seemed almost to be enjoying the experience according to a crew cut *Minneapolis Trubune* newsman who came to Turkey to interview one of them. He was shocked that the young woman from Minnesota's major request, aside from some toilet articles and clothing, was for a dildo. But he mailed it to me, and one of our vice consuls duly delivered it on his next official inspection trip to the prison.

The Turks, having made their point, released the group after a year.

There were the usual congressional visits. Richard Perle, with whom I later worked in the Pentagon, came on an inspection tour while he was an assistant to Senator Jackson. And Wayne Hayes, an infamous congressman, brought his dog and pony show to Ankara. On one memorable evening Macomber groveled with what was, even for him, an impressive servility until two a.m., insisting that I hang around in case any of the press needed anything.

Macomber had a curious patrician concern for his minions and on this evening had dismissed his marine driver. The ambassadorial limousine was an armored Cadillac infamous for burning out its brakes if stopped abruptly. After Hayes finally wound down and went to bed in alcohol-sodden stupor, Butts, as he insisted on being called, offered me a ride home, since I lived in an apartment on the same hilltop as his great mansion.

He wore glasses as thick as the bottoms of coke bottles, but I had not realized that he was close to being legally blind. We weaved our way through the mercifully deserted streets of the capital in a lethal slalom and somehow managed to get home.

In my last weeks in Ankara the U.S. military base on the outskirts of the town decided to put on a special celebration of the Fourth of July, complete with a parade, a fair and other typical American entertainment. The Turks loved this sort of thing and turned out in masses to participate. Unfortunately, nobody had informed them that a massive fireworks display would be set off at midnight.

It was an impressive show, lighting up the sky for miles. And sending the Turkish military into a state of panic. They were, for a short time, convinced that the Greeks had started a war with an attack on their capital and declared a general mobilization before they figured out what had happened.

Twenty-four

What do we do now that the orgy is over?

Jean Daudrillard

Five hundred and seventy-one charred corpses lay on their backs in the Tenerife Airport hangar. Their arms pointed toward the roof, the ligaments in their elbows contracted by the fire. Along one wall a dozen Spanish nurses in blood-spattered white surgical gowns methodically ripped open the bellies of the dead and emptied the entrails into large barrels, pouring disinfectant into the cavities and winding linen bandages around the remains which were then stacked neatly along the wall.

I had taken three American newsmen stationed in Madrid through a backdoor to view the scene. Jim Markham of The *New York Times,* Karsten Prager of *Time Magazine* and Stan Meisler of the *Los Angeles Times.* During my tour in Madrid all three had become personal friends, despite the fact that the relationship between a press attaché and foreign correspondents is essentially adversarial.

We were all in Tenerife because a Dutch Boeing 747 flown by KLM's senior pilot had taken off just as a Pan American 747 turned onto the island airport's one runway. The Dutch pilot had pulled the nose of his plane up at the last second, too late to avoid a collision. Of the six hundred people on both planes some thirty survived.

It was the worst aircraft accident in history and swarms of newsmen headed toward the scene. I was detailed with a group of twelve other embassy officers to fly down on a chartered plane to assist the overwhelmed Spanish authorities. Within hours of my arrival, the Spanish governor, a man I'd known in Madrid, had turned over de facto direction of the press operation to me.

When I arrived at the airport the Spanish Guardia Civil, the tricorn-hatted national police whose basic job had been repression of dissent throughout the Franco regime, held dozens of foreign newsmen prisoner in the small airport lounge, allowing nobody near the crash site or any interviews of the few stunned survivors. I quickly persuaded the colonel in command to allow camera pools from the television networks onto the tarmac to film the crash scene and permit them to contact the ambulant survivors.

An American hospital plane was scheduled to land, to take on board a dozen or so of the badly burned, and the colonel reluctantly agreed to allow newsmen and cameras to view the loading from a distance of more than a hundred yards. He had strung a satin ceremonial cord attached to movable brass stanchions to keep the media at bay. A line of Guardia armed with riot sticks stood behind the flimsy barricade to enforce his orders.

At the sight of the wounded being moved toward the plane, a group of British television cameramen surged forward. The colonel screamed at them to stop. "What the fuck's the barstid saying?" one of the Brits asked me.

"If you cross the rope, he'll set his men on you with those riot sticks. He means it."

The Brits were ecstatic at the thought of Spanish police beating television cameramen, and they quickly decided on a pool, with several of their number acting as sacrifices to police brutality, while the others filmed the scene which would add drama to the static shots of the wounded.

I told the colonel what they were planning, and he instantly blew a blast on his whistle which brought another two dozen Guardia, this time armed with automatic rifles, onto the scene. They spaced themselves between their comrades, armed with riot sticks, and the colonel, marching up and down between the newsmen and his little army with a stiff legged swagger, ordered me to translate.

"Tell them that the first man who crosses the rope will be shot." I started to argue with him, but in the meantime one of the Spanish journalists had done the translating. As all this was going on, two of the newsmen had surreptitiously picked up the movable poles attached to the rope and begun inching them toward the waiting hospital plane.

The Spanish troops recoiled before the advancing rope, as their oblivious colonel continued to posture between the two groups. Markham, Prager and Meisler stood on the sidelines through all this, calling out sardonic advice to me as I tried to mediate between the military maniac and a tribe of frenetic photographers ready to go to any length to get a shot of the horribly injured people being loaded on the plane.

Among the television reporters was a particularly obnoxious character who kept threatening me with an official reprimand if I didn't get him special consideration. His name was Peter Jennings. His threats finally broke through my patience, and I pointed out to the colonel that his fence was moving ever nearer to the plane.

He stared in disbelief at the two moving stanchions and screamed an order to arrest the two culprits, at the same time sending his men forward into the packed mass of journalists who scuttled to safety.

Later at the large tourist hotel where we were staying along with the few ambulant survivors, the newsmen lined up to interview the living. It was my first real encounter with the power of the camera to transform tragedy into farce. A handsome young woman, face still stained with soot from the flames, was at first dazed by the attention. But after the third interview, she began to enjoy her fifteen minutes of fame, and as the last questioner turned away, she almost reached out to hold him back. Others recounted their heroism in rescuing fellow passengers or described with increasing relish the hellish scene from which they had escaped relatively intact.

The disorganization and confusion at the Tenerife Airport was reflected throughout Spain when I arrived in the summer of 1976. Generalissimo Francisco Franco, who had ruled the country with an iron fist since the end of a bloody civil war in 1939, had died in November of the previous year. Although the young Prince Juan Carlos de Bourbon y Bourbon was Franco's designated heir, he was widely regarded as a figurehead.

Franco had intended to place real power in the hands of Admiral Carrera Blanco, but two years before Franco's death a Basque bomb blew his car six stories into the air and landed it on the fourth floor balcony of a nearby apartment house. His successor, the weak and ineffectual Carlos Arias Navarro, was soon replaced by Adolfo Suarez, a personal friend and crony of the newly crowned young king.

Although Suarez was a creature of the Franco regime, and former deputy head of the Fascist *Movimiento*, he was a key element in restraining the extreme right-wing generals from attempting the military coup d'état which everyone expected on the old man's death. He promised an election within a year and kept the promise. He also legalized all political parties, including the communists, freed political prisoners, instituted universal suffrage and legalized labor unions.

Even more important, censorship was relaxed and liberal newspapers—such as *Diario Sixteen*, led by Juan Tomas de Salas, and *El Pais*, edited by Juan Luis Cebrian—were able to publish. It was a wild ride. For the first time in almost forty years, public discourse was free and open. All this effervescence was made more piquant by the ever present possibility that the military would, as Franco had in 1936, decide to move. A major factor in this immobility in the face of repellent reforms was the generals' uncertainty about whether, if they marched, the conscript army would follow.

Memories of the brutal civil war were still vivid. Nobody wanted another bloodletting. Compromise became possible. In addition the young socialist party leader, Felipe Gonzalez, imposed a rigid discipline on his followers and gradually gained the confidence of the king and conservative elements who might otherwise have supported a coup.

The United States was an interested player in the unfolding events. Keeping the Soviet Union in check was still the major thrust of our foreign policy. Our military bases in Spain were key elements in the NATO defense plans for Western Europe. Even a hint that a leftist government might demand their removal led to panic. Above all else we sought stability in Spain.

Welles Stabler, a career diplomat of the old school, was the American ambassador. A product of private New England academies and Harvard, he affected expensive handmade British shoes cracked with age, but shined to a mirror-like finish, and Saville Row suits. He was that curious phenomenon, an American who mimicked the style and manner of a British aristocrat in a society which found such pretensions risible.

He was, nonetheless, a superb diplomat and, underneath the affected mannerisms and arrogance, a serious man. I detested him, and he returned the favor. He nonetheless used me ruthlessly. All the Spanish papers were delivered to my apartment each morning, and by seven-thirty I could expect a call from him to discuss the latest events and get orders on how to answer any criticisms of the United States. He had discovered, and enthusiastically approved, my habit, used in both Poland and Turkey, of calling immediately on any journalist who was hostile to our policies, pointing out the error of his ways.

He read my memoranda of these conversations with attention, his approving annotations before me as I write. Nonetheless, in staff meetings he would routinely disparage my comments and excluded me from the inner circle of embassy policy makers. He demanded, and received, from close collaborators more servility than I was prepared to offer. Despite our mutual hostility he nevertheless used my contacts among Spanish journalists and their connections with political leaders to balance the rigid and conventional reporting produced by virtually all embassy political sections. At this distance, and no longer having to suffer his supercilious sneer, I have to admit he was one of the few real pros I met in my diplomatic career. I was simply, in his eyes, an intellectual lackey and one whose knee would not bend.

And, like a lackey, he used me for all the dirty jobs. When governor Carlos Barcelo of Puerto Rico came for an official visit to Madrid, Stabler turned him over to me. Barcelo was an easy-going politician whose English and Spanish were both impeccable. It was his first trip to Spain, and it was more a vacation than political.

I had set up a press conference for him and made a few phone calls to make sure some Spanish journalists showed up. I needn't have bothered. I, along with everyone else in the embassy, had totally misread the importance of Puerto Rico to Spaniards of all political colorations. The room was packed, and the first question set the tone.

"Senor Governor, when will the United States' imperialists allow a referendum in Puerto Rico which would permit the people of this downtrodden colony to express their desire to return to the bosom of their native country, Spain?"

Barcelo stared at the man, puzzled, and turned to me, asking in a whisper if he'd heard the question right.

"Do not ask that CIA running dog of imperialism at your side what you should answer, Senor governor," the questioner, a correspondent for ABC, a conservative paper, with whom I had had many a pleasant drunken lunch, said. "Answer honestly from the depths of your Spanish soul."

Barcelo, a little stunned, replied that there were indeed three parties in Puerto Rico. One wanted independence, another to retain commonwealth status, both with about the same forty-five percent of the vote, and finally a very small party calling for independence. He knew of nobody who wanted to return the island to Spain. The audience erupted with rage, and the rest of the conference dealt with the U.S. dismemberment of the Spanish empire and annexation of Puerto Rico following the Spanish American War in 1898. Barcelo bobbed and weaved, slipping most questions adroitly as he was hit from every side.

When it was over he asked where we could get a martini.

Three-hour drunken lunches with journalists, beginning at one and ending at four or later, were a large part of my job, and we often met at the Alabardero, the Halbardier, a restaurant run by a defrocked Basque communist priest. It was here that Markham, Prager, Maisler and I celebrated the publication of my book, *The Last Caesar,* with a lunch that lasted into the night.

Two days later, Prager was struck by a massive heart attack, which he always attributed to the aftereffects of our debauch. Some years later he underwent a heart transplant and returned to work at *Time* as editor of the International Edition. Markham and I were once again to cross swords in friendly duels when he became the *Times* correspondent in Germany and I was counselor for public affairs in West Berlin. Later, while the paper's correspondent in Paris, he lay down one night in his luxurious ten-room apartment in the sixteenth arrondissement, put a rifle in his mouth and blew out his brains. He had just been notified of his transfer back to New York to a senior editorial position. He left no explanation. Perhaps he was simply unwilling to hang up his trench coat and give up the excitement and romance of being a foreign correspondent.

He was one of the best and the brightest. I occasionally drink a martini and turn down an empty glass to his memory.

Aside from spending endless hours trying to sell American foreign policy to skeptical Spanish journalists, my main job in Madrid sometimes seemed to be handling visiting firemen. Stabler, knowing how I hated the job, delighted in turning them over to me. "You're our publicity man, Harper," he would cackle. "Image is your job. Get it done."

One of the easier tourists was Senator Sam Nunn, a fellow Georgian, who showed up in Madrid one summer with an entourage including a former commander of U.S. forces in South Korea. Nunn, even then considered one of the great congressional experts on defense, and his group had been inspecting a thoroughly demoralized U.S. Army in Europe. The debacle in Vietnam, replete as it was with the "fragging" of unpopular officers, general indiscipline, inability of the troops or the nation to comprehend the geopolitical rationale of the war and resultant low morale, had left the military in a state of near catatonic depression.

Nunn had stopped in Madrid to draft his report and at the same time sample some of its rather tame fleshpots. We played tennis, went to Hemingway's old restaurant for suckling pig, ate tapas and drank sherry in the bars and ogled the myriad prostitutes in the cafes. It was hard to explain that nobody ate in Madrid before nine-thirty at night, and one evening we descended on a famous Flamenco restaurant long before the dancers were scheduled to perform.

Swilling Sangria—that insidious mixture of wine and fruit which tastes like lemonade and slowly paralyzes the central nervous system—as we waited for the action, had led to a certain amount of gaiety even though the restaurant was empty as a tomb. Finally the performers, reluctantly going through the motions of a hoked up tourist version of the magnificent flamenco art, began to sing and dance a little, warming up like the athletes they are.

Suddenly, as they began to dance, the door opened and a hundred Japanese men in identical suits, all bearing flash equipped cameras, stormed the restaurant. Our general, a veteran of the Pacific campaign on Saipan, growled in disgust. "Can't escape the little yellow bastards." The Japanese climbed over the furniture, took pictures with the dancers and singers and raced off to another exotic locale after their guide handed over a wad of bills to the restaurant owner.

All was not fun and games with Nunn, however. His report, rigorously researched and crisply written, was a devastating critique of the lack of combat readiness of the U.S. military in Europe. He passed it to me one evening and asked that it be sent back to his committee staff in Washington through the Embassy communications system that same night. I read it in the car on the way to the embassy and immediately called the ambassador who was about to sit down to a formal dinner.

His residence abutted the embassy, and I entered through his private entrance. We retired to the library where he read the report, face congested with rage. He tossed it across to me. "Tell the senator I cannot send such a scurrilous report through official channels. And don't interrupt me again while I'm with my guests for such trivia."

I took the report back to Nunn and conveyed the message. We are both southerners and surface courtesy covers a multitude of sins. It, unfortunately, is also sometimes taken for weakness in less polite circles. Nunn asked me to get the ambassador on the phone.

"Ambassador, I really would regard it as a personal favor if you would transmit this report of mine," Nunn said mildly. He listened to the reply.

"Yes, well, I appreciate your problem. But if that report doesn't go out tonight I think I can guarantee that we'll soon have a new ambassador in this country. Mr. Harper will be bringing it over again for transmission."

Stabler's dinner was still in progress when I reached his residence. "I thought I told you not to interrupt me while I'm with my guests."

"You want me to send the report?" I asked, ignoring his remark.

He stared at me, a diplomat for more than forty years, a man from a powerful family, an integral part of the Washington bureaucratic structure. It was all as nothing compared to the power of a senator from Georgia. He nodded, unable to speak, and left the room.

Life in an embassy was often a reality check. It was also occasionally theater of the absurd.

I had reached a level at which I did not have to stand the hated weekend duty watches which every embassy mounts to assist citizens in need. However, one of my tennis partners, knowing that I would be in town for the four-day Easter weekend, asked me if I would take his duty.

I thoughtlessly agreed. It all began on the Friday holiday. The Marine guards were told to allow no one into the embassy except in dire need, and on this morning large numbers of enraged citizens who had lost their passports, spent all their money or just wanted to talk, were told to come back on Tuesday.

My first real customer was an aging black man, brought in by a deferential Marine guard, also black. "Mr. Harper, I thought you ought to talk to this man. He's a musician. Got a gig in Denmark and can't find his passport." He was inside, and there was no way I could turn him down. He had an American driver's license and that peculiarly mellifluous accent which spoke of New Orleans, so I went outside and fumbled through the safe to find a blank passport.

I hadn't issued one in twenty years, and the machinery had changed. I quickly destroyed two of the blanks before calling one of the consuls for aid.

"I'm leaving for the coast in ten minutes, Harper. If you can't figure out how to print out a passport you ought to be drummed out of the service. Tell him to come back Tuesday."

I looked at the genial old boy, a trumpeter who had found a second life in the Dixieland Jazz bands of Europe, and took out a blank and wrote out a passport by hand, valid for only twenty-four hours, instructing him to call immediately at the Copenhagen Embassy for a more legitimate document. He was on his way.

Years later I heard from a consular officer that my passport, the first one written by hand since World War I, had been used by the old gentleman for about five years without the slightest problem. They were thinking of putting it in their little consular museum.

Saturday was quiet until I received a call from the Guardia Civil indicating that they had picked up an American in a wheel chair on the highway from Torrejon, our air base twenty miles outside Madrid, and would be delivering him to the embassy. An hour or so later a marine ushered in a quadriplegic in a wheel-chair who barely had the use of one hand.

He was an army veteran, wounded in Vietnam, who had taken advantage of the air force space available policy for veterans and bummed a ride on one of its transports from the United States to Torrejon. From there he had directed his electric wheelchair toward Madrid. He was planning, he said, to go to Malaga after a couple of days in Madrid.

I called the colonel in charge of public affairs, another tennis partner, at the base and outlined the situation to him. He agreed to have the man picked up and arrange to send him back to the States. The following day I got another call from the bemused Guardia. They had once again picked up the man tooling down the highway, and he was now demanding to be taken to the civilian airport and put on a plane to Malaga.

I decided, what the hell did he have to lose, and told the Spaniards, who were clearly admirers of his insouciant courage, to do as he asked.

I had just immersed myself in rereading volume two of Jose Maria Gironella's massive trilogy on the Spanish Civil War, *Un Millon de Muertos*, when an intimidated marine introduced a formidable looking woman in her sixties into my office. "Lady's got a dead husband in her hotel room, sir," he said, taking cover.

My first, irrational, impulse was to ask if she'd killed him. "He had a stroke and fell face down into his grapefruit at breakfast," she said. "I want his body out of that hotel room. Now."

"The hotel..."

I got no further. "The hotel is run by a bunch of incompetent idiots. They tell me the morgue is closed for Easter. People keep the bodies of the dead in their houses until Tuesday. Also, the hotel is full. They don't have a room to put him in."

She was right, of course. Everything shut down for Easter. I began making calls, finally locating a doctor I knew, another occasional tennis partner. I was beginning to think tennis was an essential consular skill.

He started to laugh when I explained the problem, but finally agreed to help. He worked out of a small Catholic private hospital specializing in child birth, but he persuaded the intern on duty to accept the body.

"You'll have to come in on Tuesday and arrange for disposal of the body," I said, explaining the situation.

"I will not," she said. "My tour leaves for Rome tomorrow at noon and I'll be on it. I've been waiting for forty years to make this trip, and I don't intend to allow anything to interfere with it.

Just get that body out of my room, young man, and ship it back to America. Here's my address."

I started to protest, but she turned on me with eyes bulging with rage. "My taxes pay your salary, young man. You'll do as I say or my senator will know the reason why you didn't." She turned on her heel and left.

Unfortunately, her threat was an empty one. Millions of American traveled overseas every year. Tens of thousands died, were jailed, turned up indigent or just lost their passports. Almost all wound up in harassed embassy consular sections, often waiting their turn with the unwashed multitudes seeking visas to the promised land. The consuls, hemmed in by laws which gave them limited ability to help, soon became inured to the tales of woe. Senatorial letters, arriving by the hundreds, were answered with routine boiler plate. After all, they were the ones who had passed the laws hamstringing us.

Sunday was calm until mid-afternoon when another Marine opened the door, grinning. "I think you'll like this one, sir," he said. I stood as she came through the door. I guess the closest I can come to describing her is the young Eva Gabor. She had lustrous black hair, a honey colored skin and the largest green eyes I've ever seen. She walked with a kind of leonine insolence, every line of her body showing through the cashmere dress.

She threw a black mink across one of the chairs and dropped into another, crossing superb legs and taking a cigarette out of a gold case. I leapt to light it, gazing down at her like a schoolboy confronted with a plate of fudge.

"I am having lost my passport, my money, everything," she said in a husky voice which bled sensuality. "You are pleasing to give me another. And some money. I have plane to catch at five o'clocks. Is no time to lose."

"Uh, you're American? I mean, a citizen?"

"Of course, citizen. O'Malley. Marina O'Malley."

"You have some proof?"

"Proof? Proof?" She was indignant. "Is not obviously I am American? I telling you, I American. You give passport." She recrossed her legs. Her stockings were the sheerest I'd ever seen. I remembered the visa applicants in Vienna.

"Where did you lose your purse?"

"Airport. I sitting down. Talking to man." She shrugged. "It gone. Man bring me to town." She smiled. I'd never seen a smile promise more. "You give passport, no? My friend in Paris. He very impatient." I could understand that.

Five o'clock was four hours away. My fantasies had begun to work overtime when the phone rang. It was the airport manager. "Please tell Mrs. O'Malley that we have found her purse. The money's gone, but her passport and tickets are in it." I coughed up enough for a taxi and watched her leave, trailing my fantasies in her delicious wake.

Madrid was, fortunately, off the beaten track for most visitors. However, Secretary of State Cyrus Vance did pass through. It was a courtesy visit. Something to placate the Spaniards who were becoming increasingly restive about our bases. Inevitable discord between the soldiers and sailors and the civilian population had increased as Spain prospered. In the beginning the bases were an economic godsend, bringing in millions of dollars, jobs and supporting a mini-economy of bars, brothels and restaurants. Now, with the flood of Tectonic tourists, they were a nuisance. Vance was there to stroke the Spaniard's pride.

Both Spain and Turkey had once been world powers, controlling large chunks of the Mediterranean in Turkey's case and most of Latin America in Spain's. Their perception of themselves was greatly influenced by history. The pride and arrogance which are part of being powerful had outlived their long lost empires. They were both much like the shell of exotic molting insects, all form and no substance.

But perception is an excellent substitute for reality if backed by inflexible will. Charles DeGaulle for years made France a player on the world's stage despite his nation's small population, crippled economy and exhausted people. Using its mildly strategic geography, an absolute indifference to the opinion, good or bad, of others and a laser-like awareness of his nation's interests and the psychological weaknesses of his opponents, he had regularly frustrated the policies of the genuine superpowers, Russia and the United States.

Spain suffered from a similar belief that it was the navel of the universe but, after the death of the astute, cynical and infinitely duplicitous Franco, the country lacked a leader who could influence events. Its new politicians cast about for policies to make Spain once more a player on the world stage.

They began a quixotic and doomed quest to penetrate Latin America and wrest its domination from American hands. Their only weapon, a common language, was in many ways a hindrance, since the haughty Castillians could not conceal their amused contempt at the Latin American dialects seeded with Indian and English words. And the Latin Americans could not forget the rapine and pillage of the conquistadors four centuries earlier.

Resentment at the United States, a worldwide phenomenon which is inevitable for a superpower, is something our leaders, and people, have always had a hard time dealing with. Americans want to be liked, even loved, while pursuing the messianistic goal of converting the world to "our way of life."

We ignore the fact that in known human history representative governments have ruled for a minuscule period in a very small number of nations. The concepts of compromise, tolerance, nonviolence and, above all, respect for the rights of opponents and minorities are alien to most societies. The core beliefs essential to a working republic are regarded with contempt by many nations, evidence of weakness and lack of the will to rule.

The Vance visit was in the tradition of American paternalistic attitudes. The president had no time to waste on such a visit, so he sent the secretary of state.

All such trips are meticulously scripted, decisions made by subordinates, communiqués written in advance and surrounded by an aura of good feeling. The Vance advance team was, like the visit, second string. The press element was headed by a tall, lanky man in his mid-twenties, Paul Costello, who had spent most of his young life figuratively licking envelopes in election campaigns.

Madrid was his first overseas trip, and he was exploding with self-importance. The visit was to be a short one. We had arranged to set up a press room in the Palace Hotel, one of Madrid's finest. It was a routine operation which my highly efficient Spanish assistant, Rafael Jerez, had done many times before. Telexes were ordered, phone lines installed, typewriters and desks set up, a podium and microphone installed for briefings, press credentials arranged. The whole schmear. All in place when Costello arrived.

I turned him over to Rafael, a gentle, intelligent man who had been a seminarian and many years later died tragically of AIDS. About an hour after I returned to the Embassy, Rafael called in a state of despair. Costello wanted to rearrange everything. Move every desk. Worse, he wanted to "paint over" the priceless mural on one wall of the room.

When I got to the hotel, chaos reigned. I took Costello aside and suggested we go to lunch at a typical garden restaurant on the outskirts of town. He spent the ride smoking a marijuana cigarette and expatiating on his importance in the Carter administration.

I order Sangria at lunch, stuffed him with superb tapas, trout and creme caramel followed by a glass of the World's finest brandy, Carlos I. As he sipped the nectar I leaned across the table.

"You know, Paul, I used to be a semi-pro boxer."

"Oh? That how you got the broken nose? Forgot to duck." He laughed at his own witticism.

"Yeah. And did you also know that I have my twenty years in and can retire any time I feel like it? Write my novels and not have to take any more chickenshit?"

He shrugged, uninterested. His world circled around Paul Costello's carefully styled hairdo.

"So, listen carefully, you insolent young asshole. You've got everything to lose, and I've got nothing. You're going to shut your fucking mouth, do what you're told, leave Rafael in peace, and we'll deliver your little trip all wrapped in red ribbon. You interfere once more and I'll break your fucking jaw."

I'll give him credit. He sobered up in a hurry, saw the logic of my threats, and on the way back to town we worked it all out. Vance came accompanied by his press attaché, a young Mississippi aristocrat named Hodding Carter. A man of infinite good nature, wit and courtesy. At the airport, on a cold winter day, he went to the secretary's plane and returned with a tray of coffee for Rafael and me and the rest of the small staff.

Vance spoke for the cameras which were mounted on a flatbed truck in order to follow him out to the plane. Costello watched the truck with the fascination of a child. He considered it a genius idea. I refrained from telling him it was routine. He shook my hand and muttered his thanks as he boarded the plane.

Twenty-five

Sincerity remains essential. Once you can fake that, you've got it made.

Samuel Goldwyn

It was eight o'clock in the morning at the Pavillon d'Honneur at the VIP arrival terminal at Orly. President Jimmy Carter's Air Force One was due to land at three in the afternoon. I had received a call from my colleague in Paris, Bill Payeff, three days earlier asking me to come to Paris and help with the visit. The deputy press secretary in charge of the advance team for the visit had insisted that I handle the press arrangements for Carter's airport arrival.

His name was Paul Costello.

Payeff and his deputy, Howard Simpson, were old friends. Wary and experienced career officers who knew that a presidential trip was a minefield. Better to remain in the shadows and use others to do the dirty work. And take the flak. If all went well, they would get the credit for superb management skills. If it screwed up they would fade away.

I'd arrived in Paris two days before the president's scheduled arrival. The trip was a big deal. The French president, Giscard D'Estaing, intended to pull out all the stops to make it a success. For once, the French were the soul of cooperation. Anything the Americans wanted, they were to get. Sumptuous ceremonies, military parades, glittering state dinners, including a reception at Versailles for two thousand, were all designed to show this little peasant what a great and powerful country France was.

Payeff, short, grossly overweight with a subtle middle eastern intelligence, greeted me in his office located in Talleyrand's mansion overlooking the Place de la Concorde. "Costello is starting the schedule of events, line by line, over at the embassy. We better get over there." He collected Simpson and the three of us walked along the edge of the great square to the embassy.

Costello, flanked by young, pretty and arrogant female aides, sat at a long table facing a room full of foreign service officers, many twice his age. Plastic briefing books were piled in front of him. After some rambling remarks, he began with the arrival.

"Ed Harper's going to handle that," he said, nodding to me across a sea of heads. "We'll have the television crews on a flatbed truck, so they can roll alongside the president as he gets off the plane and walks up to meet Giscard."

He then began a line-by-line rundown of the visit. "This is going to take more than two days to get through if I know this guy, Bill," I said. "You better do your own advance work. He's a total fuck up. And probably on acid."

"Acid?"

"Lysergic acid diethylamide. Better known as LSD." I got up to leave.

"Where you going?" Payeff asked.

"To get tickets to Cyrano at the Salle Richelieu, " I said. "And see if I can dig up an old girlfriend to have dinner with."

The old girlfriend turned out to be happily married with two children. However, the embassy had put me up at the Hotel Meridien where all the USIA officers from around Europe were thrown together with the hundreds of newsmen covering the trip. I was having a martini at the bar and contemplating my expensive extra ticket when a young woman climbed onto the stool next to me.

"I say, you are the fellow who's handling the landing aren't you?" she asked, giving her name and network affiliation. It was a British independent company which had trouble muscling in on big events.

"Yes."

"I hear there's going to be a flatbed. Can my people get aboard?"

"Sure. First come, first served after the American networks book space." I looked from her to the extra ticket. "You speak French?"

"Of course," she said. "My mother's French. Why?"

"I've got an extra ticket to Cyrano tonight. Like to have dinner and go?"

She didn't hesitate. "Give me one minute while I talk to my boss."

We saw the wonderful romantic old play and went to Bofinger's for oysters and steak au poivre afterwards, rolling into the hotel after midnight. She was married to an actor but things were not going well. She was on the road most of the time, and he had a girlfriend. My wife and I were entering what turned out to be a terminally chilly phase. When I suggested she have a nightcap in my room, she grinned.

"Sure. Why not?"

As we headed for the elevator, a pimply faced youth descended on us, grasping her arm. "Gavin's going bonkers with anxiety. We've got a team meeting. He's been screaming for you, darling. Come on."

She looked at me and shrugged. "Some other time?"

Paul Costello never did get through the schedule. It didn't really matter. The French were running things and they did it, not only with grace and artistry, but a superb attention to detail. The airport arrival ceremony was choreographed like a ballet.

I had met the young French diplomat in charge of the arrival and been provided with the plastic pass which gave me access to all areas of the terminal. He broke off discussions with his staff to invite me for a coffee, relieved that he would not have to deal with me in his good but awkward English. Our consultation, it rapidly became clear, was not a negotiation but a *fait accompli.*

He spread a diagram of the terminal across the coffee table and explained the scenario. The plane would taxi up parallel to the terminal at a distance of about a hundred yards. A red carpet would be laid from the plane to the Pavillon d'Honneur. President Carter would descend from the plane and be greeted by French President Giscard d'Estaing and presented to officials of the French government and U.S. Ambassador Hartman.

Carter and Giscard would then review the honor guard and enter the Pavillon d'Honneur to be greeted by other French and U.S. Embassy officials. Giscard would make some remarks followed by Carter. They would depart for the Arc de Triomphe for further ceremonies.

"Where will the television cameras be stationed?" I asked.

My French colleague pointed to a position next to the plane. "French television will have one camera here. All the others will be on the roof of the terminal. Pool footage will be available."

I shook my head. "The American networks will be enraged. You're going to have to let them next to the plane."

"Impossible," he said. "Even the one small camera of French television destroys the artistic unity of the arrival ceremony. To expand the site would wound it irretrievably." We argued, but it was clear that he had extremely high level backing and wasn't about to change his mind.

He was an exquisitely polite young man with a steely mind and the self-confidence of his aristocratic background. To relieve the tension, after coffee he took me on an exhaustive tour of the terminal, pointing out where the motorcade would be formed, arrangements for the secret service cars and, finally, taking me to an area to one side of the terminal where the press buses would be parked. A large wire gate shut off this area from the arrival zone. A small emergency stairwell led to the roof which would enable the television crews to move down to the press buses quickly once the ceremony was over.

We were accompanied by a colonel of the gendarmerie, the paramilitary French national police, who introduced me to the gate guards as the "diplomat handling the American press." The young lieutenant in charge of the gate saluted with appropriate respect.

After this show of courtesy, I was left pretty much to my own devices. I spent a good bit of time in a small cafeteria for the terminal staff. I had been introduced to a good many of them, and I gravitated to the police table where the young officers gathered. We drank coffee and traded funny and cynical stories of other presidential events. These men were an elite corps specially recruited and trained for such visits. I became a familiar figure, *un copain*, part of the furniture.

They were hardened to the inevitable chaos which accompanied such events, and I regaled them with tales of presidential visits to Bucharest, Belgrade and Warsaw. At one o'clock I walked out to the highway entrance to the terminal, chatting with the sentries with whom I had earlier been drinking. I hung around until our flatbed truck arrived. It turned out to be an immense machine driven by a diminutive fifty-year-old Frenchman in blue overalls, built like a Gaelic fireplug, Gauloise hanging from his upper lip.

The police stared at the truck, puzzled. He showed his papers, which had been issued by the prefect of police at the request of the embassy.

"He belongs to me," I said, climbing into the truck. "The American television people need it." Television was a magic word and, anyway, they'd been told I was in charge of the Americans. I directed him to the side gate where the press buses would be parked and explained to him what we were going to try to do. As it turned out he had a sense of humor. As we shared a bottle of red wine, which he produced from under the seat, I sketched the plan. He thought the idea of screwing the police and making a shambles of the elegant arrival scenario was hilarious. And the prospect of being on national television was enticing.

The young police lieutenant in charge of the gate came over, and I explained that the truck was for the American television cameras. One of the weaknesses of the young Frenchman running the operation was his upper class arrogance. He delegated nothing to subordinates, instilling terror, and expecting unthinking obedience. The officer shrugged and returned to his post. It wasn't his business. He, too, had been told I was handling the American press. Inside the terminal the American television producers were screaming bloody murder at my French colleague who listened in superbly tailored calm, finally waving them off to the roof.

The television producers, as rough a crew as I'd ever seen, cornered me and began the familiar litany of threats which they used to intimidate embassy personnel in crises. Producers were young thugs, hired to make the pretty faces of the correspondents look good, make sure the cameras were well positioned and, often, to write the scripts of the stars. I pulled them aside, a half dozen in all, and explained what I was going to try to do.

"What if it doesn't work?"

I shrugged, in imitation of my French colleague and said, "then you're screwed."

"Okay," one finally said. "We'll have to try it. But you fuck up, Harper, and we'll hang your balls from the Eiffel Tower." The British girl with whom I'd had dinner had sidled up to the group and grabbed me as I turned to leave.

"Can we come, too?"

"Sure. Just your crew, though. If too many start heading for those stairs Phillipe will get suspicious.

It worked. As the plane landed, the television crews pelted down the emergency stairway onto the truck and I waved to the young lieutenant to open the gate. He stared at me, mouth open to protest.

"Hurry man," I said. "Do you want to be responsible for 250 million Americans not seeing their president land in Paris? Your superiors will send you to a remote village in the Pyrenees if you do."

Fear and indecision fought on his face as he looked for help. I waved to his men to open the gate, and he finally nodded. The flatbed truck coughed to life, spewing fumes from its vertical stack and headed onto the runway just as the plane came to a halt.

I reentered the building and joined my French counterpart among a group of other second echelon diplomatic sherpas. We were watching the arrival on a small television monitor as well as over the heads of the dignitaries. Just as Carter descended the steps, the flatbed truck appeared on the right edge of the screen, cameras rolling. The driver, cigarette still dangling from his upper lip, waved gaily.

Phillipe stared at the scene in horror, a victim of the press attaché's nightmare: you can plan all you want but the asshole variable always wins in the end. I was finished at the terminal. In fact, I was finished with the trip and as my frantic French colleague watched his nineteenth century panorama dissolve, I sprinted toward the car the embassy had put at my disposal and directed it to the Arc de Triomphe where the real arrival ceremony would be held.

The Champs Elyssees, from the Place de la Concorde to the Arc de Triomphe, was a ghost street. Not a car was to be seen nor a human being. At the Arc masses of dignitaries were gathered, along with veterans of the first and second world wars and the various colonial campaigns of the post-war era. Some looked old enough to have been at the front in 1870. I climbed up onto a metal platform provided for the television cameras and stared down on a scene that only the French can stage.

Massive American and French flags hung down and blew in the stiff wind as the honor guard and the ancient veterans came to attention. A French band played "Aux Drapeaux" as the two presidents approached. As they reached the tomb the band switched to "Aux Morts". Two haunting melodies celebrating the great thousand-year French military tradition.

I'd released the embassy car at the Arc, and when the ceremony ended I headed across the now deserted traffic circle planning to walk through my beloved Paris when a bizarre scene confronted me. A short dark young woman was screaming at the top of her lungs in totally incomprehensible French at an immense police colonel who was listening to her gibberish in total puzzlement.

My first instinct was to move on, but duty overcame prudence, and I stopped. "Uh, can I help you?" The young woman turned on me in fury.

"Who the fuck are you? This bastard won't get Mrs. Carter's motorcade moving. We're going to be late." She was clearly frantic.

I spoke to the Frenchman who said he was ready to do anything she wanted but couldn't understand her.

"Tell me what you want. He'll do it. He just didn't understand you."

"Then why the fuck doesn't he speak English?" she said spitting out instructions. I translated and he waved to his motorcycles to start up. As I left, the young woman shouted after me. "Get that man's name. I'm gonna have his balls." That seemed to be the fashionable threat of her generation.

I spent the evening and most of the next day wandering through my old student haunts, eating in a superb Vietnamese restaurant in the Rue Monsieur le Prince. Then I made a mistake. Around five-thirty in the afternoon I wandered into the press room at the Hotel Meridien and watched Carter's press secretary, Jody Powell, one of the best in the business, give a press conference.

Powell was a classic southerner. Shrewd, duplicitous, courteous and vengeful. He used the tools of his office superbly, conning the romantically cynical newsmen with an oily charm and squeezing whatever goodies he could for his self-righteous egomaniacal patron. They were, in a sense, two sides of the southern coin—the congenital hustler and the deluded preacher who believes he has a telephone line to God.

As I stood admiring Powell's act, one of Costello's minions came up behind me and grabbed my arm. "I been looking for you. We gotta have somebody on the press bus for Versailles. Costello wants you." He led me, protesting to a corner of the press room where Costello sat holding court, surrounded by correspondents and cameramen. An aura of grass hung over the scene.

"Hey, Ed, baby. Great job at the airport. TV guys singing your praises. Fucking genius idea, that flatbed of yours. Use it all the time. Want you on the press bus for Versailles."

At his side stood the young woman who had screamed at the policeman at the Arc de Triomphe. "Lisa here, she'll run things, but you'll be her advisor, okay?"

"No."

"Huh?"

"If you want me to take the bus, I will. But I damn well won't work for her."

"Yeah, okay, man. Don't get your balls in an uproar. Lisa will go along to help." He pushed over a box of press credentials of different colors, each with a different number, ignoring the young woman's enraged protest. "You work it out with the guys. There are TV camera stations all along the route inside the Chateau that the president will follow."

By this time the press had begun to wear down. The coverage on Carter's visit to Normandy had been massive and the networks were cutting their losses. Versailles, once a major event, had descended on the scale. Only half as many camera teams as anticipated were on the bus. I stood up by the driver and passed out Xeroxes of the immense old palace with sites marked.

"Okay, who wants what?" In the ensuing pandemonium we sorted out sites, and I was left with a handful of credentials. "Okay fellows. You don't like what you got once we get there, you can change to these," I said, passing out the plastic cards.

"You can't do that," Lisa screamed as I passed down the aisle.

"Hey, honey," a newsman said, laughing, imitating Costello, "don't get your balls in an uproar. He already has."

I tried to make a date with the British television producer for the next day when the trip was over, but she left a note in my box at the hotel, saying she had to get back to London to edit the footage.

Twenty-six

Every strong people extends its ambitions as far as its arms can reach, and every weak people lasts just as long as its energy for defending itself endures.

Manuel Ugarte

Michael Ledeen opened the conversation with the Spanish prime minister, Adolfo Suarez, by conveying a message from former Secretary of State Henry Kissinger, expressing admiration for the accomplishments of the King and Suarez in moving Spain from an authoritarian regime to democracy. He then said Kissinger was anxious to come to Spain for the World Cup football matches in 1982. The Spanish ambassador in Washington had suggested that he play ten minutes as goalie for the Spanish team. Ledeen said Kissinger was holding out for a full half.

The interview was one more tribute to Mike Ledeen's chutzpah. I had met him some eighteen months earlier when Jock Shirley, then public affairs officer in Rome, had called to tell me an interesting character was coming through Madrid. He had worked on the margins in Rome for years for, among others, Clare Sterling and was down on his luck. Could I arrange a lecture and a modest fee?

He had a Ph.D. from Wisconsin which made him respectable. But the only profitable lecture date open was before the American Chamber of Commerce in Spain, my old employer. I set it up. The result was a total disaster. Ledeen had an uncanny ability to push people's buttons, and he gave a lecture which left his audience, men somewhat to the right of Cesare Borgia, stunned. In essence, he suggested that the Spain of Franco was a corpse. Its protectionist, mercantilist economic policies destined for the ash heap. A revolution was happening all around them. Those who didn't ride the wave would be drowned by it.

I was appalled. Knowing next to nothing about Spain, he'd gotten most of this from me over a long drunken lunch from which we had not quite recovered by dinner time. To the audience of comfortable oligarchs, shielded by tariffs and regulations from competition, his remarks were anathema, although the realists among them agreed.

We played some tennis, I added a dollop of embassy money to the honorarium of the Chamber and sent him, bedraggled but undaunted, on his way. Within weeks I got a letter announcing his appointment as executive editor of the Washington Review of Strategic and International Studies. Many years later he surfaced as a player in the Irangate hearings but escaped without being indicted, becoming in the process a respected television commentator and, incidentally, boosting his value as the representative of the interests of various African nations in Washington. He was also for a time the principal advisor on Italian politics to Secretary of State Al Haig. His enemies put about the rumor that he was an agent for Mossad, the Israeli intelligence agency.

All in all a decidedly baroque character.

But this was later. In September 1978 I got a call from him. Could I set up an interview with Suarez? It was an impossible request. Ledeen was nobody. Suarez almost never gave one-on-one interviews. What if he had a message from Kissinger? After he hung up I called Alberto Aza, Suarez' chef de cabinet with whom I'd become friendly over the years in meetings at diplomatic dinners and cocktail parties.

Aza came to attention at the mention of Kissinger whom Suarez, he said, regarded with awe. Within a couple of days I had the interview. All Ledeen had to do was come up with the message.

Suarez, a cynical opportunist, had presciently cultivated the young prince, Juan Carlos, when everybody else had ignored him as a figurehead and a fool. Ledeen and Suarez turned out to be soul mates. Dupicitous, subtle, unscrupulous realists, wreathed in the irresistible charm of scoundrels. I somehow doubt that there ever was a "message from Kissinger", but Suarez left the meeting much the wiser about U.S. motives than U.S. Ambassador Welles Stabler would ever have conveyed.

Suarez and the young king were a shrewd pair. They gradually dismantled the Franco apparat while their enemies told endless jokes such as the following.

After the old man's death, Suarez went to his immense tomb on the outskirts of Madrid to pay his respects. The bones of tens of thousands of fascists who fell in the Civil War were encased in its walls and the musty smell of death permeated the place. As Suarez knelt to pray, he heard the old man's high-pitched, reedy voice cry out: *"Traigame un caballo blanco."*

Transfixed, Suarez raced to Madrid and returned with Juan Carlos. The two knelt before the old man's tomb. Once again Franco's voice came from the sepulcher: *"He dicho, un caballo blanco, no un mulo."*

Juan Carlos may well be a lesser intellect than Franco, but somewhere in his Bourbon bones he inherited a useful shrewdness. Every decision he has made since assuming power has been brilliant, and he will go down in the history of the twentieth century as one of its truly astute rulers. In any event he may not be a Bourbon at all, but the by-blow of an American dentist rumored to have been the lover of his great grandmother.

Normally I would not have accompanied Ledeen to the meeting with Suarez, however, knowing that it would be a coup of the first magnitude for me to be present and write a first hand memorandum of the conversation, he insisted. Aza shrugged. I could do the translating, he said.

Suarez began by pointing out that the success of the last three years since Franco died were no accident. He and the King, with whom he had developed a personal friendship, had planned it all during the old man's last illness. He then launched into a bitter denunciation of American indifference to Spain, particularly its unwillingness to help it establish a special role in Latin America. Shades of Barcelo, I thought.

He noted that, although there was no question that the Soviet Union had reason to destabilize Spain, he would not allow himself even to think that the U.S. might have similar interests. It was an example of the "myth of the central position" at work once again. Spain was the navel of the universe, therefore, the United States had to have some evil agenda to keep it from power. The reality was, of course, that nobody in the American government cared what happened in Spain as long as it wasn't coming apart.

I spoke only once during the interview, protesting this absurd suspicion. Suarez laughed and said it had been a joke. It was a revealing piece of paranoia, however. Although Spaniards were not in a class with Poles for wit, recklessness and political deftness, they had lived for forty years under a dictatorship and developed some of the creative tensions, and wry humor, that such regimes engender.

One of the curious phenomena of the crumbling of dictatorships, whether of the right or left, is the abrupt decline in political humor which accompanies the turn to democracy.

Suarez typifies a desire among all Spaniards of whatever political persuasion to play a role in the Great Game, to cease to be the "Africa that begins at the Pyrenees" in that contemptuous French phrase.

Suarez, who was rumored to have sealed his relationship with the King in all-night orgies at some of Madrid's more discreet and opulent bordellos, said he and Juan Carlos were attempting to move the country to conventional democracy by preserving the legality of Francoist institutions while reforming them through civilized political process rather than risking another civil war.

He had legalized the communist party and cut a deal with the socialists to damp down some of their rhetoric which was frightening the business class. Fascist though he certainly had been, Suarez was nonetheless a key architect of the New Spain which he handed over to his opponent, Felipe Gonzalez, in free elections a few years later.

During my three years in Spain, from 1976 to 1979, rumors of a military coup were rampant. Hardly a month went by without some paunchy, aging general, all veterans of the Civil War, taking center stage by mobilizing tank brigades or parachute regiments on the city's outskirts. The press had gradually been freed, and two newspapers were fearlessly supporting the reforms.

El Pais, edited by Juan Luis Cebrian, an attractive young sympathizer of Felipe Gonzalez, and Juan Tomas de Salas, the rich owner of *Diario 16,* were fearless supporters of the King and Suarez. Even *ABC,* a ponderous conservative journal, got on board of the new reforms.

My KGB minder in Madrid was a troglodyte named Yuri V. Golovialenko, ostensibly a Novosti correspondent. We met for lunch only a few times, however, since he was a man of singular stupidity. He did, on one occasion, blurt out that there were no longer any real communists in Spain. Even La Passionaria, the heroine of the revolution, was a bourgeoise in her old age. But my dreary memcons of our talks were to become one more nail in a security coffin the FBI was later to prepare for me.

By the time I left Spain in the summer of 1979, it almost seemed as if the fragile new semi-democracy might survive and evolve into a true representative government. When I mentioned the possibility of a right wing coup to Cebrian in our last meeting, he laughed and said, "Harper, we've had our revolution. *Las Suecas,*" meaning the swarms of tall, willowy blonde northern women who had begun to descend on Spanish beaches and resorts in the nineteen sixties, leaving dazed a whole generation of Spanish men, destroying forever the nation's dour Puritanism. And bringing with this freedom all the problems of the twentieth century.

As I put Leedon on the plane back to the States I gave him an envelope containing a picture of me with Henry Kissinger, taken when his plane stopped off in Madrid on the way to Golda Meir's funeral in Israel. As he left the plane, Kissinger had spotted me and said, "Hey, Harper, where is the men's room." I asked Ledeen to get him to sign it with a line thanking me for showing him the way to the john.

Kissinger, or one of his minions, refused the request as beneath the dignity of the great man. As many men do, he had become obsessed with his historical image. Frustrated, relegated to the margins of the Great Game, he had lost the irreverent and biting sense of humor which had characterized his years of power.

The years in Spain, following the Watergate debacle, ushered in some major changes in how the world viewed the United States. Our inability to bring the Vietnam war to a satisfactory conclusion, combined with the self-destruction of the Nixon presidency, virtually destroyed the myth of American invincibility. Until the late seventies there were few effective opponents of American foreign policy on the world scene other than the Soviet Union.

Beginning at the end of this traumatic decade the American hegemony of the non-communist world began to unravel. It became progressively weaker over the next decade as we permitted Iranian thugs to take our embassy hostage without exacting quick and brutal vengeance. At the same time the image summed up by the slightly ironic German phrase *Das Land die Unbegrenzten Moeglichkeiten*—the land of unlimited opportunity—began to crack.

Europe, and particularly West Germany, had recovered much of its economic strength, and a new Goliath, Japan, was rising rapidly in the Pacific. Add to this an American journalistic community which had discovered that savagery sold newspapers and brought in television dollars and you had a recipe for propaganda disaster.

Foreign correspondents no longer reported the news. They commented on trends and wrote think pieces lightly veiled with dubious facts. Worse, the fashionable points of view of many of these men and women were often at odds with conventional American thinking and, especially, foreign policy. Just as a form of intellectual Marxism tends to be pervasive on American university campuses today, a sort of guilt-ridden, anti-American, anti-capitalist, social democratic *Weltanschauung* permeates our media. Many reporters became engaged advocates rather than detached observers and used their news stories to support their hidden agendas. Their views circulated abroad and confirmed the prejudices of those who resented our power.

The relatively sudden expansion of information which began during this period tended to jam the cross-cultural gears more than add to understanding. Pragmatic, non-ideological American constructs often met head-on with the elegant Cartesian intellectualism of the Spaniard. In a nation where style is more important than substance, grace a virtue outweighing practicality, and compromise disdained as unmanly, the "Anglo-Saxon" is stereotyped as a materialist robot, insensitive to human values, preoccupied with artifacts, uninterested in ides, puritanical, obsessed with some chimerical "progress" and unable to accept and enjoy the world as it is.

Former world powers such as France, Germany, Great Britain, Spain and Turkey will resent our sudden accession to leadership no matter what we do. Our deep desire to be loved doesn't help. To seek love is to lose power, and we have done this consistently in the post-war world.

The career foreign service, which had been through a series of so-called reforms since the mid-fifties, was undergoing another paroxysm about this time. The small elite corps which I entered in 1951 had been expanded to include large numbers of service personnel—administrators, career consular officers and specialists of one sort or another—in a move which had seriously diluted its intellectual level.

Beginning in the sixties, so-called mustang programs brought in various minority groups who were unable to pass the still rigorous examinations held for the career service. At the time I favored the goal of more diversity. The rich men's sons who dominated our diplomacy between the wars were seriously divorced from the realities of American life. They did, however, have one great advantage: they were of the same caste as most of the European diplomats with whom they came in contact.

Welles Stabler, for all his arrogance and snobbery, was more at home in this ambiance than his successor, Terence A. Todman, a black from the Virgin Islands. Ironically, given the litany of accusations of racism always directed at the United States, the Spanish press and public deeply resented the appointment of a black as ambassador to Spain.

It was a weird situation, and to his credit Stabler mobilized every resource to mute this unseemly reaction to his successor. Todman, in fact, turned out to be a retiring, dignified, enigmatic character who had little if any impact on Spain, much in the tradition of old style career officers.

In a classic bureaucratic progression, the foreign service continued to expand during these years as our influence declined and the immediacy of communications made diplomats less and less relevant. The result was an increasing mass of despatches delving into the minutiae of foreign countries which, arriving in Washington, were distilled into single paragraphs or consigned to the files.

This arteriosclerosis of the system inevitably resulted in the real power of decision passing from the Department of State to the political appointees, generally former academics, staffing the National Security Council and the White House office of the National Security advisor. The bane of any bureaucracy is overstaffing and the proliferation of useless tasks. The Department of State has become a textbook example of such excess.

Twenty-seven

Its strength was an ideology projected by power; its weakness, that the ideology was erroneous and the power never quite adequate.

Robert Conquest on the Soviet Union

Erich Honecker, the maximum leader of the East German Communist Party, returned from an overseas trip. Arriving at Schoenefeldt Airport, he found it deserted. All the lights were on, but not a soul was in sight. He walked outside and found his Zil limousine waiting, engine running. He drove quickly into East Berlin through deserted streets.

Not a soul was in sight. No automobiles moved, but the city was brightly lit. Then he saw a note attached to a hole in the wall at the Brandenburg gate. He got out of his Zil and read: "Erich, you're the last one out. Please turn off the lights."

This joke was current in East Berlin when I arrived to take over the press and cultural section of our Embassy there. It was a *cri de coeur* since nobody expected the wall to fall in the foreseeable future. The Soviet Union seemed invincible, its hold on Eastern Europe unbreakable. The Cold War was less cold but just as much a war as it had ever been.

Fear of mutual destruction held both sides in check but détente had turned out to be a chimera. Our embassy in East Berlin was a curious animal. In theory the United States did not agree that East Germany existed as a sovereign state. Neither did our West German ally. But we both maintained diplomatic missions there as a matter of pragmatism. Only West Germany called its representation the *Staendige Vertretung*—permanent mission—rather than an embassy.

While in Spain I had been promoted to counselor, one rank below minister-counselor, the pool from which ambassadors were selected. In theory the career diplomats of the United States Information Agency were as eligible as State Department officers for ambassadorships, and, in fact, some ten of the approximately one hundred and sixty positions were reserved for us. However, they tended to be in African, Asian or Latin American backwaters.

Our most realistic goal was to become public affairs officers, in charge of both cultural and press activities, in major embassies where we could operate largely outside the embassy hierarchies. I had reached this eminence in 1979. There was only one catch: East Germany allowed almost no cultural exchanges and our contacts with the press were zero when I arrived in Berlin.

Our library, located on the ground floor of the embassy, was a desert. No sign advertised its presence. We averaged two or three visitors a week, exclusively foreign students or members of other diplomatic missions. Two large guards stood on either side of the entrance to the embassy and checked identification documents. Other STASI, or *Staatssicherheitsdienst,* members in civilian clothes, lounged on the corners. We were a beleaguered fort.

The STASI was an East German combination of the FBI, CIA and, more cogently, the old Gestapo. All our East German employees, hired through a central employment office, were presumed to be STASI officers. These were highly trusted operatives, some with the treasured permission to travel to the west in the course of their duties.

One of the more bizarre incidents during my tour involved the ambassador's chauffeur. He was accustomed to driving the modest ambassadorial Chrysler through the wall at will, with or without the ambassador. He was, after all, a senior STASI officer. His job enhanced his prestige since accredited diplomats, even of the hated Western powers, were treated with the same servile respect accorded high ranking communist officials.

The chauffeur one day crossed the wall three times in the Chrysler at different checkpoints, each time taking a member of his family folded into the trunk. He then made a final trip back, carefully washed and polished the car and used his special identity card to cross the wall one final time on the subway line which connected the two parts of the city. Questioned by American military intelligence officers as to why he had risked returning to the East with the car, he replied that he did not want to offend the ambassador by not returning the automobile in pristine condition.

That American ambassador was David B. Bolen, a career officer who had served mostly in Africa. He was himself black. He was, perhaps understandably, touchy about his prerogatives and kept his distance from the staff. There was, in fact, virtually nothing for anybody to do. The political and economic sections were allowed occasional meetings with lower level government officials but were, in the end, reduced to poring over newspapers and government handouts in vain attempts to penetrate the arcane between-the-lines codes and find out what was going on.

The West German mission, led by a left-wing social democrat named Guenter Gaus, had much closer relations with the top East German leadership by virtue of the huge sums of money West Germany was pouring into the country. These bribes were a quid pro quo for the East allowing West Germans to visit the East to meet with relatives. Gaus also arranged the periodic freeing of political prisoners and unsuccessful wall jumpers at an average price of ten thousand dollars a head.

He was also the conduit for the hundreds of millions of marks the West Germans paid East Germany to repair and maintain the access routes to West Berlin, a city totally isolated within East Germany and since 1960 enclosed by the infamous wall.

Gaus, and his successor, Klaus Boelling, a former press spokesman for West German Chancellor Helmut Schmidt, were virtual proconsuls in East Berlin, presiding over opulent receptions where high-ranking East German officials fawned on them. They, along with West German Foreign Minister Genscher, delighted in sabotaging hard-line U.S. foreign policy initiatives intended to strengthen western responses to Soviet provocations. They preached a policy of appeasement of East Germany and, by extension, the Soviet Union in the belief that there was no other way to alleviate the lot of their captive fellow citizens.

For a period of almost twenty years U.S. and West German interests diverged in Central Europe, although the split was skillfully papered over with words.

The so-called Ost-Politik, or Eastern Policy, of rapprochement between the two Germanys initiated by Chancellor Willy Brandt in the early seventies had largely defanged the intense hostility between the two states. East Germany could, under the tacit blindness of other Common Market members, export its products duty free into West Germany thus becoming a de facto member of the European duty free zone. And the large West German monetary subsidies, overt and hidden, enabled the eastern regime to keep its population quiescent.

As my Viennese wife once said, bemused: "My God, all they need to do to reunify these two countries is to plug in the electricity." She turned out to have been somewhat optimistic, but when the time came, reunification happened overnight.

Under these conditions, small problems tended to become large ones. With nothing else to do, petty annoyances became tests of will. My wife's perfect German, cutting wit and steely Viennese charm were a great asset in the very active, incestuous, diplomatic social life of the capital. We were invited to a continual stream of dinner and cocktail parties. Bolen's wife, an imposing woman almost six feet tall, was particularly active and tended to give black tie affairs even though the East Germans refused to wear dinner jackets.

Although, according to strict protocol, long dresses were supposed to be worn only with tails, Mrs. Bolen had laid down a ukase that embassy wives would not wear short dresses to these affairs. My wife ignored this ruling. This impudence began to obsess the ambassador's wife. After the third or fourth violation of the dress code, Bolen called me into his office.

"Your wife will have to wear a long dress to our formal affairs, Harper," Bolen said. "Mrs. Bolen is most annoyed with her for not doing so."

It seemed a small thing, and I told him I'd bring it up with her, which I did. Our relations were, at this point, approaching a total break. Her boredom with the foreign service life, her inability to work and our deteriorating personal relations left us with nothing more to hold the relationship together but habit and the civility which we had always maintained.

"No," she said. "I'll go along with most things, but I will not be dictated to on what I wear."

I passed this message on to Bolen who a day later convoked me into The Box, a plastic bubble secure from bugging devices, which exists in all American embassies.

"Your wife is going to have to wear a long dress to our affairs, Harper. Mrs. Bolen is adamant. Either that or you will no longer be included."

Since his parties were among the dreariest in town, and I had far more contacts among East Germans than the entire embassy staff, this was an empty threat. I shrugged, said that was really unfortunate, but I was in no position to issue orders to my wife in matters of dress. Over the next week, I went through three more meetings with Bolen on the subject, one lasting more than two hours. He and his wife were clearly obsessed. In a sense these absurd scenes summed up the irrelevance of most of our diplomatic missions, encrusted as they are with outworn eighteenth-century protocol and stripped of decision making functions by the speed of modern communications.

In the end, he let the subject drop, and we continued to be convoked to his dinners and cocktail parties.

On my arrival in East Berlin I had spent a month or so of futile attempts to meet with press and cultural leaders. Finally I called on the East German desk officer for the United States, a charming young man named Teutschbein who had spent several years at the East German embassy in Washington.

I insisted that, in conformity with the agreement establishing our embassy, I be given access to leading journalists dealing with foreign affairs and cultural leaders in the university, theater and music worlds. I pointed out that his embassy had such access in the United States but that, without reciprocity, this would be abruptly curtailed if some quid pro quo was not forthcoming.

Despite his years in the United States, Teutschbein believed me capable of delivering on this threat, although there was in fact no possibility of my doing so. American scholars, journalists, musicians and museum directors would see whomever they pleased and many were curiously sympathetic to the nasty little tyranny. But the result of my empty threat was a gradual loosening of the invisible wall between me and East Germans.

I first called on the foreign editor, Klaus Steininger, of *Neues Deutschland*, the communist party newspaper, spending an hour listening to his tale of covering the Angela Davis trial and the harassment he underwent from our FBI. I managed to point out that his coverage of the upcoming American election hardly mentioned Jimmy Carter and Ronald Reagan, devoting most of its space to the Communist Party candidate, Gus Hall. Steininger was a man of considerable wit and sophistication. For some reason he was convinced that I was Jewish, and I never disabused him. Once he told me a story about the Nazi period.

"My father, a communist, was walking down the Unter den Linden one day when a dark-skinned man with a hooked nose and wearing a Kaftan came running around the corner, blood streaming down his face.

"'Hide me,' he said. 'They're trying to stone me to death.' My father pushed him into a doorway and shielded him until a band of Nazi thugs swept past.

"'You fool,' my father said. 'They're stoning you because you're not wearing the Star of David armband the way all Jews are supposed to?'

"The man looked at him, puzzled, and answered, 'But I'm a Persian diplomat.'" The story, whether true or not, is a classic example of the Berliners addiction to ironic humor.

Over the next two years I had many conversations with Steininger, all dialogs of the deaf. When I returned to Berlin in 1990, after the wall had been torn down, I called on him again, and he greeted me as a long lost friend.

"Harper," he said, "your visits broke the monotony of my days. It was possible to talk to someone from the West, to get a little feel for what was going on. You were," he searched for the word, "most amusing."

Among the other journalists I met was an attractive young woman, who shall here remain nameless, a deputy editor of the *Berliner Zeitung*, the mouthpiece of the city's communist apparat. Her face was marred by a very bad scar, the result of an automobile accident. Over a period of time it became clear that she was an immensely unhappy woman, divorced, restless, disillusioned with communism, bored with her job.

Had she been the usual beautiful young woman assigned to seduce impressionable diplomats, I would have assumed that she was, indeed, a honey-pot. But she was an unlikely candidate. My memoranda of conversation caused the local spook to salivate. Maybe, for once, he could turn somebody.

I broached defection with her, delicately, and she eventually became one of our agents. During the tense period in Poland before Jaruzelski declared martial law, she told me over lunch that an invasion was imminent. Soviet troops in East Germany were mobilizing. I was later to see vivid evidence of it.

Occasionally we were allowed to stage minor cultural events deep in the provinces. The opera house in Gera, a small city in southern East Germany, had agreed to put up a modern dance exhibit in its lobby. On the one hand I was an official guest, on the other I was the enemy. I spent a restless night in the town's best hotel which turned out to be inundated by Russian tourists. About midnight a noise awoke me. The sound of giggling Russians cavorting in bathtubs had penetrated the flimsy walls of the hotel and continued well into the morning hours. Clearly bathtubs were one of the great bonuses of trips to the west.

On the way back, on an overcast day blotting out any observation from our spy satellites, I saw hundreds of Soviet tanks rumbling across the autobahn bridges heading East. Back in Berlin, I went west and reported what I'd seen to the spooks. Immediately, teams of American soldiers belonging to the

Military Liaison Group fanned out across East Germany, returning with confirmation. The liaison group was an anachronism, a holdover from the post-war period of good feeling between the Russians and the Americans.

These agreements allowed designated units for the Soviet and Western allies to move freely through the other's occupation zones. It was a complicated world in Berlin. Nothing was what it seemed to be.

Although there were no true dissidents in East Germany, I did meet with ambiguous figures from the East German nether world, many convinced communists who for one reason or another were out of favor but not persecuted. Stefan Heym was one. A communist since he was sixteen, he had escaped the Nazi pogroms of the thirties by fleeing first to Czechoslovakia and then to the United States. There he joined the Office of Strategic Services, precursor to the CIA, a haven for refugees who spoke European languages, many of whom were communists. At the time nobody cared about their politics, since the Soviet Union was our ally.

All this changed as the Cold War deepened, and in the nineteen fifties Heym fled the McCarthy hearings to East Germany. He was by then a well known novelist, and the East Germans welcomed him with an opulent villa and other perks. Unfortunately for them Heym was a congenital trouble maker, a professional pain in the ass. He was, however, protected by his fame and tolerated, allowed to do much as he pleased.

Heym was typical of many intellectuals of his generation, both European and American. They believed benevolent socialism was the wave of the future and some distortions, such as Leninist authoritarian regimes, were worth the price of the final goal. The means justified the ends.

Over the years I have come to believe that the intellectual, either of the right, left or center, will never be able to accept that means are the only thing out there, and the goals are an ever receding chimera.

Heym and I often met in the hard currency bar of the Hotel

Metropol, a glitzy Swedish built hotel, drank the superb east German Meissner wine and debated the future of Germany and Europe, the beauty of Polish women and the decline of literature in the last decades of the twentieth century.

The Institute for International Relations was another door I managed to pry open. It was part of East Germany's diplomatic academy located in Babelsberg outside Potsdam. Here the sons and daughters of the privileged communist elite were trained as diplomats. The best and the brightest were sent to the Institute, a research organization tasked with providing foreign policy options to East Germany's leaders. Its members were the future movers and shakers of the foreign ministry.

The Institute's director, Klaus Montag, a former number two at the East German embassy in Washington, accepted my offer to bring in American foreign policy experts to lecture his faculty. Somehow he managed to convince his superiors that these young diplomats could be trusted to listen and not be taken in by the seditious westerners.

Over the next two years the Institute hosted such noted Cold Warriors as Bill Griffith of MIT and the Ambassador to Turkey, Strausz-Hupe, a rich Hungarian émigré, physically diminutive, but a giant in open-ended dialectical debate. He used a verbal rapier on the brilliant young East Germans, in a take-no-prisoners exchange for hours, interrupted only by the eighty-year-old man's retreat to the john to attend to a prostate problem.

Afterwards, I took Strausz-Hupe through West Berlin and across the famous Glinicke Bridge, where spies were exchanged with the Soviet Union, to visit Cecilienhof, the royal hunting lodge which had been the site of the Potsdam conference, and Frederick the Great's palace, Sans Souci.

Over a couple of bottles of Meissner wine in Cecilienhof's elegant restaurant, the wizened little man informed me in his charmingly accented English that being an ambassador was the only modern equivalent of the life led by Hungarian magnates before World War I.

Until Strauss-Hupe came I had proposed mostly leftist

American scholars to Montag on the theory that hard-liners might rupture the tenuous connection, since one of the panel, Rainer Hagen, was clearly a minder from the Central Committee if not the STASI. After the Strausz-Hupe visit, however, Montag seemed to have obtained permission to bring in whomever he pleased. When I proposed the Harvard scholar Stanley Hoffman, he waved him off with a remark that "we're not interested in crypto-Marxist French intellectuals. Bring us the right-wing Americans who really make your foreign policy, not academic dilettantes who are sympathetic to us."

In one of the ironies of our time, these bright young diplomats were dismissed from the diplomatic service after the wall fell and most became executives in West European and American companies eager for access to the new German provinces.

The older faculty such as Montag and Hagen, embittered and left behind by events, told me in 1990 that they felt *verraten und verkauft*—betrayed and sold out by the Soviet Union. It seemed a fair analysis then and now.

The brutal insensitivity, arrogance and vengefulness of the West Germans after the wall fell were in large part responsible for the unexpected difficulties of reunification. The particularly stupid decision not to simply nationalize all East German property, compensate monetarily its former owners and sell the properties on long term mortgages to those who occupied them, was a disaster. The resulting messy litigation, evictions and uncertainty offended everybody, East and West, and drove an unnecessary wedge between the two societies.

One of the most interesting East Germans assigned to talk to me was Heinz Kosin, a subtle, witty and sensitive man and a member of the apparat of the Central Committee. We met regularly, touring the political horizons from China to Albania to Paris. We often lunched in the restaurants reserved for the East German elites, he elbowing his way to the head of the line with that natural arrogance which so typified powerful East Germans.

Once, mellowed by vodka and wine, he leaned across the table and said: "Harper, we first thought we would build the socialist man in thirty years. Then we thought: three hundred. Now we believe one thousand."

Then there was the previously mentioned Yevgeny Bogumolov, a great block of a man with hands the size of hams. I had met him at a Soviet Embassy reception, sweat popping out on his forehead as he downed vodka and gobbled caviar. A known KGB agent, he was my assigned shadow. We lunched together about once a month for two years, covering the broad range of U.S.-Soviet problems with no holds barred.

Bogomolov, as with most of the Russians I knew, had a marvelous dry sense of humor. He had given up trying to get me drunk, and the lunches had ceased to be competitions in alcoholism. He turned out to be relatively abstemious. As we got to know each other, he often told self-deprecating jokes. One dealt with the participation of a Soviet scientist at a conference in Vienna. After the westerners had risen to recount their discoveries, the Russian stood to speak. "We Russians make great discovery. Revolutionary discovery. We take flea and put flea in left hand and say 'flea, jump.' flea jump to right hand. Then we rip off legs of flea and put in right hand. Say 'jump flea' but flea does not jump. Discovery. Rip off legs of flea, and flea cannot hear." I began to look forward to these sparring sessions.

One of my minor responsibilities was to oversee the six IREX, Board for International Scholarships, grantees resident in East Germany. This was the unique exchange program, semi-covertly financed by USIA, which sent six East German scholars to the U.S. and six Americans to the German Democratic Republic. Among those who came in my second year was a slender young man with a bad stutter who was looking for a lost Mozart manuscript. He had studied to be a concert pianist but was paralyzed with stage fright and was now a teacher.

Another was the world's greatest expert on beetles. His card carried a sketch of one of these beasts which, he said, represent one-fourth of all the world's living creatures. Still another was a singularly handsome young man who had shown up with his equally attractive Swedish girl friend and appears to have spent most of his grant time in bed with her. He was studying late 19th century police techniques in Prussia. A likely story.

Then there was a young doctoral student from Yale specializing in nineteenth century German history, specifically Prussia during the revolution of 1848. She was researching a dissertation at Yale on the role of humor in Prussian society of the time. Her name was Mary Lee Townsend. Her book based on the East German research, *Forbidden Laughter: Popular Humor and the Limits of Repression in Nineteenth-Century Prussia,* was later published by the University of Michigan Press.

The East Germans sent nuclear physicists and biochemists to the United States. There were also other, ad hoc, exchange programs. In one of these we sent an East German garbage recycling specialist to California.

"Herr Harper," he announced, during a courtesy call at the embassy upon his return, "your garbage has more BTUs than our coal."

IREX was one of the myriad organizations spawned during the Cold War by energetic hustlers to bleed the American government. It occupied luxurious offices in New York, and its director, a man named Kassof, traveled continually in the communist Eastern European countries where IREX was the counterpart to the Fulbright program. Its ostensibly private nature enabled it to escape the periodic congressional paroxysm of anti-communism and to continue the scholarly exchanges which were among the few areas of non-official contact between east and west. It was also clear that their expense reports were exempted from government scrutiny.

One evening I dined with several of the IREX scholars, and a charming young functionary of the New York office named Lucia Capodilupo. In the course of an alcoholic evening, she listened to the deferential scholar grantees praise the program, hoping for further grants. At one point, thoroughly blitzed, she began describing her training in a branch of Indian yoga.

"My guru can levitate," she announced.

"No kidding," I said, breaking the silence. "What does it look like when he does it?"

She gave me a contemptuous look. "He can't do it when somebody is looking. None of them can."

"Pity," the young woman from Yale said dryly, "If he could teach people to levitate over the wall, he could make out like a bandit."

Visitors are a bane on the existence of foreign service officers. One day Mary Lee Townsend called from West Berlin. She was notetaker at a conference there. One of the participants was the famed American historian Arthur Schlesinger, and he wanted a tour of the East. I'd read his biography of Jackson forty years earlier and admired it, so I arranged to send my car and driver over to pick the two up and shepherd them through Checkpoint Charley.

We then walked down the Unter den Linden, and Schlesinger stopped dead at the sight of the famous equestrian statue of Frederick the Great which stood in the middle of the street before the *Neue Wache*, the tomb of the Unknown Soldier.

"They took it out of storage a few months ago and put it up one night. Trying to pander to the peoples' patriotism."

"My God, I don't believe it."

I had timed our walk to coincide with the weekly changing of the guard. Schlesinger watched, incredulous, as the Rosa Luxembourg Regiment paraded down the great boulevard, its uniforms uncannily like those of the Nazis, the jangling sound of its equipment menacing, and at the command *Stechshritt marsch* changed effortlessly from the parade step into the goose step as they passed the *Neue Wache*.

Schlesinger professed to be immensely impressed with East Berlin, its cleanliness, uncluttered air and tasteful restorations. We took him to the restaurant on the 37th floor of the Hotel Stadt Berlin, another of those secret places reserved for the elites of Eastern Europe. For some reason, on this day, the elevator would not rise above the 35th floor. We left and took the stairs, but the doors to the 37th were locked. We and half a dozen East Germans descended. It was a scene from a Marx Brothers comedy as we tried for half an hour to arouse somebody's interest in our fate. At one point we all became locked in the stairwell.

When we finally arrived in the restaurant we were escorted to our table by a waiter in a powder blue tailcoat and served an impeccable meal. Schlesinger turned to me at this point, clearly enchanted with the service and food, and said, accusingly, "You set that nonsense up in the elevator deliberately to mislead me. The place runs beautifully." He was only half kidding. Another American intellectual desperately seeking to see only the good side of Eastern European socialism.

Then there was the visit of Charles Z. Wick, the *jefe maximo* of USIA, a personal friend of President Reagan's whose wife was reputedly Nancy Reagan's closest friend. Wick, who had changed his name from Zwick for obscure reasons, had once produced a feature film in Hollywood starring the Three Stooges, but he'd made his fortune in nursing homes. Although undoubtedly a shrewd businessman, he was totally at sea in the morass of the foreign service bureaucracy and soon fell under the spell of career hacks.

He had virtually no knowledge of foreign affairs, no interest, and had an attention span of about ten seconds. When my harassed colleague in West Berlin called to say he would be coming over, I awaited the worst.

Luck, as it turned out, was with me. He had very little time. I took him on a quick tour and, more or less desperately, told a couple of East European jokes. He instantly came alive, and for the rest of the visit, which included lunch at the infamous Hotel Stadt Berlin, I dredged up from memory all the wit I'd heard over the years. He listened, fascinated, at the bitter, wry jokes.

"Harper, I want those jokes collected into a book. We'll finance its publication. Be great propaganda."

I said sure and forgot all about it. A technique which was said to work marvelously with the man.

There were other, more welcome visitors. Tom Niles, later an assistant secretary of state, a bright if conventional and typically uptight foreign service officer, got the Rosie's Bar treatment. Rosie's was in the basement of what seemed to be the one building in central East Berlin which had escaped being bombed. It sat alone near the embassy parking lot, a scrofulous relic of the nineteenth century whose basement was occupied by a filthy worker's bar with excellent draft beer.

Niles stared in disbelief as we descended, ostensibly for lunch, into this dank and dismal tomb filled with sweaty overalled workers. "Not interested in the real Berlin?" I asked innocently as we drank a beer, finally relenting and taking him to the elegant restaurant reserved for diplomats just across the street.

John Vinocur, the *New York Times* correspondent in Bonn and Dan Morgan of the *Washington Post* got the full treatment before I took them to the Ganymede, a restaurant around the corner from the Brecht Theater which looked like a set for Marlene Dietrich's *The Blue Angel*. You expected to see her come on scene momentarily, threading her way through the tuxedo clad waiters to sit atop the ancient Bechstein with Professor Unrat staring in besotted lust. East Germany was in many respects a place preserved in amber. Nothing had changed since the nineteen-thirties, and the restaurants and public places of East Berlin reflected the desire of its leaders to duplicate the opulence of the pre-war rich, luxuries out of reach in their youth.

After a year in East Germany, my marriage had deteriorated beyond repair. My wife left for the States. The Yale graduate student had taken to calling at my office when she came to town from Merseburg where she worked in the Prussian archives. She was an immensely attractive red-haired young woman who, after some initial awe at being in an embassy, had allowed her natural irreverence to take over. Then the office calls stopped, and I asked my secretary what had happened to her.

"Her grant was up and she went home. Good riddance, too. Every time she came in, she filled up that great big damned cloth bag of hers with toilet paper." East German toilet paper was rumored to be manufactured by a pre-war sandpaper plant.

I quickly realized how much I missed our weekly sparring sessions. Then one day she turned up on a one-day visa, back to do more research in West Berlin. I asked her to lunch. We went to the West Berlin Press Club, a place where the leading journalists and political leaders of the city congregated. The mayor, and later president, Richard von Weizacker was there that day along with a coterie of prominent officials from West Berlin. My companion was duly impressed.

So was I. Her beauty, charm and sense of humor blossomed under the influence of a bottle of Mosel, and, to prolong the lunch, I suggested a brandy at the Cafe Einstein, a half a block from her apartment. Afterwards she invited me up. She had two rooms in a sort of communal apartment, bicycles hanging from pulleys on the twelve-foot ceilings, a poster of Adenauer being buggered by a gleeful devil resembling DeGaulle, and a painting of the Virgin Mary, nude and pregnant.

One thing led to another. It was, in her words, "like an oriental wet dream." She had the face of a virgin and the mores of a Singapore hooker, learned, she later assured me with a mischievous grin, from something called *The Joy of Sex*. She matched my sensuality and I filled her bottomless need for uncritical affection. I left her apartment in a state of dazed obsession from which I have never recovered.

She was also funny and joyous. Once, walking through the zoo to the Kempinski Grill for lunch, she burst into a childish ditty.

Never laugh when the hearse goes by,
    Or You may be the next to die.
They wrap you up in a big white sheet,
    And bury you down about ten feet

The worms crawl in
    The worms crawl out
The worms play pinochle
    On your snout

Your stomach, it turns a sickening green
    And pus comes out like whipping cream
You spread it on a piece of bread
    And that's what you eat when you are dead

Following it, in a clear, bell-like folk singer's voice, with:
Dites-moi pourquoi, la vie est belle.
Dites-moi pourquoi, la vie est gai.
Dites-moi, cher Edouard, est-ce que, parceque
Vous m'aimez.

We spent the next several weeks in a sexual frenzy. One night her phone rang at two a.m. Would I please come back to East Berlin? President Reagan had been shot and we would have to put out a press release as soon as the Embassy opened. The spooks were clearly following our affair.

This was confirmed a week or so later when the station chief in East Berlin, with whom I regularly played tennis, turned to me over a beer and said: "You realize she's not in love with you, Harper. She's got to be some sort of Communist agent."

I pointed out to him that she was an American citizen and, as such, not subject to being harassed. Then I leaned toward him, conspiratorially looking over my shoulder. "Actually, George, I'm now a member of the Red Rudy Dutschke Cell. I've got card number thirteen." Dutschke was a well known German radical.

Our own spooks were not the only ones interested in my private life. In another lunch with Bogumolov, he leaned across the table and spoke in a confidential tone.

"Harper, I am hearing since your wife left you are living with much younger womans?"

"How on earth could you know that?" I asked, poker faced.

"Is having methods," he said, also unsmiling. We were both excellent straight men. "I am giving you advice. Socialist men's having much experience, older mens younger womans."

"You're kidding," I said, trying hard to suppress a smile. Every Russian diplomat I'd met seemed to be married to a drop-dead beautiful twenty-year-old.

"No. Is not kidding. Is three rules must follow. First, never lose control. Older man, younger womans, lose control, never get back. Two, make nervous. She has womens friends. Give them bon bons. Flowers. Make jealous. Three. She is having men's friends. Avoid them. But when you must come together with them," he reached his immense hand across the table and closed it in a fist. "Squeeze them."

I found his advice useful over the years.

With nothing to lose, and increasingly obsessed with Mary Lee, I became seriously reckless. Once, on the way to a week in the Italian coastal resort of Portofino, we were held up by a miles long column of West German cars waiting to cross from East Germany after visiting relatives. As a diplomat I had the right to go to the head of the line, but the second lane of the autobahn was blocked. I turned onto the unmown grassy median strip and roared up to the checkpoint, grass sprouting from bumpers and wheels. We were lucky not to be cut down by a blast of machine gun fire. But my red diplomatic plates and identity card rescued us.

Down the Median Strip became one of our talismanic incantations.

The border guard came to a paralyzed salute and waved us through as the enraged West Germans shook their fists and pounded their horns.

Mary Lee giggled and began to sing another of the sixties songs she grew up with:

"Oh, Lord, won't you buy me a Mercedes Benz?
My friends all drive Porsches,
I must make amends.
Worked hard all my lifetime,
No help from my friends.
Oh, Lord, won't you buy me a Mercedes Benz."

Shortly after this I was scheduled to go to Washington for a week for the signing of a cultural treaty which would regulate relations between our two countries. I suggested she meet me in Paris on my way home. She agreed and offered to book the hotel.

It was on the Square Viviani across from Notre Dame Cathedral in a street called St. Julien le Pauvre. The Esmeralda. We had missed signals at the airport, and she hung out a fourth floor window as my taxi drove up, mass of red hair hanging down around her face, clattering down the narrow stairs of the fourteenth century building into my arms as the Albanian troglodyte who manned the desk in the miniature lobby watched impassively.

The next four days were a blur. At one point I mentioned that we walked a lot.

"Yeah. From the bed to the bidet and back," she said, giggling and singing a little jingle she'd made up which began:

"Nooky in the morning, nooky in the evening, nooky at suppertime..." Once, as we awaited breakfast, sated she turned lazily toward me and, grinning, said, "You know something?"

"What?"

"A woman's orgasms compared to a man's are like an AK 47 compared to a muzzle loading rifle."

I usually got up much earlier, leaving her to sleep while I walked down to the quai to run a couple of miles along the banks of the Seine. One morning a bearded clochard rose on one elbow among the empty wine bottles surrounding him and called out: *"Quelles jolies jambes. Quelles jolies jambes."*

We had breakfast in the room every morning at a rickety table looking through the windows at Notre Dame across the way. The trip was to be the end of the affair, and our gaiety was shadowed by that knowledge.

I took her to the Tour d'Argent for lunch one day, first circling the great church and walking through the Ile St. Louis. In front of Notre Dame a street photographer, with a complexion the color of a good burgundy and magnificent green eyes, immortalized us.

"Elle est jolie, n'est-ce pas?" I said fatuously, as I paid him.

He focused on her suddenly and turned to me smiling. *"Quelle chance, monsieur. Quelle chance."* At the Tour d'Argent, I tipped the matire'd at the bottom of the elevator a hundred francs just as he was about to say there were no tables. In the restaurant, the head waiter took one look at us and led us to a table by the window with a superb view of the flying buttresses of the great medieval church.

"Funny, I usually get a table by the kitchen," I said.

Mary Lee grinned. "Older means, younger womans. Trying to impress. Big tip." She was right. In thirteen years, nobody ever put us near the kitchen.

We ate and drank too much and indulged in a game which became almost a ritual in later years. At a nearby table a young man dressed in British tweeds and a wearing a bow tie lunched with a young woman, also in tweeds, without makeup. Their dress and attitude as well as the servility of the head waiter indicated their class.

"That's the Duc d'Angouleme," I said in a whisper, leaning across the table.

"And she's a rich banker's daughter he's going to marry to save the family chateau from ruin."

"But her lover is threatening to jump off the Eiffel Tower."

"And he is madly in love with a Chinese au pair."

Then she began to sing in a soft voice:

"Je suis le duc d'Angouleme
Qui ne bois que le cafe creme
Un getilhomme sans bleme
Je suis le duc d'Angouleme"

On the last day desperation began to set in. She was scheduled to leave for the States the next week. We walked arm in arm across the Pont Neuf, stopping to embrace in the middle of the Quai des Grands Augustins to the cheerful honking of horns.

"Christ, I don't want it to end," I said.

"It doesn't have to unless you want it to," she replied, tears streaming down her face.

Twenty-eight

Conquerir est notre destin.

Pierre Ambroise Choderlos de Laclos

"We will spend the Soviet empire into destruction," the slim, gray-haired, somewhat desiccated, man said with a slight Swiss accent and the fixed stare of a fanatic. His name was Fred Ikle and he was the undersecretary of defense for policy, the third-ranking man in the Pentagon. I had, as usual, arrived in his office by a curious route.

In the spring of 1981, Mary Lee Townsend had moved into my house in East Berlin after I had convinced the East German desk officer to give her a permanent visa. Up to that point we had had to go through the charade of crossing Checkpoint Charley just before midnight, when her twenty-four hour visa expired, having a drink in the Stresemann bar in the Askanischeplatz across from the ruins of the Anhalter Bahnhof and then returning to East Berlin. As with all Berlin, the ruins of the railroad station were symbolic. It was here that Hilter had greeted the leaders of countries he was about to swallow up.

The alternative was to spend the night in her West Berlin apartment. I would then drive the next morning all the way across West and East Berlin to my house in the Platanenstrasse in the East Berlin Pankow district, shower and go to the office. After six weeks of this I was a zombie, approaching terminal exhaustion.

Bolen had by this time been replaced as ambassador by Herb Okun, a charming intelligent man of my generation, sophisticated and urbane with the street smarts of a lower middle class New Yorker. We had developed a warm relationship, lunching frequently and regaling each other with comic tales of the foreign service. He was almost pathetically proud of his success, starting out as the son of Jewish immigrants, a graduate of that same New York high school my friends at the University of Georgia had called "Odessa on the Hudson", fighting his way through Stanford and Harvard and winding up an ambassador.

When he discovered my living arrangements he was at first speechless.

"You can't *do* this, Ed. My God, she's young enough to be your daughter. In any case, you can't possibly bring her to any embassy functions," he sputtered.

"Herb, she's an American. There aren't any security problems. She hates embassy functions." She had been regularly invited when she was in East Berlin and had proclaimed them abymally dull.

"But it's," he groped for the word, finally coming out lamely, "It's scandalous."

I stared at him, grinning, and finally he laughed. "Well, goddamn it, the women are all going to hate you and the men will envy you. There's certainly no law against it, although George is convinced she's in the Red Brigades."

"Why, because of her hair?" George was our lone official spook, a humorless character whose body was covered with scar tissue from being shot down in a blazing helicopter in Vietnam. He had a right to be humorless. He wasn't the only one. My co-worker, Paul Smith, had also been a crewman on a helicopter. When the machine took a direct hit, he was flung through the door and fell fifty feet, shattering a shoulder.

Once I asked him about it. He shrugged. "I was lucky. All the others died. A chopper gets hit in the right place, it turns into a torch with the flying properties of a falling safe. In those days, happiness was a cold landing zone."

Herb and I went out to lunch after our conversation, got blitzed on vodka and wine and regaled each other with foreign service scandals, but the story of the affair had moved up through the hierarchy and my tour was discreetly ended after two years instead of three. When I arrived in Washington, Jock Shirley, who, after a meteoric career, had briefly become acting director of USIA while Charles Z. Wick awaited confirmation, convoked me to his office. He was Wick's right-hand man, as counselor, the senior career foreign service officer of the agency.

"Are you going to marry her?" was his first question.

"What the fuck business is it of yours?" I answered, finally exasperated by the intrusions into my private life.

Jock threw up both hands and grinned. "I was just curious. Rumor has it that she just got out of kindergarten and is a raving beauty. However, I didn't call you in here for that. What the hell is this about an Eastern European joke book?"

"You mean he remembers?"

"Yes. He remembers. And he expects it on his desk tomorrow. I've had to send cables to all the embassies in Eastern Europe demanding jokes. Couldn't talk him out of it. We're the laughing stock of the foreign affairs community, once again. But you're going to have to put the damn thing together. Once he gets an idea, there's no way of talking him out of it."

I shrugged. "So, give me a desk and a computer and the cables. I'll check the Library of Congress for any stuff they've got and put something together. Shouldn't take long." The library, I was to discover, had no less than nine books on Eastern European humor.

"That's not all," Jock said. "He wants you to go over to the Pentagon as our liaison officer. Thinks you're perfect for the job. For some unfathomable reason he likes you."

"Liaison for what?"

"Good question. He and Defense Secretary Cap Weinberger were at dinner at the White house a few days ago, and they agreed we needed some coordination. To improve the Pentagon's image overseas."

"And you suggested me, you son of a bitch. Because nobody else would touch it with a hot poker."

Jock smiled, doing his imitation of a shark. "You're seeing the undersecretary tomorrow at ten. He's got a veto on you. Don't defecate in his hat."

At the meeting, Fred Ikle, a former professor, expatiated for the next two hours on his plan to destroy the Soviet Union through economic warfare, clearly enamored of the sound of his own voice and the brilliance of his concept. He spouted statistics on the Soviet economy, proving that more than twenty-five percent of gross national product was going directly to the defense industry and there was no way they could squeeze any more out. I thought it was an absurd figure at the time, but it turned out to be low.

Our defense budget would be doubled, tripled if necessary, and in the end they would not be able to follow. They would have to admit defeat. There was nothing new about Ikle's idea. For years there had been speculation in the academic community that excessive outlays for defense were counterproductive in the long term.

In 1987, six years after my meeting with Ikle, a Yale professor, Paul Kennedy, summed up the hypothesis in a book, *The Rise and Fall of the Great Powers*, which postulated that the United States would itself fall victim to an economic decline brought on by the massive military expenditures necessary to maintain its empire. He compared the U.S. to the Spanish, British and French imperiums which expired, according to his thesis, from the inordinate costs of their military. To compare these small feudal satrapies with a United States the size of a continent was typical academic formalism. But Kennedy's essential error was assuming that the United States, and not the Soviet Union, would go bankrupt first.

I had spent an afternoon with Kennedy, on the terrace of my house in West Berlin some years before, listening to him outline the thesis for his book. He and his wife were pacifists who had demonstrated against U.S. nuclear bases in Britain, and he was violently opposed to the emplacement of medium range missiles in Germany capable of reaching the Soviet Union.

Despite being totally in error, his book was extravagantly praised by reviewers and sold hundreds of thousands of copies, making him a millionaire. On that day, as I prodded and provoked, a little bored with this embittered British academic, it became clear that he was eaten up with hatred of the United States, an upstart nation which had usurped his country's place in the world. And in the process denied him access to the perks and power which fell to the British upper classes for three centuries. He has been extremely well treated in the United States, given a chair at Yale and, by British standards, vast amounts of money. But, as Castlereagh put it, with a cynicism typical of his time: "Gratitude is an emotion for cravens."

There was a perverse congruence between Ikle, a right-wing fanatic consumed by hatred of the Soviet Union, and Kennedy, the anti-American, crypto-Marxist, pacifist British intellectual. The thought of these vulgar colonials assuming the British role in the world was more than Kennedy could bear. The Swiss émigré, enamored of America, and the subconsciously embittered young Englishman were preaching the same formula for imperial demise but with different targets.

Ikle's plan to spend the Soviet empire into destruction worked, aided by the unexpectedly stubborn support of the so-called Star Wars program by President Ronald Reagan. Nobody believed in this visionary plan to build a defensive rocket shield against nuclear attack except Reagan and the chief of the Soviet General Staff. As it turned out, they were the only ones that mattered. The Soviet military, hypnotized by the myth of American technical superiority, believed us capable of anything and demanded the means to counter the threat.

Gorbachev looked deep into the Soviet economy and saw a black hole. He then, in Dean Rusk's inimitable phrase about Khrushchev in the Cuban crisis, blinked. And the leaders of the satellite states watched as the will drained out of the Soviet leadership. The unwillingness to invade Poland in late 1980 was, perhaps, the first sign of that loss of will. They still had the machine gun but there was increasing doubt of their will to use it.

Once tyrannies lose credibility, their decline accelerates and confusion overtakes decisiveness. Gorbachev undoubtedly thought he could hold off the United States while reforming the Communist system with a new version of the nineteen twenties New Economic Policy instituted by Lenin. But when he lifted the lid a little, the backed up steam blew it off, and he lost control of the process.

Thus, in a sense, Paul Kennedy's thesis that an exaggerated defense budget could bring down an empire was justified. He simply picked the wrong empire. In fact, however, Kennedy and his neo-Marxist ideological cohort—secretly hoping for the weakening, if not destruction, of American power—overstated the amount of money being spent on defense by the U.S. These expenditures had peaked at nine percent of the gross national product during the early sixties and never exceeded six percent in the Reagan years, an easily sustainable sum for a dynamic and growing economy.

One of the more bemusing phenomena of the post-Cold War era is the desperate attempt by former world powers such as Britain, France, Germany and Japan to reduce U.S. preeminence now that there is no Soviet danger. It is as if they can now afford to come out of the closet and allow full rein to their rage at this upstart mongrel nation which has in one generation risen from a relative backwater to the eight-hundred-pound gorilla which sits where it chooses.

But in that summer of 1981 none of this was clear to me. I thought that Ikle was a reincarnation of Doctor Strangelove. Only he wasn't in a movie but held one of the most powerful jobs in the American government, with a foreign service and research staff that far outnumbered the State Department's and the immense budgetary influence of the Pentagon behind him.

I crossed the outer office and walked, uninvited, past his secretary into Assistant Secretary of Defense Richard Perle's office, closing the door behind me. I'd known Richard when he had been a briefcase carrier for Senator Jackson, circling the globe as the senator's eyes and ears. We weren't close friends, but I'd done him some favors over the years when others had ignored him as a low ranking gopher.

Richard was an odd combination. Quiet, never raising his voice, and capable of enunciating the most outrageous ideas with an air of sweet reasonableness. I dropped into a chair across from him.

"Richard, the man's nuts. You better send for somebody with a straitjacket." I have to give him credit. He smiled instead of having me ejected from his office.

"You're wrong, Ed. We're going to do exactly what he said we would."

And he was right. They did.

My immediate problem at the Pentagon was more mundane. I had been turned over to one of the lieutenant colonels who, I discovered, really ran the place. They were a wary bunch, steeped in intrigue and attuned to the subtleties of bureaucratic power in a way few foreign service officers could match. This man had seen me spend two hours with his boss and walk in unannounced on Perle. I had to be somebody. But he had looked up my rank and discovered that I was only the equivalent of a brigadier general.

In the Pentagon hierarchy a brigadier general is one step above an office boy. Still, he rates an office with a certain square footage and none was available. I offered to take smaller quarters. He stared at me in total disbelief and rejected the heretical idea. Begin to accept something like that and the whole hierarchical edifice could crumble. Finally, after several days, I got a call at the cubbyhole in USIA where I was putting together Wick's Eastern European jokebook. They had an office.

I was led through the immense labyrinth of the Pentagon, past an inner checkpoint of armed guards, to a door with three combination locks. "This is Nuclear Targeting," my guide said. "Only place we could find space for you. Theoretically, you need," and he rattled off some Greek letter names, "clearances even to get through the door, but we got a waiver for you. Can't give you the combinations until you're cleared, though, so you'll have to knock to get in." He knocked.

It was an unimpressive place. On the left, the office of an assistant to Ikle named Dov Zakheim; on the right, my office; and in between, some five cubicles occupied by full colonels. One secretary handled everything. My guide introduced me around.

At one hallucinatory moment I thought back to a French film of the early forties called *Clochemerle*. It dealt with the disputed decision to build a street urinal in a provincial town. The contested project made its way up through the labyrinthine French bureaucracy to the office of the prime minister, then the president. Unable to decide, these august personages sent the decision up to the ultimate authority: Two old men under the mansard roof of the Elyssee Palace, who threw darts to make the decision.

The fate of hundreds of millions would be decided in a nuclear war by the pins these five obscure colonels placed in their maps.

"George does the Soviet Union; Mike, China," he said moving down the small offices, each dominated by a huge wall map full of pins indicating the targets. He then introduced me to Zakheim, a short dark man wearing a yarmulke. He was the most unlikely looking chief of nuclear targeting I could conceive of, and, in fact, he was an economist who dealt with arms purchases.

I never got a clear explanation of why these five offices of nuclear targeting were sandwiched in between two civilians who had absolutely nothing to do with it. However, the office had one totally unexpected dividend.

Two days after I moved in, Wick, whose undoubted charm was enhanced by his total lack of pomposity, often dialed his own phone numbers. The secretary outside answered his call with her standard phrase.

"Nuclear targeting?"

Wick came on the line, voice three octaves higher than normal. "Harper, you're in nuclear targeting? Jesus fucking Christ. Nuclear targeting." He was clearly awed, and at the next USIA staff meeting brought up the fact that USIA had access through Harper to nuclear targeting.

My colleagues, a little dazed tried to pump me, and several made phone calls to hear the secretary's answer. I opted for total silence, refusing to comment in any way. Even Jock's aplomb was shaken until I finally relented and explained the situation to him.

My two years at the Pentagon were a hallucinatory experience. One morning, early on, I arrived at the office to find a British vice admiral and two aides sitting on the rickety chairs in the narrow corridor connecting our offices, the secretary crammed into one corner. The Falklands war had just begun, and they were waiting for Dov Zakheim, who was in charge of supplying the British with oil and whatever else they would need to keep their fleet and troops operational.

Without U.S. help, Britain would have been unable to go to war and would have had to concede the Islands to Argentina. Looked at cold-bloodedly, that might have been a solution meeting our interests. But over the next few weeks a stream of flag rank officers came through our office, quickly made aware that Zakheim, an orthodox Jew, closed down, war or no war, from Friday at dusk until sundown Saturday.

I did absolutely no work while at the Pentagon. I had no responsibilities except to attend the morning briefing of the assistant secretary for public affairs, a charming rich man's son named Henry Catto, and report back anything suspicious he was doing to Ikle's office. Paranoia was the primary emotional dysfunction of the Pentagon and there were myriad internal spying apparatuses.

At my first meeting with Catto, misunderstanding my role, I managed to offend all the military public relations hotshots present, something for which I was never forgiven. It was announced that Weinberger was meeting with a correspondent of the German magazine *Der Spiegel* just after the noon briefing.

"It's the *Time Magazine* of Germany," his lieutenant colonel said proudly. "Good way to get our position on missiles before the German people." At the time there was a huge flap over the U.S. proposal to emplace intermediate range nuclear missiles in Germany. Massive street demonstrations were orchestrated against the plan, and one of its major opponents was Augstein, the owner of *Der Spiegel*.

It rapidly became apparent that nobody had bothered to

clear this interview with the State Department or the White House. Innocently, I intervened, pointing out that *Der Spiegel* would probably cut Weinberger to shreds in such an interview.

Catto was a decent man, but, in that inimitable Texas expression, "all hat and no cattle". He possessed virtually no substantive knowledge of anything. But he had enough shrewdness to recognize his limitations. He now looked from me to the colonel and back. "Well," he said, in his Texas drawl, "maybe we better cover our asses." He picked up the phone and put through a conference call to the press spokesmen at the White House and State. When the call was over, he looked around the room, having been thoroughly chewed out.

"Well, Mr. Harper, I have to thank you. Seems like they really would not like to have the secretary talk to this magazine."

Once again I was to discover that being right was fatal. I, a myrmidon of the hated Ikle, had made fools of his brilliant press staff. I would not be forgiven. Although I continued to attend the meetings, my opinion was never solicited and I seldom volunteered. Catto was a puppet in the hands on his staff.

His pre-briefing meetings were a case study in how to mislead the press, to misdirect, obfuscate, stonewall and lie to conceal from them the Pentagon's endless list of goofs. The duplicity of the military mind was clearly bottomless. It was a war of wits between them and the journalists. A war the newsmen usually lost because, basking in their own hubris, they underestimated their opponents.

At one briefing a short, muscular, red-faced colonel built like a stump was brought in to brief on a new anti-tank missile which was reputedly a disaster. His chest was covered with ribbons, among them a Silver Star and three Purple Hearts. He wore a paratrooper's wings and ranger badge and his resume said he was a mustang, an officer promoted from the ranks, who had served three tours in Vietnam. Not in staff jobs, but commanding troops at the company and battalion level. A fighting soldier.

"I hear this thing doesn't work too well, colonel," Catto said, in his usual courteous way.

"It's new technology," the colonel said, voice as raspy as a rusty saw blade. "Nothing works perfectly for the first year or so. But it's not doing badly. We're getting one hit out of three. In combat it would be one out of five or six."

"That doesn't sound so good," Catto said. "Wasteful."

"A missile costs about one fiftieth of what a tank does," the colonel said, face turning purple at this civilian's stupidity. He was a rare bird in the Pentagon. A blunt combat officer to whom image was bullshit. His view was: the missile was the best thing going. Give it to us until something better comes down the pike.

It was decided that Catto would bob and weave on the topic, and he did pretty well, although John McWethy, one of the television correspondents, tried repeatedly to corner him. As the briefing ended the red-faced colonel confronted McWethy, clearly enraged by the tall, elegant, exquisitely articulate young man's remarks about the weapon.

"Mr. McWethy," he said, "I've got a proposition for you. We put you in an M-60 tank and we fire one missile at you. If it hits, we win. If it misses, you do."

McWethy stared at him for a moment in disbelief, then grinned and put his arm around the much shorter man's shoulders. "Colonel, why don't I buy you a drink instead?" I had the feeling the colonel was about to have his pocket picked.

Catto could be quick on his feet. On one occasion he was harassed unbearably by a born-again minister who represented some obscure religious journal. The man was one of those gadflies whose questions were total non sequiturs but who could not be excluded from the briefings. At one point, Catto turned to the gathering and quoted in exasperation:

"Who will free me from this importunate priest?" The exchange made the *New York Times* and *Washington Post* and gave Catto an undeserved reputation as a wit. He had been fed the quote by one of his staff to use against the man in an appropriate exchange.

It was his finest hour.

About six months into my assignment, already intriguing to

shake loose, Richard Perle invited me on a two-week trip to Scandinavia which would end at the *Friedrich Ebert Stiftung* meeting in Bonn. The ostensible excuse was that I was a German expert. The *Stiftung* was a think tank of the Social Democratic Party which Perle had been invited to address.

The trip was the boondoggie of all boondoggles. We had a Boeing 707 at our disposal, and there were some twenty people in the party. The ostensible motive for the voyage was to consult with Richard's counterparts in the Danish, Norwegian, Swedish and Finnish defense ministries. And, where possible, persuade them to buy American weapons.

In reality it was a classic bureaucratic debauch. We ate mountains of smoked salmon, drank gallons of vintage wines and were entertained by the leading industrialists and politicians of each of the countries and, as far I was able to determine, achieved absolutely nothing. By the time we reached Germany the plane was overloaded with gifts and purchases. Richard's wife accompanied us on the trip along with a dozen or so of his government cronies.

In Bonn, Perle had to share the stage with Richard Burt, another golden boy of the Reagan administration, with whom he had staged a shadow play during most of my time in the Pentagon, carrying on a murky feud which the press reported with glee. They seem to have, in fact, been close friends who set the whole thing up as a joke. A sense of humor was one of the saving graces of the second echelon of the Reagan administration.

The Burt and Perle dog and pony show was wiped out by the unexpected appearance at the *Stiftung* of German Chancellor Helmut Schmidt, probably the most brilliant political leader of his time. He was certainly the most acidulous. He was in a bitter mood on this day, coming to the end of his power, and he loosed a tirade against U.S. policies which reduced Burt and Perle to cringing silence.

It was a revealing contrast between the appearance of power and its reality. The self-important young career functionaries, clever but brittle, against a man of genuine intellectual force and brutal will. A man who had also fought in all the major battles of the Second World War and spent four years on the Russian front, a fact he neither concealed, boasted of nor apologized for.

His democratic, anti-Nazi credentials were impeccable. He had fought, as many Germans did, from a misplaced sense of duty to save his country from destruction. But unlike his contemporary, Richard von Weizacker, later to be elected president—who also spend six years in Hitler's armies as a member of the aristocratic Ninth Regiment—he never groveled or beat his breast in *mea culpas*. Schmidt, a middle class youth, had had little choice but to fight.

Von Weizacker, whose father was for twelve years the highest ranking career civil servant in the Nazi foreign ministry and a willing collaborator, sniveled and squirmed, mouthing platitudes and becoming eventually a paradigm of the good German. This despite the fact that he publicly defended his father during the old man's trial as a war criminal.

A Jewish émigré once said to me: "Every time I see a German with gray hair, I wonder what he was doing during the Nazi time." While objectively unfair, it is a haunting comment.

Von Weizacker, a morally supple, charming Cambridge-educated aristocrat, somehow escaped the stigma of his past. His contemporary, Kurt Waldheim, later president of Austria, spent most of the war in an occupation backwater in Yugoslavia, never in six years rising above the rank of lieutenant. Yet he suddenly found himself demonized as a monster equivalent to Eichmann, although the record seems to show that his biggest crime, if such it was, consisted of exaggerating the effects of a wound to avoid returning to the Russian front, a classic Viennese ploy if ever there was one. But he lacked the elegant, and arrogant, self-assurance of the handsome von Weizacker. And his groveling seemed to lack sincerity.

The contortions which ambitious Austrians and Germans went through to cleanse or hide their wartime actions would fill volumes. The line between voluntary criminal collaboration in Nazi crimes and "following orders" is a fine one. Refusal to execute

Russian prisoners about to be liberated by a Soviet offensive, a routine procedure as the German retreat began, was punishable by death. Hundreds of thousands died in these slaughters.

There were also dozens of cases such as Prince Heinrich zu Sayn-Wittgenstein. This idealist, who was of French and Russian ancestry, hated the Nazis and plotted to blow himself up while being presented with a medal by Hitler. Although he grew up in Switzerland and barely considered himself German, he nonetheless shot down eighty-three allied planes before he was himself killed in 1944. Such is the power of patriotism and the warrior ethic.

Nobody, however, was forced to be a concentration camp guard. The gradations in between are gray areas where heroes and survivors dwell. It is easy to think that we could have chosen to be heroes, but none of us have ever faced the choice. With their world crumbling about them, their cities in ruins, their armies deteriorating, the Germans fought on. Including Schmidt, Weizacker, Sayn-Wittgenstern and Waldheim.

It has been argued, as Churchill privately did, that Roosevelt's unexpected and unilateral demand for German and Japanese unconditional surrender prolonged the war unnecessarily. That, with some hope of salvaging something and to keep the Russians at bay, the German July 20th military coup might have drawn overwhelming *Wehrmacht* support resulting in the overthrow of Hitler and his cronies. Perhaps. In any event, hypothetical historical scenarios are much like onanism: enjoyable but leading nowhere.

But all was not fun and games at the Pentagon. Once, in my second year, with the Sandinista problem in Nicaragua on the front burner, I ran into Nestor Sanchez, the former CIA station chief in Madrid. Nestor had been seconded from the CIA to become a Deputy Assistant Secretary of Defense responsible for Central American policy.

He was something of a legend in the covert operations branch of the CIA. Among other exploits, he had parachuted behind the lines in Korea and later had delivered the poisoned pen in Paris to the man who was supposed to use it to assassinate Fidel Castro during the Kennedy administration.

Nestor had never asked me for any assistance in isolating possible agents while we served in Madrid, as many other spooks had done over the years. As press attaché I had access to a vast number of sources, people the station chiefs often salivated to turn. He had clearly not needed my help. He now invited me to his office and asked what I was doing.

"Nothing."

He grinned. "I thought so. When I saw your name I asked what you were doing over here. Nobody seemed to know. Why don't you come out to the coast with me for a couple of days? We're having a meeting with some Nicaraguan exiles."

Obsessed as I was with Mary Lee, who hated being left alone, I had no interest in getting involved, but it was hard to turn him down. I went and drifted on the edges of the meeting. Vernon Walters, a legendary figure, former deputy director of the CIA was there, and half a dozen other famous spooks. It was one of the earliest exploratory meetings which resulted in the Contra uprising and the eventual defeat of the Sandinistas in a free election.

Looking back I suspect that Nestor took me along to see if he could fit me into the operation. My Spanish was fluent and by this time my reputation for being a wild man who was at the same time trustworthy had spread. I was a natural recruit and at another time and place I would have jumped at the chance to join him. He needed people he could depend on, since I am convinced, looking back, that Nestor was at the heart of the entire Contra effort, from recruiting to action. He wisely faded out before the scandal surrounding Oliver North ripened. Like the superb spook he was, he did his job and sought no fame, wrote no books and left no footprints. I am nonetheless persuaded that he, not Oliver North, was the guts of the ultimately successful effort.

I backed away, uninterested in the eighteen-hour days and endless meetings which absorbed the government groupies around Nestor and Richard Perle, now the tip on Fred Ikle's lance as the Pentagon budget escalated and their plan to destroy the Soviet Union and its allies matured.

In October 1982 Mary Lee and I were married, and I set out to arrange for one final tour in Germany in order for her to finish her dissertation. I was by now one of Wick's favorites, having finished the joke book as promised. But it was not to be published. The career hacks in the agency, terrified of the possible fallout, mobilized to persuade him that it was too dangerous politically to go ahead with the project which would have involved clandestine USIA funds.

As a reward, and consolation, Jock informally offered me one of the plums of the Agency, public affairs officer in Turkey, an almost certain promotion to rarefied atmosphere of minister counselor. I turned it down and asked for West Berlin, calling in all my chips.

I planned to retire from the Agency once Mary Lee had converted her dissertation into a book, which she would be able to do after three years in West Berlin, and follow her to one of the elite universities which would surely recruit her.

Twenty-nine

Ah, my Beloved, fill the cup that clears
Today of past Regrets and future Fears:
Tomorrow—Why tomorrow I may be
Myself with Yesterday's Seven thousand years.

The Rubaiyat of Omar Khayyam

Berlin 1983-86.

Days of wine and roses.

I had found a beautiful, witty, intelligent, joyous and irreverent lover who had fulfilled my every erotic fantasy. And this in middle age. I was fifty-seven; she was thirty. Wonder of wonders, I seemed to fulfill her needs as well. As Charles Ramber puts it: "The callow solipsism of the early years is gone, and the old is able to offer the awareness and stately pace so prized by fair companions." When once I pointed out that age would put a term to what was becoming a great love affair, she shrugged and said, "I'll jump off that bridge when I come to it." And she did.

The wind was in our sails. I was making more money than we could spend. The foreign service provided us with a superb villa in the elegant suburb of Dahlem, confiscated from some Nazi in 1945. Turkish gardeners manicured our large rose-and-fruit-tree-filled garden. A cheerful Yugoslav maid did the scut work.

It was my last post. I had opted out of the rat race and could relax and watch the passing parade. She, whose affection for the city and its people bordered on obsession, was able to travel to the archives in East Germany, so essential to her research, using a diplomatic passport which opened all doors. Marriage to me, she said, was a permanent Fulbright grant. During these years she wrote her first book, in German, *Humor as High Treason: Albert Hopf and the Revolution of 1848*, which resurrected a once famous revolutionary and playwright who had disappeared from the German literary consciousness. Rave reviews appeared when the book came out several years later and she was interviewed on German television.

She completed her dissertation and received her doctorate during these years, converting a monograph on the political and social role of humor in Berlin in 1848 into a highly respected scholarly book.

At the same time, I was working on a novel whose leitmotif was the love affair between an aging diplomat and a young graduate student, conducted in Berlin against the backdrop of Cold War crises and intrigues. It was never published. Editors were unanimous in saying it lacked verisimilitude.

Berlin was a unique foreign service post in many ways. First, American, British and French expenses were covered by a West German government anxious at all costs to maintain the allied military presence in the beleaguered city. Their generosity was egregiously abused. Our U.S. government entertainment allowances were minuscule, but the bills were submitted to the Germans and paid without a murmur. The result was a round of opulent cocktail parties, receptions and black tie dinners by all three occupation powers.

I walked ten minutes to my office. A fleet of embassy automobiles waited in ranks at our pleasure to take us to lunches and dinners in some of the best restaurants in the world. Each occupation power had constructed mini-malls where expensive delicacies from the homeland were sold to the occupation forces at duty free prices. Vintage French wines, subsidized for their army contingent, went for a fifth of their price in France. Superb British woolens were available at a third what they sold for in London. And American electronics, priced at cost in the PX, were gobbled up by the French and British.

The French army restaurant, Le Pavillon du Lac, was the best in Berlin. Germans were prepared to kill for an invitation to it by one of the Allied officers or diplomats. Tennis courts, a golf course and gyms were everywhere. A special American train departed each night for Bremerhaven and a French one left for Strasbourg. Passage was free. A round trip airline flight to London was fifty dollars, again all subsidized by the West Germans. Our cars ran on untaxed gas.

The Berliners, a sophisticated people, tolerated all this in the full knowledge that without the Allies they were at the mercy of a hated and feared East German regime backed by a massive Soviet army presence.

In theory the Berlin city administration was subordinate to the three generals who headed the Allied occupation forces. In fact, virtually all power had been ceded to the German civil government over the years, although the apparatus of control continued. Committees and commissions abounded, fully staffed and without any function. Useless meeting were held to ratify city legislation, and the civilian ministers of each ally, career diplomats of ambassadorial rank, comported themselves with the trappings of Roman proconsuls.

Although theoretically subordinate to the Embassy in Bonn, the State Department personnel and its subsidiaries such as USIA were, in fact, virtually independent. The American ambassador maintained a fully staffed residence in Berlin, again German financed, but rarely used it. The commanding general had, in addition to his city mansion, a large villa on the lovely Wannsee lake where an array of sailboats were at our disposal. The general's yacht was available to senior officers for entertainment purposes.

My fiefdom included a large America House, heavily subsidized exchange program and a bloated press and publications staff which put out an exhaustive daily summary of the German press in translation. I was also the Mission press spokesman. One of our main, and more onerous, jobs was providing press backup for American official visitors who came in a continual stream.

A visit by Secretary of State George Schultz was typical. It was the occasion for a series of Lucullan state dinners and social affairs. German foreign minister Hans Dietrich Genscher, a notably duplicitous political animal who delighted in poking a stick in the American eye, accompanied him. His small Free Democratic Party held the balance of power during much of the post-war period, and Genscher spent seventeen years as foreign minister, effectively controlling German foreign policy to the chagrin of various chancellors, both socialist and conservative.

Trailing in the wake of these political heavyweights was the saturnine figure of Richard Burt, the newly appointed American ambassador to Bonn, a post for which he had no discernible qualifications other than having been the only conservative on the *New York Times* reporting staff. And that he had married one of Nancy Reagan's favorite administrative assistants.

Burt spoke no German, had no real foreign policy experience outside internal State Department intrigues, and was possessed of an outsized ego which matched his ambitions. However, he had one indispensable quality which distinguishes every successful courtier. He was capable of the most abject self-abnegation in the presence of his superiors. *Oben buchen, unten treten,* as the Germans say. Bend to those above and kick those below. He practically soiled his pants every time Genscher spoke to him.

Schultz's press secretary was Bernard Kalb, brother of Marvin Kalb. My German press staff handled the visit with their usual superb efficiency. Everything ran on greased casters. Kalb was impressed. I took all the credit, although I had done nothing but stay out of the way. At midnight on the final day of the Schultz visit, with their plane scheduled to leave at six a.m., Kalb announced that he would like to go to East Berlin to see the gutted remains of the famous synagogue there.

I commandeered a mission car and, both of us three sheets to the wind after a long evening, we headed for the infamous Checkpoint Charley. The East Germans closed their wire gates at midnight and would normally open them only for diplomats and officials accredited to East Germany. I was, however, well known to the guards from my previous East German incarnation when we had crossed the border so many times after midnight.

The checkpoint was a barometer of East-West relations. It if tightened, the political climate was bad. By the same token one of the first indications that something might be cracking in the Soviet empire happened there on our first return to East Berlin after two years in Washington.

Brandt and Genscher's Eastern Policy had been highly successful in breaking down some of the barriers between East and West Germany. The price, however, was high and not only in money. In my myriad contacts among the Social Democratic Party's supporters—politicians, professors, students, activists and journalists—I never recall an instance of direct, unambiguous criticism of the German Democratic Republic and its policies.

Either the speaker found some residual Marxist virtue lurking in the social, economic or cultural policies of the GDR, or "the East was bad, but we in the West are as bad or worse in our own way." The strenuous efforts of the SPD to delay or avoid reunification after the wall came down were a continuation of the effort to save a pure "socialist" state. Kohl's quick, savage thrust for unity, leaving the GDR leaders no way out and offering massive bribes to the Russians to concur, was the mark of a prescient statesman. But all that came almost a decade later.

After we returned to Berlin in 1983 we immediately visited our old haunts in East Berlin. My wife had retained her maiden name after we married, and, as we held up our diplomatic passports to pass through the border, the East German guard, one we had seen dozens of times and who had never acknowledged our existence, grinned, saluted, and with that ironic Berlin humor murmured, "Still not married?"

He was on duty this night and smiled as he recognized me, opening the gates and waving us through. In those days, going from West to East Berlin was a bizarre experience. The West was all light and glitter, the streets filled with pulsating crowds at all hours of the day and night. The East was dark, its streets here and there still marred by the burnt out hulks of war damaged buildings, facades of even the new ones stained and cracked.

No cars moved and what few people who were on the streets seemed to slink along glued to the buildings. We drove through the wide deserted boulevards of the central city, down Unter de Linden and on to the gutted skeleton of the synagogue. Kalb sat in the car for a few moments staring at the ruin. Then he walked across the street and leaned his head against the soot-stained stones, praying silently.

Berlin is in the geographic center of Europe, excluding Russia. A superb Hitler-built highway system radiates from it in all directions. It has, in the years since the wall fell, begun to realize the potential it has always had to become the dominant continental capital. In the process it will eclipse London, Paris and the long somnolent Vienna as the magnet for scholars, intellectuals, writers, painters and musicians from both Eastern and Western Europe. The Prussians will have finally won.

The dynamism, wit and creative juices of its polyglot population, a third descended from French Protestant émigrés given asylum by Frederick the Great after the religious wars in France, will welcome the influx as it did during the wild, anarchic years of the Weimar Republic.

My lover-scholar-wife, somewhat to her own surprise, turned into a relaxed but superb diplomatic hostess. Our house was filled with a combination of my political, cultural and journalistic contacts and her young academic cohorts, at first taken aback by the luxury and excess, then reveling in it. Once we invited the entire corps de ballet of the Berlin Opera, most of whom were American or British. A sprinkling of East Germans with permission to go to the west occasionally showed up.

Wolfgang and Emoke Kohlhaase and Guenter and Petra Fisher created a sensation at one such evening. Kohlhaase had written the script and Fisher the music for the most famous film ever produced in East Germany, *Solo Sonny*. They were funny, irreverent people, convinced communists who believed that, although perverted, the system would in the end right itself and provide the paradise it promised. In the meantime, they worked it skillfully, having the best of both worlds.

Karl Heinz Roeder was a more ambiguous figure. The CIA reports on him stated unequivocally that he had been a member of the East German intelligence service in the fifties and sixties. He was now a respected historian with permission to travel to the west. Once, on a visit to Washington, I'd invited him to the Pentagon for lunch in the generals' dining room.

I put him on my visitor's list, and the secretary of nuclear targeting picked him up at the guarded gate and parked him in my office until I came back from an overlong staff meeting. Dov Zakheim came over to share a coffee and started to laugh when I introduced him. For some reason neither of us was able to take our office mates seriously, despite the fact that they held the destruction of the world in their paws.

Occasionally I would have a twinge of guilt at sticking the Germans with some ridiculous expense. Nobody else did. One cynical British officer summed up the Allied attitude. "Reparations for the war, don't you know, old boy. After all, the buggers lost, don't you know," he said, stuffing his face with Russian caviar bought in East Berlin at the diplomatic store and swilling Piper Heidsieck Brut.

Or, as the American Air Force colonel commanding Templehof Airport, a fellow southerner, once put it during a celebration there: "Boy who'da thought that two old rednecks like us would be here in Berlin, eatin' shrimp and drinkin' wine."

The colonel was talking in a room filled with historic photographs of events which had taken place in the airport. Among the pictures were shots of German aces of the First and Second World War as well as famous German generals from both conflicts. The colonel, like many military men, viewed war as a sort of game. Sometimes you won, sometimes you lost. He saw nothing wrong with honoring a defeated enemy, one of whom had shot him down over France.

One of his pet projects had revolved around a massive iron eagle's head which had dominated the airport during the Hitler period, holding in its claws a swastika and a bundle of arrows. It was an impressive piece of sculpture, singularly menacing, an almost perfect symbol of the virility of the Prussian military tradition. It had been dismantled and put in storage in 1945.

The colonel had pulled it out of storage, had the swastika and rust removed and was about to mount it on a pedestal in a garden at the entrance to the airport when I found out about it. I first invited the colonel to lunch and explained why the eagle was a bad idea. He listened politely and refused to change his plan. When I reported the impending disaster to the minister, Nelson Ledsky, the senior American civilian in Berlin, he was equally appalled. Emplacement of the statue was an unnecessary distraction serving no useful purpose and exposing us to another savage attack by anti-American German leftists.

Ledsky was a grossly fat, shrewd, unscrupulous, duplicitous man who, had he also possessed a modicum of courage, would have been a superb diplomat. But, confronted with any crisis, he sought first to define his self-interest, then that of the country. If the two coincided, and he could see no risks, he acted with decision and dispatch. If, however, there as no clear-cut decision possible but rather, as in most cases, a series of unpalatable options, he tended, as do most bureaucrats, to bob and weave, avoiding putting his gonads on the line.

Caution has its uses, but it can also be as dangerous as recklessness. When word of the Nazi eagle leaked to the press, the Germans were utterly bemused. On the left, in this city long known as "Red Berlin", it was one more proof of the basic fascistic tendencies of the Americans. On the right, there was a certain satisfaction that the eagle, an ancient German royal device, was being freed of its Nazi associations.

The bird was in fact a much more complicated animal. It embodied a series of stereotypes which modern democratic Germany still must confront at every crisis. Both a symbol of historic Prussian military prowess, as exemplified by Frederick the Great and Bismarck, and German aggression in the two World Wars, it tended to sum up all the bad images.

In an age when reality has little meaning, and image, however flawed, is all, there are few who know that Prussia under Frederick the Great was one of the most enlightened governments in Europe, offering unprecedented independence to women, an excellent educational system, relative upward mobility for the talented, a high degree of tolerance for its Jewish minority, and a haven for tens of thousands of Protestants on the verge of being massacred in France after the revocation of the Edict of Nantes. Frederick himself was the best educated and culturally sophisticated monarch of his time, offering asylum to Voltaire, playing the flute with professional skill and encouraging a wide variety of progressive government measures. He was a wry, witty, autocratic man, imprisoned by the traumas of his youth beginning with his father's execution of his best friend, who was possibly his lover.

Similarly, the much vilified Bismarck spent the years after the French defeat by Germany in 1870 in an attempt to create a balance of power in Europe which would avoid future wars among the European states. He knew that the new technology of slaughter had stripped war of any useful function.

His subtle playing off of Austria-Hungary, Russia, Great Britain, Italy and France in a roundelay of shifting alliances, exploiting their contradictory interests, was designed to avoid confrontations leading to the abattoir of modern war. And to keep Germany from having to confront a two-front war as a result of a Franco-Russian alliance. His system worked for forty-five years until the young Kaiser, thirsty for fame and full of hubris, brought on the disaster of the First World War, aided, it must be said, by the equal arrogance and stupidity of the other powers.

The colonel's iron bird would inevitably call up all these images, but the American military, with that density which seems to cloud its collective mind when it steps beyond the battlefield, insisted that it be emplaced.

Ledsky caved. However, the ceremony was modest, and the Berlin press and political class, tacitly recognizing the explosive possibilities, muted its response. Once in a while reason prevailed.

Shortly thereafter, when President Reagan visited a German cemetery holding the graves of Waffen SS soldiers killed in battle, it resulted in a massive uproar. I suspect that the same bureaucratic tone deafness of the military and the gutlessness of the State

Department were once again at work in the planning of that disastrous visit.

As these and other similar events piled up over the years, I have changed my mind about the staffing of our embassies abroad. I think in most instances intelligent and informed non-career diplomats, even if lacking detailed expertise in the nation to which they are appointed, are more likely than career diplomats to analyze political events and ascertain American interests in an objective and dispassionate way. The innate bureaucratic caution of the careerist will often paralyze his will and lead him into cautious inaction. There are plenty of policy experts and linguists at the second level to give the non-careerist the information he needs. All he has to supply is decisiveness and the will to confront his superiors with unpalatable truths.

Balls are always in short supply, which brings me to one of the more surprising events of my tour in West Berlin.

"The Germans and the Jews have always had a love-hate relationship. The Jews loved the Germans and the Germans hated the Jews," Peter Gay said, looking out over an audience that included German President Richard von Weizacker, Chancellor Helmut Kohl and virtually every prominent personality in Berlin. The occasion was the first meeting in Germany of the Leo Beck Institute, an organization of Jewish émigrés from Germany.

Gay, a short, overweight, rumpled figure in an unpressed suit bagging in the seat, was making the keynote address. He had left Germany as a lower middle class teenager in the late thirties, one step ahead of a concentration camp and death. Once in America, driven by ferocious motivation and energy, he had realized the German Jewish immigrant's dream of paradise, becoming a distinguished professor of history at Yale University where he had been the doctoral advisor of my wife.

The Beck Institute's conference was lavishly subsidized by the German government in one more of its many attempts to atone for the Holocaust. Gay's mildly spoken but brutal words irritated some of his fellow Beck Institute members who embodied the sentiment he had evoked. The fascination of these aging émigrés for the

Teutonic culture was wrapped in the horror of what had happened. Many of these gentle, highly assimilated, often non-religious people were still seeking desperately for some rational explanation of what had happened, so that they could forgive if not forget.

They were unwilling to admit what Gay insisted on facing in his speech. The fact is that a majority of Germans who lived through the Nazi period had only one regret: they lost. Anti-semitism is almost never overt in Germany today, as it is in Poland, Rumania, Hungary and the Soviet Union. But the Jew, as with the second generation Turks and Tamils, is still regarded as an alien presence, not really German. Among the German young, who are as indifferent to history as they are everywhere, there is a certain irritation at the world's continuing insistence on remembering the Holocaust. Why me? they ask. Even my parents weren't born when it happened.

Gay's speech was an admirable and courageous act. It was also, in some perverse way, very German. Beneath a seemingly relaxed and jolly facade, he was a tortured man, possessed of demons he could neither recognize nor admit. His four years of intense Freudian analysis had done little to exorcise them and had given him virtually no insights into his own dictatorial personality.

He treated his graduate students with fatherly kindness as long as they bent to his will. Not unlike his hero Freud, if they resisted he broke them. Mary Lee Townsend, beautiful, brilliant, an American aristocrat, the classic shiksa, had clearly worked her way into his subconsciousness. Although he said nothing, as did most of her friends, he was clearly astounded and offended by our affair and marriage.

My cynical, hard-edged geopolitics and Celtic stoicism clashed with his compulsive Jewish need to be loved, accepted and admired. In one memorable exchange on child rearing, after he had expatiated at length on the impossibility of persuading children to eat, I had, with a certain impatience, offered the following solution.

"When they won't eat, say nothing. Take their plate away and put it in the refrigerator and make sure they eat nothing until the next meal at which point you present them with the plate of congealed food. Repeat the process until they eat. No child has ever been known to starve itself to death. One dose of this treatment is usually enough to stop their whining."

He looked at me in horrified distaste and mumbled something about "coarse brutal fascist."

In another, even more bizarre incident during a relaxed discussion of some political incident on the American scene, I mentioned the Jewish lobby. Gay turned purple with rage. "The Jewish lobby doesn't exist. It's an anti-Semitic invention." Jim Markham, the *New York Times* correspondent in Bonn, who was present, and another Yale professor, who was Jewish, stared at their fingernails in embarrassment as Gay continued to rant, but opted out. Since my comment on the lobby had not been critical, I was astounded at the force of his reaction and the patent absurdity of refusing to admit the existence of a perfectly legitimate organization for furthering Israeli interests.

His dislike was a matter of indifference to me, until my wife entered a drastically reduced academic job market replete with brilliant Ivy League scholars bearing credentials equal to hers. Although he had described her as his most brilliant student ever, his recommendations were tepid. She was, in the end, forced to take a job at the University of Tulsa. It seemed a momentary setback at the time, but in the end it became a festering wound in her psyche.

But this somber, almost subliminal, tapestry of a German national neurosis hardly intruded on our three years in Berlin. We were deep in the grip of hormonal obsession. All was right with the world. We vacationed in Paris, London and Portofino, spent two weeks at a tennis camp in Provence on the slopes of Mount Ventoux, and three at Contrexville, a nineteenth century spa with the charm of its age. And there were three glorious weeks on Gozo, the small island north of Malta, an unspoiled, undiscovered voyage into antiquity.

We once took the French train to Strasbourg and then a special gourmet one to Paris. And we often boarded the American train to Bremerhaven for a weekend in Cuxhaven. All the while contributing to the West German budget deficit at the finest restaurants in Berlin. For a change we would visit a nameless Greek bistro and the Zur Henne, a nineteenth century German *kneipe* up against the wall in Kreuzberg. The Einstein Cafe was a favorite hangout before and after the theater.

We were besotted and obsessed with each others bodies. She had fulfilled my every fantasy and some that had not occurred to me. For diversion Berlin offered a kaleidoscope of great music, theater, opera, cabaret and ballet. Although she balked at attending the endless round of dinners, receptions and cocktail parties, she was one of the most sought after guests. Speaking perfect German, knowing far more of their nation's history that the condescending and pompous German males and not hesitant to stick it to them, she commanded a room with her brains, athletic American body and flaming mass of red hair.

If there is a certain fatuousness in these passages, so be it, for it was ever thus.

It was not, however, all fun and games. The Law of Unintended Consequences often brought some hilarity into our lives. For example, I one day received a call from a Berlin labor leader named Karl Pagels. I'd met him at one of the endless functions hosted by the mayor at the city hall. Although he declared himself a Marxist and anti-American, he became a regular at our receptions. Pagels wanted to invite Jane Fonda to speak at an immense rally on May 1, the major holiday of German leftists, anarchists, Greens and Knows God how many other oddball political sects. He asked for my help.

I gagged at the idea, since the lady was, and is, in my view not only a traitor but a paradigm of the political airhead, but my sense of humor took over, and I gave him the name and address of the head of the actor's union in Hollywood. This union had, for many years, been a hotbed of the American left but, unbeknownst to me, a right-wing group had taken it over in an electoral coup d'état. In a series of conversations Pagels had with the union's president, he was persuaded to accept a substitute for Ms. Fonda.

His name was Bruce Hershensohn, the former head of the film unit at USIA. By this time, again unbeknownst to me, he had become a famous political commentator who made Genghis Khan look like a McGovern liberal. I put my feet up on the desk and contemplated the East German poster of Le Roi Ubu which faced me, a reminder of just how weird the real world can be. I should, of course, have warned Pagels. But I didn't. Perversity, as it often did, overcame common sense.

Bruce arrived in due course, and we reminisced about our days in the film unit of USIA two decades before. He was a little grayer, but still the stoop shouldered, intense caricature of a Jew in an anti-Semitic cartoon. He was, if anything, even more ingratiating than he had been in 1967, extruding pre-détente Cold War slogans and eviscerating the left as either traitors or simple-minded. His speech was a litany of hatred for the Soviet Union and a hymn to American democracy.

Pagels, who spoke no English, met briefly with Herschensohn but did not read the German translation of Bruce's speech. On the morning of May first he was in a state of comfortable alcoholic euphoria when Bruce walked out on the balcony before a crowd of more than two hundred thousand people, black anarchist flags mingling with the red ones of the socialists and communists.

As the translator repeated his English speech in German over dozens of loudspeakers, the multitude at first became still, then restless, clearly puzzled by the virulent anti-leftist, anti-Soviet language filling the atmosphere. Then, almost as one voice, a roar arose, bottles, beer steins and rocks suddenly flew toward the speakers stand.

Bruce, a pale, lonely figure, stood his ground, threw away his speech and shouted that they were intolerant thugs, no better than the Storm Troopers of Nazi Germany, unwilling to allow freedom of ideas, intolerant fascists. I risked life and limb to grapple with him and drag him back into the safety of the building.

Pagels and his staff were stunned. "Get him out of here," he screamed. "They'll storm the building and tear him limb from limb. And me with him," he added in despair, between German curses at Herschensohn who stared at him with utter calm.

"You're nothing but a reincarnation of a Nazi Brown Shirt," Bruce told him and followed me out the back door where we faded into the crowd surging toward the speakers balcony.

I have seldom, if ever, seen anything to compare to this odd little man's calm courage during this incident. He was one more of a string of right-wing reactionaries whose grace and wit I have admired without sharing any of their beliefs. The obverse are the often intolerant, insolent, backbiting, petty, treacherous and vengeful intellectuals of the left, with whose domestic politics I totally agree.

I had a large staff, and personnel matters often took over from substance. For a period the America House director, Parker Anderson, a strange young man with a fuzzy grasp on reality, was a real problem. As was often the case, he was psychologically imprisoned by the efficient young German who really ran the operation. The difficulty with Herr Ludwig, who had studied in America, was that he had become infected with the idea that we should try to show America warts and all, instead of presenting a selectively favorable view.

Given the fact that the German media inundated the population with hostile portraits of the American scene, I was determined to make a modest effort at righting the picture. I was, however, unwilling to spend vast amounts of time supervising the cultural programs, and I opted for a shortcut. Brutality. Anderson and Herr Ludwig fought back, often successfully. I really only gained control when Anderson and his wife came apart over his German mistress.

Anderson's wife, a piece of steel from South Carolina, marched into my office one day and announced that her brother was sending her a dismantled pistol through the mail, and that she planned to put it together and blow away her faithless mate.

Gives the history of the Southern women in my family, I believed her and persuaded the agency to transfer Anderson immediately. To everyone's astonishment he resigned, giving up his government pension and moving in with the school teacher with whom he was madly infatuated. The last I heard they are living happily in Berlin.

I had the mails monitored for pistol parts but none arrived, and Anderson's wife eventually left for South Carolina.

Then there was Wolfgang Stresemann, son of the former German foreign minister in the pre-Hitler days. Stresemann was a former intendant of the Berlin Philharmonic orchestra, perhaps the world's finest, and a holy icon in Berlin where music is as important as politics. After Stresemann retired, the orchestra's conductor, Herbert von Karajan had become embroiled in a feud with the musicians and refused to conduct. Stresemann, an elegant gentleman of a past era, was recalled to settle the row which he did with impeccable calm, resigning once again once the crisis was resolved. He was, by this time, in his eighties, but with an eye for the ladies. He was enamored of my wife, utterly astounded that a woman this beautiful had wasted her time obtaining a doctorate in mid-nineteenth century German history.

On one occasion Stresemann described a tennis match with Hitler's foreign minister, von Ribbentrop. He first said the von, an indication of minor nobility, was purchased and second, that von Ribbentrop tended to cheat at tennis although he had a wicked sliced backhand. Listening to the energetic old man was like a walk on the dark side of history as he described the Nazi era in Berlin before he emigrated to the United States in 1938.

His antithesis was a young photographer, a South African, the son of Berlin émigrés. His name was Stephen Laufer, and he worked at various times for Berlin newspapers and the office of the conservative mayor, Eberhard Diepgen. I was instinctively suspicious of Laufer, not so much for his evident anti-Americanism, which was endemic among Berlin intellectuals, as for his treachery.

Years later, as the wall came down and the mission became no more than an important consular district, Laufer was hired by one of my successors, Carolyn Meirs-Osterling, a lady of singular arrogance and impenetrable stupidity. I warned her, and the then minister, of Laufer. They ignored the warning and Ms. Meirs-

Osterling made him press spokesman for the mission, a virtually unheard of appointment, since this job was always held by an American.

Two years later he was convicted of spying for the East German STASI and, by extension, the Soviet KGB and was jailed. Ms. Meirs-Osterling was soon promoted.

Perhaps the biggest drama of my West Berlin tour was the Sharansky Affair. Natan Sharansky was a Russian dissident imprisoned for his outspoken opposition to the policies of the Soviet government. After months of publicity and behind the scenes negotiations, the Russians agreed to let him go. They chose to free him on the Glinicke Bridge, a small span bridging a finger of the Wannsee on the road to Potsdam.

The bridge had been made famous as the site for the exchange of the most successful Soviet spy of his time, Rudolph Abel, and Gary Powers, the U-2 pilot shot down over the Soviet Union in 1960. Sharansky's release became a journalistic orgy. Hundreds, if not thousands, of newsmen descended on the city. The Russians had demanded that there be no press coverage as they handed over Sharansky, and we established with the help of the Berlin police a buffer zone of more than a mile between the bridge and the press enclosure.

Our esteemed young ambassador, Richard Burt, saw the exchange as a golden opportunity to burnish his image and sought out the press at every opportunity. As usual, my staff handled the operation with impeccable efficiency. At one point the journalists had broken through the barricades and were attempting to set up much closer to the bridge than was allowed.

I called them all together and held an off-the-record briefing on the rules. Off-the-record is one of the great jokes of journalism, since any journalists will violate it if the information will get him a beat. I informed everybody that they were going to have to move back to the assigned area at which point the American producers, those puppet masters who pull the strings of correspondents and cameramen, began to issue the usual threats to "get me fired", "hung by the heels", "castrated" or just plain sent to Ouagadougou as janitor.

I looked them over in silence for a while until they calmed down and, making sure there was no lighting for the television cameras, told them verbatim in the mildest possible tone that: "If you're unable to do it yourselves, the German police will be happy to assist you in moving your gear to the assigned areas. And if you don't cooperate they will escort you to the slammer." Unfortunately, I had not realized that modern technology had developed the ability of television cameras to operate with very little light. My threat appeared worldwide that evening, along with scathing criticism of my "censoring" of the news. Richard Burt was enraged that I had pre-empted his right to center stage.

One of the networks had somehow obtained a five-story cherry picker and installed zoom cameras in the miniature gondola at the top. Their producer, whom I had known from presidential trips, took its removal philosophically. Although abrasive, brutal and utterly untrustworthy, I found the producers by and large the most intelligent of the television newsmen. They often wrote the scripts for the talking heads and had complete control of content. Faceless men and women, too homely to be anchors, dressed in soiled blue jeans and, totally harassed, they were the unsung masters of the medium.

Among the correspondents covering the event were my old friend Jim Markham of the *Times* and a name from the past, Pierre Salinger, President John Kennedy's press secretary. We traded anecdotes on the vicissitudes of being a press attaché, and he then tried to hustle some special treatment. I bent some rules for him. After all, we belonged to the same union.

As in all hermetically sealed societies, there was a high quotient of petty intrigue in the Mission. On one occasion Ledsky's protocol chief, a handsome young female career officer in her mid-thirties, left Mary Lee's name off an invitation list provided to the Soviets who were inviting senior Mission personnel to visit their impressive embassy in East Berlin for a film evening.

The young woman's excuse was that she'd overlooked Mary Lee since she used her maiden name. Her real reason was irritation at the popularity my wife enjoyed among the senior members of the diplomatic and military missions. It was, she said, too late to revise the list.

I went alone and, encountering Bogumolov mentioned that Mary Lee was disappointed at having been left off the list. On the spot he arranged for us to come over the following day for a conducted tour of the embassy and lunch in their cafeteria. It was one of many examples of the profound courtesy and good manners of the Russians I met over the years when no political tension was involved.

It was, and I assume still is, a warm and giving society where friendships, hard to establish, are often much more profound once in place than in western countries.

Somewhere near the middle of my tour, I received a cryptic telegram from Washington ordering me to appear there within three days. I called the area director, an old friend, to find out what was going on. He said, with some embarrassment, that he didn't know. The day before I left the local spook asked me to meet him in the parking lot.

This man, an old friend, who had handled the running of the lady journalist I had helped recruit in East Berlin, swore me to secrecy and told me that I was being investigated as a security risk. He had been queried about me and assured everybody not only that I wasn't a risk, but was in fact a dedicated Cold Warrior under no illusions about the East.

Forewarned, I arrived in Washington and was immediately taken to what was clearly an interrogation room. Present were a graying USIA security officer and a tall, handsome character in an Italian suit and Gucci loafers. Over the next four hours I underwent an interrogation which covered virtually every inch of my foreign service career and private life.

It began with the question: "What does "oatmeal for brains" mean, Mr. Harper?"

"Why?"

"You are reported to have said that about the American ambassador in East Berlin."

"It means stupid."

"Did you say it?"

"Sure."

Things went downhill from there. The clown in the expensive suit held up a thick stack of reports and pushed them toward me. "Do you recognize these?"

I thumbed through them. "Yeah. They're Memoranda of Conversation."

"All with members of the Communist Party or Russian diplomats, a lot of them KGB agents," he said, triumphantly. "You have more of these memoranda in your file than any other officer in the foreign service. What do you say to that?"

"Well, first, it's a regulation that when you talk to a red, you write a memcon. Second, I was serving in communist countries and it was my job to talk to communists. Third, you're an insolent fucking idiot. Fourth, you moderate that tone of voice you're using or I'll first break your goddamn jaw and then get a lawyer."

He was a big guy with all the authority of the FBI behind him. He wasn't used to being talked to this way. I'm sure that the paunchy, aging diplomat who shouted at him didn't frighten him, but he was certainly shocked. He stood up.

"You'd better understand that I'm armed, Harper."

I started to laugh. The absurdity of the situation had finally come home to me. Here I was, one of the most convinced Cold Warriors in the diplomatic service being interrogated by a political idiot.

The USIA security officer intervened. "Look, Ed, you're going to have to go through the interrogation. Nobody's accusing you of anything. It's just that you've got so goddamn many contacts with Soviets and communists that it got flagged."

In some odd way the very nearly physical confrontation seemed to have impressed the young FBI man. He became genuinely courteous and even made some attempt to understand how an embassy works. About halfway through the interrogation, it became routine. When I was freed, I stopped by the area director's office, who grinned and suggested I get the hell back to Berlin as quickly as possible.

Some years later, after Stephen Laufer was arrested as a spy, two other FBI men showed up without warning at my front door in Tulsa, Oklahoma. Laufer had apparently suggested to his superiors that I was a candidate to be "turned" by a "honey pot", an especially trained seductress. The leader of this team had copies of my letters warning the mission about Laufer. He was a highly educated political scientist and specialist in German affairs. We toured the German horizon for two hours and as he prepared to leave, he thanked me for my time. I never did figure out what they expected to get out of the interview.

About the same time my novel, *The Orpheus Circle*, was published. It dealt with the Berlin Document Center, an archive of information on Nazi party members, SS and other prominent people associated with Hitler's regime. The archive was run by the American Berlin Mission under the direction of a retired army colonel. However, the staff of about forty people were all Germans. I postulated in the book that a group of high ranking NAZI SS men had changed their identities after the war and became submerged in post-war Germany. They were protected from discovery by people in the document center.

Several years after we had left Berlin, and just after my book was published, an investigation revealed that the German staff of the BDC had been using documents to blackmail war criminals in an uncanny resemblance to my plot. *Der Spiegel*, the *Time Magazine* of Germany, sent a correspondent I knew, Christian Habbe, to Tulsa to interview me. He wrote a lurid article implying that I had known about the scam before I wrote the novel.

As my three-year Berlin tour came to a close I was offered once again, the position of public affairs officer in Ankara, one of the most difficult and avoided posts in the foreign service. The Greeks and Turks, both close allies, essential to securing the southern flank of the NATO Alliance against what then seemed to be a still aggressive and expansionist Soviet Union, were at each others' throats and we were in the middle. I was fluent in Turkish. The job would probably have resulted in a promotion to minister counselor.

But I had no interest in staying in the foreign service, having agreed to take early retirement as soon as Mary Lee had found a job. However, my pension was decimated by being split with my first wife and would be barely sufficient to survive on. Mary Lee had been interviewed for a half dozen academic posts but had not received any job offers except one from the University of Tulsa in Oklahoma. Her field was glutted with desperate job seekers, most of whom were leaving academe in despair.

I toyed with the idea of going to Turkey, but in the end I urged her to take the job in Tulsa on the theory that she needed some experience in teaching and would be able to finish her books there. The alternative, a tour in Turkey, would take her off the academic screen for too long. She agreed, reluctantly, and went off ahead of me to Oklahoma while I finished the tedious business of retirement. I drove from Washington in two days, virtually without sleep, to join her.

At the last second, realizing I had no present for her, I stopped at a truck stop in southern Missouri and bought a small furry gorilla with a red heart on his chest proclaiming him to be "The Last of the Red Hot Lovers."

I presented him to Mary Lee as she came into my arms, tears in her eyes. "Lover, I want to live happily ever after."

It was not to be.

Thirty

Philosophy and the study of the actual world have the same relation to one another as onanism and sexual love.

Karl Marx

Having spent most of my life attempting to disentangle reality from its appearance—to deconstruct the Bullshit Factor—it is only fitting to sum up the results. H.L. Mencken wrote six volumes of his prejudices; I'll do mine in one chapter.

My first premise will cause the intellectual, tortured by the Talmudic subtleties so dear to his profession, to wince: human motivations are not all that complicated. Greed, gratification of the senses, the need to be loved, vengeance and domination are the universal elements.

The twentieth century has been a dark and bloody time. But what century in human history has not? For the past seven thousand years, recorded on everything from clay tablets to pentium chips, the life of most of mankind has been, in Hobbes' mordant phrase, "solitary, poor, nasty, brutish and short." True, in the midst of this bloody cauldron there evolved a few small islands of civilization when beauty, benevolence and political sanity briefly flourished. But only the most addled of optimists can find much to sing about.

Ours has been another of those periods when the tectonic plates of powerful ideologies ground against each other, in the process crushing the life out of dozens of millions of bystanders. Just as Christianity and the Koran eradicated the pagan gods, socialism and fascism pushed these beliefs to the margins in an orgy of materialism.

Secular religions offering earthly rewards instead of a paradise to come, they both enshrined a tactic which particularly appealed to the young: the means justify the ends, ignoring the reality that means are the ends for the pullulating mass of humanity. Both embodied the same paradox. They were essentially elitist, although their public appeals were to the aching needs of the masses. Their founders were theorists and intellectuals who dealt in systemic constructs having little or nothing to do with man's nature. When that nature interfered with theory, it was brutally suppressed.

Thus Marxism-Leninism's "from each according to his ability, to each according to his need" was distorted into a class system elevating a mandarin governing cadre above the herd. Calls for egalitarianism by such critics as Milovan Djilas were dismissed as "vulgar Marxism." Fascism's highly structured society, assigning its followers to an almost feudal ladder, also rewarded and glorified an intellectual-administrative elite.

The temptation to use government power to amass wealth, present in every system, was all too evident in the profoundly corrupt Soviet culture. It is no surprise that the Sandinista leaders in Nicaragua and their counterparts in Cuba, while preaching the ideal revolution, live in the confiscated houses of the rich while their followers sink ever deeper into poverty and despair.

Inevitably, the sincere fanatics, immersed in the rhetoric of revolt, were rapidly replaced by *fonctionnaires*, practical men who put their own self-interested version of the theories into effect. Nowhere in human history, other than in the wake of Attila and Ghenghis Khan, have the murderous brutalities of the Soviet and Nazi rulers been equaled.

Why?

The bottom line in political theory and practice is: power corrupts and absolute power corrupts absolutely. A cliché. But clichés exist because they are generally accurate. Deliver me from the originality of the clerks and their convoluted complexities.

Fact is, the more centralization of power, the greater the risk of tyranny. This simple truism has been has been recognized by political realists through the ages, from Thucydides to Cicero, Machiavelli, de Maistre, Hobbes and the brilliantly cynical triad of Jefferson, Madison and Hamilton. To ignore it is to court disaster.

Another bane of our age is the proliferation of words—written, spoken and conveyed in images. A desperate search for originality, drama and variety obscures the simple realities. If Capitalism, in its extreme consumerist form, is the heroin of the people, then the Word is its needle. The bland banality of the soundbite has replaced the trenchant witticism cutting to the heart of the matter. Outright lies are used to deconstruct unpalatable realities. Repeated often enough, they become the reality as Joseph Goebbels so presciently knew. Humor, the grease of civilization and deflator of flatulent pomposity, has degenerated into tasteless gags.

Where are the Lytton Strachyeys, an enthusiastic advocate of buggery, who said, with a salacious grin, when asked what he would do if he encountered a Prussian officer raping his sister: "I would interpose my body."

Or the Earl of Sandwich to John Wilkes: "Pon my honor Wilkes, I don't know whether you'll die on the gallows or of the pox."

Wilkes replied: "That must depend, my Lord, upon whether I first embrace your Lordship's principles or your Lordship's mistress."

Then there was Hegel, replying to an accusation that his facts were wrong: *Umso schlimmer fuer die Tatsachen*—so much the worse for the facts.

Or the deadpanned State Department spokesman who, when accused of ambiguity, replied: "I think that ambiguity tends to clarify the situation," and got away with it.

But humor won't go far with fanatics. And ours has been the century of revolutionary terrorism by small groups of singularly dour fanatics. Their slogans mirrored their humorlessness. The Spanish Falange marched under the absurd banner "Long Live

Death." Pere Lazarbal, a theorist of the Basque terrorists, summed up the motivation of all such movements devoted to violence in one sentence: "It is better to be the butcher than the calf," a sentiment hard to fault but irrelevant in the rollicking democracy which is present day Spain. Patrick Pierce, leader of the Irish Easter Rebellion in 1916, declared with gloomy relish: "Bloodshed is a cleansing thing, and the nation that regards it as the final horror has lost its manhood."

Looking for manhood in shallow graves is cold comfort to the troops following these prophets of death. This brings me to the guts of this final chapter. What follows is my answer to Chernyshevsky's terse demand: What is to Be Done. Although I've tried to excise prejudice, bias and ideology and adopt a neutral stance, clearly I have a point of view. Here it is.

In my youth I was offended by the brutal results of an unbridled capitalist system and seduced by the solutions offered by socialism. Government ownership of the means of production seemed to guarantee a just, equitable, egalitarian society where each shared fairly in the pool of material and intellectual goods. *Helas*, I learned quickly that life doesn't work that way. The Iron Law of Oligarchy states that all regimes are of necessity ruled by an organized minority controlling a disorganized majority. A government functionary in a pure socialist society quickly becomes a pure tyrant, his ego, ambition and greed unfettered by competing power centers. As Aristotle acutely observed: men do not become tyrants to keep out the cold.

Bureaucracy is the preferred weapon of those who distrust the voice of the people. The United States today has three million federal employees and fifteen million state and local functionaries. Their numbers increase yearly far in excess of population growth. Public employment is a cancer gorging itself on the decreasing number of productive workers. Technology, the benign goddess of conservatives and progressives alike, seems most concerned with pandering to our appetite for ever more frenzied entertainment. The whore with the credit card machine perhaps sums up manic consumerism most graphically.

Gradually, intellectually kicking and screaming, I moved toward social democracy. Let the invidious capitalists, motivated by greed and lust for the power and perquisites of money, have their head. Then use the fiscal power of government to share the rich results with their less motivated, energetic, intelligent, unlucky or just plain lazy compatriots. And in the process provide a more level playing field in equalizing opportunities for each new generation. An elegant formulation and I'll now offer my short, simple, mundane agenda for achieving it.

Since all agendas need a name, I'll call it neo-Puritanism.

First, the problems. Decaying cities; an imploding educational network; roiling ethnic hatred; an electoral system guaranteeing an increasing monopoly of power by wealthy self-perpetuating elites, of both the right and left; a hopeless and alienated *lumpen-proletariat;* the aesthetic devastation of the environment; erosion of our basic manufacturing sector; a scandalous lack of national health insurance and minimal safety net for the hopelessly incompetent; and, last but far from least, the deterioration of our international influence.

Paradoxically, despite this alarming litany of problems, we remain a remarkably vital, inventive and productive nation, offering unique opportunities to dynamic and motivated individuals. Although class and caste, as in any maturing society, have become less permeable, we still offer the precious possibility, to those with energy, motivation and brains of upward mobility unparalleled in any other advanced industrial society. We have had, over the past fifty years, four impressive successes: One, the defeat short of war of our great antagonist, the Soviet Union; two, the legal reintegration into the mainstream, imperfect though it may be in practice, of the ten percent of our population which is black; three, the opening, beginning with the revolutionary impact of the GI Bill, of our higher educational system to all classes; and four, our population enjoyed an increase in the material standard of living unparalleled in human history.

But we are also a society ruled by the Great God Greed. Its leitmotif is More More More. I suggest, now that we have a surfeit of the toys of affluence, it is time to pull back and begin to concentrate on quality rather than quantity. And this means quick and visible pain in the form of short-term financial sacrifice.

I am not, however, an oatmeal-for-brains optimist. Nothing recommended below is going to happen, since there are two linked realities which Americans are so far unwilling to confront: they insist on having essential programs such as social security, a preponderant defense force, universal medical care and a minimum safety net for societal drop outs, but they will not agree to increased taxes to pay for these programs. The inevitable long-term result of this blind greed is a debased currency, huge interest payments on the national debt and the loss of the dollar's dominant position as the world's reserve currency, a major source of our international clout.

Given this economic narcissism, the following suggestions are written in sand. Nonetheless, the search for economic sanity, much like that chimera of objectivity, is worth the effort, since there is no real alternative. And we might just some day wake up to the fact that there is no free lunch.

Money comes first; solutions flow from it. I would institute four simple, easily administered tax reforms: One, an immediate fifty-cent-per-gallon increase in the federal tax on gasoline, rising gradually over five years to a dollar after which the tax would be tied to the rate of inflation. This would reduce our imports of petroleum products and cut both our balance of payments deficit and air pollution, thus pleasing both bankers and tree huggers. Since virutally all advanced industrial nations charge taxes of two-to-three dollars a gallon on gasoline, our competitive position would hardly be affected.

Two, a national sales tax of five cents on every dollar spent on anything except food, housing and medicine. Regressive, yes. But such a tax is the bread and butter of social democrats from Sweden to Italy.

Three, impose escalating income taxes beginning at fifteen percent on incomes from $30,000 to $50,000, twenty-five percent on incomes between $50,000 and $100,000 and fifty percent on all income in excess of $100,000 up to a total of $500,000. On incomes above $500,000 up to $1,000,000 the tax would be seventy percent. On incomes above $1,000,000 but less than $5,000,000 the tax would be 90 percent and on all income above $5,000,000 ninety-five percent. A similar income tax schedule was in effect during World War II and was accepted by the population without a whimper.

The only income deduction allowed would be for interest on housing loans up to $500,000, since this program is one of the most successful in providing affordable housing to the great mass of our society, an unmitigated social good.

Four, a similarly escalating schedule on inherited wealth would deprive all heirs of ninety-five percent of fortunes above $10,000,000, not so much for the financial gains to the government, but to prevent dynastic families from accumulating the political power money conveys. The Rockefellers, Kennedys and Perots would no longer be able to buy governorships, senate and house seats and, with luck, three-quarters of the members of congress would cease to be millionaries as they are today.

All the above to be indexed for inflation and subject to a constitutional amendment to alter it. Otherwise, a craven congress and president would soon pervert its elegant simplicity with a morass of venal exceptions.

These tax schedules would abolish some of the obscene rewards now paid stock market speculators, executives of large corporations, star athletes, parasitic coupon clipping billionaires and actors. They would also pour vast sums into government coffers. Enough to finance all the programs which follow and still have something left over to pay down the national debt.

Having addressed the question of financing, I would then institute the following social, economic and cultural reforms.

The most basic is an incompetent educational system which must be fundamentally reformed. This expensive sclerotic monster is now in the hands of education theorists and teachers' union bureaucrats whose main interest is in protecting their iron grip on the cash cow the schools represent. The so-called teachers' colleges and education departments of universities across the nation demand a massive concentration of curricula on teacher training programs. Dreary, mind-numbing how-to-teach courses rather than basic subjects such as mathematics, written and spoken English, history, physics, chemistry, political science and foreign languages which should constitute the core curriculum of our schools. Since the teachers are not required to master any of these disciplines in anything but the most superficial manner, they can't possibly teach them. Teachers' colleges should be abolished and the education course requirements for teaching certificates drastically reduced.

While I am wary of the immense federal bureaucracy and would devolve many of its functions to the states, in this instance a set of minimum national norms for all students in these core subjects is essential. Even more important, teachers should meet a national standard for competency in subject matter, not procedure.

There should be a return to track systems, grouping the intelligent and motivated together, with yearly evaluations to allow late bloomers to re-enter the elite groups once they have shown their ability and desire to do so. It is a cruel but real fact of life that some people are more intelligent or energetic than others. Reducing the difficulty of academic courses to accommodate the lowest common denominator in public schools has already given unfair advantage to those educated in the private schools of the affluent.

Egalitarianism of merit should be our goal, not a spurious leveling down. At the same time immense, even disproportionate, resources in money, time and energy should be devoted to practical vocational courses for those headed for artisan jobs. These courses should be designed in close cooperation with the businesses which will hire the graduates to insure some reasonable correlation between education and the needs of the workplace.

Massive subsidized apprentice programs similar to those so successful in Germany should be set up in all industries. These apprenticeships are coveted opportunities in nations which use the system, and they turn out highly paid, skilled artisans proud of their skills and professions.

It is essential that such vocational programs not shield these students from the demands of the academic curriculum. Members of our rich and diverse society must be given large doses of the common culture rather than condemned to lives of intellectual aridity.

Obviously, the track system would not be exclusionary. Large comprehensive schools would mingle the tracks in many instances such as music and athletics. Talent and motivation would be the guiding rule.

For those unable, or unwilling, to participate in these programs, a federal America Corps, modeled on the civilian Conversation Corps and Works Projects Administration of the nineteen thirties, should be established. One section would be devoted to youths from fourteen to eighteen who have, for one reason or another, dropped out of school.

Another, and by far the larger, would be composed of adults eligible for welfare payments. In order to receive money, they would be required to register in this program and work eight hours a day. Their children would be cared for in a nationwide network of federally financed, locally administered, child care centers open to everyone. A means test would force those capable of paying to contribute to the cost of such centers. Similar systems are highly effective throughout Europe.

Finally, at age eighteen or upon graduation from high school, all able-bodied youths would be required to spend one-year in a national service program, living in barracks and serving, at their choice, either in the military or in a broad spectrum of programs designed to rejuvenate our schools, cities and the environment. Purpose of the program, aside from the immense potential of these young people to improve all aspects of national life, would be to throw together for one year people from all classes, leaving them forever with a tactile, immediate experience with their peers. There is an extreme, and politically explosive, lack of real contact between social classes in our society.

If education is the basic building block of a polity, grace and beauty follow closely. When I moved back to the United States from a fourteenth century village house in the Provence region of France, an area of almost painfully spectacular landscapes and medieval towns, I toured the United States in search of the American equivalent. I found it often in small New England and Mid-western towns, in coastal cities which had survived in the amber of poverty and in backwaters such as Boulder, Colorado, Madison and Washington, Georgia and Eureka Springs, Arkansas. There are certainly dozens, perhaps hundreds, of others.

But in between I drove through an aesthetic horror story of decaying, dismal cities and dozens of small towns whose early charm and grace had been left to decay, all life forms gathered along strip malls of fast food joints, shoddy motels and the ubiquitous obscenities of gas station architects. The leitmotif of middle America seemed to be a pervasive ugliness, a cultural desert mired in dreariness.

One of the major functions on the America Corps as well as the national service draftees would be to participate in a massive effort to rejuvenate our landscape, if nothing else by planting millions of trees among the concrete deserts and repairing the eyeless hulks of deserted buildings.

The nineteenth and early twentieth century produced commercial architecture of simple elegance. Everywhere these sturdy brick factories stand unused, windows broken, roofs collapsing. Using low cost labor they could be converted into apartment complexes, shopping centers, restaurants and artisanal shops. We could, for very little money, turn others into multi-cultural centers with libraries, film, theater and video rooms, gymnasiums and swimming pools, bringing together youth and age in a convivial environment. Such centers exist in every town and village in France and are one of the great successes of that nation's post-war effort to enliven the countryside and keep its population on the land.

Grace and beauty are more or less accepted values. Ethnicity is something else. As a mongrel, descended from Cherokee Indians, French Huguenots, Scots bondsmen and an Irishman escaping death by starvation at the hands of the British in the

Great Famine, I'm congenitally skeptical of ethnic purists. The old computer joke sums up my cynical view.

First man: My computer can answer any question you ask.

Second man: Where is my father, Alexander McGhee?

Computer: Your father is fishing off Nova Scotia.

Second man: Ridiculous. My father, Alexander McGhee, is in San Francisco.

Computer: Alexander McGhee is in San Francisco. Your father is fishing off Nova Scotia.

Or as my own father put it with his ineffable wit: It's a wise man who knows his own father.

But, as usual, my personal views are irrelevant to the American reality. The fact is that ethnic hatreds and rage continue to rise from the ashes of past crimes and discrimination like an evil Phoenix. But this validation of difference, the worship of particularity, is antithetical to the basic assumptions underlying this society. Our goal, if we are to survive, should be a cafe-au-lait colored, blue, brown or green-eyed prototype with the brains of a Jewish Talmudic scholar, the humor of an Irish trick driver, the athletic skills of a lithe black cornerback and the gentle genius of a Vietnamese trader.

Or the puckish wit of the cornerback, the lilting tenor of the Irish truck driver, the intense motivation of the Jewish boxer and the Confucian stoicism of the oriental. The ideal would be, of course, the disappearance of the above stereotypes as we spend the next two centuries engineering this national melange and developing a tolerant, educated citizenry who may differ in detail but support an egalitarian representative democracy.

It won't happen, of course, but the alternative is a discrete society of mutually suspicious, paranoid, ethnic enclaves, tearing out each others guts. Having said this, even profound cynical pessimism needs an occasional injection of hope, or at least irony. Otherwise it becomes paralyzing despair. So I will continue to define my dream world, knowing, like all dreams, it is a chimera.

At the moment the United States had acute problems which have to be dealt with here and now. Ten percent of the population are a *lumpenproletariat* locked into a repetitive Catch-22 spiral. They are unable for reasons of history, environment, education, motivation and mindless rage to break the pattern of poverty and criminality. They need special help. But society also has the right protect itself from this group's more violent members. Breaking pathological habit patterns is a long-term job. Our attempts to bribe this segment of the population into passivity have failed.

In the short-term, drastic, unpalatable measures are needed. More jails for violent recidivists are inevitable if we are to make the streets safe. The less violent, rather than being warehoused, should be confined in factory-like conditions and forced to work normal eight-hour days learning a trade. But it may well be that a whole generation will have to be written off.

To break the pattern, children of drug-addicted or otherwise anti-social families should be removed and placed in benevolent institutions staffed in part by compassionate upper middle class youths from the America Corps who would provide roll models. These children would be given affection and individual instruction designed to teach discipline and responsibility.

Obviously such Hobbesian solutions will face constitutional problems and enrage the individualism-at-all-cost elites, living in comfortable isolation in their walled, well-guarded enclaves. Tough. We've tried everything else, and our society is on the verge of cultural collapse. Draconian measures have to be tried.

Perhaps the most scandalous aspect of American society is the lack of universal, free, cradle-to-the-grave basic medical care. A national health plan paid for out of the general revenue should be put in place immediately. We are the world's most affluent society. Virtually every advanced industrial nation has such a program. It need not be imposed on anyone with the resources to opt out. Those with the means to buy private care would still have that opportunity.

Finally, our electoral system has become corrupted by money. Money doesn't just talk in our society; it shouts. Electoral campaigns at all levels, from county commissioner to president, should be required to meet strict spending guidelines based on the number of voters in the constituency. Qualified candidates would be given flat government subsidies and forbidden to use their personal fortunes or accept contributions of any kind. Strict time limits on the electoral process, maxing out at three months for the presidency, should be imposed. All primary elections, subject to the same monetary restraints, should take place on the same date.

To repeat, I am well aware that none of the above reforms is likely to be enacted. But nothing happens until ideas are put on the table and a framework for debate is established.

Domestic problems are messy and in some areas our society is close to being out of control. But we can muddle through these with our classic pragmatism, waiting until a problem becomes unbearable before we attack it.

Foreign affairs are another bucket of snakes. Our ability to impose our will is much more limited. Chaos has always been the order of the day in much of the world. *Pax Romana* and *Pax Britannica* are misnamed. Both Rome and Great Britain were in a continual state of war during the periods when they maintained a tenuous hegemony. The collapse in 1914 of the fragile balance of power established by the Congress of Vienna in 1815 led to a century of unparalleled cruelty and bloodletting.

The disintegration of the colonial empires of Britain and France after the Second World War resulted in the rise of brutal dictatorial regimes often dominated by tribal cabals which ruthlessly slaughtered their ancestral enemies. The Yoruba and Ibo of Nigeria, the Tutsi and Hutu of Rwanda and Burundi, the Moslems and Hindus of India and Pakistan and the roiling ethnic hatreds of the dissolving Soviet Union and Yugoslavia, left dozens of millions of people homeless and starving among the corpses of their clans.

As Europe recoiled back on itself, leaving the Great Game to the Soviet Union and the United States, the Cold War intervened in many of these essentially tribal struggles. Although the battle for the hearts and minds of the so-called third world was often couched in terms of capitalism versus communism, the fate of most of these countries was decided not by ideology but by age-old conflicts between traditional enemies in ruthless civil wars, with the winners slaughtering and enslaving the losers.

American foreign policy following the Second World War had two main goals: 1) restraining an expansionist messianistic Soviet Union perceived as intent on exporting its form of Leninist-Stalinist Communism and 2) establishing a world of peaceful, stable representative democracies supporting open borders and free trade.

The two goals were often antithetical. Sad to say, many of the leaders willing to suppress communist-supported insurgencies were brutal and venal dictators. And some of the supposed communists underwritten by Moscow were genuine idealists intent on improving the miserable lot of their people. In a somewhat facile generalization, the U.S. foreign policy establishment divided between realists and idealists. The first believed that the enemy of my enemy is my friend and don't ask questions you don't want answered. The idealists tended to dismiss the danger of Soviet communism as a right-wing delusion and to blame the United States for East-West tensions.

These two groups met head-on during the civil war in Vietnam. As usual in American politics, the two antagonists straddled party lines. Liberal democrats—men such as Dean Rusk, McGeorge Bundy and Robert MacNamara—in the administrations of John Kennedy and Lyndon Johnson, began and expanded the U.S. intervention. Equally hawkish republicans, led by Nixon and Kissinger, reluctantly ended it in the face of the rising opposition of a sizable minority of the American population.

Whatever verdict historians will render on this relatively minor skirmish in the Cold War, the end result was a disaster for the United States. We entered the war as the most powerful military and economic power in the world. Wherever we chose to exercise that power, we usually prevailed. Our desertion of our South Vietnamese allies, and the panicked scuttle up ladders to the helicopters taking off our diplomats from the American embassy in 1975, imprinted an image around the world of a giant with feet of clay.

Quite suddenly our influence and the ability to project power disappeared. The worst scars of this conflict are a continuing reluctance, even though we now have a volunteer army, to risk casualties when our vital interests are at stake. This, combined with a national neurosis which inhibits our using influence of any kind to further our interests, leaves us internationally impotent.

Realists have suggested a solution to the problem of injecting troops into military skirmishes, such as Somalia and Lebanon, where the sight of the corpses of young Americans in body bags forced us to scuttle away, tail between our legs.

All great empires of the past have callously used mercenaries. The Ethiopian archers of Alexander. The Scythian cavalry of the Romans. The condottieri of medieval Italy. Hessian and Ghurka troops in the hire of the British Empire. And, probably the model for any such American unit, the French Foreign Legion which after World War II was a predominantly German force employing former members of the SS, common criminals and desperate men fleeing the chaos and desolation of Central Europe. They fought superbly in the colonial wars at Dien Bien Phu and in Algeria and spared the lives of young French conscripts.

Today there are tens of thousands of such rootless men who would gladly fight and die for Old Glory for a living wage and the promise of citizenship after twelve years. No fatuous yellow ribbons would fly for corpses of such human refuse, and our statesmen could operate secure in the knowledge that force was available when needed to back up diplomacy. The American professional army officers, formed in the Spartan traditions on West Point, the Virginia Military Institute and the Citadel, would welcome the opportunity to lead troops into battle who were willing to fight and die.

Certain underlying assumptions of American foreign policy have always been flawed. First, we continue to believe in the naive concept of international "friendship." It doesn't exist. People have friends; nations have interests. Second, we persist in the arrogant belief that, given the chance, everybody would choose to be like us. This despite overwhelming evidence that representative government has throughout history been rare, fragile and short-lived. The spirit of compromise so essential in such systems is alien to most other cultures. Their preference seems to be for a sort of benevolent, efficient despotism rather than the messy anarchy of democracy.

Our attempts to cajole or bully other nations to imitate us is one of the more absurd manifestations of an arrogant insensitivity which probably results from out intolerant Puritan heritage. China is a nation of one billion two hundred million people with a rich and diverse culture dating back seven thousand years into the mists of history. To expect this proud people to kowtow to a bunch of Anglo-Saxon primitives who were living in caves a couple of thousand years ago is the height of silliness. Attempts to eradicate authoritarian and tyrannical regimes around the world, through economic and political blackmail, are equally doomed to failure.

And then there is the national yearning to be liked, even loved, as a nation. This puppy-like behavior is treated with amused contempt by older, more self-assured cultures. As the philosopher said, "when you seek love, you lose power." A corollary is the American tendency to expect gratitude for past favors. As the great British diplomat Castlereagh said: "Gratitude is an emotion for cravens." Today's reaction is likely to be "what have you done for me lately?"

The major problem we face internationally today is not nuclear holocaust. Russia, although still capable of a suicidal last gasp with its intact nuclear force, it unlikely to challenge us for world hegemony for some decades. And while an alliance between Japan and China is a worrying possibility, uniting as it would China's nuclear capacity and population with Japan's technological prowess, it seems a far-fetched scenario.

Chaos and anarchy are the plagues of our time. Although an eerie stability reigns throughout Europe, Latin America and along the Asian rim, the Middle East is still a tinderbox. India and Pakistan, both armed to the teeth, could go to war over very little. Africa is consumed by tribal conflicts and endemic governmental corruption and savagery.

Once, in a late night bull session with colleagues in Spain in the late seventies, a brilliant young foreign service officer, in his cups, offered a solution to three of the long-festering international problems. He suggested that the United States offer $50,000 and a visa to all the Protestant inhabitants of Northern Ireland. At least half would accept, and the remaining minority would be forced to join Ulster to the Republic of Ireland.

In our alcoholic daze we applauded this elegant solution.

He then proposed that we offer the same deal to the white South African minority. Again, probably half that population would have accepted.

South Africa is a highly organized modern industrial state dependent on a cadre of experienced, well educated white managers, scientists and technicians. According to recent statistics this group is emigrating at an exponential rate as the new black leaders take command.

Inevitably, to satisfy their constituency's justifiable demands for a larger slice of the economic pie, more and more whites will be driven into exile. As in other post-colonial African nations, security and productivity will deteriorate. International investors will bide their time, waiting for the economic dust to settle. Frustration among the blacks who watch the hoped for riches slip through their fingers will offer opportunistic demagogues, such as the succession of corrupt and venal leaders in Nigeria, to come to power.

At this point, with the military and police in black control, a serious possibility exists of bloody civil war between the remaining, now desperate, whites and a black community bent on revenging past wrongs. The situation in South Africa is more analogous to that in Algeria, where a million French colons left the country, than in other African nations with relatively small white populations.

It may well be that, in some not-too-distant future, the United States and Europe must be prepared to evacuate three-to-four million white South Africans and find them a refuge.

My brilliant, if tactless, young colleague then suggested a

similar solution for Israel, noting that some 800,000 Israelis had already emigrated to America. He pointed out that one of the intransigent Arab states would eventually obtain atomic weapons and the means to deliver them. A first strike with five such devices would destroy the entire population of Israel in about three minutes.

In all, the United States would acquire about six or seven million highly educated, hard working new citizens to fill up some of the immense spaces still available.

At which point a Jewish member of our group erupted with rage, pointing out the deep cultural and ancestral importance of Israel to the Jewish people and accusing the young man of anti-Semitism.

He replied, defensively, and perhaps with some justification, that the real anti-Semites were the American politicians who refused, as World War II approached, to issue visas to the Jews trying desperately to escape annihilation in Germany. While there is something tragic-comic about the intellectual simple-mindedness of such suggestions, they also contain an element of creativity sadly lacking in the traditional foreign policy establishment.

In the short term the major problems we face are a nuclear-armed North Korea and the somewhat more remote possibility that several of the rogue states of the Middle East—Iran, Libya and Syria—may obtain nuclear weapons from criminal elements in Russia. The Japanese are almost certainly unwilling to accept a hostile nuclear power on their doorstep without themselves developing such weapons. A nuclear armed Japan would destabilize the already fragile dynamic of the rapidly industrializing Asian nations and eventually vitiate American influence throughout the area.

In another age we could, in ruthless pursuit of self-interest, have surgically removed the atomic installations of North Korea. A more radical move would be to provoke them into some rash action and use this as an excuse for taking out the atomic plants, But mass democracies are incapable of acting with such duplicity. Inevitably the press would discover the ruse and blow the whistle.

As it is, a hamstrung giant, we will stand by as this criminal regime becomes a major player in Asia.

The other major Asian flashpoint, India and Pakistan, although involving almost a quarter of the world's population is almost irrelevant to American interests. The conflict is localized, and both nations are fundamentally hostile to the United States. Our support for Pakistan was predicated on its hostility to the Soviet Union while India was a Soviet ally. With the retreat of Russia from the international stage our interests in the region have altered.

The major point of conflict between the two nations is Kashmir, a small province isolated from the rest of the world, inhabited primarily by Moslems but ruled by Hindu India. It is another of those knotty ethno-religious problems with no just solution. Since we have no clear national interest at stake, other than world stability, we should probably stay out of this one, offering, if asked, our aid as a mediator if nuclear war threatens.

In the Middle East, despite the exaggerated optimism of the so-called peace process between Israel, Jordan and the West Bank Arabs, Israel continues to be, in Arab eyes, a political carbuncle which must be excised. Iran, Syria and Libya are committed to its destruction. Their more sane Arab neighbors are, for the moment and despite the bitterness of their populations, willing to declare a truce.

But let there be no mistake. It is a truce, not a peace, and as the forces of militant Islam grow throughout the region, Israel will be the focus of their hatred and a major source of their strength among the exponentially increasing populations and consequent economic misery of the region.

Americans, at least those outside the south, have no real experience of the desire for vengeance that losing brings with it. We have, as a people, a mindless belief that nations as well as people can reason together. Sometimes they can; more often they can't.

Of all the problems the United States faces, Israel is the most explosive. Our commitment is total, but our ability to protect this embattled enclave is sadly limited. The perceived humiliations of the Arab states, played upon by their fanatical leaders who are imprisoned in their own rhetoric, and the cultural tradition of exacting vengeance for past wrongs—the Bedouin belief in an eye for an eye, a tooth for a tooth—probably make genuine peace in the region an impossibility. Fortunately, and for the foreseeable future, there seems to be a world glut of oil which diminishes our vital interest in the region.

But again, as with Korea, managing the crisis will take skill, patience and a good bit of simple menace to keep tragedy at bay.

In Europe, American interests are now primarily economic. The eventual establishment of a customs union between the North American Free Trade Area of Canada, Mexico and the United States and the European Union is inevitable. Eventually, Poland, the Czech Republic, Hungary and probably Slovenia and Croatia will join the Union and NATO, posing a solid buffer against the probable resurgence of Russia as, at the very least, a regional power.

Although Germany is well on its way to becoming the dominant European power, both economically and politically, its national neuroses will probably restrain its congenital Teutonic hubris for another generation. Nonetheless, as events in the former Yugoslavia have demonstrated, the United States is going to have to remain a European power for the foreseeable future.

Even France, suffering from prolonged withdrawal symptoms as a now powerless former world mover and shaker, has recognized the need for a U.S. counterbalance to the German behemoth. All the former European Great Powers live in ambivalence about this resurgent adolescent—in their eyes—power to the west. Even the British, who are bitterly enraged at our usurpation of their world role, have tacitly agreed to our preeminence.

However, the United States, increasingly isolationist, prone to contemplate its navel rather than the great world beyond its borders, has had to be dragged kicking and screaming into the Great Game of world politics once again. Our leaders have tried to shift the burden to the United Nations, NATO, Japan and

Europe, but international relations are a brutal reality check. In the last analysis, diplomacy has to be backed with power and the perceived willingness to use it. And we are the only ones with the means to do the dirty jobs.

The last major area of American concern is Latin America. Although I spent almost nine years in Spain, I've never served south of the border, and I am most reluctant to comment on the problems there in detail. The region is obviously of first importance to the United States. Looking at it from a purely theoretical perspective, stability is probably the best we can hope for. Again, as in Europe and despite the vocal opposition of the area's leaders, we may here and there be forced to intervene, particularly in the Caribbean, although such adventures may often be futile.

Mexico has replaced an impotent and isolated Cuba, now a pathetic museum of communism's failures decorated with the flyspecked images of Lenin and Stalin, as our major concern. Its exponentially increasing population will continue to put pressure on our border areas as large numbers of desperately poor people seek to escape. The corrupt nature of its political culture seems unlikely to change over the short term. Encouraging population control and a concerted effort to increase its economic viability should be the focus of our long term efforts. Quixotic attempts at political reform will have to be left to this proud, talented and sensitive people.

Thus ends my list of prejudices and my discursive ramble through the back alleys of the century. Despite claims to realism, a good bit of it is in the romantic tradition of Cyrano de Bergerac, or, in that earthy phrase so replete with imagery, "pissing into the wind." The sad fact is that nothing a government does can guarantee its citizens happiness. Stability and economic comfort are about the best it can offer. Most memoirs attempt to find The Meaning of It All. As an existential atheist, I leave this to the believers and their search for God. As far as I'm concerned my uncle Marvin was right when, asked what comes after death, he answered: "Nothing."

The conclusions I reach in this final chapter are mostly harsh, for I have led a harsh life and am not prone to paint in pastels. Most of the characters who appear compromise with principle and lie, cheat and steal in pursuit of personal self-interest. Nature's noblemen are few. It is not a pleasant book and happy endings are rare. It is, however, as true as I could make it. A record of a full if not happy life. There are no sermons preached, no lessons read. It is a bare-bones tale of a southern peasant boy who clawed his way within sight of the rainbow. And walked away for love of a woman.

Again, in summing up, I turn to one of the great political thinkers of all time, Niccolo Machiavelli. He said:

"No government should ever imagine that it can always adopt a safe course. Rather it should regard all possible courses of action as risky. This is the way things are. Whenever one tries to escape one danger, one runs into another."

Or, the Law of Unintended Consequences almost always wins.

Epilogue

Soon cold shadows
Will close over us
And Summer's transitory gold
Be gone

Charles Beaudelaire

The mind-stretching excitement and innocent licentiousness of graduate school, and, later, the glitz and luxury of diplomatic life, were rapidly replaced for Mary Lee by the sudden transition to the daily grind of teaching at a richly endowed but second rate university with a rudimentary library and no real respect for academic excellence. The students, often intelligent, were badly prepared by the culturally barren landscape of a state which was at a nexus of the South, Midwest and West—and often summed up the worst of each. It was a crude and brutal reality check.

My modest success as a writer of Cold War suspense novels, two more of which sold within our first three years in Tulsa, paid for escapes to Pairs, Berlin, Puerto Vallarta and, finally, a summer-long hegira through provincial France in search of my last remaining fantasy—a village house in Provence.

The publication of *The Orpheus Circle* and *The Heracles Commando* also freed me from some of the stigma of retirement and helped me over the shock of living in the United States permanently for the first time in decades. I was, however, unprepared for the insolently patronizing attitude of my wife's colleagues toward a non-academic.

The history department at Tulsa was made up of embittered

Ivy Leaguers, a Rhodes scholar, refugee from Berkeley and a graduate of the London School of Economics, all hired from a market glutted with brilliant young post docs desperate for a job. Any job. In another time they would have been at Princeton, Yale, Harvard, Stanford or, at the least, Michigan, Indiana, Duke or Emory. Several antiques from another era, held in contempt by their brilliant young confreres, completed this nest of embittered intellectual vipers.

I was a natural target. A Cold Warrior, ex-diplomat, and schlock novelist. Academe, then and now, was the last redoubt of theoretical Marxism, and, although I was a Helmut Schmidt-style social democrat in good standing, I did not bleed copiously for the poor, downtrodden, brown-skinned masses. Nor did I emote at the injustices of the world or join in the demonization of right-wing politicians with whom I disagreed. Breast beating doesn't help, and there are few demons.

By the time we reached Tulsa, the Soviet Union was beginning to crumble. To my everlasting amazement, the old actor's stubborn intention to destroy "the evil empire" was succeeding. And on schedule. Star Wars, a red flag waving in the face of the American intellectual, and the immense defense buildup had frozen the new Soviet leadership in its tracks. Gorbachev, in desperation, had begun to lift the lid of repression. He bet on glasnost, perestroika and a form of the New Economic Policy of the nineteen twenties to extract Russia from an increasingly impossible economic morass.

When the process began to spin our of control, the Russian faced a momentous decision. Either he reinstituted brutal repression, as Stalin did in 1928, or he moved to the front of the new movement toward a truly reformist economic and political regime and led it. He dithered and a tidal wave rose up and engulfed him. Once again, the Law of Unintended Consequences had its way.

Pointing all this out over a dinner table in Tulsa to a group of knee-jerk academic ideologues was equivalent to committing social suicide. But, politically correct as I was on all domestic policies, I might have been forgiven for these transgressions had I beat my chest and tore my hair and sobbed at the fate of all the poor starving children of the world as I downed an excellent California Cabernet Sauvignon and ate superb steaks two inches thick.

Fortunately, Mary Lee was rescued from this morass for two years by a grant to do research at the Institute for Advanced Study in Princeton, home of Einstein and Oppenheimer and the most prestigious organization of its kind in the United States. It was a coup, recognition finally of her brilliant potential as a research scholar. Certainly now we would escape our prairie prison.

Princeton began in September, and we headed for France that summer in search of my village house. We began at Dunkirk and drove south in a rented 2 CV Citroen, a crackerbox on wheels, through Normandy, the edges of Brittany and on south to a village near Foix and a house owned by an American poet, Susan Ludwigson.

For six weeks we looked for a house, but Mary Lee became increasingly morose and finally conceded that the only place in France she could really live was Provence. For the first time in the marriage, we fought. It was short, brutal and quickly over, but the idyll had, for a moment, dissolved. It was not a battle I could win, and I should not have fought it.

We had six more weeks and headed north to Provence although I knew that the area was beyond my means. We were en route to a small town of seven thousand, north of Nimes. Uzes. Four kilometers short of the town a fortified village on a hill emerged from the summer haze. A fairy tale place preserved in the amber of poverty, a walled jewel, isolated, unspoiled. We parked and walked through its narrow cobblestoned streets into the miniature main square. The church, deconsecrated during the French revolution, was now apartments.

Then we saw the Jaguar with British plates. The Mercedes from Switzerland and a BMW from Germany. "It's hopeless," she said. "The rich Europeans have bought it all up."

Uzes, lovingly restored in the nineteen sixties by the French minister of culture, Andre Malraux, is one of the most beautiful medieval towns in France. Its five towers, the de Crussol flag flying from the tallest indicating that the countess is in residence, are stark sentinels against the deep blue of the sky. The local legend is that this lady, in her nineties when we bought Dar Dragut, was the mistress of Edouard Daladier, the French prime minister at the beginning of World War Two.

We settled into a cellar apartment in a nearby village, sharing it in uneasy companionship with a dozen or so scorpions and, outside, a male peacock who turned up each morning on the wall of the chateau next door to await being fed. We'd first heard him at night, his unearthly cry echoing through the night.

"He's calling for his mate," our landlady said. "The owners of the chateau sold it recently and the new owners turned the two birds out. His mate was last seen on the road to St. Hippolyte de Montaigu. He cries for her every night."

We looked, lackadaisically, for a house. But mostly we sought gently to repair the damage of that one and only fight. It was in these weeks when I began to realize the fragility of even the greatest obsessions.

Then one day the wife of the *notaire*, a French invention which combines all the functions of a title insurance company, administrative judge and a host of other obscure duties, took us house hunting. Prices were totally beyond our means. In exasperation, certain as she was that we, like all Americans, were millionaires, she drove us to a village four kilometers from Uzes. It stood on a hill overlooking a valley. Aureilhac.

"My God," Mary Lee said as we parked. "This is the place we saw coming in."

The house was built into the wall. Three stories high. No cross ventilation. Walls three feet thick. Only half restored. No land but a small terrace with a breathtaking view of vineyards, sunflower fields and, in the distance, the menacing dark green of the *garrigue,* the scrub forest which has taken over much of the farmland of southern France.

The price was too high. We haggled with the owner who bore an uncanny resemblance to the French actor Tati. He was desperate to sell. Over the next few days the dollar unaccountably rose against the franc. The price came down. Mary Lee loaned me five thousand dollars from a recent inheritance. We bought it. She christened it Dar Dragut, the House of the Pirate, after the corsair who sacked Gozo in 1553 and sold its population into slavery.

The house healed our wounds. We moved to Princeton where for two years she lived in a sort of academic paradise, researching her book, spending long lunches with her colleagues, brilliant older scholars, the cream of American academe. I faded into the background, wrote and published the last of my Cold War entertainments and began a serious novel dealing with an aging diplomat and a graduate student in East Berlin.

But there were no jobs for young historians of mid-nineteenth century Germany. None. We returned to Tulsa. She was sinking into increasing despair at not being able to escape. Each summer our return to Dar Dragut and its idyllic landscape lifted her spirits briefly. But her bitterness was profound. I had given her a five-year contract and we had been together thirteen years.

Imperceptibly, the difference in age, never a factor, began to intrude. Always jealous, my obsessive possessiveness became more pronounced. I watched, helpless in the grip of my demons and hers, as the great love affair crumbled and finally became a cinder, flickering intermittently into flame, but growing ever colder.

One day in the summer of the fourteenth year, she sat on a two thousand year-old wall on the Hill of the Old Mill, a magnificent field of sunflowers over her shoulder framed by the menacing deep green of the *garrigue*, tears streaming down her face, and said she loved me dearly but no longer wanted to live with me.

Dar Dragut, haunted by a green-eyed, red-haired ghost dancing and singing nude at midnight on the terrace, a glass of champagne in her hand, became a prison. It is now the fief of a pair of charming Teutons of dubious sexual orientation. I wish them the same happiness we had.

And I sometimes, like the peacock on the chateau wall, cry out in the night for a love long lost.

As a greater poet than I said, long ago and in another country:

Dites moi ou, n'en quel pays, est Flora la belle romaine,
Qui beaulte ot trop plus qu'humaine?
Ou sont les neiges dantan?

Boulder
September 1995